London has provided the setting and inspiration for a host of literary works in English, from canonical masterpieces to the popular and ephemeral. Drawing upon a variety of methods and materials, the essays in this volume explore the London of Langland and the Peasants' Revolt, of Shakespeare and the Elizabethan stage, of Pepys and the Restoration coffee house, of Dickens and Victorian wealth and poverty, of Conrad and the empire, of Woolf and the wartime Blitz, of Naipaul and postcolonial immigration, and of contemporary globalism. Contributions from historians, art historians, theorists, and media specialists, as well as leading literary scholars, exemplify current approaches to genre, gender studies, book history, performance studies, and urban studies. In showing how the tradition of English literature is shaped by representations of London, this volume also illuminates the relationship between the literary imagination and the society of one of the world's greatest cities.

A complete list of books in the series is at the back of this book

THE CAMBRIDGE
COMPANION TO
THE LITERATURE
OF LONDON

EDITED BY
LAWRENCE MANLEY
Yale University

CAMBRIDGE
UNIVERSITY PRESS

CAMBRIDGE UNIVERSITY PRESS
Cambridge, New York, Melbourne, Madrid, Cape Town,
Singapore, São Paulo, Delhi, Tokyo, Mexico City

Cambridge University Press
The Edinburgh Building, Cambridge CB2 8RU, UK

Published in the United States of America by Cambridge University Press, New York

www.cambridge.org
Information on this title: www.cambridge.org/9780521722315

First published 2011

Printed in the United Kingdom at the University Press, Cambridge

A catalogue record for this publication is available from the British Library

Library of Congress Cataloguing in Publication data
Manley, Lawrence, 1949–
The Cambridge companion to the literature of London / Lawrence Manley.
p.   cm. – (Cambridge companions to literature)
Includes bibliographical references and index.
ISBN 978-0-521-89752-5 (hardback) – ISBN 978-0-521-72231-5 (paperback)
1. English literature–England–London–History and criticism.   2. Literature and society–
England–History.   3. London (England)–In literature.   4. London (England)–
Intellectual life.   I. Title.   II. Series.
PR8471.M36 2011
820.9′358421–dc23   2011026077

ISBN 978-0-521-89752-5 Hardback
ISBN 978-0-521-72231-5 Paperback

CONTENTS

CONTENTS

ILLUSTRATIONS

CONTRIBUTORS

JOHN CLEMENT BALL is Professor of English at the University of New Brunswick and author of two books: *Imagining London: Postcolonial Fiction and the Transnational Metropolis* (2004) and *Satire and the Postcolonial Novel: V. S. Naipaul, Chinua Achebe, Salman Rushdie* (2003). He is editor of the *World Fiction* volume of the forthcoming three-volume *Encyclopedia of Twentieth-Century Fiction* (2011) and co-editor of the scholarly journal *Studies in Canadian Literature*.

PETER BARRY is Professor of English, University of Wales, Aberystwyth. He was reviews and poetry editor for *English* (the journal of the English Association) from 1988 to 2008. His books include *Beginning Theory* (third edition, 2009), *Contemporary British Poetry and the City* (2000), *Poetry Wars* (2006), and *Literature in Contexts* (2007). He is currently completing *The Pleasures of the Text: Enjoying Poetry*.

ROSEMARIE BODENHEIMER is Professor of English at Boston College, specialising in Victorian and modern fiction. She is the author of *The Politics of Story in Victorian Social Fiction*, *The Real Life of Mary Ann Evans: George Eliot, Her Letters and Fiction*, and *Knowing Dickens*. She is beginning a study of nineteenth- and twentieth-century novelists who animate London on the page in ways that challenge traditional literary accounts of the city as labyrinth or wasteland of modernity.

JAMES DONALD is Dean of the Faculty of Arts and Social Sciences and Professor of Film Studies at the University of New South Wales. He is the author of *Imagining the Modern City* and *Sentimental Education: Schooling, Popular Culture and the Regulation of Liberty*, and editor of over a dozen volumes on film, media, education, and culture. He is currently writing a book on the international significance of Josephine Baker and Paul Robeson between the wars. He is a Fellow of the Australian Academy of the Humanities.

BREAN HAMMOND is Professor of Modern English Literature at the University of Nottingham. His latest publications include a monograph on Jonathan Swift published in 2010 by the Irish Academic Press, and an edition for the Arden Shakespeare of the lost Shakespeare–Fletcher *Cardenio* under the adapted title *The Double Falsehood*.

RALPH HANNA is Professor of Palaeography at the University of Oxford. He writes on locality and language contact in medieval England, as well as *Piers Plowman* and alliterative poetry, all prominent topics in his study, *London Literature 1300–1380* (2005).

JEAN E. HOWARD is George Delacorte Professor in the Humanities and Chair of English at Columbia University. Among her books are *Shakespearean Orchestration, The Stage and Social Struggle in Early Modern England, Engendering a Nation: A Feminist Account of Shakespeare's English Histories* (with Phyllis Rackin), and *Theater of a City: The Places of London Comedy 1598–1642*, winner of the Barnard Hewitt Award (2008) for outstanding work in theatre history. One of the four editors of *The Norton Shakespeare*, she is currently writing books on Caryl Churchill and on the early modern practice of tragedy.

ADRIAN JOHNS is Professor of History and Chair of the Committee on Conceptual and Historical Studies of Science at the University of Chicago. He is the author of *The Nature of the Book: Print and Knowledge in the Making* (1998), *Piracy: The Intellectual Property Wars from Gutenberg to Gates* (2009), and *Death of a Pirate: British Radio and the Origins of the Information Age* (2010). He has written widely on the histories of science, intellectual property, and the book.

JOHN MCLEOD is Professor of Postcolonial and Diaspora Literatures at the School of English, University of Leeds. He is the author of *Postcolonial London: Rewriting the Metropolis* (2004) and numerous essays on London writing by migrants to Britain and their descendants. He has also edited *The Revision of Englishness* (2004) and *The Routledge Companion to Postcolonial Studies* (2007). A second edition of his best-selling book *Beginning Postcolonialism* was published in 2010.

LAWRENCE MANLEY William R. Kenan, Jr. Professor of English at Yale University, is the author of *Literature and Culture in Early Modern London* (1995) and the editor of *London in the Age of Shakespeare: An Anthology* (1986). With Sally-Beth MacLean he is completing a study of Lord Strange's Men and their plays.

LEO MELLOR is the Roma Gill Fellow in English at Murray Edwards College, Cambridge, and a Newton Trust Lecturer at the Faculty of English. He has written on Second World War literature, contemporary poetry, and post-pastoral nature writing. His monograph *Reading the Ruins: Modernism, Bombsites and British Culture* will be published by Cambridge University Press in 2011.

LAURA J. ROSENTHAL is Professor of English at the University of Maryland, College Park. She is the author of *Infamous Commerce: Prostitution in Eighteenth-Century Literature and Culture* (2006) and *Playwrights and Plagiarists in Early Modern Drama: Gender, Authorship, Literary Property* (1996). She has recently edited *Nightwalkers: Prostitute Narratives from the Eighteenth Century* (forthcoming) and is currently working on eighteenth-century cosmopolitanism in theatre and print culture.

WILLIAM SHARPE is Professor of English at Barnard College, Columbia University. Recipient of NEH, Mellon, and Guggenheim Fellowships, he focuses his research and teaching on the intersection of art, literature, and the growth of the modern city. He edits the 'Victorian Age' volume of the *Longman Anthology of British Literature*, now in its fourth edition. He is the author of *Unreal Cities: Urban Figuration in Wordsworth, Baudelaire, Whitman, Eliot, and Williams* (1990), and co-editor of *Visions of the Modern City: Essays in History, Art, and Literature* (1987). His most recent book is *New York Nocturne: The City after Dark in Literature, Painting, and Photography* (2008).

CYNTHIA WALL is Professor of English at the University of Virginia. She is the author of *The Prose of Things: Transformations of Description in the Eighteenth Century* (2006, and Honorable Mention for the James Russell Lowell Prize) and *The Literature and Culture of Restoration London* (1998), as well as an editor of Defoe, Pope, and Bunyan.

SHEARER WEST is Professor of Art History at the University of Birmingham and Director of Research at the Arts and Humanities Research Council of the UK. She is the author and editor of a number of books, including *The Image of the Actor*, *Fin de Siècle*, *The Victorians and Race*, and *Portraiture*. Her current work is on eighteenth-century pastel portraits and eccentricity, laughter, and visual culture in Britain.

CHRONOLOGY

1045	King Edward the Confessor moves his palace from the Wardrobe near St Paul's to Westminster to supervise the building of a new abbey.
1066–75	Building of the White Tower of the Tower of London by William the Conqueror, who recognises rights of the London commune in place since the time of Edward the Confessor.
1189–1211	Henry Fitzailwyn, chief magistrate of the commons of London, the first to be designated by the term 'mayor'.
1215	King John bestows a charter allowing the right of self-government to the citizens of London; the practice of electing a mayor from among the Aldermen of the City of London's twenty-four wards begins.
1340	London population estimated at between 40,000 and 50,000.
1348	The Black Death kills 40 per cent of Londoners.
1376	Court of Common Council formed to assist the Lord Mayor, Sheriffs, and Aldermen in governing the twenty-four wards of the City of London.
1381	The Peasants' Revolt. Rebels from Kent and Essex march on London and, with the aid of London mobs, threaten anarchy until the rebel leader, Wat Tyler, is slain by Mayor William Walworth.
c. 1390	Death of William Langland, author of *Piers Plowman*.
1407	The Company of Merchant Adventurers of London chartered for international trade in cloth.
1476	William Caxton, governor of the Company of Merchant Adventurers of London, sets up a press at Westminster and prints Chaucer's *The Canterbury Tales*.
c. 1500	William Dunbar's 'London, thou art of townes *A per se*'.

1550	Southwark, designated 'Bridge Without', incorporated as a ward into the City of London.
1557	Company of Stationers established; printing of books restricted to London and the university presses of Oxford and Cambridge.
1576	'The Theatre', London's first purpose-built theatre, erected in Shoreditch.
1581	Levant Company organised for trade to the Near East.
1587	The Rose Theatre built on the Bankside in Southwark.
1598	John Stow, *A Survey of London*.
1599	The Globe Theatre built on the Bankside.
1599	Thomas Dekker, *The Shoemaker's Holiday*.
1600	London population estimated at 200,000; East India Company chartered.
1605	*Eastward Ho* by Ben Jonson, George Chapman, and John Marston.
1606	Virginia Company of London established.
1610	Ben Jonson, *On the Famous Voyage* published with Jonson's *Epigrams* in his *Works* (1614).
1616	Death of William Shakespeare.
1618	Under the direction of Inigo Jones, planning begins for the development of Lincoln's Inn Fields.
1631	Fourth Earl of Bedford begins development of Covent Garden.
1632	James Shirley, *Hyde Park*.
1636	Attempts to incorporate rapidly growing suburbs around the City of London; with the discontinuation of these measures by 1640, the continually expanding surburban area remains without effective government for a further 200 years.
1637	Hyde Park, previously hunting ground and recently a haunt of gentry, is opened to the public.
1642	Under mounting pressure from hostile London crowds, King Charles I flees from Whitehall; 100,000 Londoners fortify the city against royalist troops; under Puritan influence, Parliament orders closing of London theatres.
1644	John Milton, *Areopagitica*.
1649	Execution of King Charles I outside Westminster Hall.
1652	First London coffee house opened in St Michael's Lane, Cornhill.
1660	Entry of Charles II into London marks restoration of the monarchy; establishment of the Royal Society of London for the Improvement of Natural Knowledge; on 1 January, Samuel Pepys, a clerk in the Navy Office, begins the diary he will keep until poor eyesight forces him to abandon writing in 1669.

1661	Edmund Waller, *A Poem upon St James's Park, as Lately Improved by His Majesty*; by 1672 John Wilmot, Earl of Rochester, writes 'A Ramble in St James's Park', and in the same year William Wycherley's *Love in a Wood; or, St James's Park* is performed.
1663	First theatre at Drury Lane, rebuilt by Christopher Wren 1674.
1665	Outbreak of bubonic plague kills between 70,000 and 80,000 Londoners, one-sixth of the city's population.
1666	The Great Fire of London, 2–5 September, destroys 400 acres of London, including much of the historic City and 13,200 houses. John Dryden publishes *Annus mirabilis*.
1675	William Wycherley's *The Country Wife* acted at Theatre Royal, Drury Lane.
1678	John Dryden, *MacFlecknoe*.
1694	The Bank of England created to fund government expenses at interest to the Bank's subscribers.
1700	London population estimated at between 575,000 and 600,000; William Congreve, *The Way of the World*.
1710	Jonathan Swift, 'A Description of a City Shower'.
1711	*The Spectator* is established as a daily publication by Joseph Addison and Richard Steele and runs for 555 issues and is briefly revived 1714.
1713	Alexander Pope, *Windsor Forest*.
1716	John Gay, *Trivia; or, The Art of Walking the Streets of London*; Lady Mary Wortley Montagu, *Town Eclogues*.
1722	Daniel Defoe, *Moll Flanders*.
1728	First version of Alexander Pope's *Dunciad* (final version 1743); John Gay, *The Beggar's Opera*.
1732	William Hogarth, *A Harlot's Progress*.
1738	Samuel Johnson, *London*.
1743	Gin Act provokes London riots against taxation of cheap liquor.
1747	Samuel Richardson, *Clarissa*.
1751	William Hogarth, *Gin Lane*.
1768	Founding of the Royal Academy.
1777	Richard Brinsley Sheridan, *The School for Scandal*.
1778	Fanny Burney, *Evelina*.
1780	Gordon Riots: 50,000 Protestants rise against toleration of Catholics; Hannah Cowley, *The Belle's Stratagem*.
1790	Joanna Baillie, 'London'.
1794	William Blake, 'London'.
1799	Creation of West India Dock Company begins development of original London Docklands.

1801	Census: population of inner London and outer boroughs 1,096,000, making London the world's largest city.
1802	William Wordsworth, sonnet 'Composed upon Westminster Bridge'.
1804	Wordsworth writes Book VII of *The Prelude*; the seven-book *Prelude* is published in 1805.
1807	Slave Trade Act abolishes the slave-trade in the British empire.
1812	Gas-Light and Coke Company chartered to light the City, Westminster, and Southwark.
1821–3	Pierce Egan, *Life in London*.
1829	The Metropolitan Police Act, introduced in Parliament by Robert Peel, creates from a patchwork of constabularies a professional metropolitan police force.
1833	Slavery Abolition Act abolishes slavery throughout most of the British empire.
1837	Building of Euston, first intercity railway station in London.
1842	*The Illustrated London News* becomes the world's first weekly illustrated newspaper.
1845	Friedrich Engels, *The Condition of the Working Class in Britain*.
1851	Census: population of inner London and outer boroughs 2,651,000; first edition of Henry Mayhew's *London Labour and the London Poor*; the Great Exhibition opens in Hyde Park.
1852–3	Charles Dickens, *Bleak House*.
1854	Outbreak of cholera begins in Soho.
1855	Following the discovery that cholera is a waterborne disease, the Metropolitan Board of Works is created to improve sewerage.
1856	Elizabeth Barrett Browning, *Aurora Leigh*.
1863	World's first underground railway offers service between Paddington and Farringdon Street.
1866	James McNeill Whistler begins his series of London *Nocturnes*.
1872	Blanchard Jerrold and Gustav Doré, *London: A Pilgrimage*.
1878	Electric street-lighting begins.
1886	Robert Louis Stevenson, *The Strange Case of Dr Jekyll and Mr Hyde*.
1888–91	'Jack the Ripper' becomes a public sensation in connection with the unsolved murders of prostitutes in Whitechapel.

1889	London County Council formed to provide the first elective government for the larger metropolitan area; George Gissing, *The Nether World*; Amy Levy, *A London Plane-Tree*.
1890	Arthur Conan Doyle, *The Sign of Four*.
1893	William Ernest Henley, *London Voluntaries*.
1896	Arthur Morison, *A Child of the Jago*; the Empire Cinema and Theatre, London's first cinema, established in the Leicester Square premises of the former Royal London Panorama (1881).
1901	Census: population of inner London and outer boroughs 6,507,000.
1903	Jack London, *The People of the Abyss*.
1907	Joseph Conrad, *The Secret Agent*.
1908	Walter Sickert, *The Camden Town Murders*.
1914–18	First World War; first aerial bombardment of London occurs in 1915.
1922	T. S. Eliot, *The Waste Land*.
1925	Virginia Woolf, *Mrs. Dalloway*.
1930	Evelyn Waugh, *Vile Bodies*.
1939	Population of inner London and outer boroughs 8,615,000.
1940–1	'The Blitz', the sustained bombing of London by Nazi Germany.
1941	Patrick Hamilton, *Hangover Square*; film version directed by John Brahm released in 1945.
1943	Graham Greene, *The Ministry of Fear*; film version directed by Fritz Lang released in 1944.
1947	*Hue and Cry* released by Ealing Studios.
1948	British Nationality Act gives Commonwealth citizens free entry into Britain; SS *Windrush*, carrying immigrants from the West Indies, arrives at Tilbury.
1951	Festival of Britain opens on South Bank.
1955	Heathrow Airport opens.
1956	Samuel Selvon, *The Lonely Londoners*.
1961	Census: population of inner London and outer boroughs 7,991,000.
1965	Greater London Council, replacing the London County Council (1889), created to provide elective government to thirty-two boroughs comprising the County of London, most of Middlesex, and portions of Essex, Kent, and Surrey.
1967	V. S. Naipaul, *The Mimic Men*.

1968	*Time Out* magazine begins publication.
1973	Edward Brathwaite, *The Arrivants*.
1975	Iain Sinclair, *Lud Heat*.
1981	Major race riot in Brixton.
1985	Hanif Kureishi, *My Beautiful Laundrette*, directed by Stephen Frears.
1988	Salman Rushdie, *The Satanic Verses*.
1998	Val Warner, *Tooting Idyll*.
2000	Greater London Authority created to provide an elected Mayor and Assembly for the entire London region; Zadie Smith, *White Teeth*.
2002	*Dirty Pretty Things*, directed by Stephen Frears.
2004	Andrea Levy, *Small Island*.
2005	On 7 July, suicide bombs aboard three London Underground trains and a London Transport bus in Tavistock Square kill 52 and injure 700; Ian McEwan, *Saturday*.
2007	London population 7,560,000.

LAWRENCE MANLEY

Introduction

Noting that 'the literature of London ... to a large extent ... also represents the literature of England' and that 'English drama and the English novel spring out of the very conditions of London',[1] Peter Ackroyd states a maximal case for the pervasive influence of London on English literature. A correspondingly maximal case for the influence of English literature on the experience of London was offered by John Buchan, author of *The Thirty-Nine Steps* (1915), when he said that 'every street corner' of London was 'peopled by ghosts from literature and history'.[2] In keeping with these claims for the reciprocal influence of London and literature, it is the premise of this volume that to study the representation of London in English literature is to explore not only variations on a compelling and pervasive topic but a defining element in what has been called the 'topography' or the 'atlas' of English literature.[3] Just as, for reasons explained below and discussed throughout this volume, 'the *idea* of London is central to the self-image of the British people', and just as the idea of London 'deeply penetrates the rest of the world's view of British life',[4] so, through manifold instances, the imaginative representation of London has helped to shape British literature and, to a significant extent, world literature in English.

Although the chapters gathered in this volume are organised by a chronological sequence typical in the study of English literature, they are powerfully informed by spatial or geographical methods recently developed in the humanities and social sciences. Recognising that literature is, among other things, what Malcolm Bradbury has called 'a mapping of the world',[5] they concern themselves with the 'place-bound' aspects of literary expression,[6] with the psychogeographical traits of literary forms and genres, and, over time, with the recurrent ideas, memories, and emotions that characterise the imagination of London in literature. They proceed from an understanding that the spaces we inhabit are neither simply physical nor static, that they are, rather, phenomenological, defined as much by varieties of mental experience and changing social practices as by physical location.

In keeping with this dynamic way of thinking about space, the chapters in this volume are distinguished by the manner in which they combine, in varied permutations, theories and methods derived from the social sciences and concerned with the nature of cities and urban life; historical consideration of the particular developments and circumstances that account for the changing identity of London; and literary-critical analysis of the techniques, themes, traditions, and innovations that characterise the significant body of English literature in which the representation of London plays an important role. This combination of perspectives and methods is demanded by the nature of the problem, since the London that is imagined through literary representation (a space in literature) is inseparable from the London that shapes imagination (or literature in space).[7] The urban environment in which (and in response to which) so much of English literature has been written has itself been constructed in many respects *by* its representation in that literature – by the ideas, images, and styles created by writers who have experienced or inhabited it.

The city, urbanisation, and the imagination

To understand this paradox, and before discussing London as a city in particular, it will be useful to examine some key aspects of the way that modern thinkers have described 'the city' and the process of urbanisation in general. Theories of the city may focus (as they did in the classic work of Max Weber) on the combinations of institutions, structures, and forms of relationship (such as markets, laws, administration, and provisions for security) that establish the conditions for the stability, freedoms, and opportunities of communal life. Alternatively, theories may focus on those aspects of political economy – such as the flow of goods and the accumulation of capital (including intellectual capital) – that enable cities to establish dominance over their surroundings. Some theories describe the laws of urban ecology, i.e. the patterns of settlement, growth, and differentiation that characterise cities according to their various types and developmental phases. But in addition to these considerations, a principal concern in the field of urban studies during the past century has been the nature of 'behavioral urbanization',[8] the process of human adaptation whereby evolving moral and behavioural technologies – working alongside institutional, demographic, and infrastructural developments – have helped to organise and equip populations for cohabitation and cooperation in settlements of almost inconceivably massive scale. Thus, according to Robert Park, one of the founders of the so-called Chicago School of urban sociology, the city is 'something more than a congeries of individual men and social conveniences' and 'something more ... than a mere constellation of institutions and devices'. It is, rather, 'a state of mind, a body of customs and traditions, and of the organized attitudes and sentiments that inhere in these customs and are transmitted with this tradition'.[9]

If the city is a state of mind or a body of custom, then the customs that constitute the city are susceptible to sharply opposed variations. On the one hand, going back to the Hebrew Bible and to Cain, the first murderer and the first man to build a city of refuge apart from the God whose retribution he fears, the creation of the city and its ways of life has been seen to rest on forces of compulsion, violence, and inhuman sacrifice.[10] Hence the Psalmist speaks of violence and strife in the city.

> Day and night they go about it upon the walls thereof: mischief
>   also and sorrow are in the midst of it.
> Wickedness is in the midst thereof: deceit and guile depart not from
>   her streets.   (Psalm 55:9–11)

Friedrich Engels, observing that 'the inhabitants of modern London have had to sacrifice so much that is best in human nature', saw 'in the frantic bustle of the great city' 'the disintegration of society into individuals' and 'human society ... split into its component atoms' by the modern capitalist system.[11] On the other hand, theorists have also emphasised the compensatory freedoms and enlarged human capacities that come with assimilation to urban life. Max Weber, citing the German proverb 'Stadt luft macht frei' ('city air makes free'), saw in the structural conditions of medieval and early modern European cities the basis for individual creativity and social innovation. Georg Simmel, Weber's student, explored more extensively the ways in which the 'quantitative aspect of life is transformed directly into qualitative traits of character' at the point where a city transcends its visible expanse and 'becomes the seat of cosmopolitanism'.[12] Beginning with the 'objective' and 'rational' nature of the money economy and the quickened pace of life that drives the metropolis, Simmel identified impersonality, intellectuality, reserve and the calculated indifference of the 'blasé attitude' as belonging to the state of mind of the modern metropolite. But 'what appears in the metropolitan style of life directly as dissociation', he went on to explain, is in reality 'only one of its elemental forms of socialization', since it 'promotes differentiation, refinement, and ... growing differences within the public'. The result is a detachment from tradition and the development of an 'individual freedom' expressed 'in the working-out of a way of life'. Whereas for Simmel this 'elaboration of individuality' involved a disconnection from others and, in the face of the numbing tempo of urban life, a purely subjective freedom to pursue 'tendentious peculiarities' and the 'specifically metropolitan extravagances of mannerism, caprice, and preciousness', Park saw in the extraordinary complexity of urban life, with its multiple demands, affiliations, and commitments, the impossibility of being dominated by any single code of behaviour and thus the opportunity for creative deviance through the multiple alliances formed in the city's varied 'moral regions':

> In the long run every individual finds somewhere among the varied manifestations of city life the sort of environment in which he expands and feels at ease; finds, in short, the moral climate in which his peculiar nature obtains the stimulations that bring his innate dispositions to full and free expression ... Neither the criminal, the defective, nor the genius has the same opportunity to develop his innate disposition in a small town that he invariably finds in a great city. (p. 126)

The role of the city as a stimulus and arena for human development is a primary reason for its cultural significance and thus for the important place in urban theory for the analysis of the city's cultural life. Thus Henri Lefebvre, a force in the recent 'cultural turn' of urban studies, emphasised that 'the production of space' involves an ongoing triangulation of the spatial practices of a society (the routines and networks that unfold in geographical spaces) with both 'representations of space', as these are abstractly conceptualised by planners and other authorities, and the 'representational spaces' or imagined, symbolic, and associational frames through which space comes to be inhabited psychologically by individuals. Whereas concrete 'spatial practices' and abstract 'representations of space' define the ways in which space is perceived and conceived, 'representational spaces' render

> space as directly *lived* through its associated images and symbols, and hence the space of 'inhabitants' and 'users', but also of some artists and perhaps of those, such as a few writers and philosophers, who *describe* and aspire to do more than describe. This is the space ... which the imagination seeks to change and appropriate. It overlays physical space, making symbolic use of its objects.[13]

Lefebvre thus creates, in his theory on the production of urban space, an important domain for culture. For Walter Benjamin, whose work has also been similarly important for the cultural turn in urban studies, the meaning of urban life is embodied in the interaction between the physical spaces of the city – its architecture and its many distinctive spaces – and the mental life of those who experience them. In its built forms, its mixture of styles and functions, each city becomes a repository of the traditions, fantasies, and unconscious commitments that govern its life. As a result, 'reading the urban text' is for Benjamin 'not a matter of intellectually scrutinizing the landscape: rather it is a matter of exploring the fantasy, wish-processes and dreams locked up in our perception of cities'.[14] Though Benjamin understands these fantastic dimensions of urban life largely through their negative effects, in terms of the manipulation of consciousness by the mechanisms of mass culture and capitalism, media and advertising (which adjust 'reality to the masses and … the masses to reality'), he also recognises, in imaginative writing and critical thinking, possibilities for understanding the role of cultural fantasies in the process of urbanisation.[15]

This way of approaching the culture of cities, then, points to numerous roles for the imagination and the arts, including literature, in the creation of urban life. It illuminates the ways in which literature contributes to collective images of the city, to the formation of urbanites and their behaviour, and to the uniqueness of the individual imagination amid urban surroundings. It is to our understanding of the last of these that Michel de Certeau contributes in his account of 'Walking in the City', where he contrasts the 'planned and readable city' of cartographers, planners, and government authorities to the expressive nature of the 'migrational or metaphorical city', a city that is formed by the individual movements and experiences of 'the ordinary practitioners of the city' as they 'follow the thicks and thins of an urban "text" they write without being able to read it'. Applied to the conscious process of literary expression, de Certeau's model for the individual appropriation of the urban environment, and for the transformation of geographical place into cultural space, can serve also as a model for the representation of the city in literature, for its creation of 'a second, poetic geography on top of' – but never in isolation from – 'the geography of the literal' and the collective.[16]

Much of the theory discussed above was developed to account for aspects of modernity and the modern metropolis, but where literature is concerned it may be usefully extended backward in time and adapted to the changing techniques of the literary medium. The interplay of collective with individual, objective with subjective, is perhaps the central problem engaged by the city in literature. Julian Wolfreys, playing on the double meaning of 'invention' as both 'that which is found' and 'that which is created', speaks of the 'impossible ontology' of the city in literature, an entity with links to an objective, historical existence and to a collective, cultural tradition that is nevertheless always singular, *someone's* (and *some one*) imagined London.[17] The essence of the problem explored by the chapters in this volume can be found in Jonathan Raban's observation that

> Cities … are plastic by nature. We mould them in our images: they, in their turn, shape us by the resistance they offer when we try and impose a personal

form on them ... The city as we might imagine it, the soft city of illusion, myth, aspiration, nightmare, is as real, maybe more real, than the hard city one can locate in maps and statistics, in monographs on urban sociology and demography and architecture.[18]

London *and* English literature

The particular significance of London and its role in English literature is perhaps most easily summarised by way of statistics, beginning with the observation that 'London has dominated the settlement hierarchy of England and Wales for more than a thousand years and now accounts for between 25% and 40% of the population of these two countries.'[19] The problem of setting fixed boundaries for London, a definitional problem discussed more extensively below, contributes to the fuzziness of such statistics, but their import is clear: the history of London is undeniably the story of its domination of the rest of the nation. Already three times as large as Bristol, the second-largest English town in the fourteenth century, London had become by 1520 ten times as large as Norwich, then in second place.[20] By 1600, when London's population roughly tripled that of its ten largest rivals combined and when the high mortality rates in the city required that London's expansion be sustained by steady in-migration, one-eighth of the English people lived as Londoners at some point during their lifetimes. London was home to roughly 10 per cent of the population of England and Wales in 1750, to 13.2 per cent in 1851, and to 16.4 per cent in 1901, or nearly one in six.[21] The growth in London's proportion of the national urban population was reversed by the growth of the industrial towns during the early nineteenth century, although this too was arguably a function of the development of transport, commerce, and finance centred in London, and of London's role in driving a more general process that has been called 'the urbanization of the human population', the process whereby societies become *predominantly* urban.[22] By 1900, when London had already been for a century the largest city in the West, Britain became by this definition the world's first 'urbanised' society, and it remains today, with the Netherlands, the most urbanised society in Europe.

Although the population of London peaked above 8 million on the eve of the Second World War, the pattern of declining population and economic stagnation that characterised the later twentieth century began to reverse itself in the 1990s, and, in contrast to former industrial towns in continuing decline elsewhere in the UK, London's population once again began to grow. Information technology and the emergence of a global economy contributed to 'a new geography of centrality and marginality' favouring services over manufacturing and technology over manpower.[23] As a result of these economic changes, though it had slipped in rank below the two dozen most populous of the world's cities, in 2007 London was ranked above its chief competitors – New York, Tokyo, and Hong Kong – as the world's most economically important city. Hosting 25 million visitors per year, it anchors a metropolitan region that generates 75 per cent of the nation's wealth.[24]

Throughout its history as capital, market, entrepôt, imperial metropolis, and global city, London has developed through a paradoxical combination of centripetal and centrifugal effects: consolidation and cohesion at the centre have always been linked to expanding influence at the peripheries, to increasing heterogeneity, mobility, and specialisation within a national and multicultural public. Several factors contribute, then, to the fascinating *in*definition of 'London' and to the indefinite extension of its influence – its domination of the national economy and, in connection with this influence, an identity, as capital, that 'has always been straddled between locality and nation';[25] tentacular vectors of growth that for centuries have given London its physical character as a 'monster' or 'monstrous city' (as Defoe, Smollett, and Mayhew, among others, described it);[26] a history of relatively weak governmental systems – from the ancient 'City' and Corporation outstripped by its suburbs to the London County Council (1889), the Greater London Council (1965–86), and the Greater London Authority (2000). Formal jurisdictions have rarely matched up with the realities of the city's changing life. But the malleable and heterogeneous definition of London is also a consequence of its role in English literature, where a composite formed from an immense variety of inevitably singular and partial perspectives has extended its influence through a verbal medium of indefinite spatiotemporal extension.

Indeed, as the chapters in this volume attest, literature and other technologies of communication were themselves inseparably linked to developments in London – to the clerical culture of courts, schools, scriptoria, and manuscript circulation that developed there in the later Middle Ages (Hanna); to the production, in the early modern period, of printed books by the national monopoly of the London Company of Stationers; to the public theatres and the cultures of ceremony and performance that developed in early modern London (Howard, Rosenthal); to the culture of journalism, conversation, and persuasion that, in connection with the London printing trade and the city's coffee houses, formed 'the practical core of the rise of public reason' and a national 'public sphere' (Johns); to the growth of a 'cultural marketplace' of diversifying styles, genres, and decora that created new opportunities for burlesque, parody, and pastiche (Hammond); to a culture

of improvement, instruction, and self-cultivation, whose nonfictional genres (topographies, travelogues, diaries, and periodicals) helped to shape
the techniques of fictional narration and the canons of realism (Wall); to a
mechanising and industrialising landscape, whose constant motion, nocturnal activity, polluted atmosphere, and miasmal slums transformed the techniques of visual and verbal communication (Sharpe, Bodenheimer, West);
and to the development of broadcasting and film industries, centred in
London but reaching throughout the globe (Mellor, Ball, McLeod, Donald).
In the course of exploring how London is represented in works of English
literature, the chapters in this Companion have much to say also about how
and why London helped to produce that literature and why London became
a presence in so much of it.

London *in* English literature

The earliest literary representation of a city, the Egyptian hieroglyph *niw.t*,
depicts a cross within a circle. The medieval economic historian Robert
Lopez, seeing in this hieroglyph an intersection or crossroads enclosed by a
protective moat or wall, took it as a definition of a fundamental dialectic:
'Communication plus togetherness, or, a special aptitude for change combined with a peculiar feeling of identity: is not this the essence of the city?'[27]
But in addition to the pattern that fascinated Lopez – the way that intensified exchange and collective identity create each other – one might see other
features of the city in this symbol. The crossroads that converge inward at
the centre of the circle, for example, imply extension outward as vectors for
bi-directional movement beyond the walls, thus pointing to the hinterlands
to which the city is linked in countless ways. In their segmentation of the
quartered space within the circle, the crossroads also differentiate and divide, reflecting the processes of specialisation and disassociation that shape
the urban environment, economy, and populace. At their point of intersection, the converging lines produce a singular, privileged site or *punctum* that
can imply connection to a vertical dimension and to the accumulated, subterranean layers of the past and to the heavenly powers that make the city, as
both burial tumulus and temple, a sacred space. The intersecting lines might
also suggest the crosshairs of the *Lotfernrohr* 7, the Luftwaffe bombsight,
or the converging courselines plotted on the charts of military planners.
When it takes representational form, then, the city is almost by definition
a 'heterotopia',[28] a space in which many different spaces, and many different times within these spaces, can be superimposed. As the chapters below
demonstrate, the London of English literature, in and through the countless
works that depict it, is just such a heterotopia.

As Ralph Hanna explains in the chapter that opens this volume, the London represented in later medieval English literature was in several respects a 'liminal' space, i.e. an emerging *conception*, first of all, whose marginal position in late medieval literature mirrors the emerging influence of the city itself (a community of roughly 50,000 souls at the death of Chaucer in 1400). Defined primarily by its defensive walls and by the jurisdictional limits of its civic freedoms, the City, consisting of merchants and other commoners, was the social and imaginative 'other' to the dominant estates of clergy and nobility and thus to the primarily religious and chivalric tenor of much medieval literature. 'Much more aware of London's edges than its contents', medieval literature thus concerned itself with the paradox that the new powers concentrated within London's boundaries (powers celebrated in the ceremonies and hierarchical arrangements of London's guilds) were also powers that threatened at every turn to usurp those boundaries – in the city's economic encroachments on its hinterlands, for example, in the 'magnatial' ambitions of its leading merchants, in the mixture of rapprochement and contention that characterised the city's relations with the crown, and in the predation of merchandising on the lavish habits of aristocrat *dépense*. If the comic fate of the hapless hero of *Bevis of Hamtoun*, an intruding knight hemmed in by the narrow lanes, locked gates, and chained passageways of the well-policed municipality, points toward the transformation of chivalry by the comedic and mock-epic potential of the city in literature, the perception of Langland's Conscience that the order of merchandising is an order of *mis*representation and falsehood points to the fascinating incompatibility of urban life with the ideal of 'trouth' espoused in the mainstream of medieval literature and culture. This is perhaps a way of saying that the depiction of London is a threshold that marks the beginning of the end of medieval literature.

If so, it is also, as Jean E. Howard demonstrates in her chapter on the roles of London on the early modern stage, a threshold opening onto the 'performative élan' of early modern social and theatrical life. The playwright Thomas Heywood famously declared in his *Apology for Actors* (1612) that 'playing is an ornament to the Citty',[29] and in 1631 Edmund Howes could boast that there had been seventeen stages or common playhouses 'new made within the space of threescore yeeres within London and the Suburbs', among them the Theatre in Shoreditch (1576), the Curtain (1577), the Rose (1587), the Swan (1596), the Globe (1599), and the Fortune (1600).[30] By 1595 an estimated 15,000 people per week were attending performances in London. The rise of theatricality and especially the representation of London life on stage, Howard explains, were inseparable from the demographic and economic changes of the period – the rapid growth of London (200,000 by

1600), the transformation of the medieval craft guilds into international trading consortia, and the new social mobilities that 'put pressure on the traditional status system'. Destabilised relations between city and country, merchants and gentry, denizens and strangers, husbands and wives, masters and servants all contributed to narratives and social types through which the stage attempted to render the bewilderments of urban life intelligible. Yet no master-narrative emerged; rather, Howard demonstrates, different genres supplied a variety of scenarios, each of them marked by its own complexities and ambivalences: 'citizen' plays like *The Shoemaker's Holiday* (1600) and Heywood's *1–2 Edward IV* (*c.* 1599) offered pseudo-historical portraits of the heroic exploits and civic benefactions of legendary Londoners while also raising anxious questions about the relationship of royal power and aristocratic privilege to merchant life; domestic tragedies dealing with real-life crimes like the murder of George Sanders by his wife's lover or the gruesome dismemberment of the chandler Thomas Beech by his innkeeping neighbour Thomas Merry juxtaposed the criminality and danger of contemporary London with the reassuring presence of civic surveillance and justice; city comedies by William Haughton, Ben Jonson, Thomas Middleton, and others, built around erotic and financial intrigue, raised without answering the question of whether rectitude or clever performance, morality or materialism, were the key to happiness and success.

If the commercial stage was one innovation of early modern London, the printing press was another. Taking note of the 50 to 100 million volumes printed by London presses during the politically tumultuous period between 1642 and 1700, Adrian Johns examines the civic and intellectual awareness that, in the decades of the English Civil War, Interregnum, Restoration, and Glorious Revolution, made Londoners confident in their 'ability and indeed right to engage in judgment on all conceivable topics'. By examining the localised dynamics of the book-trade, the importance of the bookseller's shop and the coffee house, and the increasingly rapid tempo of serial news publication and political pamphleteering, Johns shows how a transcendent regime of print and public reasoning – a 'public sphere' in the terms of Jürgen Habermas – emerged from local knowledge, face-to-face relationships, and the London publisher's workplace. If there is a single literary image that captures the London of Johns's essay, it is 'this vast city ... the mansion house of liberty' praised in Milton's *Areopagitica* (1644), where writers and thinkers are 'sitting by their studious lamps, musing, searching, revolving new notions and ideas' while countless others are 'as fast reading, trying all things, assenting to the force of reason and convincement'. In keeping, however, with Milton's view that intellectual and moral 'trial is by what is contrary' Johns stresses that 'London was not a single entity, then or now,' that reading and writing were 'stratified and dispersed' (from the legal bookshops of the Strand and Temple Bar to the fashionable literary shops of Covent Garden and Drury Lane to the downmarket pulpshops of Grub Street) and that 'the rise of public reason' was therefore a process of contestation that involved 'the making and breaking of plausibility'.

Departing from a similar emphasis on the process of differentiation, Brean Hammond tracks the impulses of praise and blame in poetry across a range of developments that includes the widening literacy of public life, the variegation of the literary marketplace, and the imbrication of London in eighteenth-century party politics. His focus is the topographical imagination in poetry, whereby the potential materials of 'place realism', the built fabric of the city and its various locales, 'are made to signify in symbolic ways' through the framing effects of poetic genre, style, allusion, pastiche, and parody. He demonstrates, for example, how a classical literary genre like epic could be adapted to contrasting treatments of London in the 'august' Virgilian manner of Dryden's *Annus mirabilis* (1667) and in the mock-epic ridicule of the same poet's *MacFlecknoe* (1682). In weirdly hybrid genres like the urban eclogue and georgic he shows unexpected uses of tradition yielding new 'ways of responding to urbanisation', while in the savage indignation of the age's greatest satires, Samuel Johnson's 'London' and Alexander Pope's *The Dunciad* (1728–43), the noxious conditions of urban life point to the greater outrages – the corruption of the nation and of the human mind – in which the city is implicated. The crossing of poetic styles and genres with urban life results in a 'fantastic imaginary place', a 'heterotopia' or superimposition of spaces in Foucault's terms: hence the 'oneiric' qualities of *MacFlecknoe*'s London, the 'pornotopian' nature of Rochester's, and the 'hyperspacing' of Pope's in *The Dunciad*.

Ethical as well as spatial displacement defines the 'discrepant cosmopolitanism' that, according to Laura J. Rosenthal, was developed by the Restoration and eighteenth-century stage to represent female experiences of London. If 'discrepant cosmopolitanism' designates first of all the paradoxical linkage of migration with sedentarism, travelling with dwelling, and country with city in the London of the period (and thus to the creation of urban sophistication from its rural opposite) it points also to the ways in which an innovative character like Wycherley's Margery Pinchwife, a country wife who acquires an admirable sophistication in her experience of London, could modify prevailing narratives – stories of bumpkin gentlemen outwitted and innocent maidens seduced into the 'harlot's progress' – to yield a new or 'discrepant' evaluation of the city's impact on rural innocence. At the same time, however, the theatre was confronting, in its ambivalent treatment of women going 'upon the Town', all 'the pleasures and hazards of urbanisation', which is why Rosenthal finds such 'discrepant' *kinds* of urbanity and cosmopolitanism distinguishing the brilliant heroines of *The Country Wife* and Hannah Cowley's *The Belle's Stratagem*, the 'innocence' of the Cockney underworld's Polly Peachum in John Gay's *The Beggar's Opera*, and the pathos of the wicked and fallen Sarah Millwood in George Lillo's *The London Merchant*.

In her essay on narration in the long eighteenth century, Cynthia Wall, too, examines three fictional heroines – Daniel Defoe's Moll Flanders, Samuel Richardson's Clarissa Harlowe, and Fanny Burney's Evelina Anville – negotiating the spaces of London in ways that connect the qualities of moral experience to the complexities of movement in the urban landscape. But where Rosenthal focuses on the relationships of dramatic plots and characters to actual patterns of migration and urbanisation, Wall links the very forms and styles used for the fictional narration of movement through the cityscape to a variety of nonfictional genres, such as topography, journals, diaries, letters, and essays, in which writers were attempting to trace out the vectors and trajectories of movement that brought the physical dimensions of the city into the realm of consciousness and character formation.

Already a challenge to human powers of description in the early eighteenth century, when Defoe found 'this monstrous city' spreading out 'in a most straggling, confused manner',[31] nineteenth-century London, whose population increased from 1 to 7 million over the century, was rendered physically unrecognisable by massive expansion over hundreds of square miles and by the mechanised upheaval of its fabric and population. In essays on London in the poetry, fiction, and visual arts of the period, William Sharpe, Rosemarie Bodenheimer, and Shearer West examine the implications of this upheaval. Focusing on the physical conditions (constant motion and a murky, polluted atmosphere), social obstacles (the multitudinousness of lives, the obscurity of poverty), and artistic biases (toward ideals of pastoral serenity and organic unity) that turned London's literal 'invisibility' into a powerful metaphor for poets of the early and mid nineteenth century, William Sharpe demonstrates how this metaphorical blindness toward the city yielded a new, impressionistic poetics of the 'artificial sublime' by the end of the century. Sharpe tracks this process through the many re-writings of Wordsworth's sonnet 'Composed upon Westminster Bridge, Sept. 3, 1802' – by Matthew Arnold, James Thomson, Amy Levy, Alice Meynell, and William Ernest Henley, among others – and through the uncharacteristically positive responses to 'this live throbbing age' by later women poets like Elizabeth Barrett Browning, Levy, and Meynell.

The 'intermittent visibility' of London's transformation, Bodenheimer demonstrates, was a product of techniques developed in the novels of

Dickens – their fascination with 'chaotic, unfinished borderlines of every description', their combination of widely dispersed perspectives with omniscience in narration, their management of changing atmosphere and diurnal rhythms, and above all their plotting of the movements and intersecting pathways by which Londoners (including Dickens's peripatetic heroines) form hidden networks beneath apparently random motion and trace connections across fissures in the physical and social landscape. In their excavation of these human patterns occulted below the threshold of London's visible expanse, the novels of Dickens created new possibilities for the 'subterranean' perspectives of urban genre fiction, including the gritty East End crime novels of Arthur Morrison, the urban gothic of Stevenson's *Strange Case of Dr Jekyll and Mr Hyde* (1886), the detective fiction of Sir Arthur Conan Doyle, George Gissing's 'ethnographic' studies of working-class suburbia, and Joseph Conrad's exploration of London anarchy and terror in *The Secret Agent* (1907).

Victorian visual culture, Shearer West explains, was similarly concerned with 'the mysterious, unknowable, or desired city', the city of imaginative experience 'present just underneath the familiarity and exactitude of represented urban space'. Drawing on de Certeau's distinction between the mapping of place and the moral experience of space, West describes the 'mixture of specificity and fantasy' in Victorian 'visual myths' of London. Indebted to a moralising visual tradition descended from Hogarth, influenced by the outpouring of contemporary literature on London, and participating in a popular visual culture enriched by the possibilities of the lithographic magazine, the panorama, and the photograph, visual artists represented a London 'as much imaginary as real'. The paradoxical result, with the emergence of the modern impressionist style, was a recognition that *only* the artist's partial, subjective viewpoint could render the city as it is actually seen.

In his account of twentieth-century poetry explicitly 'localised' by its interactions with London, Peter Barry demonstrates how various styles of modern poetry, from aestheticism, Imagism, Modernism, and beyond, can be coordinated with historical experience of the city. Linking the Imagism of Pound's London to the stylish life of Edwardian Kensington and to the 'suburban georgianism' of poets in the prewar period, Barry contrasts this impressionistic style of 'seeing' with the 'envisioned' London that, in response to wartime trauma, was historicised, and mythologised into a more philosophic space by Modernists like T. S. Eliot, Louis MacNeice, and Hilda Doolittle. Among the subsequent styles adapting poetry to an ever-changing environment, Barry explains, are the bi- and multicultural perspectives in Afro-Caribbean poetry of the postwar migration, the return of the loco-specific in the documentary lyricism of psychogeographical and situationist poetry of the 1970s, and the superimposed temporal perspectives of contemporary *noir* and elegiac poems.

In his survey of popular genre fiction and high Modernist prose of the earlier twentieth century, Leo Mellor explores a new preoccupation with subterranean and aerial perspectives on London. Though it goes back to Elizabethan depictions of the London criminal underworld and to the Victorian ethnographies of poverty discussed by Bodenheimer, the subterranean perspective comes to include, in the modern period, the literal spaces of the Tube and the bomb shelter, as well as the metaphorical spaces of espionage, gay sexuality, and the Freudian subconscious. Aerial perspectives that had only been metaphorical in the earlier conventions of the map and bird's eye view became realities (and new possibilities for literary representation) with the developing technologies of flight and aerial bombardment. In showing how these perspectives combine and interact in the London of modern English literature, Mellor complicates de Certeau's distinction between the 'readable city' of cartography, planning, and government and the 'metaphorical' city of human experience and consciousness. Abstraction and intimacy, engineering and sensing, converge in a literature (and a city) in which a single explosive instant can open an abyss into layers upon layers of ruin. In the futuristic imagination of the period, Mellor concludes, the vision of a post-urban world of ruin engenders new forms of pastoral.

A prominent and transformative feature of London fiction in the postwar period is the writing of urban fictions by West Indian, African, and south Asian authors who arrived in the metropolis during the wave of immigration from the British colonies that followed the Second World War. Elsewhere in this volume Peter Barry, John McLeod, and James Donald explore the longer-range impact of postwar immigration on poetry, film, and contemporary London writing. In 'Immigration and postwar London literature', however, John Clement Ball explores the more immediate context of fiction by a first generation of arrivants that included, among others, George Lamming, Samuel Selvon, and V. S. Naipaul. If postwar immigration was a stage of 'mutual involvement' that began with empire, the 'mutual involvement' represented in these earliest works of postcolonial literature was often restricted to relationships within the separate communities formed by racial barriers or to the attempt, on the part of arrivant writers, to reconcile the clashing experiences of London and the colonial homelands. The literature of postwar immigration, Ball demonstrates, was often a literature whose spatial perspective on London was taken from behind closed doors, in the confined spaces of domestic interiors and segregated communities. But in terms that he borrows from theorists of postcoloniality, Ball underlines the more expansive dimensions of this literature as well – its inclusion of the perspectives of women and women writers, including Buchi Emecheta (from Nigeria), Joan Riley (Jamaica), Beryl Gilroy (Guyana), and Anita Desai (India); its appropriation, through a process of 'reverse colonialisation', of both London and the English language to the expression of migrant identities and aspirations; and its ability to 'speak back,' in critique and resistance, from the empire to the metropolis. Resistance and critique remain features in contemporary postcolonial London literature, just as barriers of discrimination remain for the descendants of postwar immigrants and for postcolonial expatriates – the conflict of 'Native and settler, that old dispute'[32] is not resolved in Salman Rushdie's *The Satanic Verses*, as Ball points out. But 'the mutual involvement' that began with empire continues to undergo mutation, as the fashioning of transnational identities contributes to London's status as a global city.

Suggesting that a sense of London as 'a site of transformative social and cultural encounter' is the major contribution from the twentieth century's postcolonial diaspora to the writing of a multicultural London in the twenty-first century, John McLeod joins contemporary writers in asking whether the city's multicultural potential can survive the new challenges of global conflict and terror. Against the multicultural, heterotopian London of Zadie Smith's *White Teeth* (2000), Andrea Levy's *Small Island* (2004), and Gautum Malkani's *Londonstani* (2006), McLeod juxtaposes the darker vision of contemporary works responding to the threats of terrorism or exploring the 'spectral communities of undocumented Londoners' whose lives are shaped by the traumas of forced migration, by the vast inequities in the contemporary service economy, and by a global traffic in human bodies. Through the London of contemporary literature, McLeod implies, we look at problems global in scope.

Closing the volume with a chapter both autobiographical and theoretical, James Donald takes up the question of where and how London exists. If London exists in the connections between location and the mental archives of individuals, he argues, those personal resources are in turn shaped by a shared archive of representations in various media, including, in our own time, film as well as literature. Drawing at once on social and literary theory, personal memories and feelings, and critical analysis of works of film and literature, Donald's essay exemplifies even while it attempts to explain the reciprocality of perceptual, conceptual, and representational space as described by Lefebvre. In the fact that these ways of experiencing the city may be as often dissonant as they are mutually reinforcing (i.e. in the disjunctions of practice, knowledge, and feeling, each from the others) Donald finds a basis for the reflective and critical distancing that is the mark of literate urbanity.

In the course of his chapter, Donald opens up a space in his personal memory that, linked to the physical unearthing of the city's layered past in the bombsites of postwar London, turns out to have been shaped by the first Ealing comedy, *Hue and Cry* (1946), whose plucky East End lads, though stirred immediately to action in the film by a radio broadcast, owed some of their enthusiasm, over the longer run, to the patriotic East-Enders of Humphrey Jennings's wartime propaganda films and, beyond these, to the East End slum-dwellers who spoke in their own voices in the pioneering documentary *Housing Problems* (1935), directed by Edgar Anstey and Arthur Elton. The line of influence could be traced further back in time, of course, to Charles Booth's *Life and Labour of the People in London* (1889–1903) and Henry Mayhew's *London Labour and the London Poor* (1861). Or, to follow a different pathway, it might be traced all the way back, by way of the first essay in this Companion, to the hue and cry set upon Bevis of Hamtoun by the feisty commons of London protecting their well-guarded city from aristocratic intruders:

> The folk him folwede al to hepe,
> And al þai setten vp a cry:
> 'Aȝilt þe, Beues, hastely,
> Aȝilt þe, Beues, sone anon,
> And ells þow schelt þe lif for-gon!'   (lines 4424–8)

Benjamin's conception of the city as a museum-like embodiment of collective fantasies, or Foucault's conception of the heterotopian overlap, within one space, of many different spaces and of different times within those spaces, are ideas that answer to what it is like to experience the physical city. But they also suggest what it is like to experience the tradition of English literature through the representation of London. They suggest what it is like to read forward, for example, through the 'hooded hordes swarming / Over endless plains' in T. S. Eliot's *The Waste Land* to

> Jerusalem Athens Alexandria
> Vienna London
> Unreal

or to read backwards with Bernardine Evaristo, in her verse novel *The Emperor's Babe* (2001), to the Roman Londinium of AD 211; or to ponder the interleaved layers of literary London past in Iain Sinclair's *Lud Heat* (1975) or Peter Ackroyd's *Hawksmoor* (1985); or to walk the streets of London, in turn, with Moll Flanders, Little Dorrit, and Clarissa Dalloway. In other words, if the cultural turn of urban social science has underlined the importance of the literary imagination to the study of cities, then examples like these show also why the imagining of London is so important to the tradition and the study of English literature.

Notes

1 Peter Ackroyd, *London: The Biography* (New York: Anchor Books, 2003), pp. 763, 754.

2. John Buchan, *Memory Hold-the-Door* (London: J. M. Dent, 1984), pp. 90–1.

3 Franco Moretti, *Atlas of the European Novel, 1800–1900* (London: Verso, 1998), pp. 4–8, Chapter 2.

4 Keith Hoggart, 'London as an Object of Study', in *London: A New Metropolitan Geography*, ed. Keith Hoggart and David Green (London: Edward Arnold, 1991), p. 1.

5 Malcolm Bradbury, ed., *The Atlas of Literature* (London: De Agostini Editions, 1996), p. 8.

6 Moretti, *Atlas of the European Novel*, p. 5.

7 The distinction between literature in space and the space of literature derives from *ibid.*, p. 3; but see also Pamela K. Gilbert, 'The Idea of the City: Afterword', in *The Idea of the City: Early-Modern, Modern, and Post-Modern Locations and Communities*, ed. Joan Fitzpatrick (Newcastle upon Tyne: Cambridge Scholars, 2009), p. 218; and Gary Bridge and Sophie Watson, 'City Imaginaries', in *A Companion to the City* (Oxford: Blackwell, 2000), p. 7.

8 Jan De Vries, *European Urbanization, 1500–1800* (Cambridge, MA: Harvard University Press, 1984), p. 14.

9 Robert Park, 'The City: Suggestions for the Investigation of Human Behavior in the Urban Environment' (1916), in *Classic Essays on the Culture of Cities*, ed. Richard Sennett (Englewood Cliffs, NJ: Prentice-Hall, 1969), p. 91.

10 Jacques Ellul, *The Meaning of the City* (Grand Rapids: William B. Eerdmans, 1970), Chapter 1; Hannah Arendt, *On Revolution* (New York: Viking, 1963), p. 10. George M. Shulman, 'The Myth of Cain: Fratricide, City-Building, and Politics', *Political Theory* 14 (1986), 215–38.

11 Friedrich Engels, *The Condition of the Working Class in England*, trans. W. O. Henderson and W. H. Chaloner (Stanford: Stanford University Press), pp. 30–1.

12 Georg Simmel, 'The Metropolis and Mental Life', in Sennett, *Classic Essays on the Culture of Cities*, pp. 47–50.

13 Henri Lefebvre, *The Production of Space*, trans. Donald Nicholson-Smith (Oxford: Blackwell, 1991), pp. 38–9.

14 Mike Savage and Alan Warde, *Urban Sociology, Capitalism, and Modernity* (London: Macmillan, 1993), p. 133.

15 Walter Benjamin, 'The Work of Art in the Mechanical Age of Reproduction', in *Illuminations: Essays and Reflections*, ed. Hannah Arendt, trans. Harry Zorn (New York: Schocken Books, 1968), pp. 223, 236–7.

16 Michel de Certeau, *The Practice of Everyday Life*, trans. Steven Rendall (Berkeley: University of California Press, 1984), pp. 93, 105.

17 Julian Wolfreys, *Writing London: Volume 3. Inventions of the City* (Basingstoke: Palgrave, 2007), pp. 1–3.

18 Jonathan Raban, *Soft City* (London: Hamish Hamilton, 1974), p. 10.

19 Andrew M. Warnes, 'London's Population Trends: Metropolitan Area of Megalopolis', in Hoggart and Green, *London: A New Metropolitan Geography*, p. 156.

20 Peter Ramsey, *Tudor Economic Problems* (London: Gollancz, 1963), p. 54.

21 Roy Porter, *London: A Social History* (Cambridge, MA: Harvard University Press, 1995), pp. 136, 205.

22 Kingsley Davis, 'The Urbanization of the Human Population', in *The City Reader*, 2nd edn, ed. Richard T. LeGates and Frederic Stout (London: Routledge, 2000), p. 5; on the volatile position of leading cities in the global network, see Manuel Castells, 'The Space of Flows', in *The Castells Reader on Cities and Social Theory*, ed. Ida Susser (Oxford: Blackwell, 2002), pp. 316–20.

23 Saskia Sassen, 'A New Geography of Centres and Margins,' in LeGates and Stout, *The City Reader*, pp. 208–12.

24 Richard Burdett, 'London: The Coolest City', in *Metropolis Now! Urban Cultures in Global Cities*, ed. Ramesh Kumar Biswas (Vienna: Springer, 2000).

25 David Feldman and Gareth Stedman Jones, 'Introduction', in *Metropolis-London: Histories and Representations since 1800*, ed. Feldman and Stedman Jones (London: Routledge, 1989), p. 5.

26 See Porter, *London: A Social History*, pp. 162, 186.

27 Robert Lopez, 'The Crossroads within the Wall', in *The Historian and the City*, ed. Oscar Handlin and John Burchard (Cambridge, MA: MIT Press, 1963), p. 28.

28 Michel Foucault, 'Of Other Spaces', trans. Jay Miskowiec, *Diacritics* 16 (1986), 22–7 (25–6).

29 Thomas Heywood, *An Apology for Actors* (London: Nicolas Okes, 1612), sig. F$_3$.

30 Edmund Howes, *Annales, or A General Chronicle of England. Begun by Iohn Stow: continued and Augmented … By Edmund Howes* (London: R. Meighen, 1631), fo. 1004.

31 Daniel Defoe, *A Tour through the Whole Island of Great Britain*, ed. Pat Rogers (Harmondsworth: Penguin, 1972), pp. 287–8.

32 Salman Rushdie, *The Satanic Verses* (London: Viking, 1989), p. 353.

I

RALPH HANNA

Images of London in medieval English literature

'London, thou art of townes *A per se*'. So, around 1500, an unknown Scots poet – the poem was long confidently ascribed to William Dunbar – begins his encomium to the greatest town he knew. The poem continues in the laudatory vein struck in its opening line for seven 'Monk's stanzas'; each ends with a refrain emphasising a superlativeness not just urban, but imperial: 'London, thou art the flour of Cities all.'[1] 'Monk's stanza' is one of those forms invented in English by medieval London's greatest poet, Geoffrey Chaucer. But the most important thing, I suspect, about this quite detailed poem is its belatedness; only at the end of the Middle Ages was it possible actually to see England's greatest City in a literary context or directly as a literary subject. Before that date, London was indeed, in David Wallace's phrase, an 'absent city', not simply for Chaucer (Wallace's subject) but nearly every literary figure.

The detail of 'London, thou art' deserves attentive examination. A great deal of this might be described as thoroughly traditional. The City is identified by two names, not simply its modern title, of which more in a moment, but 'Troynovaunt' or 'New Troy' as well (lines 9, 10, 19). This name alludes to the powerful historical myth of both local and national foundation, largely an invention of Geoffrey of Monmouth in his *Historia regum Britanniae* (1130s).

As 'Troynovaunt', London is truly imperial, Rome's first cousin (and not her inferior). Britain has its own Aeneas, its own founding exile from the fall of Troy, the eponymous Brut. He established 'Trinovantum' overtly to be his capital and to recreate directly (as Rome manifestly did not) the very laws and customs of the epic destroyed city from which the exiles came.[2] This account may actually predate Geoffrey; it became increasingly popular as a history of London's foundation from the 1380s. In the same spirit of evoking a tradition of the antique heroic, the Scots poet provides other classicising detail: for example, an account of the Tower of London as founded by that ancient paragon Julius Caesar and seat of the god 'Mars victoryall' (line 38).

Equally traditional is the Scots poet's tendency to harp upon the edges of London. After all, the place's abiding name, in Geoffrey's Troy-based history, is derived from a compound on the order of 'Lud's-town'. This king of Britain, every bit as imaginary as his predecessor Brut, allegedly renewed the walls of Brut's city and ordered its beautification.[3] The most long-lived toponym associated with his London presence is 'Ludgate', the old western gate in the original City walls, leading from Ludgate Street into Fleet Street and the western suburbs.

Londoners, authors, and citizens alike, are always deeply conscious of the place's borders, for they define an area with a special legal status and unique local laws. Traditionally, this is the very small area within the medieval walls, still generically called 'The City'. Within this precinct, in contemporary perception, London defines itself as inherently different from (and fiercely independent of) its surround. Typically, this different surround includes England's 'other capital', the second city a mile or so to the west along the Strand (of the Thames), royal Westminster.

Perhaps the medieval City is less 'absent' than it is 'liminal'. At least traditionally, literary language tends to be restricted to mapping London's edges and borders, while it is chary of offering definitions of what is within them, or at least chary of doing so in public to outsiders. Hence much of the Scots poet's description addresses conventional checkpoints on an itinerary of the City's bounds. We hear of the river Thames, the City's natural defence to the south (lines 25–30, 43); London Bridge, the great crossing point from the southeast; Kent, and the Cinque Ports serving the short passage to France (lines 33–34); the Tower, which forms the City's southeast corner (lines 37–9); and, of course, the enveloping circuit of the City walls (lines 27, 41).

Although the poem includes many such traditional details, it has far greater surprises and unexpected perceptions to offer. Unlike many other accounts, this London is not just an external surface, a boundary turned to the world; consider 'Of merchauntis *full of substaunce* and of myght' (line 7, my italics), or its reprise, 'Rich be thy merchauntis in substaunce that excellis' (line 45). The Scotsman's City actually contains something, and he recognises that there is activity within the walls – activity in the main commercial, and yet paradoxically conferring, nobility. That full mercantile 'substaunce' is clearly wealth, the profit of trade, and it is not here contemptuously dismissed. When the Scot sees London Bridge, he sees not simply an entryway, but the shops that, like those of Florence's Ponte Vecchio, line the way. The impressive 'pylers white' support, not just a road, but 'merchauntis full royall' (lines 33–4).

Such details actually engulf the poet's version of the sparer traditional account. Indeed near the centre of the poem, the poet comes very close to unveiling his central conceit in calling London 'Swete paradise precelling in pleasure' (line 23). In this account, urban London has been subsumed into a very different kind of literary space, one Chaucer can present only as fabliau parody, in the Lombard merchant/knight January's *faux Romance of the Rose* walled garden in 'The Merchant's Tale'. But rather than enclosing a totally private space, as in Chaucer's tale, or shutting the world out, in this poem London's walls surround a true garden of natural wealth. Moreover, they invite the reader to penetrate, to enter, to sample a plenitude of rich wonders. This treatment begins in the first stanza with the enumeration of the City's inhabitants, as if the Great Chain of (social) Being extended from 'royaltie' (line 3) to those 'substaunce'-stuffed merchants I have already mentioned.

And it is particularly the mercantile that draws the Scotsman's eye. His Thames does not just have swans, but palpably mercantile shipping (lines 29–30). Knights are not known here for their prowess, but their outfits, 'velvet gownes and cheynes of gold' (line 36), the sumptuary luxuries supplied them by local tradesmen. Indeed, merchants more closely resemble persons in touch with garden nature than do the nobles in the place, the traditional connoisseurs of garden poetry:

> For manly power, with craftis natural
> Fourmeth none fairer sith the flode of Noy.   (lines 14–15)

These lines, roughly 'No town has developed more beautifully in terms of male force and natural skills', form an extraordinary compliment to local artisanship, hard work, and profusion of products. Moreover, as the poem nears its end (lines 46–8), merchants, not dukes or barons, become, quite counterintuitively, given what we know of medieval demographics, the progenitors of hereditary lines of beauty and distinction. And, in climactic final position, the poet applauds the City's double 'governaunce', both the multiplicity of its churches (line 44) and the wisdom of the inhabitants (line 42), and his final stanza (lines 49–56) praises mayoral government as 'pryncely'.

'London, thou art' reveals that it had become possible, on the edge of the early modern period, to appreciate openly what in the Middle Ages may have been too problematic for discussion. A great many medieval literati, both authors and readers, will have found, as we will see, mercantile culture a problematic concept, if not an outright oxymoron. And as was certainly true in many later periods, the roots of the wealth that might sustain merchants' grandeur will have been subject to deep antipathies, both social and moral.

Furthermore, although the Scots poet applauds London's mayor and civic government as surpassing in dignity and honour those of great continental cities, and although he may actually recall a Florentine text, adapted in the early fourteenth century for London use – Brunetto Latini's image of the cultivated *podestà* as learned mayor and ruler – London civic government was not in fact representative but oligarchical. Moreover, it was inward-looking and most fully committed to its own self-perpetuation. Rather than conceiving a single unified commune, the aldermanic lords of the City were usually deeply antipathetic toward, not supportive of, the aspirations of the majority, journeyman/apprentice inhabitants. Finally, in spite of repeated claims from the late fourteenth century on that London was the king's *thalamus* or bridal chamber, a New Jerusalem conjoined to a Westminster King of Kings, London historically had founded its identity upon anti-royalist independence and rebellion. It may well be significant that 'London thou art' is actually the utterance of a tourist, someone whose Scots language marks him as not only from outwith the City but outside the realm itself.

In this chapter, I want to move backward from 'London thou art' to examine a few more customary medieval representations of the City. I hope that this sequence of analyses will suggest something of the breadth of writing about London, as well as the scrappy quality of rather chance references across a range of texts. Few medieval writers addressed themselves, as the poet of 'London, thou art' did, directly and protractedly to the City and its most usual activities. Moreover, the sample of analyses I arrange unduly exaggerates the importance of and the interest in London in medieval English writing. My selection will also suggest the ambivalence the City inspired from an early date.

I choose to begin by looking at two interlocked topics associated with London as an enclosed place, one perhaps most normally visible as a surface or boundary outlining an ill-defined core. One qualification to this view of the bounded enclave suggests itself immediately. While the City was deeply sensitive to incursion, it equally required it, indeed had actively to seek it. Like all medieval cities, investment in diversified yet centralised trade and industry rendered London 'land poor'. In a society where survival was predicated on grain harvests, this left the City, overbuilt and without open arable spaces, dependent upon a broad hinterland for its food supplies. For example, Langland's Hawkin, a speciality baker whose trade relies on the steady and predictable flow of grain imports from without, describes the dire conditions of 1370, when drayage from the mills of rural Stratford was interrupted.[4] The sheer survival of London and its industry required that the City breach its own walls, that it become a predatory imperialist in its region, that it suck in for urban use the commodities of relatively distant rural locales.

Moreover, given quite substantial urban mortality throughout the period, the City had to imperialise the country not just for food, but for population as well. Persistent economic growth required a growing labour force, and London essentially drew this from the entire southeastern quadrant of England, so far away as Leicester and southern Lincolnshire. The walls that promised protection and enclosure were always necessarily permeable – and they needed to be so, attractive, rather than repulsive, for the City's health and survival.

Yet London did not simply draw into itself, it spewed outward as well. A great deal of civic pride actually depended on the ability to intervene in non-City space, to control activities in removed suburban areas. One of the oldest efforts to describe London (1173), William FitzStephen's prologue to the life of the local hero Thomas Becket, is a fine example. When he looks within the City, FitzStephen can scarcely see its commerce; his description emphatically highlights the abundant clerical institutions, schools, and churches, with a side look at the grandeur of the City's victualling trades. Most of FitzStephen's exercise praises the City for its ability to use neighbouring, entirely extramural commodities; London's glory is its ability to encroach, largely for recreational purposes and without limit, into spaces that properly belong to others.

FitzStephen's selection of such activities is various, but strikingly focused. In addition to suburban agriculture, he describes a range of extra-urban leisure activities: hunting rights the 'barons' of the City enjoyed in surrounding areas; the livestock markets held in Smithfield, here most fully evoked as the site of aristocratic connoisseurship of horseflesh and racing; a wide range of sports that traverse neighbouring areas. And FitzStephen's list is far from complete. For example, London claimed rights, not only over the Thames, but several neighbouring rivers, as far as the Medway. Civic ordinance controlled fisheries, not only to ensure the City's food supplies, but to keep rivers unblocked for its mercantile navigation. To the north, the City protected its water supply through the river Fleet by policing offal disposal by the butchers of West Smithfield.

As the majority of these accounts will indicate, mercantile appropriation of London's hinterland was multifaceted. What was being appropriated was not just other people's space, but their customs, and customs not necessarily those of the locales invaded. The City's leaders always styled themselves 'barons', the equivalents of lords of the realm. This is, of course, scarcely the way they are generally perceived in literate society, where mercantilism bears no resemblance to an aristocracy of birth, but rests on either skilled manual labour or deft skills at exchange.

Hence, in Fitzstephen's text, merchants come to use extramural space, originally an agricultural site, not necessarily a magnatial one, to express their aristocratic fantasies. Insofar as this is the leisure expression of mercantile culture, it is entirely appropriative, the emulation of a status not publicly conferred on its practitioners outside the walls. (Londoners were indeed renowned – a fact FitzStephen glosses over – as generally failures at those military activities, the foundation of England's aristocratic glory; village boys made much better soldiers.) And at the most extreme, many successful merchants, whose families had been drawn to the City originally by the lure of profit, wished to cap their careers by emigration. Purchasing a country estate and perhaps even totally disengaging from London's walled enclosure would ensure such a person might be considered gentry, no longer involved in trade.

On further, special occasions, London invited another type of incursion. Perhaps it would be more accurate to describe this movement within the walls as invasive or penetrative only, a passage through urban space – and out of it again. Both historical accounts (Latin chronicles, as well as the English *Brut* and London chronicles) and literary ones (Richard Maidstone's *Concordia*, Lydgate's *Entry of Henry VI*) repeatedly describe the City's processional route, which figures routinely in public performative acts, most normally those involving royal entries. The route comes from the southeast, typically through Blackheath and Southwark; it crosses London Bridge and follows the great commercial axis of the City, along Cheap to the metropolitan church, St Paul's. Thence it passes westward *from* the City, either through Ludgate or Temple Bar, and at last ends in 'the other city', Westminster, at its abbey and adjacent royal palace.

Within the City, the route describes a balance, indeed a fusion, between commercial and spiritual space, Cheap and St Paul's. The City becomes sacralised; it represents the ultimate holy city, Jerusalem, not Troy the great. The processional figures the royal entry as the coming of a holy king to his adoring and loyal people – either historically, as David's entry dancing before the Ark (2 Kings 6), or prophetically, as the vision of the New Jerusalem that will be. As a form of idealising play (and frequently, down to 1392, as a symbolic finale to what the account most surely does *not* enact, regal–urban hostilities), the procession is intent on representing what is not normally present.

Thus, these occasions present elaborate dress-up, the activities of holy day/holiday, but not every day. The shopping fronts that normally define Cheap are hidden behind elaborate decorations for the processions, and the public fountains that usually offer sustaining water run with luxury wine. Given the frequent imagery of the marriage of the king with his city, or the city as royal bridal chamber, one is supposed to be reminded of Jesus' first miracle, at the wedding in Cana (John 2).

But the one thing that is manifestly not on show on such occasions is the City as it is. For example, Maidstone's elaborate processional of the City's guilds⁵ may draw upon an idea of civic plenitude, an evocation of power and vitality, in insisting upon the sheer number of organisations on display. And the poet evokes as well a concept of variegated beauty in alluding to the diverse ceremonial liveries made visible on the occasion. But the very insistence upon the 'separateness' of the guilds and their various degrees that impels Maidstone's description manages simultaneously to recall the facts of daily guild life – fractious jurisdictional disputes among greater and lesser practitioners of similar trades, warring coalitions (the victuallers against everyone else), the frequent sunderings and reamalgamations of 'fellowships' among various crafts.

Moreover, it remains unclear to what extent the processional actually heralds rapprochement of civic London and royal Westminster. For it equally – and especially in the supposedly serene religious aspects of the ceremony – might be perceived as re-enforcing deep rivalries. In the overtly spiritual portion of the civic procession, the king enters St Paul's to make his offering to the City's patron, St Erkenwald, a famous Anglo-Saxon bishop of London. But near the procession's conclusion, the king effectively atones for any possible dereliction from or dilution of proper royal religious sympathies by a stop at Westminster Abbey. There he offers to a saint of greater renown and perhaps power, Edward the Confessor, construction of whose shrine here had exhausted the energies of a great royal patron, Henry III. Erkenwald is virtually unknown outside the City walls, and insofar as he is supposed to attract royal attention, he might be perceived as offering – as did other objects of Paul's veneration, for example the magnate rebel Thomas of Lancaster, executed in 1322 – a challenge to royal national interests.

The royal procession also had its own, decidedly anti-holiday parody, although Thursday 13 June 1381 was the feast of Corpus Christi, a day given to processions. The invading peasants of Kent and Essex essentially followed the route of royal processional when they invaded the City. They gathered in Blackheath, passed through Southwark despoiling and opening prisons, and got across London Bridge, in spite of efforts to bar their way. A certain sense of complicity with local dissolute elements appears as well in the peasants' most prominent acts of despoliation. Like Londoners, they attacked prominent alien traders, Italians and Flemings especially. Moreover, although their activities were generally and ubiquitously destructive, the peasants' most shocking depredations occurred in suburban areas and the extra-urban 'liberties' that dotted inner City space. Outstanding examples of their pillage and murder that impressed themselves upon a range of chroniclers included the burning of John of Gaunt's Savoy Palace in the Strand, the destruction of St John's Priory in Clerkenwell, the massacre of Flemings in Southwark, and the siege of the Tower. Ultimately, the whole affair ended in a space almost over-determined for such a climactic scene, suburban Smithfield. There the peasant leader Wat Tyler displayed an unduly familiar longing for royal companionship and, in a site well known for mercantile play at aristocratic pursuits, the Lord Mayor, William Walworth, actually performed like a knight and smote Tyler down for his insolence.

As I have indicated, medieval literary presentations seem much more aware of London's edges than its contents. Certainly, there are exceptions to this rule, and they concentrate in a few vital areas. In the remainder of the chapter, I want to glance at three repeated topics: labour and merchandising, revelry and the City as place of quasi-licit delights, and (a topic related to the last) the City and the loss of a stable personal identity.

One of the most striking depictions of London as a contained area occurs relatively early in the Middle English tradition, in the final episode of a romance of *c.* 1300, *Bevis of Hamtoun*. The titular hero ends up in London largely by accident, at a lodging in Tower Street, after he has been rebuffed in the royal Court at Westminster. But the City provides the estranged knight no refuge; indeed, in a typically humour-laced episode of this most ebullient of narratives, London provides the antithesis of chivalric endeavour. Just as the locale is too built-up and developed to offer space for agriculture, the City's labour and merchandising offer only minimal room for warfare and heroic action.

Bevis is pursued into London by his adversary from the royal Court, the king's perfidious steward. As he rides out in Cheap, London's great shopping district, the steward subjects him to specifically urban persecution; he puts 'the hue and cry' on the unfortunate knight, has him hunted as 'traitor' but uses the mechanism conventional to prevent market thievery. At the hue and cry, all within earshot are to drop what they are doing and attempt to apprehend the criminal. Yet Bevis has clearly stumbled into an arena of labour and sales; once aroused by the steward, no one has proper weaponry to take up. In the unarmed, nonmilitarised City, people rely upon clubs, traditionally the weapon of the churlish Daunger of *The Romance of the Rose*, for self-protection. Clearly, but for their massive number, the citizens do not really form an efficacious fighting force, and the outcome of this battle should be predictable.

But that is to reckon without urban space. In this account, the City is a rabbit warren of small lanes, fine for foot traffic but too narrow for Bevis to turn his great steed Arundel. Moreover, in an area overrun by 'properties', private houses that also make do as shops and warehouses, all ways seem capable of being barred. Bevis is progressively hemmed in by locked gates and roadways blocked by chains.

In a probable allusion to a contemporary London romance, *Richard Coeur de Lyon*, Bevis can only escape by slicing through the chain that pins him within 'Godes Lane', a baying crowd behind. Like Richard, Bevis is a king (in the faraway orient), and he will eventually be reconciled with the king of England. Moreover, Richard's cutting a cable also frees up urban space; by this mechanism, he opens the harbour of besieged Acre and relieves the beleaguered Christian army there. Similarly, once he has freed himself from this constraint, Bevis and his sons can slaughter the citizens who have been cheeky enough to attack him. For the author of *Bevis of Hamtoun*, London is no place for a nobleman, and its citizens are only upstart irritants.

Perhaps the medieval London poet par excellence was not a native at all, but the western immigrant William Langland. *Piers Plowman*, in spite of its agrarian title, probably contains more resonant images of the City and its labours than any other Middle English text. Indeed, as I have already mentioned, Langland's great representation of busy urban life (B-text, passus 13 especially) centres upon a London figure, Hawkin the active man.

Hawkin has two alternative professional titles; he is both 'wafrer' and 'mynstrall'. The first identification links him with London's powerful victualling trades, and perhaps especially bakers. Yet 'wafers' are a luxury product, rather like Belgian waffles, and as party food, they connect Hawkin with a world of professional entertainment and entertainers, minstrels.

Hawkin's problem, as he describes it, is that those who provide the refreshments at these feasts for great lords do not obtain the same rich rewards as the entertainers. Thus, he finds himself consistently underpaid, undervalued, underpatronised. In the absence of remunerative lordly connections, Hawkin describes himself as a workaholic, perpetually engaged in his craft – the expenditure of energy necessary to meet a broad demand, in the absence of more leisurely endeavour with well-paying upper-class patronage. As he compulsively bakes away the predawn hours, the very opposite of the penitential Piers Plowman who undertakes to 'wep[e] whan I sholde slepe, though whete breed me faille' (B 7.125), he loses himself. In his overinvestment in the world of work(s), Hawkin's graceless state appears in his badly soiled baptismal gown. As a figure of civic industry, Hawkin is committed to providing pleasure and satisfaction; the only person apparently never satisfied is Hawkin himself.

But the gravest dangers of London labour are not, like Hawkin's, selfinflicted, but acts that damage others. Medieval conceptions of labour and consumption typically, as we will see, imagine as an ideal a zero-sum game, in which money and benefits simply flow between producers and consumers in equal measures, yet opposed directions. In such a conceptualisation, the real danger is not Hawkin's dissatisfaction, but capitalistic success. Entrepreneurial profit and wealth must, in such a model, imply loss somewhere else, among those who consume.

Langland's figure of Covetise provides a resonant example of this reading of guild and merchant labour. At the head of this deadly sin's confession, he describes part of his early training:

> [D]rough I me among drapiers my donet to lerne,
> To drawe the list along, the lenger it semed.   (B 5.207–8)

A 'donet' is a generic term for a basic Latin grammar (from 'Donatus', the great classical grammarian), the text from which young boys are taught the rules fundamental to reading and composition in the language. By extension, it could mean a basic introduction to any study. But Covetise, while rather typically offering a figural extension of the term, equally provides a grammatical joke, concerning a training in the unregulated and impermissible. He seeks to pass off a short piece of cloth for a longer, and thus more substantial and expensive, one. In essence, he is learning how to construct a 'solecism', a grammatical error; in strict 'donet' terms, he seeks to create a Latin verse line with its syllables in the wrong order and positions. Rather than attend to proper grammatical rule, to the agreed communicative functions of language, he invents his own private (and perverse) speech-system.

In Langland's perception, trade, Covetise's *métier*, rests on similar rule-violations. As Conscience, a particularly strait-laced Langlandian creation, remarks:

> In marchaundise is no mede ...;
> It is a permutacion apertly, a penyworth for another
> (B 3.257–8).

If there is 'mede' ('reward', here synonymous with 'profit') involved in trade, it must depend upon some sharp practice, for example, adulteration of materials. When he makes a short cloth into a long, Covetise essentially attenuates the fabric, weakens it and decreases the wear it will sustain. In Conscience's perception, products that confer profit must similarly reflect things offered and purchased as something other than what they actually are, and profit will be directly proportionate to the degree of misrepresentation involved. (Figures like Conscience make no concessions for quality of workmanship, or for entrepreneurial reward, extra cash for a winning and attractive product conception.) Langland is far from unique in presenting such a view of London trade and artisanship; it underlies such representations as Chaucer's discussion of alchemy in 'The Canon's Yeoman's Tale' and the depiction of marketing practices in the fifteenth-century 'London Lickpenny'.

Such a presentation will indicate why, in the medieval period, severe doubts might exist as to whether there could be such a thing as 'mercantile (literary) culture', or some poetry of the City. In Langland's formulation, merchant language is unrecognisable as a properly ruled discourse. (Tellingly, Covetise mistakes his very English interlocutor Repentance for a French speaker.) Merchant-speak is a persistent stream of impropriety; at its basis, quite in distinction to either learned/clerical or chivalric idealisms, is no regulation, no proper sense of linguistic – or, because it is a construction built upon the linguistic, literary – form at all.

Moreover, in the lines I am discussing, the merchant Covetise comes to resemble his cloth. The fabric is drawn along to make it attractive to a purchaser; he has been drawn into the cloth-trade for his educational formation as a profit-maker. It is no accident that Langland presents Covetise physically as a mass of distensions, like his cloth (and the purse its sale will fill): 'And lik a letheren purs lolled hise chekes' (B 5.191). The figure is a grotesque, and the only literary form into which he could possibly fit is the fabliau, the genre of medieval tale involving bawdry and low decorum. The fabliau is predicated, moreover, upon deceitful plots, the presentation of objects and situations as they are not (like cloths of the wrong measure). And it is a genre in which those proprieties dear to socially creditable learned and chivalric literature become hopelessly muddled. Chaucer's 'Shipman's Tale', although it is associated with Paris, not the English City, well illustrates the problem. There love, sex, and financial profit all become commodified and confused in the 'tailing' and 'tallying' of the tale's rigorously quantitative conclusion.

But Covetise's potential for criminality is not simply limited to magical or fraudulent misrepresentation of product. Covetise resembles Gower's single discussion of the City, the description of urban criminality in *Vox clamantis*, his Latin satire prompted by the Peasants' Revolt of 1381, where he combines sins of 'marchandise', the misrepresentation of wares, and usury/'(h)oker' (5.12–15).[6] His winnings from his first 'trade' prove capable of capitalist transformation and obscene multiplier effects. Reinvestment of profits magically produces yet more profits – and serious social disruptions, more civic incursions into the countryside. As usurer, Covetise is a valuable servant to noblemen, socially prominent but cash-strapped (B 5.237–53). But as both Gower and Langland argue, Covetise's favourite transactions involve the potential for foreclosures on aristocratic country estates, the disruption of proper rural lordship in order to enrich a distant and uninterested urban landlord. Ultimately, as Langland claims, such acquisitions send the ill-equipped and uncouth urban entrepreneur off to play country squire:

> And sopares ['shop-keepers'] and here sones for suluer han be knyhtes
> And lordes sones here laboureres and leyde here rentes to wedde.[7]

But trade does not just harm those outside London. While it provides the glory of the City, its local benefits are selective and uneven, mostly for those large-scale entrepreneurs who inevitably form the London aldermanic ruling class. Thus, civic glory paradoxically contributes to the demise of anything like civic solidarity. The ruling rich may be out to double their profits, and they may frequently ruin knights, those supposed pillars of feudal society. But they equally exploit their fellow citizens and seek profit from the local poor.

Protection of consumers was one fundamental purpose of civic government and thus a persistently repeated theme of civic legislation and record. Guild statutes, in the fourteenth century recorded as part of municipal record, sought to ensure quality of workmanship. City courts showed a commensurate zealousness in prosecuting those responsible for shoddily produced, or wrongly measured, goods, especially prepared foods.

The City government operated the stocks or pillory in Langland's Cornhill in order to display such malefactors (and their products) to public abuse. Among the most basic crimes were sharp practices in violation of parliamentary statute. This 'assize of bread and ale' regulated proper pricing of the most ordinary prepared foods; the costs of bread and ale were fixed to correspond to the going price of the raw materials, the grains that were the basic ingredients. In essence, profiteering out of need, the hunger of citizens, was a crime – and one that, like Covetise's lengthened cloth, involved adulterating a proper product, skimping on those raw materials that should comprise the sold foodstuff.

At *Piers Plowman*, B 3.76–100, Langland describes a situation in which civic government becomes complicit with civic malfeasance. The character Mede convinces London's mayor, in return for a bribe, to ignore the law, the assize of bread and ale. Instead, as a servant of the victuallers, the mayor will allow 'brewers and bakers', among others, to 'selle somdel ayeins reson'. The moderation and due measure that are supposed to define retail pricing will be ignored.

Worse is yet to come, however. Like Covetise, food-traders prove capable of double profiteering, in this case a double victimisation of the urban poor. The mayoral acquiescence in profiteering creates excess, and this is susceptible to further monstrous transformations. Food-tradesmen reap a double profit from the needs of the poor by real estate speculation. The surplus cash generated by their adulterated foodstuffs goes into the land market, the purchase of slum housing, which is then capable of being rented to the needy as excessively overpriced tenement housing.

But Langland's perception, that urban wealth depends on picking the urban poor clean, is really rather far from the truth. The major driver of urban fortunes was aristocratic surplus, loose money from rural agricultural exploitation that could enable purchases wildly sumptuary. A customary way of expressing aristocratic status was excess spending, ostentatious luxury. City fortunes, in their turn, were created for those able to supply appropriately splashy goods, things like unusual oriental spices and richly embroidered tapestries or wall-hangings.

In the Middle Ages, authors show a deep ambivalence about such excessive spending and the surplus that allows it. But, whatever the obvious moral pangs about 'waste', in a world that essentially depended upon subsistence agriculture, excess remained deeply fascinating and potentially attractive. In far too many places in the Middle Ages, starvation was only a dodgy harvest away; in such a context, a full belly, indeed too much to eat and drink, was a prospect nearly heavenly. When one adds to the picture the overwhelmingly carbohydrate-based diets frequent in medieval society, the prospect of good food – a balancing portion of fruits, or a full serving of chicken – might provoke a, for us, surprising rhapsody. It is no wonder that perhaps the greatest commercial site of the City FitzStephen can imagine is a well-stocked public kitchen, or that the street cries at the end of Langland's Prologue emphasise reasonably expensive meat and drink.

Langland's predecessor poem *Winner and Waster* offers a particularly rambunctious analogous description. For the poet of *Winner and Waster*, London represents that place 'Ther moste waste es of wele' – in this poem's terms, the greatest opportunity for an expensive party. In Cheap, Bread Street, and the Poultry, the poet imagines a rich supply of meats and drinks on offer. Waster is to address himself solely to knights, 'botet beryn[s]', men booted for riding; in locales like these, they can find ample outlets for their loose cash – taverns with ale and wine, markets offering both lamb and an array of birds. One pays, not simply to enjoy the fine tastes, but to do so in comfort; fine service, with boys to set the table and to bring food, adds to the sense of excess.[8]

Instructively, this vision of plenty is strongly class-marked. Just as they are suitable victims for urban usurers, rural aristocrats are the proper people to waste their substance on delicacies. Much as the beleaguered poor might wish for such delights, moralists would deny them the opportunity. When they opt to spend their money foolishly on the non-necessities, they are perceived as sinful.

Langland's depiction of Glutton (*Piers Plowman*, B 5.296–362) might typify a range of such portrayals. Aristocrats can have heroic enjoyments in cook-shops, but the homey tavern is a place whose moral status is over-determined, 'the devil's church'. Glutton is dragged in while on his way to confession and mass, and his leisure activities parody the deeply serious business of getting right with God that he has chosen not to perform. The happy camaraderie he enjoys is deliberately marked as urban play; Glutton shares space with a whore from Cock's Lane, a Cheap street-cleaner, and a man from Garlickhythe. But while the upper classes can have their enjoy-ments, for the lower it remains a sinister business, emphatically identifi-able as sinful temptation. It is, of course, 'revel', one of the cries of the rebels of 1381. And Glutton is not the only literary figure engaged in such allegedly criminous and soul-destroying urban actions; one might also point to Chaucer's Perkin (even surnamed 'Reveller') in 'The Cook's Tale' or to the early onset of the mental troubles of Thomas Hoccleve, which are linked, in that poet's 'La Mal Regle', to indulgence in tavern delights.

Hoccleve's breakdown raises a more serious charge against the city and urban revels, the potential loss of one's identity in a large, bustling, indiffer-ent, and anonymous place. Inferentially, medieval texts would seem to imply that before migration to such a centre as London, one had, in one's rural village, a secure identity and a place. The City, in contrast, is no-place – the scarcely governable urban bustle, the mob-scenes that, for example, fill the background of the alliterative *St Erkenwald*, a poem celebrating London's legendary Anglo-Saxon bishop. Equally, as John Gower argues in his *Vox clamantis*, the City is the locale of detraction, rumour, and talebearing (5.16). Along with misrepresentation of product, from diluted, under-strength ale to stretched textiles, goes verbal misrepresentation, the identification of things and persons as something other than what they are, the loss of 'trouth'. After all, it is emphatically in Cornhill and London that Will Langland, the satiric observer of City sin, becomes indistinguishable from his targets, the bogus 'lollares and lewede ermytes' that infest the place (C 5.1–104). Like them, the hero comes to appear self-created, someone seeking to escape the role proper to him and to enter a life of parasitic self-indulgence.

Will's uncomfortable discovery – he is not unequivocally, as he believes, a sanctified individual, but representative of a probably criminous urban type – offers a properly paradoxical image with which to conclude. In the Middle Ages, London was a great draw, with its promises of opportunity and freedom not available elsewhere. But within the City's walls, which apparently enclose and protect this promise, one is just as apt to find a fre-quently indescribable cultural image, one of both vitality and threatening instability.

Notes

1 All citations of the poem are from Arthur Quiller-Couch, ed., *The Oxford Book of English Verse* (London: Oxford University Press, 1919), no. 19.

2 See especially Geoffrey of Monmouth, *The History of the Kings of Britain*, 1.17, ed. Michael D. Reeve, trans. Neil Wright (Woodbridge: Boydell Press, 2007), pp. 28–31.

3 See *ibid.*, 3.53, pp. 66–7.

4 William Langland, *Piers Plowman: The B Version. Will's Vision of Piers Plowman, Do-Well, Do-Better, and Do-Best*, ed. George Kane and E. Talbot Donaldson (London: Athlone, 1975), 13.263–70. Further references to the B-text are to this edition.

5 Richard Maidstone, *Concordia (The Reconciliation of Richard II with London)*, ed. David R. Carlson, trans. A. G. Rigg (Kalamazoo: Medieval Institute Press, 2003), lines 79–101.

6 John Gower, *Vox clamantis*, 5.12–15, in *The Complete Works*, ed. G. C. Macaulay, 4 vols. (Oxford: Clarendon Press, 1899–1902), Vol. IV, pp. 220–5.

7 William Langland, *Piers Plowman: The C Version*, ed. George Russell and George Kane (London: Athlone, 1997), 5.72–3. Further references to the C-text are to this edition.

8 *Winner and Waster*, lines 472–95, in *Alliterative Poetry of the Later Middle Ages: An Anthology*, ed. Thorlac Turville-Petre (London: Routledge, 1989), p. 64.

2

JEAN E. HOWARD

London and the early modern stage

The changing city and the commercial stage, *c.* 1600

It is a curious fact of London theatre history that around about 1598 play-wrights quite suddenly began to write plays that in a sustained way depicted aspects of contemporary London life. London streets and London places began to be mentioned prominently in theatrical dialogue, and those famil-iar streets and places became the setting for stories about London economic life, the struggles among various social groups for dominance within the city, and the domestic disputes and intrigues that percolated through London households.

While prior to 1598 there had certainly been plays with scenes set in London, such as *Richard III*, and others, such as *The Three Lords and Three Ladies of London* (1590), that evoked London as a place to be redeemed from sin, nonetheless, 1598 marked a real change in how and how frequently the city was staged. Dramas such as William Haughton's *Englishmen for My Money* (1598) and the early comedies of Ben Jonson did not treat London as an abstract landscape populated with allegorical figures, nor did they set the occasional scene within the city; rather, they luxuriated in 'place realism', that is, in the depiction of a particular city-scape and its contemporary inhabitants. Most of these plays were comic in form, and they are generally known as city comedies, or London comedies, in recognition of the fact that they constitute a distinct subgenre of comedy in general.

These plays of London life used conventional characters and story forms to create the feeling of place realism that was their hallmark. They drew, for example, on social types such as the hardworking artisan, the grasping mer-chant, the high-spirited and independent urban wife, and the feckless gentle-man who has lost his land but not his taste for luxury. Through narratives about these social types, the stage rendered urban life intelligible and made the city comprehensible as a place where certain kinds of things happened to certain kinds of people. In this process, genre was crucial, for the 'London' represented on the early modern stage looked quite different depending on whether it was rendered as tragedy, history, or comedy.

An immediate question, however, is why the sudden interest in the late 1590s in the theatrical depiction of contemporary London life? There is no single answer, but rather a suggestive series of partial answers that together speak to the changing nature of London commercial theatre at the end of the sixteenth century and the changing life of the city within which it was embedded. First, both the city and the theatre were being impacted by profound commercial and demographic changes. In 1550 London had a population of approximately 55,000 people; by 1600 that number was close to 200,000. A city of such size and scope was, in England, a new phenomenon, something requiring interpretation and representation if it was to be cognitively and emotionally comprehended both by those who inhabited it and also by those whose acquaintance with the city was less intimate. Theatre was a popular form of entertainment, available to the literate and the illiterate alike, and well-suited to render the city legible to its inhabitants and, in the form of playbooks, to spread ideas of contemporary London life to readers across England.

The commercial theatre certainly depended upon London's burgeoning population to sustain its growth. In the 1590s playing occurred six days a week in several large amphitheatres and in smaller venues such as inns. Only a large metropolis could have provided the audiences with so much theatrical activity. The availability of London capital to construct and sustain large theatrical enterprises was also crucial. Throughout the sixteenth century London was experiencing the effects of an increase in commercial activity of all sorts, including an uptick in international trade. As a port city, it was linked by sea-trade to entrepôts in Europe, North Africa, the Levant, and increasingly to the Far East and the Americas. Much of this trade was organised by ambitious joint stock companies, such as the Levant Company, in which shareholders made investments in expensive overseas ventures and together shared the risks and the profits they entailed.

International trade affected London life in a number of ways. It brought many new products, from American tobacco to Indian pearls to Sumatran spices, into the London marketplace. Many were luxury goods, but some were priced for purchase by people of the middling ranks, creating new consumer tastes and making it possible for people to acquire goods once exclusively reserved for the elite. The increase in the scale and pace of commercial life put pressure on the traditional status system, allowing people to cross-dress, for example, in clothing inappropriate to their rank, and transferring power within the city's commercial ranks from the leaders of the traditional craft guilds to the leaders of the overseas trading companies. Such trade also made the city more cosmopolitan, both because of the influx of exotic goods and also because it brought merchants and travellers from other nations into the London city space.

The commercial London theatre participated in, affected, and was affected by all these changes in urban life. Theatres were themselves often financed and structured as joint stock companies with shareholders spreading the risk and the profits of company ownership among themselves. This was true of Shakespeare's company, the Lord Chamberlain's Men, later called the King's Men, in which Shakespeare was a shareholder. Perhaps more strikingly, the playhouses became in the eyes of many the epitome of the shapeshifting practices associated with the loosening of the social system under the pressure of market forces and of geographical mobility. Anti-theatrical writers attacked players who 'jetted' themselves in the clothing of kings and noblemen, and attacked boy actors who, on the all-male stage, wore the garments of women.

The most profound way in which the theatres registered their urban location was in the kinds of dramatic fictions they created, fictions that in the case of London comedy focused on key aspects of city life: commerce, social mobility, petty crime, and the interactions between gentlemen and citizens, citizens and foreigners, men and women. When we look at particular London comedies written after 1598, it will quickly be apparent that they return again and again to certain narrative motifs and stock situations. Many plots revolve around economic struggles and scams – clever gentlemen, for example, attempt to siphon off the money of prosperous artisans and merchants, sometimes by winning favour with their wives, or city merchants connive for the lands held by prodigal gentlemen. Women are often positioned as counters in struggles between those whose social prestige is based on birth and claims to land and those whose power springs from commercial sources. Comic plots frequently pit native-born Londoners against those born elsewhere: either those, called foreigners, who were born outside London and were therefore not London citizens, or those, called strangers, who were born outside England altogether. Frequently linguistic difference (a funny accent) separates outsiders from insiders, whether those outsiders are from Africa, France, Holland, Wales, or just from the northern counties of England itself. Together, the recurring situations dramatised in London comedies speak to the complexities of an urban existence in which crowded streets, alien bodies, escalating commercialisation, and an astonishing array of new commodities were affecting the way daily life was understood and experienced.

London history plays and London tragedy

It is a mistake, however, to think that the 'invention' of London comedy *c.* 1598 constituted the only way in which the city was foregrounded on the London stage at the end of the sixteenth century. In August of 1599 an interesting two-part play was entered in the Register of the Company of Stationers and described as follows: 'Twoo *playes beinge the ffirst and Second parte of* EDWARD *the IIIIth and the Tanner of Tamworth With the history of the life and deathe of master* SHORE *and* JANE SHORE *his wife as yt was lately acted by the Right honorable the E[a]rle of* DERBYE *his servants.*'[1]

What is unusual is the space given, not to the typical monarchical protagonist of a national history play – here Edward IV – but to the comic character John Hobs, the tanner of Tamworth, and, more importantly, to a London guildsman, Matthew Shore, and his citizen wife, Jane. In the 1590s the English history play, including such popular works as Marlowe's *Edward II* and Shakespeare's *Richard III* and *1 Henry IV*, had foregrounded late medieval monarchical protagonists and their struggles to attain and defend their thrones, their military actions at home and abroad, and the dynastic disputes that complicated the legitimacy of their rule. As the Tudors consolidated central governmental functions, and as a sense of national identity intensified as a result of events such as the threat posed by the Spanish Armada, the national history play became a genre in which the origins of the English state could be dramatised and pride in England's dynastic history given expression. In some of these dramas, as the historical record dictated, London plays a part. In *2 Henry VI*, for example, the rebel Jack Cade invades London with his lower-class followers, raping, murdering, and plundering. In *Richard III*, the Tower of London is where Richard has his two young nephews, rivals to his throne, put to death; and in another scene, Richard's noble supporters call on the people of London to acclaim Richard as king. In both cases, however, while London is where certain events happen, it is not itself a protagonist in the play, nor are its citizens. The spotlight remains firmly fixed on the contenders for monarchical supremacy and on their noble followers.

Edward IV is a very different kind of history play. Rather than focusing mainly on Edward, it pays equal attention to Matthew and Jane Shore and to the London citizen culture of which they are a part. When rebels invade London, it is Matthew Shore and other London citizens and apprentices who drive them off. The king arrives after the battle is finished. Moreover, when the king disguises himself to woo Jane Shore in her husband's shop, he is figured less as the defender of the nation in the manner of Henry V and more as an intruder into the sanctity of citizen homes. The emotional centre of the play lies with the Shores as Matthew Shore's life is ruined by the King's adulterous sexual conquest of Jane, and she suffers piercing remorse for the loss of her honour and the downfall of her household.

Two things are new about this pair of history plays. The first is the displacement, in affective terms, of the monarchical story by the citizen story. The second is the rooting of the citizen story firmly in the particulars of London geography and in the city's guild culture. The play is place-rich. When the rebels think about invading the city, they mention specific city sites – Leadenhall, Cheapside, the Mint, the Tower, Lombard Street, St Paul's, Westminster – they will occupy and plunder. The citizen defenders in their turn talk about defending the eastern entrances to the city, especially Aldgate and Bishopsgate, gather for consultation at the Guildhall, and drive the rebels back to Mile End.

The citizens deeply inhabit this urban landscape. For example, Heywood presents the play's mayor, John Crosby (who according to the historical record was sheriff of London but never actually mayor), as steeped in knowledge of the city's history. When urging the apprentices to repulse the rebels, he evokes the example of William Walworth, a London mayor during Richard II's reign who stabbed a rebel dead in Smithfield and was knighted for the deed. According to an apocryphal but fervently held legend retold by Shore himself, a red dagger was incorporated into the arms of London as a result of Walworth's noble act. The deeds of London citizens thus live on in an urban coat of arms that rivals the coats of arms proudly displayed by noblemen. Crosby presents himself as a complete creature of the city. Having been found abandoned as a baby by Cow Cross in Islington, he reports that he was given the name Crosby (by the Cross) by the shoemaker who found him and took him to the nearby charitable hospital to be raised. Later in life, as a prosperous member of the grocers' guild, he endowed a poorhouse in Bishopsgate Street and called it Crosby House.[2] The play links the mayor with the geography and the edifices of his city, especially the charitable institutions that aided the poor and were erected by successful citizens to show forth their good works and London's greatness. Similarly, at the end of 2 *Edward IV*, after Jane Shore has died in a ditch at the city's edge, the people who loved her for her many deeds of charity name the spot of her death Shore's Ditch or Shoreditch. This is also an apocryphal story, but it again speaks to the play's impulse to read the city through the deeds of its citizen heroes and to read those citizens through the streets and buildings of the metropolis they inhabited.

Providing the city with a history of its own, the London history play fore-grounded the deeds of Lord Mayors, famous merchants, and study citizens rather than the deeds of kings. It thus drew on and contributed to a citizen culture that had its own defining myths, heroes, and profound attachment to the physical geography of the city. Many of these London histories, such as Thomas Dekker's *The Shoemaker's Holiday* (1599) or Part 2 of Thomas Heywood's *If You Know Not Me You Know Nobody* (1605), are, like *Edward IV*, tinged with nostalgia in that they depict a London that at least on the surface is dominated by traditional guild life. By the end of the sixteenth century that dominance was threatened by a variety of forces: the economic power of the overseas merchants, the presence of unregulated labour in the suburbs, and the social pull exerted by gentlemen who came to the city for Court employment, for urban pleasures and vices, or simply to escape the tedium of country life. For the most part, *Edward IV* ignores this cast of characters in favour of the loyal citizens who defend London from invasion and uphold its civic traditions.

That such plays were popular is indicated by a speech made by a grocer in a satiric London comedy, Francis Beaumont's *The Knight of the Burning Pestle* (1607), in which the grocer, attending the theatre, decries plays that make fun of citizens and celebrates his affection for dramas (most now lost) that made historical London citizens into heroes. His favourites are *The Legend of Whittington* (the story of Dick Whittington, the humble London apprentice who rose to be Lord Mayor), *The Life and Death of Sir Thomas Gresham, with the Building of the Royal Exchange* (about a merchant who built a splendid bourse in the Cornhill area of London that rivalled the most elaborate markets of Europe), and *The Story of Queen Elenor, with the Rearing of London Bridge upon Wool-sacks* (which celebrated the merchants of the wool-trade and the revenue derived from that trade that financed the building of London Bridge).[3] While some of these plays, and I would include *The Shoemaker's Holiday* among them, acknowledge the tensions and competing economic currents that put traditional guild culture under pressure, they nonetheless collectively represent London as a space dominated by productive guilds and hardworking citizens.

A different and more dangerous London, however, emerges in several other plays of the 1590s. Rather than histories, these plays are London tragedies, and they construct the city as a place of criminality where dangerous and uncontrollable passions are stirred by the sexual and economic temptations of urban life. The anonymous *A Warning for Faire Women*, printed in 1599, dramatises an historical event: the murder of a London merchant, George Sanders, by his wife's lover, George Browne. Robert Yarington's *Two Lamentable Tragedies*, printed in 1601, also dramatizes another actual crime – the murder of a chandler of Thames Street, Master Thomas Beech, and his servant – by his neighbour, Master Thomas Merry, a tavernkeeper. The cause in this case is avarice; Beech has boasted of the money he has saved through his trade, and the more impecunious Merry wants it.

Critics now call both plays domestic tragedies, that is, tragedies that focus on the downfall of characters not of noble rank and that pivot on the murderous tensions within households and neighbourhoods between masters and servants, husbands and wives. Some of the best known of these plays, such as Thomas Heywood's *A Woman Killed with Kindness*, are set in rural England; but both *A Warning for Faire Women* and *Two Lamentable Tragedies* are located with remarkable specificity in a recognisable London. Together, they speak to what historians have identified as a concern about crime that accompanied the growth and expansion of the city in the late sixteenth century, and they explore the motives and emotions that lie behind these crimes. In the case of *Two Lamentable Tragedies*, both the crime and its discovery are mundane and deeply rooted in the circumstances of London life. Though Merry owns a tavern, has a loving sister and faithful servant, and by his own admission may in time grow to greater wealth, he nonetheless is not content. The city offers him the spectacle of men with more money than he and of goods he would like to buy. He complains in particular about the fact that he has no store of cash through which to take advantage of bargains that suddenly became available. When Merry's neighbour makes the mistake of talking out loud about the score of pounds he has salted away, Merry can not overcome his envy and greed. Eventually, in a paroxysm of violence, he kills Beech, striking him fifteen times with a hammer; later, to avoid detection, he also attacks Beech's man, this time leaving the hammer lodged in the servant's head.

The play mitigates the horror of this violence by bringing the criminals to detection and thus showing that London, if endangered by crime, is nonetheless ultimately tractable to the ministrations of justice. Urban population density, the proximity and careful surveillance of neighbours, and the peculiarities of craft production all make it hard for murderers to get away with their crimes. Thus, if the conditions of urban living incite crime, they also thwart it. When Merry attempts to kill Beech's boy, the boy makes such a cry that the murderer flees the scene for fear the neighbours will hear, leaving the weapon behind and the job not entirely finished. Indeed, Beech's neighbours prove relentless in their pursuit of the murderer. After Merry kills Beech in a room upstairs above his tavern, he is constantly afraid that neighbours will hear him or see him trying to dispose of the body, which he hastily dismembers and stuffs in two bags. One bag he ferries across the

Thames and drops in Paris Garden ditch in Southwark; the other he leaves by the stairs leading down to the Thames by Baynard's Castle.

Alas for him, Merry's methods of body disposal take no account of the overcrowded urban landscape. Two watermen stumble over the bag containing Beech's head and legs as they are going to get in their boats to begin their work on the river. Meanwhile, the water spaniel accompanying a gentleman walking by the Paris Garden ditch comes across the bag containing Beech's trunk. Merry has vainly attempted to commit and conceal a murder in a densely packed London where few places afford escape from the intrusions of men, sometimes of men and their dogs. Moreover, the bags in which the body was stuffed bear the mark of the craftsman who made them and prove easily traceable.

In *A Warning for Faire Women* crime is given equally homely and equally urban roots, though this time sex enters into the equation when a predatory gentleman, George Browne, pursues a city wife from Billingsgate, Ann Sanders, and for her love slays her husband. Their story is complicated by economic and class factors quite common in theatrical depictions of contemporary London life. While Sanders's husband is a merchant who spends much of his time at the Royal Exchange in Cornhill, Browne is a gentleman who in the latter part of the play attends the Court. Tension between gentlemen and men of commerce thus play out over the body of a woman. At the same time, Ann is associated with the acquisitiveness often attributed to London wives. Calling a milliner and a draper to her, she arranges for the purchase of linen, an Italian purse, and gloves, only to have her desires thwarted by her husband's servant, who tells his mistress that all of Master Sanders's money is tied up in an obligation at the Exchange. Furious both at being ordered about by a servant and at having to forgo the purchase of the goods she craves, Mistress Sanders suddenly becomes susceptible to the suggestion that she might, in future, take a gentleman for a husband. Browne is conveniently at hand.

These London tragedies construct the city in a particular way, as a place of criminality and danger, but also as a place where order is eventually restored and the secrets of sinful misconduct revealed. The city that seems by its size and complexity to conceal crime is ultimately revealed as a place of encompassing surveillance where neighbours, magistrates, and even hunting dogs detect wrongdoers. These plays also lay down templates for defining the causes of criminality. Economic envy and a hunger for 'things', they suggest, impel both men and women toward violence. Avarice and envy of Beech's wealth set Master Merry on his murderous course, and affection for Italian purses and gloves propels Mistress Sanders into the catastrophic events that end with her husband's murder. London emerges in these plays, not as a place where sturdy citizens erect poorhouses and defend their city against invaders, but as a place where overpowering desires are released, desires so urgent that they destroy the bonds that connect husband and wife, neighbour and neighbour. It is no wonder that each play so firmly counteracts the entropic force of these desires by bringing the criminals to account, eliciting their confessions, and killing them off.

London comedy

If London history constructs a city dominated by successful citizens, the edifices they build, and the good works they do, and if the London tragedy focuses on the household and neighbourhood crimes that test and ultimately confirm the orderliness of the city presided over by London's good burghers and magistrates, then London comedy, the richest and most fully developed of the subgenres depicting London life, works differently. First, its primary register is imaginative, rather than documentary. That is, it does not stage crimes that have actually happened, like Beech's slaying of Merry, or historical figures, like Jane and Matthew Shore. Instead, London comedy develops a rich array of fictive types and narrative templates, endlessly worked and reworked, for representing the interactions among social groups within the urban context: men and women, Londoners and country folks, Londoners and those born abroad, citizens and gentlemen, wits and fools. As with most forms of comedy, love plots are central to London comedy, but in this genre love is almost never separable from monetary concerns, nor, perhaps surprisingly, are marriageable young maids the only women of interest. City wives often emerge as key figures in London comedy as, with avidity or reluctance, they tend their husband's shops, dally with gallants, confirm or put at risk their own reputations and their husbands', and broker marriage deals for their children.

What has been called the first of these city comedies, William Haughton's *Englishmen for My Money*, foregrounds the marriage fortunes of three young daughters of Pisaro, a 'Portingale' (or Portuguese) merchant who married an English woman, settled in London, and has become extremely wealthy by extensive overseas trade. A place-specific play that depends for much of its humour and its realistic effects on constant reference to London streets and buildings, *Englishmen for My Money* makes Pisaro a key figure at Sir Thomas Gresham's Royal Exchange, the Cornhill bourse erected as a meeting place for big overseas merchants to facilitate their trade. As is typical in many ensuing London comedies, this great merchant and his children have different ideas about the girls' proper marriage partners. Perfectly assimilated to English ways, they want to marry three penniless English gentlemen, all in debt to their father. Pisaro, in his turn, wants them to marry three stranger merchants: a Frenchman, an Italian, and a Dutchman.

A key question for all London comedies is: who has the cash and who the cachet? In *Englishmen for My Money*, the three girls will bear Pisaro's fortune into their marriages, making them attractive marriage partners both to wealthy foreign traders and to cash-starved English gentlemen. The daughters dote on their impecunious English suitors whose rank and nationality enhance their desirability, while they regard the stranger merchants with disgust, in part because they can't speak fluent English. Their stage speech is heavily marked by thick accents. As one daughter says: 'If needes you marry with an *English* Lasse, / Woe her in *English*, or else sheele call you Asse.'[4] The foreign suitors do prove themselves asses by their incompetent wooing, while the English gentlemen engage in a number of clever wooing tricks that confirm their status as the smartest men in the room. In the end, the Englishmen get the girls, and the threat that the foreign suitors will capture both Pisaro's daughters and his money is repelled.

At one level the wooing plot of *Englishmen for My Money* follows the New Comedy pattern of having clever young men and their servants outwit the aged fathers of their intended brides. But that basic template is complicated by other concerns typical of London comedy. The first is economic. While Pisaro is a merchant, the wooers are gentlemen; and the young men's success marks the transfer of significant economic assets from one class to another. Perhaps more importantly, Pisaro is himself of foreign birth, and his economic pre-eminence in the play speaks to an anxiety about the power of alien merchants within London's merchant community, including their power to buy up the land of impoverished English gentlemen. Pisaro is too powerful simply to be rendered comic, and he never forfeits his place of pre-eminence at the Exchange. The play handles the threat he poses more obliquely by ensuring that through his daughters' marriages his wealth will eventually end up in English hands. Moreover, with this wealth the young English suitors will be able to regain the land that, the play suggests, is the true guarantee of their worth. While London must make room for Pisaro, the powerful Portingale merchant, it makes the feckless English gentlemen the beneficiaries of his commercial labour.

In *Englishmen for My Money*, social and economic conflict arises between native and foreign figures, merchants and gentlemen, parents and children. Ensuing London comedies ring changes on these conflicts and invent others. In some of the most sophisticated of them, struggles for supremacy within the city do not have clear-cut resolutions since within the urban context competing systems of value are set against one another in ways that make it difficult to assess actions by a single and unvarying standard. *Eastward*

Ho (1605), a collaboration by Ben Jonson, George Chapman, and John Marston, is an especially good example of such competing codes. As in *Englishmen for My Money*, the play deals in part with the disposition of wealth through marriage. A wealthy London goldsmith, Touchstone, has two daughters. One, Gertrude, makes a rash marriage to a debt-ridden knight, Sir Petronel Flash; the other, Mildred, makes a prudent marriage to the virtuous apprentice, Golding, who serves in her father's shop. Flash is a gold-digger who uses Gertrude's marriage portion to finance an ill-advised venture to Virginia that ends in a shipwreck at the mouth of the Thames. Golding is a thrifty and dutiful apprentice who, having wed Mildred, makes a spectacular rise through the ranks of his guild and establishes himself as a leading man of the City.

The play at first glance thus seems to be a fairly conservative reprise of the worldview of a play like *Edward IV*, with its celebration of guild life and its scorn for women like Gertrude, who wants to leave London, rise above her class, and live in a castle in the country. If London offers temptations to over-consumption, illicit sex, and disruptive social climbing, those temptations are to be eschewed. Yet to make this point, *Eastward Ho* so energetically and entertainingly depicts the doings of those who live by other rules that the moral compass of the play is thrown off kilter. *Eastward Ho* is not alone in projecting ambivalence about the status of the urban vices it depicts. To decry the seamier side of London life, London comedy had to depict it; and in many London comedies satire has an odd way of verging toward celebration. This is particularly true of *Eastward Ho*. To make my point, I want to look further at how the play handles two characters: the foolish daughter, Gertrude, and Quicksilver, a second apprentice within Touchstone's household.

Everything about Gertrude is written in an excessive register. While her sister creeps about being good and demanding nothing, Gertrude wants everything: a husband with a title, a castle in the country, a maidservant, a coach, and a way to lord it over her mother and her sister. The play delivers her a dreadful comeuppance. Eventually she is reduced to selling her clothing for food and living in her coach, Sir Petronel having run off with her wedding portion and his castle in the country having proven to be a fiction. But the soaring passions unleashed by the allure of a title and a coach do not, as in the London tragedy of Ann Sanders, lead to crime. Instead, they make Gertrude an oddly attractive figure. Thwarted in her desires, Gertrude keeps hoping, longing that eventually fairies will come and leave money in the street for her to find. Any actress worth her salt would prefer to play Gertrude rather than Mildred. Although portrayed as naïve and often comic, she is still a scene stealer whether she is trying on the fancy clothing she considers suitable for a knight's wife or flouncing off to her coach before her neighbours' astonished eyes. There is no question that Mildred is the 'better' child judged in moral terms. Yet in Gertrude the play creates a figure who embodies the desires unleashed by the economic and social disruptions that marked London life around 1600. The play presents the two girls as a study in contrasts, but the contrasts end up being posed in theatrical and performative, as well as moral terms. The quick and the dead, as well as the sinful and the virtuous, are labels one might use to parse the difference between these daughters. At its best, London comedy renders its judgments on urban life with exactly the complexity one finds in *Eastward Ho*, where being good is juxtaposed to the complex pleasures of being alive to the possibilities for self-display and self-transformation that the city affords.

This complexity is amplified in *Eastward Ho*'s depiction of Quicksilver, the bad apprentice. A flambuoyant figure who hates the drudgery of the shopkeeper's life and prefers to play tennis and go to the theatre with his courtly friends, Quicksilver is eventually dismissed from Touchstone's establishment and throws in his lot with Sir Petronel Flash's ill-fated Virginia adventure. Usury, prostitution, drink – Quicksilver is familiar with all these urban vices, but he is above all a prodigal who lives beyond his means. As a result, Quicksilver eventually finds himself locked up in the Counter, one of London's main debtors' prisons. To win release, Quicksilver does something unexpected. He confesses his sins and repents, seemingly aligning himself with the pious behaviour of Golding and Touchstone.

The mode of Quicksilver's repentance, however, calls into question what it really means, for Quicksilver repents with a performative gusto that rivals Gertrude's gusto at playing 'lady'. In a paroxysm of reforming zeal, he cuts off his long hair, sign of his aspiration to gallant status; gives away his rich apparel; wears a rough garment signalling his abjection; asks to be put in the Hole, the worst accommodation the Counter affords; willingly eats out of the alms basket provided for the poorest prisoners; and takes to singing Psalms and ballads of repentance and telling stories of Christian piety gleaned from John Foxe's *Book of Martyrs* (1563) and Thomas Becon's *Sick Man's Salve* (1558). This exaggerated performance of repentance melts the hearts of his jailors and eventually of Touchstone himself, and the play ends with Quicksilver's emergence from the dank debtors' prison into the bright daylight of Cheapside.

The question is: what is being rewarded – the repentance of a sinner or the sinner's performative skill? Critics divide on this question, and the play is coy about its ultimate judgment on the bad apprentice. On the surface, morality prevails, and the virtuous and the reformed triumph. But the exuberant theatricality of figures like Gertrude and Quicksilver hints that there is more than one standard of judgment at work in this drama. A stern morality would suppress much that the play suggests makes city life alluring and fun: theatricality, social aspiration, performative élan. In inviting an audience to feel the tension between the two the London comedy registers and gives expression to some of the deepest tensions of the age, for the struggles of the genre are not just between social groups but also between systems of value. If some plays, like *Edward IV*, cling to traditional moral frames, others, like *Eastward Ho*, juxtapose those to newer norms, ones arising from the unstable, performative, and often crassly materialistic elements of urban life. In the rub between the two, some of the most vital drama of the period emerges.

Thomas Middleton, one of the most prolific writers of London comedy, exemplifies the iconoclasm and deep irony that permeate some city plays and bring into question traditional standards of value. A common Middleton theme is the tension between clever city types and country gentlemen new to London. His *Michaelmas Term* (1607) explores this tension largely through the character of Master Easy, an Essex gentleman who, his father being dead, arrives in the city to enjoy its pleasures. Almost immediately he is ensnared by the henchmen of Quomodo, a scheming woollen draper and moneylender who wants to get his hands on Easy's estate. Because of Easy's unfamiliarity with London ways, Quomodo drags him into a financial quagmire, and for a while it looks as if the clever tradesman will have his way with the country naïf. Simultaneously, in another plot an upstart adventurer named Lethe brings a young woman from the country to be his mistress while he pursues the daughter of Quomodo in marriage. Again, it looks as if London will be the site of country ruin as the country wench exchanges her innocence for some fashionable clothes.

An anxiety common to the period was the fear that London was a snare and a pit, drawing people and resources into its maw and leading to the depopulation and impoverishment of the countryside and the decay of rural hospitality. *Michaelmas Term* stokes these anxieties by its depiction of Easy's entrapment, the country wench's ruin, and Quomodo's fantasy of cutting down the logs on Easy's estate. The play ultimately mitigates these worries, however, and the resolution is brought about largely because of Quomodo's hubris. Wanting to see what his son and heir will do with his money after his death and wanting to see his wife, Thomasine, mourn for him, Quomodo gives out that he is dead. In a series of complex plot developments, the trick used to entrap Easy is revealed at the same time that all of Quomodo's dependants, from his wife to his servants to his son, make plain their indifference to his death. Once Thomasine believes him dead, she rushes to marry Easy, exerting an independence of mind and will typical of many city wives.

Moreover, Quomodo's daughter refuses to marry Lethe, her father's choice, choosing instead another gallant favoured by her mother. Lethe is ordered by a judge to marry the country wench.

This complicated resolution is rich in the ironies that mark Middleton's brand of London comedy. The balance between city and country is nominally restored, since Easy regains possession of his country estate and foils Quomodo's appropriation of it; and the country wench is saved by marriage from being sucked into London's illicit sexual economy. It nonetheless remains true that the city has exerted its centripetal force over all the country characters, and that pull can't be erased; moreover, city morality – or lack of it – marks this ending. The country wench undergoes a mindboggling alteration from whore to wife, and the same judge who gives her in marriage to Lethe also determines that Thomasine must be returned to Quomodo. In the interim, though, Thomasine has been the wife of another man. Middleton, in a different way than in *Eastward Ho*, but to much the same effect, seems bent on pointing out how the city lives by rules that pose a challenge to traditional customs and values. Even when city villains are foiled, the return to custom is never a seamless one, the strains in this case made most evident by the way the play challenges the assumption that a good wife must be virginal before marriage and chaste thereafter, or that the country, for all its virtues, can really outmatch the allure of the city.

While the heyday of London comedy is typically taken to be the period between 1598 and 1615, in actuality the theatre kept turning out London-based comedies right up until the closing of the commercial theatre in 1642. In the Caroline period, in particular, new themes and preoccupations were added to the genre's repertoire, and its geographical centre shifted to the fashionable West End. Many Caroline London comedies are set in new places of fashionable congregation: Hyde Park, Covent Garden, the New Exchange, ballrooms, and academies of manners. As in earlier London comedies, these plays are preoccupied with social pre-eminence: who has power within the urban world? Rank and money continue to matter, but so increasingly does mastery of the fashionable conduct that could be displayed while walking in Hyde Park or dancing at a ball. A strong distinction emerges in these plays between boors and cosmopolitans, between those who can't dance with elegance, give compliments, or wear their clothing with grace, and those who can.

James Shirley's *Hyde Park* (1632) marks out some of the new terms through which these Caroline plays constructed their version of London. In Shirley's world, manners matter, and women play a major role in arbitrating between the mannerly and the boorish. This is made clear when the play's highest-ranking figure, Lord Bonvile, walks with a young woman named

Julietta in Hyde Park. Opened to the public in the 1630s, the Park quickly became a place of entertainment (horse races and foot races are featured in the play) as well as social display. As *Hyde Park* opens, Julietta is wooed by Trier, a gentleman who, unbeknownst to her, has decided he will test her virtue by leaving her in Bonvile's company in the park. Bonvile behaves badly, leading Julietta into the park's less-frequented parts, asking for a kiss, and suggesting that the two of them engage in a sexual dalliance. Julietta staves him off, saying that his titles are worth nothing without virtue and that her own innocence sets her above him. Virtue trumps rank as a mannerly woman of modest rank reads a lecture in proper conduct to the play's most socially prominent figure. Julietta is also severe with Trier for exposing her to Bonvile's unmannerly assault, informing him that his lack of trust in her has proved him no fit suitor. Properly shamed, both men vow reform, and Julietta emerges as the arbiter of manners and social worth.

The verbal exchanges between the men and women of the play suggest new forms of social interactions between the sexes in this fashionable world, interactions that construct men and women on terms of greater equality than was typical of earlier city plays despite the scope they had given to London women's wit and will. If Julietta brings a powerful moral seriousness to her scenes with Bonvile and Trier, another woman, Carol, is most notable for her compelling wit. An overt scorner of marriage, Carol nonetheless has a number of suitors whom she teases and torments. One, Fairfield, is her match. He tricks her into promising that if she will fulfil one request, he will leave her alone. He stipulates that she is able to forbid him to ask anything that would offend her. She reels off a long list of things that would impinge on her autonomy. He is not to ask her to marry him; love him; sleep with him; spoil her face; ride naked through the city; fast; wear a hairy smock; give him her parrot; pray before dinner; desist from card games, the theatre, and other places of public pleasure; say how old she is before company; cease teasing her suitors; or listen to his sonnets. When he agrees, she grants him his wish, which, to her astonishment, is that she will never seek his company again. Attracted by his independence, Carol immediately begins to pursue him. In the end the two finally admit their love, but not before they have in effect enacted a contract to respect each other's autonomy. Recalling Benedict and Beatrice in their witty repartee, and anticipating Millamont and Mirabel in their careful delineation of separate spheres of autonomy, Carol and Fairfield intimate the shifting codes of behaviour that defined interactions between the sexes in Caroline London.

The stage and London were inextricably intertwined in early modern London, nowhere more visibly than in the many different plays – histories, tragedies, and comedies – that took London as their setting. Each genre created its own types and narrative conventions to express and negotiate the social changes that came with the city's wildly expanding population, its evolving economic practices, and the instabilities that arose when established social groups won or lost pre-eminence in the urban milieu and when new actors emerged on the scene. Revelling in the naming of London places and in the retailing of its history, delighting in the energy released by the changing city, the playwrights of the time made the city their own. If we think of early modern London today, it is often in the terms these dramatists provided: a place where strangers jostled against native-born citizens; where trade and consumption caused a flowering of sharp practices, flamboyant consumption, and shapeshifting; and where, finally, there emerged the tasteful culture of the West End with its fashionable theatres, parks, and gardens. Perhaps at no other time in English history was the theatre more central to the urban culture of which it was a part and to which, in its London plays, it gave lasting expression.

Notes

1 Thomas Heywood, *The First and Second Parts of King Edward IV*, ed. Richard Rowland (Manchester: Manchester University Press, 2005), p. 58.
2 Again, Heywood somewhat alters the historical record; see *ibid.*, pp. 159–60, notes to lines 11–31.
3 Francis Beaumont, *The Knight of the Burning Pestle*, ed. Michael Hattaway (New York: Norton, 2000), Induction, lines 16–22, p. 12.
4 William Haughton, *Englishmen for My Money*, ed. Albert Croll Baugh (Philadelphia: University of Pennsylvania Press, 1913), II.iii.1092–3.

3

ADRIAN JOHNS

London and the early modern book

For the first two centuries of its existence, the printed book in England was overwhelmingly an artifact of London. With a few relatively specialised exceptions, the university presses of Oxford and Cambridge being the most important, before 1695 printing was restricted by law to the capital city. While the letter of the law was not always decisive – the Marprelate Tracts, for example, came from clandestine operators who moved about the country, and Charles I's army trundled along a royalist press operated by Leonard Lichfield as it marched[1] – for the most part the production of books was a practice in and of the metropolis. In consequence, as the city grew into a great European capital and as print developed into a central element of its everyday life, the character of the one substantially shaped the character of the other. Markets, modes of publishing, genres, audiences, literary sensibilities, reading practices – all these and more came into being as aspects of London life, and in turn London life was transformed by them.

This was more than a matter of location alone. What emerged by the end of the seventeenth century – having been ringingly and prophetically proclaimed by John Milton half a century earlier – was a citizenry confident in its ability and indeed right to engage in judgment of all conceivable topics (politics being but one) by virtue of its mastery of an arena of printed argument. But this confidence had been hard won, and its foundations remained questionable even after 1700. In fact, during the mid-seventeenth-century upheavals and the Restoration a sustained debate had taken place on the question of whether (to what extent, on what basis) readers could responsibly treat the representations produced by print as authentic, accurate, truthful, or trustworthy. That debate addressed not 'print' in the abstract, but printing and bookselling as London crafts and trades. To be a skilled user of the printed book, it helped to be as familiar as Milton with London itself – its diverse places, people, and customs. The public sphere, such as it was, rested on practices that were socially complex and ever-shifting, but that took their shape from the metropolitan context.

Topographies

Printed materials – not just, or even particularly, books – were a constant presence in seventeenth-century London. Sheer numbers provide an impressive indication of how much so. It has been estimated that in the period from the collapse of royal regulation at the beginning of the Civil War to the end of the century, London printers produced about 100,000 titles; if print-runs were typically about 500 to 1,000 individual copies, that makes for between 50 and 100 million volumes.[2] About 1.3 million Bibles alone had been printed by mid century – sufficient for every English household to have a copy of Scripture – and perhaps a million catechisms.[3] To those totals one needs to add periodicals, of which between 1620 and 1695 almost 700 discrete runs appeared, totaling some 24,000 separate numbers, and therefore, again, perhaps 10 to 20 million copies. This proliferation of serials is especially notable because it began from a standing start: the genre was unknown in 1600, but by 1700 had become a defining element of the contemporary public sphere. The rise had not been steady – there were pronounced peaks of production at moments of political crisis – but it had proved ultimately irreversible.[4] And, above all, any such estimates necessarily miss the innumerable small, workaday printed objects – posters, tickets, forms, bills, and other 'job' work – that poured from the presses, almost none of which survived for long. As an economic enterprise, printing was first and foremost a matter of these kinds of documents, not of books. There is simply no way to gauge the scale of this kind of material, but it certainly greatly exceeded that of books and serials.

By the seventeenth century, therefore, Londoners lived lives that were super-saturated by print. Ships sailing into the capital's port documented their cargoes on printed bills; druggists and apothecaries marketed their wares by posting printed placards; polemicists provoked their antagonists by tacking printed challenges to their door-posts. The authorities exhorted readers in printed proclamations, and preachers exhorted them by publishing their sermons. Citizens learned about their relation to each other from conduct books, and about their relation to providence and the Almighty from printed Bibles and from John Foxe's *Book of Martyrs*. Ballads and broadsides surrounded them with songs and images (a cottage industry existed to convert images from books into pictures to hang on the household walls). They plotted their daily affairs by jotting notes in printed almanacs, and treated their families' illnesses by following printed books of secrets. Their children learned how to think and act from printed ABCs and catechisms. From the early 1640s, they could also track events through newspapers, either by reading them themselves or by hearing of their contents from others. In every respect, Londoners placed and shaped themselves by reference to the printed materials that surrounded them on all sides.[5]

'London' was not a single entity, then or now. Its inhabitants habitually resolved the city into streets, precincts, parishes, and wards, many of them distinct in terms of population and character. They knew from experience the differences between these locales, with quite a fine degree of resolution. This makes it worthwhile to begin by asking what may seem a banal question: where were the different objects of print to be found, and how did their locations shape their characters and uses?

Across the capital, there were particular streets and precincts in which bookshops congregated. The most notable was the area known as St Paul's Churchyard, just south of the Cathedral. This had been a locale for the trade since long before the invention of the press. It remained a major social hub for genteel Londoners. At its western boundary stood Stationers' Hall, the headquarters of the company charged with overseeing the commerce of print in general. In Paternoster Row, to the north, could be found taverns and coffee houses where the grandees of the trade began to hold the 'trade sales' that would define the literary property and publishing regime of the eighteenth century. To the east, bookshops clustered again in the thoroughfare of Cornhill. The area was one where gentility, commerce, and spirituality converged.

Other areas known for bookshops stood in the cultural shadow of St Paul's Churchyard, but they might have their own reputations for particular subjects or genres. The Strand and Temple Bar were good for legal works. Covent Garden became a centre for drama and novels toward the end of the seventeenth century, with the westward movement of the city's elites. Little Britain, to the northeast of St Paul's, enjoyed a brief moment of dominance after the Fire of 1666 and was especially known for the sciences. Bookshops specialising in maritime affairs (mathematical sciences, navigation, and the like) clustered around the Tower of London, those in mercantile practices and accounting around the Exchange, and those in law and politics at Westminster. Finally, if one walked northeast from St Paul's Churchyard, one might stroll along a road the very name of which would come to signify the lower end of commercial literature: Grub Street. At its far end one would emerge into Moorfields, a place of risqué entertainments outside the city walls. Here second-hand dealers laid out books for passers-by 'on the rails' – that is, on the fencing that surrounded the park. Although they were associated primarily with Grub Street fare, they could also include some quite elevated and esoteric work: Robert Hooke bought mathematics there, and was dismayed to find books from

Robert Boyle's personal library exhibited at Moorfields after his one-time master's death in 1692.

Returning back into the city proper, to find books in the making one would need to venture off the main streets. Printing houses tended to occupy less expensive and prominent lodgings. Some clustered to the south of St Paul's, for example, in a warren of lanes and courts leading down to the Thames. The largest of all, the King's Printing Office, stood just to the southwest. But others were scattered through the city. In principle, the government and the Stationers' Company maintained strict limits on the number of master printers permitted to operate – usually around twenty at any time. But these limits were never matched by reality. Even in 1668, when the regulatory effort was probably enjoying one of its more effective moments, a survey found twenty-nine established houses; it omitted at least four others that we know of. They ranged in scale from the King's Printing House (six presses) and the patentee Miles Flesher's (five) down to several with only one.[6] Doubtless some opposition printers had no 'house' at all, but moved about constantly so as to remain ahead of the authorities.

No printing house survived solely by producing books. A master had to keep the presses operating as continuously as possible in order to keep cash flowing and workers employed. Even the more substantial houses carried on jobbing work from day to day to pay the bills. Learned and genteel authors regularly bemoaned how this practice delayed and compromised their more substantial works, which were constantly being set aside in order to churn out the latest pamphlet. But the printers' economic survival – and therefore their works' very existence – depended on it. This means that printers were tied all the more tightly into a very local world of commerce and sociability, because it was from that world that their jobbing work probably came. Printers lived cheek-by-jowl with bakers, alehouse-keepers, joiners, apothecaries, butchers, and, in the case of Ichabod Dawks, a storehouse dedicated to collecting the city's abundant night-soil. Gentlemen and international merchants might also live alongside, in the close-packed manner so characteristic of the early modern capital. It is plausible to suggest that all these neighbours were prominent among the customers whose needs for tickets, bills, and so on made the difference between viability and disaster for a printer.[7]

What happened when one entered a bookshop or printing house? London buildings varied, obviously, but they had a broadly typical vertical arrangement with store or workshop on the ground floor, domestic rooms on the first and second, and servants' (or apprentices') chambers in the attic. For a bookshop, the ground floor was a semi-public space, with a prominent sign and an open door. Title-pages were often laid out on tables or tacked to door-posts to tempt in passers-by. The bookseller seems to have been a constant presence, asking about wants and suggesting possible purchases. The ability to browse solo seems to have been quite limited. Valuable books might be behind a counter; dubious books, under one. And the conversations that took place in the bookshop, with the bookseller or other customers, were liable to be overheard. In the so-called 'battle of the books' that occurred at the end of the century over the spurious *Epistles of Phalaris*, the Whig scholar Richard Bentley found himself in a confrontation over just such conversations. Bentley's alleged incivility to scholars was published and set against the conduct of the Tory bookseller Thomas Bennet, who resided at the Half-Moon bookshop in St Paul's Churchyard. The feud was cast as a clash of manners between librarian and bookseller, with Bentley being accused of insulting Bennet at the Half-Moon. Bentley indignantly denied this, and insisted that as a gentleman his word should be believed. The reputation of Bentley himself, and that of the Phalaris book, came to rest on whether it was.

The battle of the books exemplifies the point that the London bookshop became a location for the making and breaking of plausibility. To become an author, one usually had to attend at such a place; going upstairs into the actual household might well be essential. As a result, becoming an author meant subordinating oneself to some extent to the civility and interests of the bookseller who might be undertaking the publication, and gentlemen complained frequently of what that implied. Once published, too, the credit of printed materials might depend on where they were made and sold, and by whom. A telling indication of this is provided by the many cases in which booksellers advertised that sceptics could visit their shops to see the factual evidence proving an author's claims. Thus John Wood's *Practicae medicinae liber* (1596) urged that 'if anyone has any doubts about the preparation of any remedy described in this book, or about the apparatus needed', he should 'go to the printer, who will, for a consideration, demonstrate more clearly … the method'.[8] The Presbyterian bookseller Michael Sparke, worried that readers might suspect him of having added 'a new *poyson*' to the documents for his history of the reign of James I and thereby altered 'the *truth* of the *story*', first reminded them that the licenser could confirm its fidelity, and then invited them to inspect the original documents at his shop.[9] So when at the end of the century Bennet lodged manuscript testimonials as to his and Bentley's conduct in the battle of the books, he was doing nothing at all unusual. Readers were quite accustomed to being invited to the bookshop to examine for themselves the manuscripts (or medicines) that lay behind printed books. The practice is unheard of in the modern age, of course. But in the seventeenth century the fidelity of print was not to be taken for granted, and tying a book to a specific place – Sparke's shop at the sign of the Blue Anchor in the Old Bailey, Bennet's at that of the Half-Moon in St Paul's Churchyard – was a way to secure it.

Going into a printing house, the visitor faced a rather different set of issues. These began with whether access would be granted at all. The threshold here was at the doorway to the street, not at the foot of the stairs into the home. By all accounts London printing houses were awfully cramped. A fully equipped house would have needed a lot of space – not only for the presses themselves (ideally at least two, each braced to the ceiling with the heavy joists shown in contemporary prints) but for type and paper. They rarely had enough in the small, often rented premises available to them. Printing houses were therefore crowded and noisy (and smelly too). Crammed together, the journeymen, 'devils', and apprentices would constitute themselves into a 'chapel' peculiar to each house. Chapels were moral communities. They maintained ritual calendars and complex internal codes of conduct, including prescribed roles for each participant and punishments ('solaces') for those failing to play them. Their rules sustained the creative craft by which written words were converted into print. Chapels themselves were therefore prized by their members, who always seem to have seen them as under threat. Outsiders who presumed to venture into a chapel and did not know the rules were liable to pay a price. But would-be authors notoriously felt that they had to brave the prospect. Country-dwelling authors especially were well advised to come to London for the duration and live with the printer. Tales were legion of those who did not, and found that their work was re-crafted out of recognition as it passed through the printing house and became a book.

Because London printing houses were small, vulnerable, and overworked, books of any size were rarely produced in just one. Any volume longer than a pamphlet was likely to represent an alliance of houses. There were no hard and fast rules governing such concurrent printing, but it certainly happened routinely. It explains why many sizable volumes – William Prynne's *Histriomastix* (1633), for example – emerged with irregular typography and discontinuous pagination. Moreover, after about 1660 large books were increasingly printed for partnerships of booksellers too, rather than for individuals acting alone. Compare, for example, the *Works* of Samuel Daniel, 'printed for Simon Waterson' in 1601, with the *Reports* of Sir George Croke, 'printed for A. Roper, T. Collins, F. Tyton, J. Place, J. Starkey, and T. Basset' in 1669. Again, there were at first no fixed conventions governing this kind of alliance. But as such conventions emerged, so the alliances developed into more stable and enduring combinations, called 'congers'. The origins of the eighteenth-century trade's high notion of literary property lay in this practice. In the meantime, people had to move back and forth down city streets and across thresholds in order to bring a late-seventeenth-century folio into existence. Such a book therefore can be seen as a physical embodiment of collaborations in both finance and craft that extended into intimate domestic households and out across the capital.[10]

Finally, much of the commerce of the book occurred in no fixed location at all. The book-trade itself depended on a constellation of placeless figures. Mercury-women, in particular, were itinerant wholesalers who carried pamphlets and books from shop to shop to sell to retailers. They were often the widows of printers, and were rather notorious as channels of secret information about the information flows of seventeenth-century London. Hawkers, by contrast, dealt directly with customers. Government officers suspected them because they might go into places of conversation like coffee houses to sell their pamphlets there, where they seemed likely to find a ready audience. Chapmen traversed relatively regular routes beginning at a few key London locations and extending all across the nation. All of these types were a cause of constant anxiety to Whitehall and to the propertied booksellers. The Stationers' Company repeatedly sought either to embrace or suppress them. The latter was a futile ambition, and would have severely damaged the Stationers' own interests had it ever been achieved.

These are only a few of the ways in which the spaces of early modern London affected the constitution of print. A lot more could be said. The topographical approach, pioneered by Pat Rogers in his study of Grub Street in 1972, has developed into something of an orthodoxy since the 1990s. A number of individual and collective projects, often using digital technologies, have allowed us to see in unprecedented detail exactly where printing and bookselling happened – down to the level of individual rooms within buildings. Thanks to these efforts, we can finally appreciate once more how deeply the book – and print in general – participated in the same richly textured culture as did scientific, medical, and political activities in early modern London. When we do so, we find that print manifested a topography of trust, which hugged quite closely the social contours of the city itself.

The fellowship of the book

Early modern citizens recognised printing as a craft. That meant that it could be accommodated in the same kinds of ways that other crafts were subsumed within a well-ordered commonwealth. In many cities this meant that a community of practitioners ought to be gathered together into a social body – a corporation or guild – by which it would be integrated into the hierarchical structure of contemporary political order. So it was in London.

If printers and booksellers were members of extremely local communities, at the same time they were also participants in a city-wide trade fraternity. It was this fraternity that established what it meant to act properly in their capacity as members of the book-trade, and sought to bring them back into line when they did not.

A fraternity of bookmakers and -sellers had existed for generations by the time printing arrived in the late fifteenth century. In due course (with the encouragement of Queen Mary, who saw it as a useful tool of regulation) the trade was given a royal charter as the Worshipful Company of Stationers. This company was intended to contain all craftsmen of the book – booksellers, printers, typemakers, binders, and even the various kinds of itinerants. All of these would then become subject to oversight by their peers. For example, the company (like its counterparts in other trades) policed apprenticeships to ensure that a sufficient – but not excessive – supply of properly civilised Stationers was maintained. More interestingly, it also oversaw the journeymen and master printers thus produced. This meant creating and sustaining a form of civility to which they should commit themselves. Central to this was a register book – a large manuscript volume held under lock and key at Stationers' Hall. At first, this book was meant to record merely the fact that a Stationer wishing to publish a certain book had had it properly licensed. But it soon came to manifest a form of exclusivity. That is, a member who had 'entered' a given title in the register claimed that he or she alone could publish it. This was a customary right – it had no real legal standing, at least until mid century – but on the other hand it was also unlimited in time. An entry in the Stationers' Register constituted, by custom, a kind of property that endured indefinitely. By the end of the century this customary property was being referred to internally as a 'copy right'.

Printers, booksellers, binders, and founders were thus all meant to be 'Stationers'. This was necessary for them to take their place among the well-regulated crafts of an early modern city. The company integrated the crafts of print into the institutions of civic governance in general. It was by virtue of this integration that certain central elements of the printed book, like 'copy rights', came to be securely established. Needless to say, however, like any community, that of the book had its internal disagreements. When printers and booksellers clashed, they were supposed to bring their feuds to a court of the Company's grandees that met every month in Stationers' Hall. The proceedings of this court were to be kept secret, preserving for outsiders the image of an intrinsically harmonious craft. But throughout the seventeenth century unauthorised reprinting was prominent among those concerns, along with questions of apprenticeship and seditious work.[11]

One increasingly acute cause of dissension within the Company was the relative ascendancy of the booksellers over the master printers, and in particular of copy-owning booksellers over the rest. By the mid seventeenth century, the Company's register had become the index of a new kind of enterprise, resting not on craft skill but on financial and speculative acumen. Certain booksellers realised that they could make secure incomes by holding onto key titles and repeatedly undertaking editions of them, if necessary by collaborating with other Stationers to share the costs and risks. None abandoned retailing, as their successors a century later would do in creating the role of the publisher. But those who invested most successfully in this exploitation of customary property became a wealthy elite in London's book-trade. They came to dominate the marketplace for literature – or at least, that for polite literature – and to monopolise the higher echelons of the company itself. Their origin, perhaps, lay in the upheavals of the Civil War, when printing and bookselling expanded dramatically in the wake of the overthrow of royal restraints on numbers, and the end of royal authority overthrew existing patent rights to particular books and genres. Law-books and Bibles, hitherto the preserve of royal appointees, now fell to the company and its members. Other cultural properties saw their value change radically. A few booksellers – Henry Herringman being perhaps the first – were able to capitalise and make fortunes by gathering copies to themselves. In so doing, they set the foundations for the oligarchy of publishing that came into its own toward the end of the century and would entrench monopolistic literary property in the age of Pope.

During the Restoration two great rifts thus came to divide the book-trade: that between forms of property – registration versus royal patent – and that between property and craft – publishing bookseller versus master printer. These two causes of conflict inflected each other in shifting and not always predictable ways. For example, the printers' chapels were inclined to cast their support to the absolutist cause of royal patentees. They did so to defy the booksellers, who they feared would reduce them to wage-labourers. The booksellers thus found themselves upholding the claims of an autonomous craft (one they no longer exercised) against royal control. In this conflict, every aspect of the Stationers' realm came under examination. It stood accused of virtual sedition. The booksellers defended the trade by seizing for the first time upon a principle of authorial property. Why did their register deserve respect? Because, they said, authors *created* works by the labour of their hands and minds, and in doing so they gave rise to a natural property that the register merely recorded. The idea of an author's natural right in literary works arose not from Lockean philosophy, but from the politics of company, craft, and commerce in Restoration London.

Surveying the press

The standard assumption about any well-ordered London trade was that it should be self-policing. The book-trade was no exception. The Stationers' wardens were empowered to enter members' premises and inspect materials – a right not shared by constables – and this they did quite frequently. What exactly they were looking for, however, varied. Sometimes it was shoddy work or unauthorised reprints. On other occasions they were looking for libellous, seditious, or blasphemous work – work, that is, which concerned church or state. In that context the company's protocols intersected with a system of regulation that Whitehall had developed in the sixteenth century and that persisted (on and off) until what turned out to be its final abolition in 1695.

The defining practice of this regulatory regime was licensing. Initially adopted under Henry VIII, licensing meant the submission of a work to an official reader for approval prior to publication. Licensers would, in theory, vet proposed publications for various kinds of transgression – principally religious and political – and could insist on changes. Once approved, a work obtained an *imprimatur* (literally, 'it may be printed'), which was supposed to be recorded at the beginning of the printed text. Entries in the register were only to be made once a work had been licensed, so the emerging system of property was from the outset inextricable from this system of regulation.

Licensing was administered not from Stationers' Hall, but from Whitehall, Lambeth Palace, and St Paul's Cathedral. Licensers were appointees of the Secretaries of State, the Archbishop of Canterbury, and the Bishop of London. (A few other authorities appointed licensers too – the Universities, the College of Heralds, the Royal Society – but these were for relatively specialist areas of publishing.) In practice, being a licenser seems to have been a thankless task. There was no London counterpart to Cardinal Bellarmine, who took charge of regulating the book in Counter-Reformation Italy.[12] England's licensers were junior personnel on their way up the hierarchy. Chaplains and secretaries, they could have only a broad notion of what should be suppressed, and all too frequently fell foul of changes in the political wind. The fall of licensers punctuated the history of the practice more, it now seems, than the fall of the printers they were supposed to keep in line. Moreover, the work itself was long, hard, and thankless. And the Leveller sympathiser Gilbert Mabbott indicated another basic flaw when he resigned the position, complaining that 'many thousand' tracts had been printed with false licences, incriminating him while showing no sign of having been intimidated by his authority.[13]

In truth, licensing, like printing and bookselling, was often a matter of face-to-face contacts. The best-known case in point is that of Henry More, one of the 'Cambridge Platonists', the group of Cambridge philosophers who stressed the primacy of 'Reason' in religious and philosophical issues. Having had one work heavily truncated by a licenser, More found it advisable to travel down to Lambeth in person and have dinner with the Archbishop, at which point his next work sailed through on mere sight of the title.[14] We have no way of knowing how many times that kind of experience was repeated, because at the crucial moment the historical record obviously falls silent. But it does seem that licensers themselves needed some kind of contact. Many instances are known of licensers running into trouble when they lacked such contact, and the best licensers used contacts to keep abreast of the flow of politics and the interests of the Stationers alike. The Restoration's Surveyor of the Press, Sir Roger L'Estrange, in particular, was an adept, largely because he was himself a press-maven. He ran newspapers and churned out Tory polemics. Henry Oldenburg, by contrast, was not – despite being an expert editor, diplomat, and secretary. Oldenburg lacked L'Estrange's social contacts on both sides and was never sure what line he was supposed to toe.

In practice, licensing was consequently eminently tractable. Some books were suppressed, to be sure, and others truncated. But most books issued by the London book-trade in the seventeenth century seem never to have been submitted for licensing at all, and did not suffer any consequences. What, then, was its overall significance? The great Marxist historian Christopher Hill was inclined to grant it a major role in suppressing dissent – when London erupted in the early 1640s, Hill believed, it was because the censorship regime had broken down and a panoply of already brewing convictions could finally burst forth. But of the roughly 100,000 titles that, according to Donald Wing's *Short-Title Catalogue of Books Printed in England, Scotland, Ireland, Wales*, were published in London between 1641 and 1700, only about 400, D. F. McKenzie later found, can be shown to have attracted hostile attention from the state. The extent of recorded censorship is therefore tiny. McKenzie himself concluded that the regime had 'virtually no impact' on the economy of the book-trade. That is probably true – although the fact that McKenzie's statistics started in 1641 deserves emphasis – but it does not follow, and McKenzie did not claim, that it had no impact on culture, politics, and literature.[15] For one thing, it is obviously impossible to say how many or, more to the point, how significant were the works unpublished because they could not be licensed (Oldenburg for one said that he regarded it as his duty to reject many more titles than he accepted). For another, licensing was often said to serve a positive epistemic purpose as well as a negative one. That is, licensed books bore an endorsement, sometimes likened to the face of the king on a coin. An imprimatur attested that this was a book produced under conditions of propriety and responsibility, amid a marketplace widely thought to be plagued by inauthenticity and falsity. Efforts at policing were rare in normal times, but ramped up dramatically at moments of political stress. 'Normal' times being evanescent in seventeenth-century London, at any moment some crisis might well blow up that might lead to a crackdown. At that point, the omission of a licence became a useful rationale for searching out opposition books. This was in practice often the real utility of the system: it provided a justification for searchers to cross the threshold of the printing house and bookshop. The fate of opposition printing and publishing often hung on what they found there.

Censorship enforcement was yet another practice dependent on neighbourhood knowledge and metropolitan contacts. L'Estrange, Messenger of the Press Robert Stephens, and the Company's wardens all relied on locals for their ability to intervene in the world of print. Even knowing where to search, let alone mounting a successful operation, required their help. Moreover, both the state and the company had an interest in preserving good order, but the tendencies of that interest often diverged. Senior Stationer officials surreptitiously turned round and resold seized books for their own profit. And L'Estrange even found himself engaged in an extremely bitter clash with his own assistant, Stephens. Stephens had been trained as a printer himself, so he knew where to look and what to look for. But his sympathies were with the Whigs, the nascent political party formed in 1679–82 to exclude Charles II's Catholic brother, James, Duke of York, from the succession, and he became a bitter enemy of L'Estrange, calling him a 'black-mouth'd dog' who, if he were ever to be hanged, would be a disgrace to the gallows. He charged L'Estrange with showing preferable treatment to Catholics, while Stephens himself assisted the circulation of Marvell's *Account of the Growth of Popery and Arbitrary Government in England*, one of the earliest statements of what became the central lower-church Protestant beliefs of the Whigs. Such entrenched enmity severely hampered any attempt at a functional policing of the press in politically fragile times.[16]

The regulation of print required both rights of access (which the wardens possessed) and rights of arrest (which were the preserve of constables). The claim of such officers to enter and search what were Londoners' homes aroused bitter and sometimes violent opposition. Before the Civil War, puritan Stationers like Michael Sparke might arrest the searchers. After it, John Streater's chapel mounted a near-riot in defiance of a search. Radical Whigs like Francis 'Elephant' Smith could argue that searches violated the defining freedoms of a metropolitan citizen. Smith and his allies particularly objected to the general warrants that L'Estrange and Stephens aspired to obtain. They maintained such warrants to violate the rights of Londoners that had been upheld in Magna Carta itself. Such arguments sometimes found a surprisingly sympathetic hearing in the Restoration courts.[17] In effect, an important element of the freedom of the press originated in these cases as a distinctly London form of liberty.

Reading and reason

'Behold now this vast City', commanded John Milton in the most famous of all evocations of the culture of the book in early modern London. Milton's *Areopagitica* (1644) portrayed the capital as a city at work. Some of its citizens were 'sitting by their studious lamps' nightly, labouring to present new knowledge; others were 'as fast reading, trying all things, assenting to the force of reason and convincement'. Knowledge and faith, he insisted, flourished through 'exercise', and all that was needed to create and sustain 'a knowing people' was a population of such willing and faithful 'labourers'.[18] *Areopagitica* was about this – the providential identity of the reader as a worker – as much as it was about licensing, its ostensible subject. But if the culture of the book in early modern London was that which has been sketched out here, what did that imply for this arduous kind of work? To put it another way, what was it to be a 'good' reader in early modern London?

There was no one answer to that question. Reading practices, just as much as those of printing, bookselling, and licensing, involved face-to-face interactions in specific city locations. Moreover, throughout the century innovations in reading occurred in specific, often new, places: conventicles, coffee houses, the Royal Society, the libraries that sprang up in the Augustan period. Revolutionary developments in genre – those producing the newspaper, the periodical, and the novel – took place as part of the same process.[19]

Coffee houses are perhaps the best-known case in point. Originating in the Interregnum years, they proliferated at an extraordinary rate in the Restoration. They took on individual identities, often reflective of the neighbourhood in which they stood; particular clienteles frequented those close to the Exchange, for example. They provided a venue at which reading could be done silently and alone, or aloud and to others. Either way, reading became a social act, as conversation about what was being read inevitably followed. 'Coffee-houses make all sorts of people sociable', John Houghton claimed at the end of the century, and to powerful effect: for 'an inquisitive man, that aims at good learning ... may in short space gain the pith and marrow of the others' reading and studies'.[20] Such learning from others threatened to produce unpredictable but consequential interpretations of even quite familiar and orthodox books (one observer described a coffee-house crowd making 'Havock' of Machiavelli and Plato). But its greater implication concerned new, periodical uses of print. The newspapers of the age were produced largely with this readership in mind. Several of the best-known Restoration coffee houses were linked physically to bookshops, indeed, and in the 1720s an incipient rivalry between coffee and ink would come to a head in a struggle for supremacy between the newspapermen and the coffee-house proprietors. The newspapermen won, in a victory that may conveniently be taken as signalling the ascendancy of commercial print.

Coffee-house reading and its associated effects might seem dangerous to the Court and to officials like L'Estrange. It is rather telling that oversight of coffee-houses was another task deputised to the Surveyor of the Press himself. But there was little he could do – Charles II did once try to suppress the coffee houses altogether, to no real effect. Even L'Estrange was reduced to assailing them in pamphlets and journals that adopted exactly the forms suited to coffee-house perusal. In fact, L'Estrange's policing of the press in general was financed by his legal monopoly on that most characteristic product of the mixing of ink and coffee, 'news'.[21]

This combination of coffee, print, and sociability is as good a candidate as any for the point of origin of the much-discussed 'public sphere'. A combination of things had to coincide for such a sphere to become possible and respectable: not just print, but cheap print, shared practices of reading, places in which to exercise that practice, and a routine of feedback by which readers' convictions could themselves be submitted to the commerce of print. That is, periodicity of publication was almost a sine qua non for public reasoning. No less, however, did there need to be faith in the accumulated products of print itself. That is, not only did a marketplace of books, pamphlets, and periodicals have to exist, but publications had to manifest some degree of 'reason', if not in absolute terms then at least by comparison with the alternatives available at the time. Periodicity helped achieve this, because the speed of response allowed for printed claims to be reinforced or undermined with some speed and at predictable locations. But the marketplace of print was not enough on its own – the Civil War period, with its gallimaufry of incredible printed facts, suggested that much. There was also a need for readers to be skilled, critical, and laborious. The one-time secretary to Fairfax and Cromwell, John Rushworth – who knew from experience what he was talking about – despaired of his ability to discern whether any one amid the clashing pamphlet accounts of the Civil War era could be accounted truthful, and retreated to a triangulation strategy of 'concrediting' the various opposing versions one against the other.[22] How many readers did this it is impossible to say, but it is plausible that many saw the need.

This was a public sphere, then – but a public sphere rather different from that often invoked in modern writings. It was a realm in which plausibility was a major and fragile achievement. The question for contemporaries, and therefore for us, was how plausibility might be sought, affirmed, attributed, and maintained under criticism. Moreover, the reading public was constantly searching for, and trying to articulate, bases for its own existence. Milton's is just one contribution to what was a long-drawn-out debate on these.[23] Even the upholders of licensing were participants in the debate, for one of their principal contentions was that without regulation from above the credit of printed materials in general would be jeopardised.

What this means is that the very potential of print to supervene locale and make possible a cosmopolitan 'sphere' of public discourse depended – at least in its London variant – on the most local of communities. The plausibility of a broad realm of public reason depended, paradoxically, on the local integration of print into city culture. And what was true of London was by the same token true also of Paris, Amsterdam, Venice, Dublin, and so on. The transcendent 'order' of books that came to be so remarked upon in the eighteenth century required distinctly worldly premises: neighbourhood knowledge, face-to-face relationships, chapel customs, and the proprieties of parish and ward. If authorship became a stable, bankable asset, that was because wardens, clerks, beadles, and even (in the seventeenth century) licensers could draw upon such local knowledge to register and defend it. That is, a social history of transcendence lay behind the rise of public reason, and London life was its practical core. Knowing this was the key to becoming a good, 'judicious' reader – a reader fit to participate in Milton's providential cause.

Notes

1 See L. Lichfield, 'The Printers Conclusion to Her Majestie', in *Musarum oxoniensium epibathpia serenissimae reginarum Mariae* (Oxford: L. Lichfield, 1643), sig. D4v.
2 D. F. McKenzie, 'Printing and Publishing 1557–1700: Constraints on the London Book Trades', in *The Cambridge History of the Book in Britain: iv. 1557–1695*, ed. J. Barnard and D. F. McKenzie (Cambridge: Cambridge University Press, 2002), pp. 553–67, esp. p. 566.
3 K. Konkola, '"People of the Book": The Production of Theological Texts in Early Modern England', *Papers of the Bibliographical Society of America* 94 (2000), 5–34; I. Green, *The Christian's ABC: Catechisms and Catechizing in England c. 1530–1740* (Oxford: Clarendon Press, 1996), pp. 46–51, 67.

4 C. Nelson and M. Seccombe, 'The Creation of the Periodical Press 1620–1695', in Barnard and McKenzie, *Cambridge History of the Book in Britain*, Vol. IV, pp. 533–50, esp. pp. 534, 550.

5 P. Collinson, *The Birthpangs of Protestant England: Religious and Cultural Change in the Sixteenth and Seventeenth Centuries* (Basingstoke: Macmillan, 1988), pp. 116–17.

6 Barnard and McKenzie, *Cambridge History of the Book in Britain*, Vol. IV, pp. 794–6.

7 M. Harris, 'Print in Neighbourhood Commerce: The Case of Carter Lane', in *The London Book Trade: Topographies of Print in the Metropolis from the Sixteenth Century*, ed. R. Myers, M. Harris, and G. Mandelbrote (London: Oak Knoll Press/British Library, 2003), pp. 45–69, esp. pp. 53, 58.

8 J. W. Binns, 'STC Latin Books: Further Evidence for Printing-House Practice', *The Library*, 6th series 1 (1979), 347–54, esp. p. 354.

9 M. Sparke, *Truth Brought to Light and Discovered by Time* (London: M. Sparke, 1651), sig. a2r–v.

10 D. F. McKenzie, 'Printers of the Mind: Some Notes on Bibliographical Theories and Printing-House Practices', in *Making Meaning: 'Printers of the Mind' and Other Essays*, ed. P. D. McDonald and M. F. Suarez (Amherst: University of Massachusetts Press, 2002), pp. 13–85; N. Hodgson and C. Blagden, *The Notebook of Thomas Bennet and Henry Clements (1686–1719), with Some Aspects of Book Trade Practice* (Oxford: Bibliographical Society, 1956), pp. 85–91.

11 A. Johns, *The Nature of the Book: Print and Knowledge in the Making* (Chicago: University of Chicago Press, 1998), pp. 190–248.

12 D. MacCulloch, *The Reformation: A History* (New York: Penguin, 2003), p. 407.

13 Gilbert Mabbott, *A Perfect Diurnall* 304 (28 May 1649), p. 2531.

14 M. H. Nicolson, ed., *The Conway Letters: The Correspondence of Anne, Viscountess Conway, Henry More, and their Friends 1642–1684*, rev. and ed. S. Hutton (Oxford: Clarendon Press, 1992), p. 303.

15 McKenzie, 'Printing and Publishing 1557–1700', esp. p. 566.

16 L. Rostenberg, 'Robert Stephens, Messenger of the Press: An Episode in Seventeenth-Century Censorship', *Papers of the Bibliographical Society of America* 49 (1955), 131–52, esp. 145–8.

17 Johns, *The Nature of the Book*, p. 132.

18 J. Milton, *Areopagitica*, in *Complete Prose Works*, 8 vols. (New Haven: Yale University Press, 1953–82), Vol. II, pp. 543, 553–4.

19 R. Weil, 'Matthew Smith versus the "Great Men": Plot Talk, the Public Sphere and the Problem of Credibility in the 1690s', in *The Politics of the Public Sphere in Early Modern England*, ed. P. Lake and S. Pincus (Manchester: Manchester University Press, 2007), pp. 232–51.

20 John Houghton, *Collections for the Improvement of Husbandry and Trade* 461 (23 May 1701).

21 B. Cowan, *The Social Life of Coffee: The Emergence of the British Coffeehouse* (New Haven: Yale University Press, 2005), pp. 99, 195–6; M. Harris, *London Newspapers in the Age of Walpole: A Study of the Origins of the Modern English Press* (London: Associated University Presses, 1987), pp. 30–1.

22 John Rushworth, *Historical Collections of Private Passages of State*, 8 vols. (London, 1680–1701), Vol. 1, sigs. Bv–b2r.

23 Johns, *The Nature of the Book*, pp. 353–4; M. Knights, *Representation and Misrepresentation in Later Stuart Britain: Partisanship and Political Culture* (Oxford: Oxford University Press, 2005), pp. 272–334; J. Rushworth, *Historical Collections*, Vol. 1, sig. b2r.

4

BREAN HAMMOND

London and poetry to 1750

In 1635, the poet Edmund Waller wrote in celebration of the new, albeit highly incongruous, porticoed west front added by Inigo Jones to 'Old' St Paul's Cathedral. In Waller's poem 'Upon His Majesties Repairing of Pauls', Charles I is credited with completing his father's vision of improving the Cathedral's dilapidated state. The steeple was never repaired after being toppled by the violent thunderstorm in June 1561, and the extensive damage to the roof was inadequately addressed: Waller could justly call the old Cathedral 'Our Nations glory, and our Nations crime'.[1] The poem is a canny performance. Waller's task is to celebrate a not altogether satisfactory piece of restoration in a context where others were calling for an entirely new building – a proposal that carried divisive political overtones. Eschewing 'Ambition' that would 'affect the fame / Of some new structure; to have born her name' (lines 27–8), the king displays both the modesty and greatness of his mind 'to frame no new Church, but the old refine' (line 36). In tacit response to Puritan attacks on Laudian reform, Waller presents Charles as a moderate whose innovations are of a piece with the original architecture of the church. Throughout, the poem celebrates the king's effortless grace and refusal to resort to coercion. Like a good husband and peaceful monarch, Charles seeks a 'bloodless conquest'; and in support of this representation, the poet enlists the help of the Amphion legend – according to which Amphion built the walls of Thebes without physical effort, using his golden lyre, the gift of Hermes, to charm the stones – to convey a quasi-magical sense of Charles's achievement:

> He like *Amphion*, makes those quarries leap
> Into fair figures from a confus'd heap:
> For in his art of Regiments is found
> A power like that of harmony in sound.   (lines 11–14)

Decades later, in the early years of the eighteenth century, a very different poet, Jonathan Swift, used the Amphion myth to comment on a very different architectural project. Much of the palace of Whitehall had been destroyed in a fire in 1698, and taking shameless advantage of this, the playwright and herald John Vanbrugh had gained permission to build personal accommodation on the site. The house that resulted was dubbed the 'Goose-Pie', from its awkward shape and proportions. To Swift, this house represented an abuse of personal influence and an indication of the power of a corrupt Whig clique, as well as an affront to taste. Unlike the prestigious public building projects that followed the Great Fire of London in 1666 (including Wren's new St Paul's Cathedral), this one was a blot on the landscape. The poem 'Vanbrug's House', drafted around 1703 but revised around 1708, sets the tone with a burlesque forcing of the Amphion myth, making comical connections between poetic genres and architectural detail:

> In times of old, when time was young,
> And poets their own verses sung,
> A verse could draw a stone or beam,
> That now would overload a team;
> Lead 'em a dance of many a mile,
> Then rear 'em to a goodly pile.
> Each number had its different power;
> Heroic strains could build a tower;
> Sonnets, or elegies to Chloris,
> Might raise a house about two storeys;
> A lyric ode would slate; a catch
> Would tile; an epigram would thatch.[2]

As the poem goes on to explain, however, those Amphionesque powers were rescinded by Jove, who realised that they were ruining builders: and nowadays, 'wits' are confined to the element of air, where they can build as many castles as they like! Vanbrugh, however, petitions Jove to have the old powers back. The request is granted, but the resultant building will be in proportion to Vanbrugh's 'wit' – his ability as a dramatist. Since he plagiarises and patches up old French farces, his talent is too meagre, it turns out, to build a decent house. His plot is worth only a cellar, his acts build a couple of apartments, and the final act provides a low roof, while the epitaph creates no more than the privy. All that Vanbrugh's farcical wit can contrive is 'A thing resembling a goose-pie' (line 104), 'A type of modern wit and style, / The rubbish of an ancient pile' (lines 125–6). Small and insignificant though Vanbrugh's house may be, the poem mordantly notes, it offers ample accommodation to 'every wit in Britain's isle' (line 117).

Both poems use familiar London landmarks, but it should be stressed that we are not dealing here with any kind of photographic realism. The verses by Waller and Swift discussed above cannot be mistaken for neutral, value-free loco-descriptive poems. They speak not only to the altering circumstances of London's topography, but to the poets' desire to appropriate such circumstances for a set of ideological positions by means of imaginative transformation. Buildings and their environments are made to signify in symbolic ways: St Paul's in Waller's poem for the *imperium*, the manner of wielding power of a peaceful, responsive, and moderate monarch, and Vanbrugh's house in Swift's poem for a philistine and degenerate deformity that could only have been sanctioned by a corrupt ministerial clique. Waller's poem was written at a time when there was a vogue for 'place-realism' in the theatre. In Ben Jonson's later plays, and in plays by Richard Brome, James Shirley, and Thomas Nabbes, very sharp and accurate 'photographs' are given of topical and changing London locations, so that Brome's *The Weeding of Covent Garden* (c. 1632), for example, begins with extensive and accurate reference to the new architectural development in that area, while Shirley's *Hyde Park* was presented to mark Charles I's opening of the royal grounds to the public in 1637, and makes full use of its location. As Matthew Steggle argues, however, in his study of Brome, 'the photograph is not a photograph at all'.[3] Distinguishing between 'place' and 'space' enables an understanding of how location is transformed in the imagination, of how London locations are put to contested use in the poetry that deploys them.[4]

In mode – panegyric in the one case and satire in the other – the two poems discussed above represent opposed ways of responding to urbanisation, while both are generated by the phenomenon itself. Poetry written by writers living in London during the period under survey, whether or not it deploys London locations explicitly, situates itself along a spectrum of praise for, or revulsion from, the urban experience that is its generating matrix. Individual temperament plays its part in the expression of such attitudes, as does the writer's understanding of literary genre and desire to pay homage to distinguished predecessors; but to a considerable extent the varieties of urban expression are created by supra-individual factors such as changes in social organisation and in the conditions and purposes of writing.

In the decade before the turn of the seventeenth century, there was a brief but very powerful burst of anti-urban satire produced by a group of writers – John Marston, Everard Guilpin, Joseph Hall, and, most famously, John Donne – who were all from genteel backgrounds and attached to the Inns of Court, but were at the time of writing on the margins of such privileged urban communities as the church, the law, and the Court. Unrealised ambition and attention-seeking are partly responsible for the tone of satire that creates personae similar to the figure of the 'malcontent' in contemporary plays. Of John Marston, Alvin Kernan remarks that he 'has a fixation or obsession of some unhealthy variety. He seems to delight in seeking out and describing in loving detail the most unpleasant functions of the human animal.'⁵ That is not the whole story, however. In Donne's *Satyre* IV, the satirist describes a visit to Court as such a state of purgatory that hell itself is to it a 'recreation'. Donne's hell is, like Sartre's, other people: those he meets on the way, those he meets in the queen's presence, even those who populate his hellish Dantesque visions of Court when he is 'At home in wholesome solitarinesse' (line 155).⁶ Much of the poem is occupied by meeting a tatterdemalion fop such as Ben Jonson would satirise later as Sir Politic Would-Be in *Volpone*. He is a 'Macaron', whose dress, language, demeanour, and conversation proclaim him to be a traveller or citizen of the world, but who is to the satirist 'A thing more strange, then on Niles slime, the Sunne / E'r bred' (lines 18–19). Here and elsewhere in Donne's *Satires*, the poet is crucifyingly bored by the *flâneur*-types whom the chance interactions of the urban environment force him to encounter. City locations – the sites of such encounters – structure the satire and point the jokes. The painful interlocutor tries to persuade the satirist to abandon his superior stance, to enjoy Court life and gossip about kings. The poet responds that the guide at Westminster Abbey is good for that kind of talk, and 'The way to it, is Kingstreet' (line 80). With this punning sarcasm, the poet points the interlocutor his separate way, desperate to rid himself of his plaguing would-be crony. And yet, the satirist's posture of being among the crowd, but not *of* them ('Shall I, nones slave, of high-borne, or rais'd men / Fear frownes?'; lines 162–3) is at several points undermined by the realisation that he does not have the lordly independence at which he connives: ''Tis ten a-clock and past; All … are found / In the Presence, and I, (God pardon mee.)'(lines 175–9). 'And I': the poet here acknowledges that he is not truly offstage from the visual drama encoded by the poem, not entirely the passive victim of such cruel bores. The satire depends on a new kind of spatialisation of the city, one in which mobility and social encounter make for the necessity of choice. Permeable boundaries between those of different social ranks and differing degrees of intelligence are dramatised in such encounters, and in such an environment, where time has been commodified, choices about how to spend it are forced on the would-be moral subject. There exists also the possibility, recognised in the haunted, fear-ridden quality of the poems, that no such differences in value between one individual and another can actually be sustained.

From this brand of metropolitan angst, the *Epigrams* of Ben Jonson, probably written a little after Donne's *Satires*, are largely emancipated. In this group of around 130 mainly short poems, Jonson 'transformed the earlier satiric manner into a newly resilient anti-satiric resource'.⁷ The poet of *Epigram* ci, 'Inviting a Friend to Supper', for example, far from sharing Donne's sense of being lonely in a crowd, is rather the confident urbanite, assured that in the metropolis anything and everything is available. In contrast to Donne's failure to find a kindred spirit, Jonson's poem celebrates selectivity: choice, not just of 'cates', but of company. From the city's sea of faces, the poet forms a close domestic circle of like-minded friends, selecting only those who are not government agents, and (rarer still) those who are capable of intellectual friendship and free conversation:

> my man
> Shall read a piece of Virgil, Tacitus,
> Livie, or of some better book to us,
> Of which wee'll speake our minds, amidst our meate[8]

In the early years of the seventeenth century, then, the major templates for responding in verse to urban experience were in place: the agitated satirical rejection of metropolitan vulnerability that Donne drew from Horace, and the blasé celebration of urban opportunity that Martial inspired in Jonson. We will find the templates recurring, but with considerable variety and modulation. The largest city in Europe by 1716, London's population mushroomed between 1600 (200,000 inhabitants) and 1700 (over half a million), rendering it as much as 20 times larger than its nearest population rival in England.[9] This resulted from the concentration of the nation's legal, political, and economic life there. During the period, a notable deepening of attachment to objects of material culture developed into a more fully fledged market capitalism. The status of merchants and shopkeepers rose as the moral problems attaching to profit and sumptuousness were gradually addressed. Literary expression of social change moved in two opposite directions. On the one hand, the anti-satiric manner of Jonsonian panegyric modulated into the more public manner of the 'august style', as imaginative writing set itself the task of, in Manley's words, 'inter-legitimat[ing] city and nation, bourgeois community and royal seat'.[10] On the other hand, satire took a firmer hold not only of verse but of imaginative writing in general. Satire and the city were in natural alliance because the city provides the conditions of human carnival upon which it thrives, but that alliance was very much assisted by the prevailing circumstances of post-Restoration London. The growth of London, its increasing domination over the provinces, the development of capitalism and of new kinds of socio-economic interaction that came with it – all combined to produce a wider and more complicated form of public life in which praise and blame took new forms.

Improving possibilities for free expression of those new forms of public utterance developed between the Civil War and the Glorious Revolution. Developing the pioneering work of Jürgen Habermas, historians and cultural critics have commented on the emergence of a 'public sphere', discourses created by and for new forms of public space such as coffee houses, museums and galleries, and circulating libraries, where opinions could be canvassed that were not licensed by the official agencies of Court, church, and state. This is characterised by what Charles Taylor has called a new 'social imaginary': a virtual space that is an inclusive, socially equalised sphere of print and orality, where men – almost exclusively men – could come together and discuss their concerns.[11] Actual physical spaces developed to give the new forms of polite conversation a local habitation and a name. New collectivities – clubs and societies – developed from the rolling back of the state and the development of new spatialisations answering the needs of domesticity.

The hub of this political life and of the discourses generated in the public sphere was of course London. The key developments in this process – urbanisation, incipient capitalism, freedom of expression, and the development of political parties whose supporters articulated their views in the 'social imaginaries' of the public sphere – find their most eloquent poetic embodiment in the oeuvre of John Dryden. Dryden's work is central to the civilising mission of the august style. In his writing, attitudes at both ends of the spectrum of response to urbanisation can be found. His reputation as a poet was made with *Annus mirabilis: The Year of Wonders, 1666*, a long poem written in cross-rhyming quatrains, the function of which was to celebrate the glorious conduct of the war against the Dutch and the providential salvation of London from the scourges of plague and fire. A recalibration of the importance of trade and of London's local government is written into every line of the poem, commencing with its surprising dedication to 'the Metropolis of Great Britain, the most Renowned and late Flourishing City of London, in its Representatives, the Lord Mayor and Court of Aldermen, the Sheriffs and Common Council of it'.[12] Dryden is aware of the novelty of such a dedication, which he justifies in terms of the perfect union between the king and the notables of London in bringing the city through its appalling trials – a mystical, divinely sanctioned delivery from evil. The poem itself begins and ends with trade. But where the poem's emphasis on trade begins with England's Dutch economic rivals 'scarce leaving us the means to claim our own' (line 3), it ends with a glorious Virgilian vision of London rising from the fire as a phoenix from the ashes, becoming itself the major artery of world trade. Maiden queen rather than blushing shepherdess, its river, the Thames, outstripping the Tagus, Seine, and Rhine in importance, the rebuilt and beautified London becomes the entrepôt and 'famed emporium' of the world, able to captivate and convert its enemies by its wealth and grandeur alone:

> Me-thinks already from this Chymick flame,
> I see a City of more precious mold;
> Rich as the Town which gives the *Indies* name,
> With Silver pav'd, and all divine with Gold.
>
> (lines 1169–72)

The stanzas describing the Fire of London centre on the cooperative efforts of the citizens of London and their king, who is represented not only as shedding tears of pity for his subjects' plight, but as getting his own hands dirty with the rescue efforts. What is efficacious, though, is not his manual labour, but divine intercession in answer to the king's prayer. Supernatural relief is not, however, instantaneous and is not without its embarrassments, such as the ruin of St Paul's Cathedral. Here, Dryden refers back to the Waller poem and the Amphion myth, and puts his own ideological spin on the reason why God should have permitted the destruction of St Paul's:

> Nor could thy Fabrick, *Paul*'s, defend thee long,
> Though thou wert Sacred to thy Makers praise:
> Though made immortal by a Poet's Song;
> And Poets' Songs the *Theban* walls could raise.
> The dareing flames peep't in and saw from far,
> The awful beauties of the Sacred Quire:
> But, since it was prophan'd by Civil War,
> Heav'n thought it fit to have it purg'd by fire.
>
> (lines 1097–104)

In this allusion to the fire's origins, the poet puts satire at the service of panegyric. At first confined to 'mean buildings' (line 858), the fire finds its way to 'Palaces and Temples' (line 860) before its destructive power can be recognised. In this respect, it resembles 'some dire Usurper Heav'n provides, / To scourge his Country' (849–50): thus Cromwell's rise comes within satiric range. But in its dominant panegyrical note, the poem is a very suave performance. The Anglo-Dutch war was a stalemate at best; neutral observers might have said that the Dutch were winning it, and they certainly did so in the year following the poem. Trading on the king's personal popularity, going the audacious length of actually scripting his conversation with the Almighty, Dryden provided ravaged Restoration London with its hoped-for future.

Dryden's vision of national expansion following a *pax Britannica* is indebted to Virgil as mediated by seventeenth-century English poets such as Waller and Denham. His reference to 'Old Father *Thames*', helpless or unwilling to assist in dousing the flames (lines 925–8), picks up on the 'fluvial' or river-poetry element of earlier English writers such as Edmund Spenser, whose marriage poem dedicated to the Earl of Worcester, *Prothalamion*, includes the famous invocation to London's arterial river: 'Sweet Thames! run softly, till I end my song'. Alexander Pope was to pick up on Dryden's vision of London's peaceful world-domination through trade and the stability conferred by a Stuart dynasty beloved of its people, in the poem *Windsor-Forest* (1713). There is a clear 'laureate' line of descent here.

And yet Dryden was also a trail-blazer in representing the city satirically. In *MacFlecknoe*, written in the late 1670s to ridicule the literary efforts of his rival dramatist Thomas Shadwell, Dryden begins the work of mythologising those mean streets of London unfortunately overlooked by the fire as the breeding ground of an army of incompetent literary functionaries: an area that came to be known as Grub Street. In the poem's mythology, Shadwell's mock-coronation as King of the Dunces takes place close to the ancient site of London's Romano-medieval tower, the Barbican. Already a place of literal prostitution, it is also the nursery of literary prostitution. Dryden sites an acting school here, frequented only by the second-rate. To this location, bad writers and their publishers and promoters flock, coming from symbolically named precincts, such as Pissing Alley and Bun Hill, that cement an association between expression and excrement, poetry and pissing. Dryden's major achievement in the poem, one that Alexander Pope would build upon and extend massively, is to create a new means of imaginatively transforming the city's space. In the early years of the century, as we have seen, poetry and drama in which a city setting *constitutes*, rather than merely *stages*, the forms of experience was already being written. Dryden goes beyond such place-realism by overlaying upon it entirely imaginary transformations of space. Shadwell (MacFlecknoe), the poetical son of the hack Richard Flecknoe, is to be crowned, but his kingdom is the 'Realms of Nonsense'. *Mise-en-scène* in this fictive realm is synthesised out of past events, locales from Shadwell's plays as well as real London locations, but without entirely realistic coordinates. The reader finds it difficult to determine exactly where s/he is at any given point and the overall effect is of a hazy, oneiric apprehension of space that enables the poem's mythos to succeed. In real life, Thomas Shadwell was no dunce: he was a jobbing professional writer whose comedies were more successful than Dryden's. That is not the impression one takes away from *MacFlecknoe*, in large part because the poem succeeds in its creation of a London of the mind, where low-brow cultural industries are nurtured and commence their work of subverting genuine literacy.

Even in its satirical mode, the higher decorum of Dryden's 'august' style is clear if we compare *MacFlecknoe* very briefly with the near-contemporaneous 'A Ramble in St James's Parke' by the Earl of Rochester. From the outset,

Rochester is determined to shake his rakish, epicurean, profaning credentials in our faces:

> But though *St James* has the honor on't [i.e. of naming the Park],
> 'Tis consecrate to *Prick* and *Cunt*.[13]

Rochester turns the park into a pornotopia, a meeting-ground that enables promiscuous mingling of all ranks and status-groups in a sexual free-for-all. To the extent that it would be difficult to imagine this happening anywhere other than in a city – to the extent that pornography benefits from the anonymity of the participants – the poem is a response to urbanisation:

> Unto this All-sin-sheltring *Grove*,
> *Whores* of the *Bulk*, and the *Alcove*,
> Great *Ladies*, *Chamber-Maids*, and *Drudges*,
> The *Rag-picker*, and *Heiresse* trudges:
> *Carr-men*, *Divines*, great *Lords*, and *Taylors*,
> *Prentices*, *Poets*, *Pimps* and *Gaolers*;
> *Foot-Men*, fine *Fops*, do here arrive,
> And here promiscuously they swive.   (lines 25–32)

But St James's Park is really only a flag of convenience for the poet's observing his mistress's infidelity with three town gallants, and the poem is a Juvenalian revenge-fantasy that enables Rochester, from his superior aristocratic position, to trample on the proprieties of any reader who happens to have them.

An aspect of metropolitan consumerism developed in the later seventeenth and eighteenth centuries was the appetite for reading, which generated a market for imaginative writing and a cadre of professional writers willing and able to supply that market. This has been extensively studied with respect to the novel, and it has been perhaps too easily assumed that poetry remained a relatively elitist form. But just as theatre and prose fiction were responding to demands from bourgeois consumers to see themselves in action – domestic stories with which they could identify because they dramatised problems that the citizens themselves had encountered or plausibly could – there were marked developments that made poetry more available. As Paul Hunter insists, 'poetry ... was neither a badge of the elite nor a code that outsiders had to crack; it was a standard option for all kinds of topics and levels, and it invaded all kinds of printed texts'.[14] He points to the proliferation, after 1695, of miscellanies such as those of the publishers Jacob Tonson and Robert Dodsley, that harvested the most attractive of contemporary poetry for busy consumers. Between the Restoration and the 1730s, the social provenance of the major poets shifted decisively downward, with several representatives of the labouring classes (amongst them

Stephen Duck, Mary Collier, Mary Leapor, Ann Yearsley, and Robert Burns) achieving considerable acclaim. Poetry was much less patronised at Court and by fewer powerful aristocrats than it had been, and writers looked increasingly to the commercial market or to hybrid forms of publishing such as publishing by subscription.

One very significant sign of the altering demographics of poetry was the clamour for authoritative translations of the classics: Dryden's Virgil and Pope's Homer were more important, perhaps, than any achievement in original writing in determining the cultural complexion of the period. Alongside the availability of English versions of the classics developed some emancipation in the nature of the homage paid by English writers to their classical heroes: freer translations, burlesques, and mocking versions of earlier cultural icons became popular. Using classical forms such as the eclogue and the georgic, London-based poets would filter the rural, agricultural sensibilities of those genres through urban templates of experience, in such poems as Swift's 'A Description of the Morning', 'A Description of a City Shower', and the co-authored 'A Town Eclogue'; John Gay's much longer *Trivia; Or, The Art of Walking the Streets of London* (1716); and the *Court Poems* of Lady Mary Wortley Montagu (1716). The results could be satirical, or more quietly observant and humorous. 'A Town Eclogue', for example, by William Harrison and Jonathan Swift, uses the trappings of bucolic poetry – a dialogue between Corydon and Phyllis – to satirise a sordid cameo of a woman impregnated and betrayed by her lover, despite his promises that 'When I forget the favour you bestowed, / Red herrings shall be spawned in Tyburn Road, / Fleet Street transformed become a flowery green, / And mass be sung where operas are seen'.[15] More complex are the effects of 'A Description of a City Shower' (1710), which alludes to rainstorms in Virgil's *Georgics* I and *Aeneid* II in describing the intensifying effects of a rainstorm on the behaviour of London citizens caught out in it. The poem rises to an almost apocalyptic crescendo, with overtones of biblical flood as the filth and effluent of the city are swept into a malodorous tsunami:

> Sweepings from butchers' stalls, dung, guts and blood,
> Drowned puppies, stinking sprats, all drenched in mud,
> Dead cats and turnip-tops come tumbling down the flood.
>
> (lines 61–3)

In early-eighteenth-century polite discourse, developed through periodicals such as Addison and Steele's *Tatler* and *Spectator*, personal and moral objections to city life do not become overtly ideological: directed, that is to say, at the underlying systematic reasons for their existence rather than the unpleasantness they cause for individuals. For the consumer of the city, there are down sides, and that is as far as we need go. John Gay's *Trivia; Or, The Art of Walking the Streets of London* presents vastly elaborated material on how to survive the unpleasantness and discomfort of the city as a pedestrian, and it occasionally moralises that theme, but it does not reach even so far as the jokey coherence of vision that provides Swift's climax. Gay's friend Dr Arbuthnot, jesting snidely at the commercial success of *Trivia*, put his finger (as all good jokers do) on a serious point: 'Gay has gott so much money by his art of walking the streets, that he is ready to sett up with equipage [a carriage and horses].'[16] This is an especially good line because Gay's poem sets up a clear, almost Orwellian moral schema – L E G S G O O D, W H E E L S B A D – according to which the Walker has not only a health advantage but a clear ethical superiority over those who drive:

> See, yon' bright Chariot on its Braces swing,
> With *Flanders* Mares, and on an arched Spring,
> That Wretch, to gain an Equipage and Place,
> Betray'd his Sister to a lewd Embrace.[17]

Arbuthnot counters, however, that Gay's poem (a product of the luxury economy if ever there was one) has actually enabled him to join the ranks of the rich roadhogs that he affects to despise – expressing a paradoxical reading experience to which successive generations of readers also testify. Although it constantly looks as if we will be able to make out of the poem's detail a larger moral or emblematic pattern – for instance a set of instructions on how to live a pure life in the city – such expectations are frustrated. Even topographical expectations are frustrated. Anyone who tries to base a walking tour on specified locations that survive will soon be as lost as is Gay's rustic confronted with the Seven Dials (2.77ff). The poem seems to play one poetic mode off against another, implicitly suggesting its own status as a luxury commodity produced only as an entertainment for those who have leisure to read it. As John Brewer points out in *The Pleasures of the Imagination*, there is a symbiotic relationship between the growth of the cultural marketplace and the prominence of the metropolis as a theme for creative artists. London was 'more than a place of streets and houses, rackety districts and aristocratic quarters; it was also a fantastic, imaginary space' that, as it developed, became itself a source of artistic representation as it gained the power to shape the cultural life of the nation as a whole.[18]

One can make a cost–benefit analysis of living in town as against living in the country, as many eighteenth-century poems in the 'town mouse and country mouse' mode did. And one can be dimly, contradictorily aware that some of the unpleasantness of city life is not the fault of its immediate agents, but requires a more systematic analysis. Such an apprehension underlies the contradictions of Gay's *Trivia* and may be refracted in the poem's extreme aversion to mud, noticed by Clare Brant.[19] But the melioristic climate of Whig-sponsored politeness had been operating for some years before an opposition to it developed. Samuel Johnson's debut poem 'London' (1738) presents a developed ideological critique of what the city was becoming under a Whig political dispensation. By the 1730s and early 1740s, in Johnson's 'London' and in the poetry of Alexander Pope, the city had become a counter in the partisan battle between the Whig establishment and the spectrum of Jacobite Tories, Hanoverian Tories, independents, 'Country' supporters, and Whig malcontents, who combined in an ultimately successful attempt to oust Sir Robert Walpole from office. London's dirt and stink, its roughnecks and its whores, its opportunists and its leaders, are concocted by Johnson and Pope into forms of 'corruption' and nemesis that, unchecked, will bring the city to its knees.

Reading Johnson's 'London' today, one can be a little surprised that contemporaries regarded the poem as a brilliant debut announcing a major new talent when it appears no better than a somewhat mechanical updating of Juvenal's third *Satire*. In Juvenal's poem, the protagonist Umbricius has decided to leave Rome to live in the lonely colony of Cumae, because the capital has become uninhabitable to the ordinary man bent on making a decent living. Crime is rife; the lick-spittle Greeks have insinuated themselves into all influential positions (they become, inevitably, the French in Johnson's version); the city is descending into a chaos of fires, careening traffic, airborne rubbish, and marauding ruffians. Speaking for the poor, freeborn Roman, Umbricius presents him as being tyrannised by plutocrats who make his decent poverty his burden. Johnson adopts much of this social programme, but it gains impact from being expressed through what, by 1738, had become the unmistakeable political code of the so-called 'Patriot' opposition to Walpole: opposition to infrequent elections, standing armies, bribery, and manipulation of government employment, all practices that were gathered together under the masthead of 'corruption':

> Here let those reign, whom Pensions can incite,
> To vote a Patriot black, a Courtier white;
> Explain their Country's dear-bought Rights away,
> And plead for Pirates in the Face of Day;
> With slavish Tenets taint our poison'd Youth,
> And lend a lye the Confidence of Truth.[20]

Passages like this express more than moral disgust at a metropolis that has lost the innocence and tranquillity still to be found in rural life, an ideal represented in the poem by the 'elegant Retreat' where the refugee from the city can 'prune thy Walks, support thy drooping Flow'rs, / Direct thy Rivulets, and twine thy Bow'rs' (lines 216–17). Johnson's readers would have recognised even in something as incidental as the reference to Queen Elizabeth's birth at Greenwich (lines 22ff.) a nostalgic glorification of English history that went hand-in-hand with the representation of the present as in the grip of unprecedented corruption. Walpole's system was stigmatised by his opponents as a highly technical, sinister, and specialised subversion of ancient liberties. The only antidote was a return to the courage, wisdom, and strength of the ancient Briton, to the time when 'A single Jail, in Alfred's golden Reign, / Could half the Nation's Criminals contain' (lines 248–9).

It is Alexander Pope's *Dunciad* (1728–43), however, that catches in its comprehensive net all the cultural crosscurrents of its time, transforming them imaginatively into one of the greatest achievements of metropolitan poetry. Developing what we might term an 'IMAX' version of Dryden's *MacFlecknoe*, the poem sets out to persuade the reader that such armies of low-brow professional writers as Dryden imagines attending the anti-monarch Shadwell have the potential to destroy literate culture. In the early versions of Pope's poem, those platoons of cultural Goths are led by the Shakespearean scholar Lewis Theobald, who is replaced by the actor-manager-impresario Colley Cibber in the later version. The poem is a negative epic, its heroes negative versions of the heroes of classical epics, its action an ironic mirror of the Virgilian epic journey from Troy to Rome, as the writers and entrepreneurs of the publishing industry in Pope's poem spill out from their breeding-grounds and workplaces in the City, heading toward the more fashionable purlieus of Westminster.

In content and in form the poem is a mock-homage to the state of modern publishing. The text is preceded by an advertisement, letter to the publisher, epigraphs, testimonies of authors, and a critical essay by its supposed editor Martinus Scriblerus; and is followed by a similarly exfoliating set of appendices. When the reader finally reaches the poem, s/he is at once confronted, before its opening line, by an extended debate between 'Theobald' and Scriblerus over whether the spelling should be *Dunciad* or *Dunc[e]iad*. Satire on contemporary publishing and scholarship is built into the construction of the poem. The poem's major triumph, however, lies in the way it uses London. James Joyce aspired in his *Ulysses* 'to give a picture of Dublin so complete that if the city one day suddenly disappeared from the earth, it could be reconstructed out of my book'.[21] On that documentary level, *The Dunciad* is just as successful. Pope's research into his swarm-culture of jobbing writers is impeccable; but it is the imaginative transformation of this that is so profound, and particularly with respect to the city's space. Mock-epic in its very nature works with *produced* spaces. To appreciate Pope's hilarious depiction of mock-Olympic games in Book II, where *jeux trouvés* are devised out of the nonce materials to hand (the Fleet River – or whatever), the reader needs simultaneously to hold in mind accounts of games held in purpose-designed arenas described in classical epics. Space is always dual – that is to say, always overlaid:

> Amid that Area wide she [the Queen of Dulness] took her stand,
> Where the tall May-pole once o'erlook'd the Strand;
> But now, so ANNE and Piety ordain,
> A Church collects the saints of Drury-lane.[22]   (1729 version, 2.23–6)

In this passage, and typically, Pope trades not only on the perceptible aspects of the site, but also on what the reader might know of its history. As Valerie Rumbold, Pope's modern editor notes, this site had been reserved for communal merry-making, but its huge maypole had been removed in 1713 at Queen Anne's express order, to make way for the Church. As originally designed, the Church would have had a statue of the Queen on a 250-foot-high pillar, designed by the architect James Gibbs.[23] Thus, the passage implicitly contrasts the Queen of Dulness's indulgence in the trivialities of play with the killjoy higher seriousness and soaring ego of a recently deceased monarch. Pope's poem 'hyperspaces' real material space, devising a provoking way of overlaying upon one another different kinds and conceptions of space. It is a peculiar *layering* effect, through which Pope utilises the reader's personal knowledge of a particular material space, but superimposes on that space events that could not possibly take place within it – events that the reader's very knowledge of the nature of the space renders impracticable and impossible.

As in the cases of the poets discussed earlier, some of the conditions for Pope's imaginative transformation of urban London reside in his response to changes in the material base of the city; specifically, the rebuilding of the City of London after the Great Fire, and the development of the 'Town' or west end of 'suburban' London. For at least a decade after the final embers were extinguished, the City of London was an area unusually transparent, its infrastructure and the relation between social forms of living and the architectural environment peculiarly open to view as a giant building site. The rebuilding of the City accelerated the process of suburbanisation and the westward migration of established tradesmen, professionals, and artisans into Lincoln's Inn Fields, Covent Garden, and the Strand, which in turn shifted the gentle and the titled into Soho, St James's, and Mayfair. The 1660s and 1670s saw large-scale development by aristocrats of great palaces and estates close to St James's into fashionable residential housing – the areas of Piccadilly, St James's Street, the Haymarket, and Pall Mall, which came to be spoken of as the 'town'. First Covent Garden, then the development of the great squares – Hanover, Berkeley, and Grosvenor; Cavendish, Portman, and Manchester; Bloomsbury, Bedford, and Russell: by 1800, the east–west divide in London was accomplished and patent. As on the ground, so on the page, London becomes increasingly stratified and hierarchised into a pecking order – court, town, city, and country – that appropriates for the imagination processes actually occurring in material space and social practice.

Cynthia Wall has perceptively analysed the changing grammar of space in topographical and narrative representations of post-1666 London, as its denizens adjusted from a fixed, static conception of their city to one that reflected its bewildering new mobility. This new conception, as she argues, 'includes, not surprisingly, a nostalgic oversimplification of its own past'; and of Pope's *Dunciad*, her argument is that it asserts and defends an old order that no longer exists, while lending energy to new shapes of space.[24] The poetry tries to *contain* change, but as the contemporary significance of London streets was visibly altering, 'the ambiguities and ambivalences of the streets themselves seep into the poems' (p. 124). Pope does more than attest to that transformation through a series of culturally conservative acts of fixation that try to arrest it. The poem is one of extraordinary spatial deliquescence. Long passages of it are set in spaces that have no precise 'chronotopes' (time–space coordinates) other than the poet's imagination or that of his main characters, the dunces Lewis Theobald and (later) Colley Cibber, through whom the cityscape is envisioned. His spaces are not confined to past spaces and/or spaces in the process of becoming. They are spaces on the cusp of the psychic and the real: impossible spaces that are mosaics of the possible. In a fuller version of this account of the manipulations of space in Pope's *Dunciad*, I have called upon and tried to justify Michel Foucault's term 'heterotopia' as a means of characterising it.[25]

Yet however powerful Pope's indictment of popular culture, however successful his representation of marketed, degraded entertainment, *The Dunciad* is finally as much a celebration of metropolitan energy as it is a critique of it. The poem is fed by the swarming, formicating liveliness that it affects to despise. Neither Pope nor Johnson was expressing personal or confessional views of the city. Johnson was using the dysfunctional city to articulate an oppositional, anti-government manifesto. Pope's vision of the eclipse of all knowledge in a new age of barbarism shares that manifesto, but transcends it in the creation of a cityscape that mythologises poor scribblers, those who employ and those who patronise them, as the enemies of civilised culture.

Pope's death in 1744 had the effect of precipitating anti-urban tendencies that were beginning to be apparent in poetry as early as the 1730s in the writing of such as James Thomson, William Shenstone, and John Dyer. Only Charles Churchill, whose poetic career flourished between 1761 and 1765, made significant efforts to continue the Popean vein of satire, capitalising on the resources of the city and its notable personalities to do so, in such poems as his theatrical satire *The Rosciad* (1761). Fatigued by politics and the urbane, finding no sources of inspiration in public affairs, much more concerned with the complexities of the individual self and the shaping of that self by formative influences, the generations of poets who succeeded Pope did not write as if the twin impulses of celebration and satire were two sides of the same coin. Country upbringing was perceived to be superior, and the rural–urban split intensified.

Where Pope and his contemporaries had derived vast energy and pleasure from the forms of urban behaviour that they simultaneously proscribed, later poets used London to attack debased city mores. Where Dryden, Swift, Gay, and Pope could satirise the city from a position of relative affection, writers such as Cowper, Blake, and Wordsworth rejected the nationalistic London-based metropolitanism of that era, promoting instead the local and the regional. It was William Cowper who, in his lengthy, digressive, and unclassifiable poem *The Task, a Poem, in Six Books* (1785) gave the most striking and forceful expression to the later eighteenth-century orthodoxy that rural living was ethically superior to urban living:

> God made the country, and man made the town.
> What wonder then, that health and virtue, gifts
> That can alone make sweet the bitter draught
> That life holds out to all, should most abound
> And least be threatened in the fields and groves?
> Possess ye therefore, ye who borne about
> In chariots and sedans, know no fatigue
> But that of idleness, and taste no scenes
> But such as art contrives, possess ye still
> Your element; there only, ye can shine,
> There only minds like yours can do no harm.
>
> (lines 749–74)[26]

In Cowper's reference to 'chariots and sedans' (770) as an unnatural, eco-unfriendly aspect of city life, the wheel has, so to speak, come full circle. Sedans were newly introduced to London in the 1630s: 'the Hand-barrowes? what call you 'em the Sedams?' (Act 1 sc.3) cause enormous excitement in Richard Brome's play *The Sparagus Garden* (performed 1635) as a new form of urban mobility, and are integral to the plot.[27] By

1716, they are to John Gay in *Trivia* merely a means of travel less reliable than one's own two legs: 'Or, box'd within the Chair, contemn the Street, / And trust their Safety to another's Feet'.[28] For Cowper, they are a target of his fierce, environmentalist commitment, a new departure in literary responses to London.

Notes

1   Edmund Waller, 'Upon His Majesties Repairing of Pauls', line 4, in *The Workes of Edmund Waller, Esq.* (London: Thomas Walkley, 1645), p. 3.

2   Jonathan Swift, 'Vanbrug's House', in *Jonathan Swift: The Complete Poems*, ed. Pat Rogers (Harmondsworth: Penguin, 1983), lines 1–12.

3   Matthew Steggle, *Richard Brome: Place and Politics on the Caroline Stage* (Manchester and New York: Manchester University Press, 2004), p. 47.

4   Henri Lefebvre, *The Production of Space*, trans. D. Nicholson-Smith (Oxford: Basil Blackwell, 1991), pp. 38–9.

5   Alvin Kernan, *The Cankered Muse: Satire of the Renaissance* (New Haven: Yale University Press, 1959), p. 102.

6   John Donne, *Satyre* IV, in *The Poems of John Donne*, 2 vols., ed. Herbert J. C. Grierson (Oxford: Oxford University Press, 1963), Vol. I, p. 164.

7   Lawrence Manley, *Literature and Culture in Early Modern London* (Cambridge: Cambridge University Press, 1995), p. 502.

8   Ben Jonson, *Epigram* CI, lines 20–3, in *Ben Jonson*, 11 vols., ed. C. H. Herford, Percy Simpson, and Evelyn Simpson (Oxford: Clarendon Press, 1925–52), Vol. VIII, p. 65.

9   David Harris Sacks, 'London's Dominion', in *Material London ca. 1600*, ed. Lena Cowen Orlin (Philadelphia: University of Pennsylvania Press, 2000), pp. 20–54.

10   Manley, *Literature and Culture*, p. 524.

11   Charles Taylor, *Modern Social Imaginaries* (Durham, NC: Duke University Press, 2004).

12   John Dryden, *The Poems of John Dryden*, 4 vols., ed. James Kinsley (Oxford: Clarendon Press, 1958), Vol. I, p. 42.

13   John Wilmot, Earl of Rochester, 'A Ramble in St James's Parke', lines 9–10, in *The Works of John Wilmot, Earl of Rochester*, ed. Harold Love (Oxford: Oxford University Press, 1999), pp. 76–7.

14   J. Paul Hunter, 'Political, Satirical, Didactic and Lyric Poetry (1): From the Restoration to the Death of Pope', in *The Cambridge History of English Literature, 1660–1780*, ed. John Richetti (Cambridge: Cambridge University Press, 2005), p. 163.

15   William Harrison and Jonathan Swift, 'A Town Eclogue', lines 20–3, in Swift, *The Complete Poems*, p. 115.

16   John Gay, *The Letters of John Gay*, ed. C. F. Burgess (Oxford: Clarendon Press, 1966), p. 27.

17   John Gay, *Trivia; Or, The Art of Walking the Streets of London*, 2.573–6, in *John Gay: Poetry and Prose*, 2 vols., ed. Vinton A. Dearing and Charles E. Beckwith (Oxford: Clarendon Press, 1974), Vol. I, p. 159.

18 John Brewer, *The Pleasures of the Imagination: English Culture in the Eighteenth Century* (London: HarperCollins, 1997), pp. 31, 54–5.

19 Clare Brant, 'Artless and Artful: John Gay's *Trivia*', in *Walking the Streets of Eighteenth-Century London: John Gay's* Trivia, ed. Clare Brant and Susan E. Whyman (Oxford: Oxford University Press, 2007), pp. 109, 112.

20 Samuel Johnson, 'London', lines 51–6, in *Complete English Poems*, ed. J. D. Fleeman (Harmondsworth: Penguin, 1971), p. 60.

21 James Joyce to Frank Budgen, quoted in Frank Budgen, *James Joyce and the Making of* Ulysses [1935] (Bloomington: Indiana University Press, 1960), pp. 67–8.

22 Alexander Pope, *The Dunciad*, 1729 version, in *The Poems of Alexander Pope: Volume 3*. The Dunciad *(1728)* & The Dunciad Variorum *(1729)*, ed. Valerie Rumbold (Harlow: Pearson Longman, 2007), 2.23–6.

23 Alexander Pope, *Ibid.*, p. 45.

24 Cynthia Wall, *The Literary and Cultural Spaces of Restoration London* (Cambridge: Cambridge University Press, 1998), pp. 97, 124.

25 Brean S. Hammond, 'The Dunciad and the City: Pope and Heterotopia', *Studies in the Literary Imagination* 38.1 (2005), 1–13.

26 William Cowper, *The Task, a Poem, in Six Books*, lines 749–74, in *The Poems of William Cowper*, 3 vols., ed. John D. Baird and Charles Ryskamp (Oxford: Clarendon Press, 1995), Vol. II, p. 136.

27 Richard Brome, *The Sparagus Garden* (London: F. Constable, 1640), sig. B4v.

28 Gay, *Trivia*, 2.513–14.

5

LAURA J. ROSENTHAL

Staging London in the Restoration and eighteenth century

In 1673, an anonymous writer warned a young country gentleman headed for London that he would surely see himself lampooned on the stage:

> Thou hast often ... heard of a sort of despised Animals, call'd Country Gentlemen: if thou frequentest the Play-House, thou hast there seen us brought in with a high-crown'd Hat, a Sword put through the wast-band of our Breeches, and a pair of antick tops; where we tamely stand, whilst the learned man of Humours practises upon us with his sleights, and intrigues.[1]

During the Restoration and eighteenth century, London grew at an unprecedented rate, attracting men and women in search of pleasure, work, entertainment, marriage, opportunity, and adventure. Mr Spectator celebrated the multicultural bustle of the Royal Exchange; James Boswell hoped London would polish his manners; Samuel Johnson declared those tired of London to be tired of life. But not everyone recommended the trip. Critics decried the city's immorality and dissolution; they warned against whores, gamesters, and thieves. Visitors from the country, they declared, would fall victim to the 'tricks of the town' as well as to contemptuous ridicule from smug libertines. Further, they would confront these ills immediately, for any visitor's first stop in London would be the theatre.

Restoration playwrights tended to celebrate urbanity and, as accused, show little mercy for those outside the charmed circle of wit; in the eighteenth century, however, the stage made a more serious attempt to negotiate with London's critics. In certain ways throughout this period (1660–1800), though, the theatre epitomised everything dangerous and alluring about London: it brought together men and women in a commercial venue for the explicit purpose of enjoyment, admitting friends and strangers alike. Theatre had an inherent stake in London: print could disperse novels and newspapers far and wide, but theatre didn't travel as well or as often. The Restoration stage, then, scrappily defended itself against moralistic assaults. In Thomas Shadwell's *Epsom Wells* (1673), Mr Clodpate, 'A Country Justice, a publick, spirited, politick, discontented Fop, and immoderate hater of *London*'[2] (and possibly the character to whom the opening quotation refers), heads a long line of country boobies who bumble and curse their way across the London stage, forever inadequate before the urban wits.

But while many playwrights indulged in the all-out mockery of unfashionable tourists, others created more complex liminal figures. Clodpate remains a discontented fop and hater of London from beginning to end, but William Wycherley suspends his Margery Pinchwife, as I will later discuss in more detail, between rural and urban identities for much of the play. While she never fully becomes a London wife, Margery nevertheless scrutinises and tries to imitate – with some success – the practices of city ladies. Margery embodies a comic version of the rural–urban transition still in progress for many members of Wycherley's audience, from the country gentlemen trying to cut a figure at the theatre to the town women, not long ago plucked off the wagon, seeking their attention. The country bumpkins document certain tensions between country and city, but Margery's liminality suggests the broader historical process of urbanisation. In the Restoration, as Raymond Williams has shown, the country and the city belonged inextricably to the same economic system: wealthy theatre-goers paid for urban pleasures with the profits from their rural estates.[3] Anti-Londonists, as we will see, pointed to these economic ties in their attempt to awaken these squires turned fops to their place in a 'moral economy'. Later in the period, while landed families certainly continued to produce feckless heirs who found their way to London, Britain's capital, with its traders, stock market, shops, lawyers, fashions, imports, and exports, became a more significant centre of wealth in its own right. George Lillo's enormously popular tragedy *The London Merchant* (1731), which shifts attention from men of pleasure to men of business, registers this change, as do many other popular plays. Eighteenth-century plays no longer represent London as a lurid playground from which some of the characters will virtuously or grudgingly retreat, but instead as itself contested terrain. In the context of this changing theatrical assessment of London, Margery Pinchwife acquired a powerful afterlife. To be sure, Wycherley was not the first or only playwright to find comic potential in the urban confusion of a feminine outsider. But as I will show, Wycherley's Margery offered a distinctive perspective on this tension: Margery becomes compelling for her liminality, for belonging by the end of the play neither fully to the city nor fully to the country. While she grudgingly bids farewell to London, she continues to suffer from the 'London Disease'.[4] 'Country wives', who appeared throughout this period's drama, allowed playwrights to explore, satirise, and appreciate London through the eyes of an outsider who has not necessarily come to town willingly or eagerly. While the

Clodpates betray rural ignorance in order to produce comic effects that flatter urban audiences, Margery and her after-images cut in more than one direction, revealing the transplant's lack of sophistication but also the darker aspects of her new environment. Through their gendered liminality, country wives explore not just the naïveté of the country and the hypocrisy of the city, but the process of urbanisation itself.

Urbanisation had its triumphs and its fallout. Margery Pinchwife's movement from country to city paralleled a migration pattern attracting considerable attention: a steady stream of country girls apparently coming 'upon the town' – the common phrase in the period for turning to prostitution as a last desperate resort. Going 'upon the town' was generally represented as the bottom of a slippery slope that began with seduction, moved to a 'keeping', slid to a series of temporary situations with different men, and finally ended with indiscriminate availability as a streetwalker, the most dangerous form of prostitution. Of course, a girl could grow up as a native to London and still be said to be 'upon the town'. Yet the phrase itself underscores the popular belief, possibly promoted by London bawds and perhaps even sex workers themselves ('town ladies'), that before their families abandoned them or the commons was enclosed, they too were country girls like Margery.

The Restoration

While Charles II was installing his mistresses in Whitehall and actresses on the newly reopened stage, moralists were warning against the trip to London through a steady stream of tracts, pamphlets, and advice books. In one prominent exchange, an anonymous author forcefully advises a young gentleman named 'T. L.' to stay home.[5] Men in London, the author of *Remarques on the Humours and Conversations of the Town* cautions, lead 'vicious, sottishe, and prophane' lives; they congregate at the theatre to practise those qualities and to produce their own vicious, sottish, and profane plays, which encourage atheism, whoring, dissipation, and debauchery. Country gentlemen drawn to London ruin their bodies and their fortunes, thus failing to marry or cultivate their estates. A narrative poem called *Gallantry a la Mode* (1674) offers a similar warning: a young man travels to London and visits a house of ill repute, where the proprietor offers him a girl fresh from the country. Discovery of a venereal infection, however, convinces him that he has been cheated. He then commits himself to corrupting others, and, by the end of the poem, he has become a consummate rake. *The Country Gentleman's Vade Mecum* (1699) cautions young men that city pleasures will leave them broke, humiliated, and diseased. The author grudgingly admits that drama offers the one true urban enjoyment, but the playhouses themselves ruin the experience: 'in one part of it you'll see the Judges, and the Wits, with abundance of Hangers-on, and Interlopers, censuring and mistaking the Scene', and every now and then the audience breaks down into riots: 'who but a mad Man would run the risque of being stab'd, or trode to Death, to gratify himself with an empty, insignificant Curiosity?'[6] Better to buy a copy of the play, bring it back to the country, and read it in front of a warm fire.

These copious anti-London publications direct their attention to one particular kind of reader: the country gentleman curious about urban pleasures. Mr Pensive in *The Humours and Conversations of the Town* (1693) sums up the country gentleman's case against the city:

> whilst the Youth of the Town are in chase of Ruin and Rottenness, ours in the Country are improving in the knowledge of their own Affairs, and thinking of an honest and wholsom propagation of their Families, by marrying with some Innocent and Virtuous Lady of equal Quality, who brings not only unsophisticated Beauty, but a good Fortune too; whilst the man of Mode here in Town, after he has spent, or at best, weaken'd his Estate with Drinking, Gaming, and Whoring, takes up with a damn'd Jilt at last for a Wife, who instead of repairing the Breaches of his Fortune, makes 'em wider, till he's quite ruin'd in his Purse as well as Reputation and Happiness.[7]

Mr Pensive and others explore many consequences of urban debauchery, but they ultimately return to one central point: better to marry a country wife – an 'unsophisticated Beauty' – than get mixed up with town ladies. The word 'sophisticated' has come to suggest the cosmopolitan freedom from naïveté; in this passage and in much seventeenth-century writing, however, it refers literally to impurity. Adulterated water, for example, was 'sophisticated'; a 'sophisticated' literary text has been altered in the course of copying or printing. These advice books propose the country estate and the hoped-for marriage that continues the family line as the most significant economic unit. While young people in different times and places travelled to big cities for a variety of reasons, the authors of Restoration-period advice books warn against the 'tricks of the town' because they worry that young country heirs will dissipate their estates and contaminate (or end) their family lines through whoring and theatregoing.[8] They worry that such men, once corrupted, will never settle down with an 'unsophisticated Beauty'.

The stage often singled out the same group of men, but played their urban ambitions for biting comedy. Henry Neville Payne's Muchland in *The Morning Ramble; or, The Town-Humours* (1673) comports himself with dignity, but this doesn't prevent him from getting drawn into a duel when another character harasses him: 'Alas, alas, the Gentleman's lately come out of the Countrey, he doth not understand good breeding.'[9] In John Crowne's

The Countrey Wit (1675), Sir Mannerly Shallow longs to breathe the air of London and displays a map of the city in his study. He exuberantly travels to London to claim his bride-to-be, who loves the libertine Ramble and can't abide marriage to a bumpkin. Sir Mannerly falls for London's charms but can't defend himself against its tricksters. After numerous comic errors – he gets lost and then asks for directions to his aunt's house at a tavern, as if everyone in London knew everyone else – Sir Mannerly lives out the worst nightmare of the advice-book authors when he is tricked into marriage with the daughter of an apple-woman in the place of his intended heiress. Shadwell's Clodpate also ends up married to a woman beneath him in status who wins him over by pretending to share his hatred of London. These men turn their backs on unsophisticated beauties and ruin their estates in the process.

In the midst of the advice books and the stage bumpkins, William Wycherley presents Margery Pinchwife, whom Mr Pinchwife has married precisely for her presumed lack of sophistication. Pinchwife has settled in the country, but spent most of his forty-nine years in London indulging in the vices against which the conduct books warn. Pinchwife resembles Clodpate in his rejection of town ladies, but while Clodpate comes to this conclusion through prejudice, Pinchwife has come to it through experience. Sir Mannerly Shallow should have read one of the advice books; Pinchwife, however, could have written one. In part parodying popular anti-London sentiments, Wycherley has Pinchwife reveal the city's temptations to his country wife through excessive warnings against them, as perhaps (the play implies) the conduct books do as well. Pinchwife ultimately becomes a cuckold because his rival Horner manipulates his excessive suspicion and hatred of the city. Margery's country upbringing leaves her comically unprepared for urban temptations: she immediately falls in love with the theatre, including its fine-looking actors. Neither buffoon, curmudgeon, nor island of purity, Margery embodies the geographical equality of desire; her comic errors expose not only her naïveté, but also the hypocrisy of elite London society. For example, after leaving her husband for Horner, Margery has no plans to return home: not only would she be literally unable to find her way back through the London streets, but she has also decided to become Horner's wife rather than Pinchwife's. In response to Horner's explanation that marriage doesn't work like that, Margery points out that she sees London wives change husbands all the time. Here and elsewhere in the play, Margery's enthusiasm for London vices lays them at the doorstep of her London audiences. She comes to London as an unsophisticated beauty in all senses: ignorant of the pleasures of sex and theatre, she has no moral or cultural framework that would suggest they were shameful. In this sense she remains unsophisticated to the end, although London teaches her the art of strategic falsification.

Margery also differs from the Clodpates of the Restoration stage by her gender. As we have seen, most of the anti-London publications at this time assume a male traveller; in the plays, the classic country ignoramus is male. Moralists address their warnings to gentlemen facing the choice between improving themselves through travel or improving their estates through supervision. Yet with Margery, Wycherley creates what we might call, borrowing James Clifford's resonant phrase from another context, a 'discrepant cosmopolitan':[10] she arrives in London out of necessity rather than choice. Restoration plays notoriously explored the closed world of the propertied elite; with Margery, however, Wycherley juxtaposes the kind of high-profile journey of the male search for pleasure against a less deliberate female version that, as mentioned earlier, found its most prominent articulation in the prostitute narrative. William Hogarth later visualises this narrative in his series *A Harlot's Progress*, in which a wagonload of young women arrives in London, greeted by a bawd who inspects the contents of the wagon (see Figure 5.1). In one commonly repeated narrative version, captured satirically by John Cleland in his *Memoirs of a Woman of Pleasure* (1748–9), a young country girl falls into poverty and/or to seduction, forced then to take the inevitable trip to London.

Wycherley explicitly ties Margery's urbanisation to more scandalous ways of 'going upon the town'. When Margery resists writing to Horner a letter falsely denying her attraction to him, Pinchwife pulls out a knife and threatens to carve the word 'whore' into her face. As James Turner points out, this moment of misogynistic violence evokes the historical practice during this period of men slashing the faces of prostitutes as well as attacking and pulling down bawdy-houses.[11] Coming to London exposes Margery to new pleasures, but it also exposes her to new dangers as well. Being (almost literally) branded a whore by her husband becomes inseparable from her 'Londonisation': when first asked to write this letter to Horner, Margery laughs at the absurdity of sending an epistle to someone in the same town. Letters go *between* town and country. But she quickly learns that in London people write letters to each other, and then figures out that texts can be manipulated – an epiphany that comes in handy later as well. From the Fidget ladies, Margery learns about dividing desire from marriage, a version of the prostitute's skill in separating sex for pleasure from sex for profit. Her London experience teaches her the necessary forms of alienation that the Fidget ladies have mastered. Even the virtuous Alithea, often hailed as the single figure of honesty in the play, is not above strategising: she hesitates to reject her foppish suitor Sparkish because his utter lack of jealousy,

Figure 5.1 William Hogarth, *A Harlot's Progress*, Plate II (1732).

she reasons, would give her a better chance at getting to stay in London. Unlike so many Restoration playwrights who celebrate London culture at the expense of outsiders, but also unlike the anti-theatrical moralists, who insist that London holds nothing but tempting dangers, Wycherley leaves the value of going upon the town as an open question. Has Margery improved her lot by learning to be a London wife? Would she have been better had she never met the Fidgets or Horner, never seen a play, and never walked on the mall?

Margery Pinchwife, of course, does not literally become a prostitute, yet her transition from country wife to London wife, in which she learns the invisible yet binding parameters of urban behaviour, dramatises the much-commented-upon migration of women to urban centres. Further, by turning from the country gentleman bumbling his way through London streets to a young woman fascinated by the city but threatened by countless dangers visible to the audience but not to her, Wycherley begins to explore the deeper ambivalence toward London that the stage expresses throughout the eighteenth century, as playwrights returned to various 'country wife' plots to negotiate the delicate balance between embracing the town and going upon it.

The eighteenth century

Eighteenth-century audiences may have resisted the scandalous implications of *The Country Wife*, but they embraced various reincarnations of Margery Pinchwife. Through the figure of a woman going 'upon the town', the stage continued to confront the pleasures and hazards of urbanisation and created the period's most enduring trope for the fallout from urban modernity. In his *Miss Lucy in Town* (1742), Henry Fielding renders more explicit than Wycherley the convergence of the country wife's journey with the presumed fate of other girls going upon the town. Fielding's farcical after-piece offers a stripped-down version of Wycherley's more subtle and complicated maneouvrings: a young woman newly married arrives in London with her husband and happens upon the establishment of the bawd Mrs Midnight, who has been forced to let out rooms because London wives are putting the whorehouses out of business. Mrs Midnight immediately sees in Lucy the opportunity to renew her business by acquiring this 'new face'. Lucy's country freshness will become her main selling point. Like Margery, Lucy seeks city entertainment, but must have her pleasures redirected: one of the prostitutes responds to Lucy's initial interest in the standard tourist attractions by explaining that only the 'vulgar' visit Bedlam, Parliament, and the Tower; 'fine ladies', by contrast, attend 'ridottos, masquerades, court', and, of course, 'plays'. Lucy wants nothing more than to become a fine lady: she first accepts the attentions of the wealthy Jew Zorobabel, who promises to shower her with gifts, but she quickly gives him over in favour of Lord Bawble. Margery figures out by observation that city ladies need not stay with their husbands; at Mrs Midnight's house, Lucy learns that fidelity has become unfashionable and unprofitable.

The most popular country wife figure in the early eighteenth century, however, never goes upon the town. One of the most lucrative plays of the century – John Gay's *The Beggar's Opera* (1728) – proposes the urbanisation of an entire genre with a strangely unsophisticated beauty at its centre. In this 'Newgate pastoral', Gay creates in Polly a heroine whose country-like innocence, optimism, and naïveté go comically unexplained by her London upbringing among thieves, whores, and a family of criminals. Polly falls in love with the rakish 'gentleman of the road' Macheath, and expects to marry him, a possibility that horrifies her parents. Macheath could ruin them by learning the secrets of their criminal operation, and Polly herself, they feel, would prove more profitable as a resident temptress. Like Margery, Polly inadvertently satirises urban corruption through her naïveté. Gay, however, targets a different London: while Wycherley exposes the cynicism behind the elite urban marriage market, Gay attacks through the figure of Polly a

London economy in which all property has become mobile, alienable, and tawdry. Wycherley's characters visit the theatre and the mall; Gay's inhabit jails, taverns, and whorehouses. By juxtaposing high and low, legitimate and illegitimate, Gay proposes to strip the urban elite of their cosmopolitan self-justification. In the midst of this criminal underworld that embraces, like the 'legitimate' society it parallels, universal commodification, Polly embodies the pastoral values of priceless purity, standing alone as an unsophisticated misfit. In its insistence that high life only differs from low life in that the wealthy escape from punishment, Gay offers a darker vision of London unrelieved by the genteel pleasures that Restoration characters pursue. Gay deflates key Restoration distinctions between the crude and the refined when he recasts the opera form to suit London's criminal underworld, thus removing – even satirising – the theatre's traditional claim to its contribution to urban culture.

In the eighteenth century, then, even the theatre at times scrapped the traditional defences of London. The Restoration defence, however, depended on a stratified world in which elite women might cuckold their husbands and thus act like 'whores', but the true town women (who have neither inheritances or settlements) for the most part only appear in the margins. With the increasing importance of London as not just a centre of sophistication but also a centre of business, playwrights more directly confronted the transformative power of commercial exchange. Gay and other Tory writers exposed the brutality of this world in a range of genres (poetry, satire, plays), and Whig writers responded with a qualified defence. Although Joseph Addison and Richard Steele warned their readers against the dangers of the city in their periodical essays, they embraced London's cosmopolitanism. Mr Spectator celebrated the Royal Exchange for 'making this Metropolis a kind of Emporium for the whole Earth'. Rural landownership was not enough: 'If we consider our own Country in its natural Prospect, without any of the Benefits and Advantages of Commerce, what a barren uncomfortable Spot of Earth falls to our Share!'.[12] A similar defence of global commerce enabled by urban cosmopolitanism opens George Lillo's *The London Merchant*. Here the merchant Thorowgood, for reasons that have nothing to do with the plot, explains how the London merchants have recently joined together to persuade Genoese merchants to refuse a loan to Spain, thus saving the English from an attack by the Spanish Armada. While Mr Spectator exalts in the sheer pleasure of exotic commodities, Lillo's Thorowgood insists on the public usefulness of commerce. For Thorowgood, London merchants must renounce their own pleasure for public good.

Lillo's hyper-idealised Thorowgood is served, however, by a young apprentice who should have read some of the warnings about London's dangers.

Lillo's apprentice George Barnwell, who has been sent to the city by his wealthy uncle, becomes a kind of 'country wife' in this play, and his amorous inclination falls prey to the predatory Millwood's seductive advances. While lamenting Barnwell's fall from innocence to guilt, Lillo nevertheless does not attribute this tragedy to the unmitigated corruption of London – Lillo's London is not a Swiftian city of open sewers or Gay's world of thieves, whores, and pirates. For Lillo, as for Addison and Steele, the new urban middle classes must be trained to distinguish the virtues of the town from the threats posed by the women who have gone upon it.

In some ways, Lillo returns to the earlier, advice-book model of the dangers that await men rather than women. Barnwell, however, doesn't go to the theatre, gamble, write plays, or become a rake. He straddles the class definitions invoked by the traditional coming-to-London narrative: he belongs to the elite (apprenticeships to merchants being quite expensive), but at the same time shares with other apprentices limited access to cash. So the worry with Barnwell is not that he will end his family line by dissipating his wealth, but that he will fail to profit by his apprenticeship to the virtuous Thorowgood and fail to contribute to the stronghold of virtue within London itself. Millwood, by contrast, has long been upon the town. Like the women featured in eighteenth-century prostitute narratives, Millwood at a crucial moment reveals her own story of seduction and betrayal. In the reformist prostitute narratives that Millwood's confession anticipates, women tell their stories in part to demonstrate the challenging circumstances they faced and to explain that they have ended up on the town out of need rather than inherent corruption. Lillo doesn't take Millwood's story to the point of sentimentalisation; nevertheless, her confession generates a flash of sympathy. Millwood's confession alludes to another narrative that preceded the current drama, in which she was once drawn to London's complexity with the enthusiasm and naïveté of a Margery, a Lucy, or a Polly, but with the result that material circumstances failed her. Men seduced her and left her in poverty; in a tragic version of Margery's remarks on London marriages, Millwood concludes from experience that virtue counts for nothing and that only those with money earn freedom from contempt. At the same time, while Margery's damning observations go uncontested, Thorowgood insists virtue rather than vice is the true path to wealth. Lillo thus juxtaposes these two 'merchants' who offer two different perspectives on London. In this way, he allows for a certain level of danger in the city (particularly to women, but also to men who then fall into the hands of these damaged women) while at the same time insisting on the fundamental soundness, safety, and even justice of London's commercial system.

In spite of their political disparity, however, both *The London Merchant* and *The Beggar's Opera* overlap in one significant point of representation. While Restoration plays represent London as the location of pleasure and danger (often at the same time), these eighteenth-century plays view London primarily as a place of business. Both plays dramatise, among other things, the complexities of passing along a business rather than an estate from one generation to the next, with George Barnwell and Polly Peachum both failing parental expectations. The advice books change as well. Eighteenth-century moralists worry less about heirs who will end their family lines through dissipation and more about the need to negotiate a newly permeating commercial system centred in London. The visible increase in street prostitution – a phenomenon much commented upon by contemporaries – seemed to pose the constant threat that the city belonged less to the Thorowgoods than the Millwoods, the figure for the new kind of 'London disease', with the city itself in need of a cure.

Richard King's *The Frauds of London Detected* (1779?), for example, lists a range of urban dangers, but lavishes considerable detail on the proliferation of streetwalkers. 'To the disgrace of humanity, sense, and religion', he writes,

> to the disgrace of this once flourishing kingdom, and the scoff and ridicule of our neighbours the French and Germans, it is said, and too truly, that there are more depredations, Frauds, thefts and whoredoms committed in modern London in one week, than were in ancient Rome in a twelve month; which may be easily accounted for – London is become luxurious, and, notwithstanding the salutary laws enacted against vice and immorality, luxury begets dissipation, and consequently the evils we complain of; whereas Rome was, while virtuous, free from luxury and the mischiefs produced thereby.[13]

An engraving on the inside of King's volume shows a man handing *The Frauds of London Detected* to his children in preparation for their journey to the city: the author clearly envisions this book as a new kind of warning to youth. The overwhelming population of street prostitutes struck a foreign visitor:

> Women of the town [in London] ... are more numerous than at Paris, and have more liberty and effrontery than at Rome itself. About night-fall they range themselves in a file in the foot-paths of all the great streets, in companies of five and six, most of them drest very genteely. The low-taverns serve them as a retreat, to receive their gallants in: in those houses there is always a room set apart for this purpose. Whole rows of them accost passengers in broad daylight; and above all, foreigners. Their business is so far from being considered as unlawful, that the list of those who are any way eminent is publicly cried about the streets: this list, which is very numerous, points out their places of

abode, and gives the most circumstantial and exact detail of their features, their stature, and the several qualifications for which they are remarkable. A new one is published every year, and sold under the piazza of Covent-garden, with the title of the *New Atalantis*, and the name of the author, M. Harris, in the title-page. There are likewise to be seen in the same place two other poems, one entitled, *The Meretriciad*, the other *The Courtesan*, both very fit to be annexed to the above list.[14]

Steele and Lillo early in the century defend urbanity by essentially suggesting that newcomers need to learn how to distinguish town women from unsophisticated beauties, both of whom may be found in London. In Gay, by contrast, almost everyone is upon the town. While these eighteenth-century plays thus differ in many respects from those in the Restoration, they nevertheless retain and intensify the use of the female figure as the barometer for corruption or purity.

Later in the eighteenth century, however, a few plays begin to foreground and interrogate the role of gender in the dramatisation of the migrant's experience. In his *The West Indian* (1771), Richard Cumberland proposes a version of the country wife in the colonial male. Naïve but good-natured, Belcour travels from his plantation in the West Indies to the metropolitan centre. Cumberland's Belcour combines elements of the naïve Margery with elements of the classic Restoration rake. While Belcour possesses the libido of a Horner, he lacks his wiles. Upon landing in the city, Belcour is attracted to Louisa and chases her through the London streets, where she easily loses him (all the houses in the city look the same to the West Indian). He quickly falls into the hands of the trickster Mrs Fulmer. Where the naïve Margery finds the city delightful though puzzling, Belcour at first is overwhelmed: 'unless a man marched with artillery in his front, 'tis more than the labour of a Hercules can effect to make any tolerable way through your town'.[15] He causes a massive brawl upon landing, for 'accustomed to a land of slaves, and out of patience with the whole tribe of custom-house extortioners, boatmen, tide-waiters, and water-bailiffs, that beset me on all sides, worse than a swarm of mosquitoes, I proceeded a little too roughly to brush them away with my rattan'. In spite of this confusion, however, Belcour ultimately 'applaud[s] their spirit' as fellow subjects. He later expresses even greater appreciation for the city's commercial excitement: London is 'a great, rich, overgrown, noisy, tumultuous place: the whole morning is a bustle to get money, and the whole afternoon is a hurry to spend it' (III.vii.15–19).

Like London itself, the elusive Louisa turns out, upon closer inspection, to be more virtuous and orderly than initial appearances suggest. Belcour at first treats her as a prostitute because Mrs Fulmer had convinced him that Louisa's favours were for sale (and that she, Mrs Fulmer, would secure them for him in exchange for his diamonds). Eventually, however, the West Indian learns to treat Louisa and London with appropriate respect, learning manners suited to 'the land of beauty, of arts, and elegancies' (I.v.59). From the beginning of the play – and in contrast to the eighteenth-century travellers warned against London's chaos – Belcour is challenged to free himself of his West Indian indiscretions, assimilate to the civilised ways of London, and to govern his spending 'with a temperate and restrained authority' (I.v.67). Like Margery, Belcour undergoes a process of sophistication, although Cumberland represents Belcour's change with less ambivalence. Certainly, Belcour could have benefited from a little warning about London's illicit commerce; in the end, though, the play suggests that accounts such as King's and Grosley's mischaracterise London. In this play, London's most dangerous frauds are French (Mrs Fulmer and her husband), and the woman whom he sees on the street but who loses him in an urban maze flees him to protect her virtue rather than raise her price. Cumberland, then, embraces the playwright's traditional role since the Restoration of defending London against moralistic attacks. For John Gay, the city in its current form has little redeeming social value, and in the sequel *Polly* he sends his unsophisticated beauty out to the West Indies, where at last she finds virtue in a Native American prince. The farther from London one gets, Gay seems to suggest, the greater the chance of avoiding corruption. Cumberland, by contrast, suggests that while London certainly has its pitfalls, it can ultimately polish and restrain the wild manners of a West Indian with a good heart. In the Restoration, London's pleasurable but suspect cosmopolitanism draws people to the city but exposes them to its vices; in the eighteenth century, however, sophistication can itself become a form of virtue.

This new urban possibility of virtuous and mannerly sophistication can by the end of the century extend to women as well. Some playwrights, of course, repeated the enduring gendered divisions, although with updates appropriate to London's commercial culture. An old bachelor of 50 (Pinchwife is 49), Sir Peter Teazle in R. B. Sheridan's *The School for Scandal* (1777) falls in love with a country girl, marries her, and brings her to London. Once in town, Lady Teazle dedicates herself to the rules of fashion: she buys hothouse flowers in the winter; she refuses to obey her husband; and, worst of all, she joins a circle of scandal-mongers who gather to destroy reputations. Joseph Surface, the rascal posing as a man of sentiment, tries to persuade Lady Teazle that it is a practice of fashionable London ladies to find new lovers as well as new dresses. The exposure of their almost consummated affair and the revelation that her husband, in spite of his complaining, cares for her after all inspire Lady Teazle to renounce London society and retire with Sir Peter to the country. In Sheridan's play, London awakens the country wife's commercial rather than sexual desires, which ultimately cause less permanent damage. In *The School for Scandal*, while urban dangers remain gendered in familiar ways, it nevertheless becomes possible for a country wife to come to town without going upon it.

In 1780, however, Hannah Cowley rethinks the theatrical negotiation of women, urbanity, and cosmopolitanism, proposing in both plots of her play, *The Belle's Stratagem* (1780), the cultural advantages of sophisticated ladies. The play's secondary plot revisits and revises the classic warning against a country wife going upon the town. Lady Frances and Sir George resemble the Teazles and the Pinchwifes, with their familiar age difference and the attention the couple receives from the London ladies of fashion. The city ladies, as in the other plays, convince the newcomer that conjugal affection has gone out of style; nevertheless, Lady Frances, unlike Margery or Lady Teazle, has no interest in her rakish suitor Courtall, who pursues her at all the fashionable entertainments to which the London ladies drag her. (At an auction, characters bid on a little wax model of London, among other items, perhaps suggesting the play's attempt to reclaim the city it depicts.) Courtall can only get close to her by disguising himself as Sir George: in contrast to earlier country wife figures, Lady Frances's exposure to danger is entirely inadvertent. After this close call Sir George insists on taking her back to the country. The long-time admirer who rescues her from Courtall's plot (Saville), however, makes the case that women like Lady Frances should stay in the city so that their virtue and charms can benefit London and the court: 'society has claims on Lady Frances that forbid' this retreat from London.[16] Unlike Margery and Lady Teazle, then, Lady Frances stays in the city.

While the Lady Frances plot thus refigures the traditional country wife tensions, the main plot of *The Belle's Stratagem* demolishes them. Here Letitia wins back the love of her newly cosmopolitan fiancé through strategic performances of naïveté and sophistication. Doricourt and Letitia had been engaged at a young age but haven't seen each other for years. Meanwhile, Doricourt has returned from the grand tour with a parcel of French footmen and a taste for glamorous European women, in comparison to whom Letitia now seems provincial. Doricourt would follow through on the marriage for the sake of honour, but Letitia refuses to settle for a lukewarm husband. First, in order to strengthen Doricourt's antipathy before turning it to love, Letitia performs an extreme version of a naïve country wife, adopting crude manners and comically provincial interests. This has the intended effect of horrifying Doricourt with the prospect of such a wife and perhaps also satirises the London stage's fetishisation of unsophisticated beauties. Later, however, Letitia piques Doricourt's interest at the masked ball by disguising herself as a city lady, rumoured to have been on the town, and perhaps other places as well. In disguise, Letitia embraces cosmopolitanism for the sake of love: for the right man, she would 'change my country, my sex; feast with him in an Eskimo's hut or a Persian pavilion; join him in the victorious war dance on the borders of Lake Ontario or sleep to the soft breathings of the flute in the cinnamon groves of Ceylon' (IV.i.320–5).

Through Letitia's performances Cowley transforms female sophistication from a consistently negative attribute to something used productively in the service of domestic happiness, and she reverses a long moralist tradition advocating the superiority of unsophisticated rural beauty. At the end of the play Letitia agrees to settle somewhere between rusticity and worldliness, thus revealing that she, and perhaps other women, can perform any position on the spectrum of sophistication. Yet such a range of performances itself demands a level of sophistication that transcends any one of her impersonations. The female rusticity so valued by Pinchwife and Restoration moralists becomes in Cowley's hands absurdly unattractive and even dangerous: Lady Frances would have been better off with a little more suspicion. By realigning values attached to gendered traits, however, Cowley not only asks her audience to embrace female sophistication, but also to celebrate London itself. Both women in this play become associated with a positive revaluation of London and urban life. All agree that Lady Frances would be better off in London, and that London would be better off with Lady Frances. Letitia, though capable of performing any point on the spectrum of sophistication, becomes associated with London life as the ideal compromise between a foppish cosmopolitanism and rural ignorance.

Finally, since so many of these plays about country wives going upon the town use the dreaded figure of the prostitute as a trope for the corrupting influence of urban life, it might be instructive to end with a glimpse at these town women and how Cowley inserts one into her play. Fielding gives us the comic side: a bawd insatiably driven by profit who laments the sexual laxity of London ladies because they undercut her business. Lillo captures the tragic version of prostitution: Millwood had been seduced as a young woman, and vows as a result to seek revenge on all of mankind. The only security, she concludes, can be found in wealth – a point on which she might find agreement with Jenny Diver, who sells Macheath out to Peachum. In *The Belle's Stratagem*, Courtall (disguised as Sir George) brings home a woman he thinks is Lady Frances, but Saville, to save Lady Frances, has disguised a prostitute to take her place. When Courtall's acquaintances invade his house to see the lady he has cornered, 'Lady Frances' unveils herself as the notorious Kitty Willis, whom the other characters immediately recognise. Courtall is so humiliated that he skulks off to Paris the next day. Clearly his disgrace lies in seducing a well-known prostitute when he thought he was bedding the virtuous Lady Frances. But this town lady is not only a prostitute, but, interestingly, a celebrity with whom all these respectable men are familiar. Kitty seems to enjoy embarrassing Courtall for his pretensions as much as anyone else; she is not depicted as an alien 'other' here, but rather joins with the others as part of the joke on this would-be rake. Further, as has often been noted, the name 'Kitty Willis' recalls Kitty Fisher, one of the best-known and wealthiest courtesans of high society in eighteenth-century London. Now certainly Cowley isn't trying to erase the difference between Lady Frances and Kitty Willis, even though they are easily confused; nevertheless, her town lady is neither tragic, alienated, rapacious, nor verging on poverty. Letitia herself, in fact, suggests through her dancing and dress that the mysterious stranger she pretends to be might be a woman of the town (a rumour to this effect circulates). Though this possibility distresses Doricourt, he nevertheless viscerally prefers the city lady over the country wife. While moralists had long held out the figure of the town woman as an emblem for the dangers of London and urban life, Cowley suggests the ways in which Britain's great city benefits from its creation of a wide range of sophisticated ladies.

Notes

1 Anon., *Remarques on the Humours and Conversations of the Town: In a Letter to Sr. T. L.* (1673), 'To the Reader'.
2 Thomas Shadwell, *Epsom Wells: A Comedy Acted at the Duke's Theatre* (1673), dramatis personae.
3 Raymond Williams, *The Country and the City* (New York: Oxford University Press, 1973), Chapter 5.
4 See Maximillian E. Novak, 'Margery Pinchwife's "London Disease": Restoration Drama and the Libertine Offensive of the 1670's', *Studies in the Literary Imagination* 10.1 (1977), 1–23.
5 Contributions to this particular exchange include anon., *Remarques on the Humours and Conversations of the Town*; *Reflexions on Marriage, and the Poetick Discipline: A Letter, by the Author of the Remarques on the Town* (1673); *Remarks upon Remarques; Or, A Vindication of the Conversations of the Town, in Another Letter Directed to the Same Sir T. L.* (1673); *Animadversions on Two Late Books, One Called Remarques, &c. To Which Is Added Notes on Some Humours and Conversations of the Country. The Other Called Reflections on Marriage, and Poetick Discipline, in Two Letters to Sir T. L.* (1673).
6 Anon., *The Country Gentleman's Vade Mecum; or, His Companion for the Town* (1699), pp. 47, 49.
7 Anon., *The Humours and Conversations of the Town, Expos'd in Two Dialogues* (London: printed for R. Bentley, 1693), p. 28.
8 On this concern, see the anonymous *Youths Safety; or, Advice to the Younger Sort, of Either Sex: More Valuable than Gold* (1698); *The London Bully; or, The Prodigal Son* (1683); *A Satire upon the Town: Address'd to a Friend in the*

Country, Disswading Him from Coming Up (1693); *Remarques on the Humours and Conversations of the Gallants of the Town: Two Letters by a Person of Quality* (1673).

9 Henry Neville Payne, *The Morning Ramble; or, The Town-Humours* (1673), p. 35.

10 James Clifford, *Routes: Travel and Translation in the Late Twentieth Century* (Cambridge, MA: Harvard University Press, 1997), Chapter 1.

11 James Grantham Turner, *Libertines and Radicals in Early Modern London: Sexuality, Politics and Literary Culture, 1630–1685* (Cambridge: Cambridge University Press, 2002), p. 24.

12 *The Spectator* 69 (19 May 1711), in *The Commerce of Everyday Life: Selections from* The Tatler *and* The Spectator, ed. Erin Mackie (Boston, MA: Bedford/St Martin's Press, 1998), p. 203.

13 Richard King, *The Frauds of London Detected* (London: Alexander Hogg, 1779), p. v.

14 M. Grosley, *A Tour to London*, trans. Thomas Nugent, 2 vols. (1772), Vol. 1, p. 55.

15 Richard Cumberland, *The West Indian* (1771), in *British Dramatists from Dryden to Sheridan*, ed. George H. Nettleton, Arthur E. Case, and George Winchester Stone, Jr. (Carbondale: Southern Illinois University Press, 1969), 1.v.25–8. Further citations are to this edition.

16 Hannah Cowley, *The Belle's Stratagem* (1780) in *The Broadview Anthology of Restoration and Early Eighteenth-Century Drama*, ed. J. Douglas Canfield and Maja-Lisa von Sneidern (Peterborough, ON: Broadview Press, 2003), v.v.111. Further citations are to this edition.

6

CYNTHIA WALL

London and narration in the long eighteenth century

> As I am now near the Centre of this Work, so I am to describe the
> great Centre of *England*, the City of *London*.
> Daniel Defoe, *A Tour thro' the Whole Island of Great Britain*[1]

London is in fact at the centre of many, many literary works of seventeenth-
and eighteenth-century Britain, not just as a setting or backdrop but as a
shaping force – of plot, character, and narrative itself. Narrators describe the
city, inhabit the city, walk the city, write the city. The circuits Defoe as trav-
eller-narrator takes in his epistolary documentary *A Tour thro' the Whole
Island of Great Britain* (1724–7) begin and end in London, and London
is its centrepiece, expanding as we read: 'We see several Villages, formerly
standing, as it were, in the Country, and at a great Distance, now joyn'd to
the Streets by continued Buildings, and more making haste to meet in the
like Manner.'[2] And he draws – or rather, follows – a 'Line of Measurement'
about the city, a line that actively 'runs' and 'passes' and 'crosses' and 'turns'
and 'goes away' and 'comes to':

> From *Tottenham Court*, the Line comes in a little *South*, to meet the *Bloomsbury*
> Buildings, then turning *East*, runs behind *Montague* and *Southampton* Houses,
> to the N.E. Corner of *Southampton House*, then crossing the Path, meets the
> Buildings called *Queen's Square*, then turning *North*, 'till it comes to the N.W.
> corner of the Square, thence it goes away *East* behind the Buildings on the
> *North* side of *Ormond Street*, 'till it comes to *Lamb's Conduit*. (2.2.99)

The movement of the city's outline seems to generate the movement of
the syntax, the fluid line of the sentence mapping and matching the fluid
line of London's fast-changing boundaries. Similarly, the prose patterns in
Defoe's novels follow his characters' footsteps through their topographic-
ally detailed London plots – Moll Flanders flees from thoughts of murder
in an arc around the prison that will eventually get her; the saddler H. F.
anxiously retreats to his house and then finds himself back outside tracking

the ebb and flow of the plague; Roxana hides her darkest scenes in London almost literally beneath her paragraphs; all the characters digress, repeat themselves, and circle round their points in ways that map directly onto the city's streets.

But Defoe is not the only author to pattern his genres on the patterns of London. In some ways we could say that London generates genres to tell itself, and this chapter will look at forms of narration – topographies, travel narratives, diaries, periodical essays, and novels – that deliberately mould themselves to the contours of London. 'Up, and to the 'Change' – Samuel Pepys's diary entries typically open with an excursion (in this case to the Royal Exchange for news) that only closes at the end of the day: 'and so to Bed'.[3] Young James Boswell maps his days in 1762 based on his readings: 'I was full of rich imagination of London, ideas suggested by the Spectator ... which I strongly feel and am ravished with' – and in turn becomes Macheath, Addison, John Bull, while his narratives expand with his successes on the street or in bed.[4] The popular topographies from John Stow (1598) to John Strype (1720) and the travel narratives of Celia Fiennes (1685–1712), Defoe, and Mary Delany (mid eighteenth century) supplied a vocabulary of visual description that was quickly absorbed into the novels of Samuel Richardson and Frances Burney. London is central not only to the content but to the form of its narratives, and the variety of those narratives suggests an endless fascination with the ways of telling London.

Topographies

Perhaps the most basic way to narrate London is to describe it to the traveller or visitor – or to describe it *as* a traveller or visitor. Personal experience of London becomes a public relation: this is what you will see; this is what I have seen. Topographies and travel narratives alike share an audience wanting to *see* the face of London; readers intend to go there, actually or imaginatively. The first really systematic description of London was *A Survey of London* in 1598 by John Stow, 'Citizen of London'. The *Survey* went through several editions in Stow's lifetime and became the template for a surge of topographies in the seventeenth and eighteenth centuries – particularly after the Great Fire of September 1666 destroyed four-fifths of the original medieval centre of the city in three days. The *Survey of London* opens with sections on the history of the city, on its walls, bridges, gates, towers, schools, charities, sports, customs, and on the 'Honour of the Citizens, and Worthiness of Men in the same', but the bulk of the treatise is a street-by-street encompassing of its twenty-six wards. The streets are named, their stories told; the density of habitation is matched by thickness of description. Stow gives us London past bound up in or buried beneath London present, and each section is infilled with a combination of architectural description and local history. Up toward the end of Tower Street, for example, is

> a fayre house sometime belonging to one named Griste, for he dwelled there in the yeare 1449. And Iacke [Jack] Cade, captaine of the rebels in Kent, being by him in this his house feasted, when he had dined, like an unkinde guest, robbed him of all that was there to be found worth the carriage. Next to this is one other fayre house, sometime builded by Angell Dune, Grocer, Alderman of London, since possessed by sir Iohn Champneis, Alderman and Mayor of London. He builded in this house an high Tower of Bricke, the first that euer I heard of in any priuate man's house, to ouerlooke his neighbours in this Citie. But this delight of his eye was punished with blindnesse some yeares before his death: since that time sir Percevall Hart a jolly Courtier and knight, harbenger to the Queene, was lodged there, &c.[5]

For Stow, it's as if London as entity engages directly with its inhabitants: build that tower too high, try to see too much, and it will replace you with a jolly courtier.

The stories are not just in the streets – their very *names* are stories. Cornhill Ward is 'so called of a corne Market, time out of minde there holden' (p. 188). Or you have Lombard Street, 'so called of the Longobards, and other Marchants, strangers of diuerse nations assembling there twice euery day, of what originall, or continuance, I haue not read' (p. 202). Pudding Lane is so called 'because the Butchers of Eastcheape haue their skalding House for Hogges there, and their puddinges with other filth of Beastes, are voided downe that way to theyr dung boates on the Thames' (p. 212). Mountgodard Street is so called 'of the Tippling houses there, and the Goddards [goblets] mounting from the tappe to the Table, from the table to the mouth, and sometimes ouer the head' (p. 345). There were in Bread Street formerly bakers; goldsmiths in Goldsmiths Row; 'wantons' in Love Lane; and in Pissing Alley … Every street name tells its own history, names its occupants, describes their behaviours.

Stow is interested in *everything* to do with his city – churches and houses, rich and poor, open space and crowded stalls, history and gossip, antiquity and innovation. The *Survey* is not a tour of the Wonders of London but a moving portrait of a living, seething place; it offers both a bird's-eye view and a sidewalk perspective, pulling back and zooming in. And that comprehensiveness, that voraciousness for local detail, defined the genre of London topography for well over 150 years. Indeed, treatises such as James Howell's *Londonopolis* of 1657 or John Brydall's *Camera regis* of 1676 were little more than happy plagiarisms, recycling the same stories in the same sentences – because they worked so well. At least John Strype's *Survey of the Cities of London and Westminster* in 1720 cites Stow on the title page. In Strype, as in some earlier topographies, we are moved inside the text created by the city's history: 'Then you come to Bethlem, vulgarly called Bedlam, and now Old Bedlam, a Lane, wherein stood an ancient charitable House, for the Keeping and Cure of Lunatics.'[6] The intermixing in London of the prosperous and the destitute, the grand and the mean, the good and the naughty, is captured in the very sentence structures of Strype and Stow and Defoe – not even syntax will be zoned for propaganda: '*Newgate-street*, well inhabited by good Tradesmen; it comes out of *Cheapside* and *Blowbladder-street*, and runs to *Newgate*, the City Gaol for Malefactors; as also for the County of Middlesex for the like Criminals, and likewise for Debtors. It is a large Prison, and made very strong, the better to secure such Sort of Criminals, which too much fills it.'[7]

Strype himself would be recycled throughout the eighteenth century, although the comprehensiveness (*A New and Compleat Survey of London,* 1742; *A New and Universal History, Description and Survey … of London,* 1776) would often step aside for selectivity: *The Companion to Every Place of Curiosity and Entertainment* (1767); *The Curiosities of London and Westminster Described in Four Volumes* (1786); *The Antiquities of London: Comprising Views and Historical Descriptions of Its Principal Buildings* (1814). But whether surveying the entire city or just landing on its landmarks, the topographies supplied the most popular *official* narrations of London's most public spaces.

Travel narratives, letters, and diaries

But London was privately narrated as well. Visitors and occupants alike found their lives and letters shaped by their experiences of London. Celia Fiennes (1662–1741), for example, born into a wealthy, well-connected family (her grandfather was the first Viscount Saye and Sele), travelled around England on horseback between 1685 and 1712, avidly recording everything she saw. Her accounts of her journey weren't published until the nineteenth century, but she had in mind an audience of readers and recommended that 'all persons, both ladies, much more Gentlemen' should travel over their native country and 'make observations of the pleasant prospects, good buildings, different produces and manufactures of each place' in order to form a clearer 'Idea of England'.[8] Her narrative style has been criticised as haphazardly quilted, associatively rather than linearly organised, but as Joanna Picciotto argues, Fiennes's style is patterned on her method:

It is hard to say where Fiennes's desire for physical exertion stops and her investigative ambitions begin; for her, the call to experiment *is* a call to exercise, and as she takes her solitary way through the country on an open-ended pilgrimage, riding seems to become her writing. Abandoning punctuation for long stretches, she favors parataxis that enacts a studious lack of 'prepossession' about what should be subordinated to what.[9]

Thus Fiennes's bird's-eye view of London lands on its geographical situation – on the Thames – and then swims directly into the Thames itself:

It cannot be thought amiss here to add some remarke on the metropolis of England, London, whose scituation [is] on so noble a river as the Thames; this is very comodious for shipps, which did come up just to the bridge, but from carelessness the river is choaked up that obliges the shipps to come to an anchor at Blackwall; all along this river are severall docks for building shipps of the biggest burden; six miles from the town the last yeare was built the Royal Souveraign which is our greatest ship.[10]

Fiennes enters every corner of her itinerary with sharp-eyed enthusiasm, noting the smallest detail and investigating every curiosity. In one paragraph concerning noblemen's houses, for example, she circles in from the past, marking the demolition of some great houses and the rebuilding of others, and then goes inside to see things for herself:

There was formerly in the Citty several houses of the noblemens with large gardens and out houses, but of late are pulled down and built into streetes and squares and called by the names of the noblemen, and this is the practise by almost all; excepting Northumberland and Bedford House; Lord Mountagues house indeed has been new built and is very fine; one roome in the middle of the building is of a surpriseing height curiously painted and very large, yet soe contrived that speake very low to the wall or wanscoate in one corner and it should be heard with advantage in the very opposite corner across – this I heard Myself.   (p. 223)

Fiennes sweeps through London and Westminster, noting the 'sumptuous Buildings', the parks, the markets, the sculptures, the piazzas, combining memory with observation, as in her description of Queen Anne's clothes, and not omitting the menagerie in the Tower of London. Fiennes's menagerie of prose, her profusion of detail, is not unlike the densely inhabited paragraphs of Stow or Defoe. London is profusion, and profusion guides its narration.

Mary Delany (1700–88) was as enthusiastic a traveller and travel-writer as Celia Fiennes. She had a keen eye and a sharp wit, and spent much of her early life in London before being exiled to a dilapidated castle in Cornwall with a gouty old husband, Alexander Pendarves, at the age of seventeen. Occasionally he would bring her to London, and then her letters to her sister spill over the page as London fills in and overflows with bustle and business:

SOMERSET HOUSE, 29th *Feb.*, 1727/28

To-morrow is the Queen's birthday. Great preparations are made for it: abundance of embroidery. I once thought of going, but upon second thoughts I changed my mind. We are just going to Northend to avoid the bustle of the day, and return on Sunday night to be ready for the entry of the Dutch Ambassador on Monday. Yesterday Mrs. Peyton and I went to Court in the morning; I afterwards dined with the family of the Peytons and Dashwoods, and supped. Sir Tom was brighter than ordinary, which makes me fancy Cymon has met with an Iphigenia. We were very merry, and sung the Beggars' Opera, talked, and wished for my mama and you, but all in vain. By Monday's coach I will send the chocolate and tea, and the new plays, and a tippet [i.e., hat] of my own making and invention, which I desire your acceptance of.

After the birthday I believe everybody will go into colours, except at Court; if there is any alteration in the fashions I will tell you. The *curly murly* fashion of the hair is not much worn now. The town is mussy, though very full. I have not been at an *assemblée* this winter, but I will go to my Lady Strafford's to put me in mind of some happy hours I have had there with you; though they never are out of my memory, but I love those places best where we have been together. The Opera will not survive after this winter; I wish I was a poet worthy the honour of writing its elegy.[11]

Delany's London colonises the country, influencing pastimes, music, literature, fashion, and gossip. Politics and ceremony, dining and sewing, reading and writing, observing and critiquing, constitute the life of an upper-class young lady in London. The private letter to her sister records their public diversions as well as private engagements. London sets the tone and the *ton*.

Mary Pendarves Delany was already *there*, already intimately acquainted with people at Court (she would later be a favourite of the king and queen); London was familiar, known, welcoming. But for others, such as young James Boswell, future biographer of Samuel Johnson, it tantalised as promise. Down he came from Scotland in 1762, at the age of twenty-two, with the reluctant permission of his father, hoping to wriggle out of a legal future by getting a commission in the Footguards (an almost entirely domestic – *safe* – military service), for which he needed a patron. His father, Alexander Boswell, Lord Auchinleck, gave him an introduction to the Duke of Queensberry, and off young Boswell went. He found himself respectable lodgings in Downing Street, bought himself a new pink suit and handsome sword, and courted courtiers and actresses. He adored London (except when he didn't), and he very self-consciously recorded the London textures of his days:

SUNDAY 28 NOVEMBER. I breakfasted with Mr. Douglas. I went to St. James's Church and heard service and a good sermon on 'By what means shall a young man learn to order his ways', in which the advantages of early piety were well displayed. What a curious, inconsistent thing is the mind of man! In the midst of divine service I was laying plans for having women, and yet I had the most sincere feelings of religion. I imagine that my want of belief is the occasion of this, so that I can have all the feelings. I would try to make out a little consistency this way. I have a warm heart, and a vivacious fancy. I am therefore given to love, and also to piety or gratitude to GOD and to the most brilliant and showy method of public worship.

I then walked in the Park and went home to dinner, which was just a good joint of veal and a pudding. This they told me was their usual fare, which I approved of. I found my landlord rather too free. Therefore I carried myself with reserve and something of state.[12]

When he had no friends to dine with nor dukes to appease, Boswell would linger in coffee houses, reading newspapers and listening to his neighbours. He soon made a little habit of recording overheard dialogues, and he watched himself perform the man-about-town, the sophisticated urbanite, acutely delighted with 'the pleasures of London':

SATURDAY 18 DECEMBER ... I then went to Louisa's. I was really in love. I felt a warmth in my heart which glowed in my face. I attempted to be like Digges, and considered the similarity of our genius and pleasures. I acquired confidence by considering my present character in this light: a young fellow of spirit and fashion, heir to a good fortune, enjoying the pleasures of London, and now making his addresses in order to have an intrigue with that delicious subject of gallantry, an actress. (p. 94)

Boswell records London's streets and parks, its churches and monuments (he famously took a prostitute on Westminster Bridge), its conversations and habits, and to his Scottish friends 'declaimed on the felicities of London' (p. 123); his *London Journal* is a diary of a young man's love affair with London.

One hundred years earlier Samuel Pepys, perhaps the most famous London diarist of all, had devoted seven years of paper to his habitual peregrinations of London: 'Up, and to the office'; 'Up and to St. James'; 'Up very betimes and walked'; 'Up, and to church'; 'So home and to bed'; 'so home to supper and to bed'; 'then home to bed'.[13] In between these temporal punctuation marks is all of seventeenth-century London. Pepys itemises his spaces, measuring his day through the streets of the city; his routes can be traced from his words. London has a very physical texture in Pepys's diaries, as in this account of visiting the Bear tavern at the Southwark end of London Bridge:

Dark when we came to London [from a trip to Woolwich], and a stop of coaches in Southworke; I stayed above half an hour and then light; and finding Sir W. Batten's coach, heard they were gone into the Beare at the Bridge-foot, and thither I to them. Presently, the stop is removed; and then going out to find my coach, I could not find it, for it was gone with the rest. So I fain to go through the dark and dirt over the bridge, and my leg fell in a hole broke on the bridge; but the constable standing there to keep people from it, I was ketched up, otherwise I had broke my leg – for which mercy the Lord be praised. So at Fanchurch I find my coach staying for me, and so home.[14]

Like London Bridge itself, overbuilt with houses and shops, Pepys's paragraph is a collage of intersections and interactions: traffic stopping and starting, coaches lost and found, taverns mentioned and entered, patterns of light and dark. In a sense, Pepys falls through a hole in the city itself, and narrates it. The rhythms of 'up ... and so to bed' mirror his urban patterns out and about.

Pepys's last entry of 31 May 1669, before going abroad to try to ward off incipient blindness, inscribes the urban circle of his day in the narrative circle of his paragraph:

[Up] very betimes, and so continued all the morning, with W. Hewer, upon examining and stating my accounts ... Dined at home, and in the afternoon by water to White-hall, calling by the way and Michell's ... And here yo did besar ella, but have not opportunity para hazer mas with her as I would have offered if yo had had it. And thence had another meeting with the Duke of York at White-hall ... Thence to the World's-end, a drinking-house by the park, and there merry; and so home late.[15]

Morning at home, accounting, dining, to court, with a little sexual dalliance on the way (coded in the *lingua franca*), more business with the duke, then a tavern, and home – to the World's End in the end of the diary. Pepys's diary, and his life, are extended along the lines of London; its patterns are London's.

Periodical essays and satires

The early eighteenth century was the Age of the Coffee House – a new kind of social space in which people (mostly but not entirely men) from a wide range of professions and classes gathered to drink coffee, argue politics or literature, and read the newspapers or periodicals. These small humming worlds within London were in a sense an architectural counterpart to that most popular of early-eighteenth-century genres, the periodical essay – that short, lively commentary on the cultural moment. Like the coffee house, and very much a part of it, the small essay was its own neat little world, self-enclosed around a story, a moral, a scene. Joseph Addison's and Richard Steele's *Spectator* essays (1711–12), though not the first of their kind, were sweepingly popular throughout the eighteenth and nineteenth centuries, promising to bring 'Philosophy out of Closets and Libraries, Schools and Colleges, to dwell in Clubs and Assemblies, at Tea-Tables and in Coffee-Houses'.[16] The invisible but omnipresent narrator, Mr Spectator – seen but never recognised – slips incognito among the coffee houses, observing and recording:

> sometimes I am seen thrusting my Head into a Round of Politicians at *Will's*, and listening with great Attention to the Narratives that are made in those little Circular Audiences. Sometimes I smoak a Pipe at *Child's*; and whilst I seem attentive to nothing but the *Post-Man*, over-hear the Conversation of every Table in the room. I appear on Sunday Nights at St. *James's* Coffee-House, and sometimes join the little Committee of Politicks in the Inner Room ... My Face is likewise very well known at the *Grecian*, the *Cocoa-Tree*, and in the Theatres both of *Drury-Lane* and the *Hay-Market*.[17]

The little textual world of roughly 2,500 words per essay was *of* London and addressed *to* London; as Mr Spectator expressed:

> It is with much Satisfaction that I hear this great City inquiring Day by Day after these my Papers, and receiving my Morning Lectures with a becoming Seriousness and Attention. My Publisher tells me, that there are already Three thousand of them distributed every Day: So that if I allow Twenty Readers to every Paper, which I look upon as a modest Computation, I may reckon about Threescore thousand Disciples in *London* and *Westminster*.[18]

Mr Spectator and his circle of friends move through London society, commenting on fashion, finance, families, and folly. Often the essays would centre on letters from readers, creating little dialogues, capturing different voices across the city. (Boswell often imagined himself as a *Spectator* character.) And while the foibles of Londoners might be gently and wittily chastised, London itself is consistently celebrated. Its street signs, coffee houses, professions, street cries, and neighbourhoods are all replayed in its pages. The fascination with recreating London life in small but sweeping compass never flags.

At one point, Mr Spectator rises early from his home in the country and takes a boat down the Thames to the city, 'with a Resolution to rove by Boat and Coach for the next Four and twenty Hours'.[19] He's on a sort of anthropological mission to delineate demographies:

> The Hours of the Day and Night are taken up in the Cities of *London* and *Westminster* by Peoples as different from each other as those who are Born

in different Centuries. Men of Six-a-Clock give way to those of Nine, they of Nine to the Generation of Twelve, and they of Twelve disappear, and make Room for the fashionable World, who have made Two-a-Clock the Noon of the Day.[20]

He chats with the melon-sellers on their way to Covent Garden fruit and flower market, passing hackney-coachmen off home after the night shift. Covent Garden itself is full of fruits and 'agreeable young Women'; and as the day opens wider, 'the Day of People of Fashion began now to break, and Carts and Hacks were mingled with Equipages of Show and Vanity'.[21] The happy bustle pleases him enormously, and only increases with the day as he 'move[s] towards the City; and gay Signs, well disposed Streets, magnificent publick Structures, and wealthy Shops, adorned with contented Faces, made the Joy still rising till we came into the Centre of the City, and Centre of the World of Trade, the *Exchange* of *London*'.[22] Like Defoe ten years later, Mr Spectator has no bashfulness in ascribing the utter centredness of London to itself, the country, the world:

> Our Ships are laden with the Harvest of every Climate: Our Tables are stored with Spices and Oils, and Wines: Our Rooms are filled with Pyramids of *China*, and adorned with the Workmanship of *Japan*: Our Morning's-Draught comes to us from the remotest Corners of the Earth: We repair our Bodies by the Drugs of *America*, and repose our selves under *Indian* Canopies. My friend Sir ANDREW calls the Vineyards of *France* our Gardens; the Spice-Islands our Hot-Beds; the *Persians* our Silk-Weavers, and the *Chinese* our Potters.[23]

The small world of the periodical essay spills over with the plenitude of London; it becomes a daily mirror of self-celebration, a morning dose of optimism and self-satisfaction. *The Spectator* of course addresses other issues – social, literary, religious, political, and the ills as well as the glories of society (illegitimate children, prostitutes, the poor, seducers) – but London itself sits in a prominent position of triumph in these essays.

The Spectator has its obverse in Ned Ward's *The London Spy*, originally issued in eighteen monthly parts between November 1698 and May 1700. Like Mr Spectator later, the Spy roves through London and sees profusion, but not the same profusion. His is a darker, fouler London, and his pages are not the clean little spaces of *The Spectator* but rather nasty sewers of bad-smelling waste. The Spy introduces himself as a country scholar with an 'itching Inclination' to visit London and 'expose the Vanities and Vices of the Town'.[24] So 'with a Fig for St. *Austin* [Augustine] and his Doctrines, a Fart for *Virgil* and his Elegancy, and a T—d for *Descartes* and his Philosophy', away he goes, in prose as full as similes as London is full of swinging signs.[25] And those similes make a different London. Hardly a sentence passes by without one; everything is tied to everything else, and in the process all is contaminated.

The Spy roams everywhere: the East India Company, a widow's coffee house, Billingsgate fish market, the Monument to the Great Fire, Gresham College (home of the Royal Society), Bedlam (the hospital for the insane), the Royal Exchange, the Quakers' streets, Newgate Prison, the court at the Old Bailey, the royal Court at St James's, Bartholomew Fair, alehouses and dark-houses. Each place casts a cultural shadow; there is no real place of light. Even when 'the Streets [are] all adorn'd with dazling Lights' and the bells are ringing and the street cries are of 'Hot Bak'd Wardens and Pippins', there will be 'some Odoriferous Civet-box perfum[ing] the air' as if it were (the infamously stenchy) Edinburgh, inundated with 'Sirreverence' (excrement); or some 'Deadmongers Waggon, Laden with a stinking Corps' will rumble by.[26] There is no clean space in the Spy's London.

The Spy's similes yoke meaning to place; each part of London defines some aspect of character or profession. Like Mr Hyde to Stow's Dr Jekyll, the Spy sees London defining its citizens through its sorriest or nastiest significances. 'Oaths' in a tavern fly about 'like Squibs and Crackers in Cheap-side, when the Cuckolds-all-a-Row March in Splendor thro' the City'.[27] One old prostitute calls after him: 'You white-liver'd Son of a Fleet-street Bumsitter, begot upon a Chair at Noonday, between Ludgate and Temple Bar'.[28] At St Paul's Cathedral there are 'as many Smutty Prints ... staring the Church in the Face as a Learned Debauchee ever found in Aretino's Postures'.[29] Everything that looks nasty, is nasty; everything that looks decent and respectable, is nasty: the Spy's Exchange is not the space of happy global commerce in The Spectator, but the site of 'Swarthy Buggerantoes, Preternatural Fornicators, as my Friend call'd them', 'Bumfirking Italians', 'strait-lac'd Monsters in Fur', 'Lank-Hair'd Formalists', garlicky Spaniards, and mincing French.[30] The similes tie clean to dirty: in the Preface to the Reader, the Spy ties the ornaments of authors to those of Puritan and whore: 'Some Authors are meer Beaus in Writing, and Dress up each Maggotty Flirt that creeps from their Mouldy Fancy, with a fine Dedication ... thinking their Pigmy Product looks as Naked without these Ornaments, as a Puritan without his Band, or a Whore without her Patches.'[31] The similes contaminate; London is pulled inside out, and it's only in Bedlam where 'Truth ... flies hither for sanctuary, where she sits as safe as a Knave in a Church, or a Whore in a Nunnery.'[32] Like the Spectator essays, Ward's are complete little textual worlds of London, but unlike the Spectator's, the narration luxuriates in filth while offering little celebration.

Novels

In a novel, the London glimpsed by the topographies, experienced in the diaries, and compressed into the essays, can expand into full imaginative habitation. There are as many novelistic Londons, of course, as there are other narrated kinds, or, for that matter, as there are Londoners themselves. In Defoe's *Moll Flanders* (1722), the plot often depends on the heroine knowing the streets; in Samuel Richardson's *Clarissa* (1747–8), the plot often depends on the heroine *not* knowing the streets; and in Frances Burney's *Evelina* (1778), the plot often depends on which street the heroine happens to be in. And in each case, the narrative plays out the experience: the first-person story of Moll expands and contracts, is leisurely or rushed, full of things or full of space, in the wake of her elation or fear; in the epistolary novels *Clarissa* and *Evelina*, the former shows a London exerting a spatial control over the circulation of the correspondence, while the latter demonstrates Evelina forlornly changing her postal headings with her changing fortunes.

After Moll is widowed and impoverished, she becomes adept in a new career of stealing. And to be a successful thief in London requires knowing the streets intimately – as sites of promise and routes of escape. So Moll prowls. When her eyes are open for possibilities, her narrative is expansive and her London references well spaced:

> It was now a Merry time of the Year, and *Bartholomew* Fair was begun; I had never made any Walks that Way, nor was the common Part of the Fair of much Advantage to me; but I took a turn this Year into the Cloisters, and among the rest, I fell into one of the Raffling Shops: It was a thing of no great Consequence to me, nor did I expect to make much of it; but there came a Gentleman extreamly well Dress'd, and very Rich, and as 'tis frequent to talk to every Body in those Shops he singl'd me out, and was very particular with me ...[33]

She allows herself to be talked into a coach ride with him to Spring Gardens, in Knightsbridge, 'where we walk'd in the Gardens, and he Treated me very handsomely; but I found he drank very freely' (p. 225), and one thing leads to another – to a house, in fact, where the combination of his drinking and her yielding leads to a ride home in which he falls asleep and she searches him 'to a Nicety; I took a gold Watch, with a silk Purse of Gold, his fine full bottom Perrewig, and silver fring'd Gloves, his Sword, and fine Snuff-box', and nimbly steps out of the coach as it stops 'in the narrow Street beyond *Temple-Bar*' (p. 225). Moll's prose is stuffed as full of collected objects as the Royal Exchange is of goods; the ramble from the fair through the streets to the gardens produces a nice little collection of wealth.

But Moll's prose – and her London – can shift under her feet. In the same neighbourhood where she fleeces the rich gentleman, she comes across a little girl with a gold necklace, and the temptation not only to steal but to kill sends her spiralling terrified into a tightly named network of streets:

> here, I say, the Devil put me upon killing the Child in the dark Alley, that it might not Cry; but the very thought frighted me so that I was ready to drop down, but I turn'd the Child about and bad it go back again, for that was not its way home; the Child said so she would, and I went thro' into *Bartholomew Close*, and then turn'd round to another Passage that goes into *Long-lane*, so away into *Charterhouse-Yard* and out into *St. John's-street*, then crossing into *Smithfield*, went down *Chick-lane* and into *Field-lane* to *Holbourn-bridge*, when mixing with the Crowd of People usually passing there, it was not possible to have been found out; and thus I enterpriz'd my second Sally into the World. (p. 194)

Defoe's sentences are generally a series of clauses stitched together with colons and semicolons, but this is a *remarkably* long one (I've only quoted half). The whole scene is related in one long paragraphical breath; the moment of seeing the child in Aldersgate is syntactically connected to the moment of seeing the gold necklace and geographically connected to the long run toward Holborn Bridge. The event and the streetspaces are compressed, and in fact in their conceptual and topographical centre nestles Newgate Prison, the place Moll fears, the place her route unwittingly encircles, and the place where for a time she does end up. But knowing the streets intimately even in her panic keeps her for the moment outside the prison's sphere.

Clarissa, on the other hand, ends up imprisoned for *not* knowing the streets, in a way. Young, beautiful, virtuous Clarissa Harlowe, desperate to escape the mercenary marriage arranged by her power-hungry family, finds herself carried to London by her adoring suitor, the young, handsome, aristocratic, wealthy, and witty Robert Lovelace. Clarissa hopes that London is of the Fieldingesque kind – the kind that will conceal her. And it does – in the wrong way. The problem is that Lovelace's adoration is not of the distant variety; he plans to 'test' her virtue by seeing if he can't seduce her when she is tucked away at Mrs Sinclair's in Dover Street. But as her best friend Anna Howe learns all too late,

> my dear, you are certainly in a devilish house! – Be assured that the woman is one of the vilest of women! – nor does she go to you by her right name – Very true – her name is *not* Sinclair – nor is the street she lives in, Dover Street – Did you never go out by yourself, and discharge the coach or chair, and return by another coach or chair? If you did (yet I don't remember that you ever wrote to me, that you did), you would never have found your way to the vile house,

either by the woman's name, Sinclair, or by the street's name, mentioned by that Doleman in his letter about the lodgings.[34]

But Clarissa doesn't get this letter in time – because Lovelace has figured out how to intercept and forge her letters to Anna and Anna's to her, exerting his control through his network of spies who work the streets and run the house. He is finally unable to seduce her, but his thirst for vanquishing her must be slaked; in the end, after she has escaped from London, he recaptures her, tricks her back into the city and back into Mrs Sinclair's, then drugs and rapes her.

Clarissa escapes again, to a glove shop in King Street, Covent Garden, and her letters are unleashed again to the actual world, though as ineffectually as if they had still been imprisoned. Her lodgings are a sanctuary for a time, let by Mr and Mrs Smith – 'Two neat rooms, with plain, but clean furniture, on the first floor, are mine' (p. 1022): humble, but comforting – until Mrs Sinclair has her arrested for debt as she ventures out to church, and she is taken to an officer's house in High Holborn. 'I know not where High Holborn is: but anywhere, except to the woman's [Mrs Sinclair's] ... Looking about her, and seeing the three passages, to wit, that leading to Henrietta Street, that to King street, and the fore-right one, to Bedford Street, crowded, she started – Anywhere – anywhere, said she, but to the woman's!' (p. 1052). Too many streets, too many people, too many directions to choose, too many ways to get lost. These newest lodgings are comfortless indeed, as the rake Belford describes to his friend Lovelace: 'A horrid hole of a house, in an alley they call a court: stairs wretchedly narrow, even to the first-floor rooms: and into a den they led me, with broken walls which had been papered, as I saw by a multitude of tacks, and some torn bits held on by the rusty heads' (p. 1064). Not knowing Dover Street, not knowing High Holborn, not knowing London, leads her into the worst rooms of the city, its darkest possibilities. London as well as Lovelace has a hand in the death of Clarissa.

Clarissa is a tragedy, *Evelina* is a comedy, but both connect London with the determination of fate. For Clarissa, most London addresses are tragic; for Evelina, London locations also, though on a smaller scale, organise various levels of happiness or embarrassment. Like Clarissa, Evelina is a young country girl, but unlike Clarissa, she actually wants to go to London and presses her guardian for permission:

> They tell me that London is now in full splendour. Two Play-houses are open,— the Opera-House,—Ranelagh,—the Pantheon. —You see I have learned all their names. However, pray don't suppose that I make any point of going, for I shall hardly sigh to see them depart without me; though I shall probably never

meet with such another opportunity. And, indeed, their domestic happiness will be so great,— it is natural to wish to partake of it.³⁵

Evelina resides first in Queen Anne Street, in an upper-class neighbourhood, where she embroils herself in a few embarrassing situations at balls and ridottos, knocking against the invisible furniture of city etiquette, but in the meanwhile attracting the attention of handsome Lord Orville, rakish Sir Clement Willoughby, and spiteful Mr Lovel. With the Mirvans she walks in the parks, shops in the shops, attends the plays and concerts, and generally has a grand time. Until in Volume II her vulgar, mercenary, Frenchified grandmother, Madame Duval, pounces on her and bears her off to High Holborn among her vulgar, mercenary, and selfish relatives the Branghtons: 'My direction is at Mr. Dawkins's, a hosier in High Holborn' (p. 173). 'Direction' plays in both senses: it is her new address and it determines how her life will now unfold:

> O Maria, London now seems no longer the same place where I lately enjoyed so much happiness; every thing is new and strange to me; even the town itself has not the same aspect:—my situation so altered! my home so different!—my companions so changed! ... Indeed, to me, London now seems a desart [sic]; that gay and busy appearance it so lately wore, is now succeeded by a look of gloom, fatigue, and lassitude; the air seems stagnant, the heat is intense, the dust intolerable, and the inhabitant illiterate and under-bred. At least, such is the face of things in the part of the town where I at present reside.   (p. 174)

Madame Duval and the Branghtons belittle her new-found London expertise; they presume on her friendships; and display that it's not their class but their nature that makes life wretched. In one of the worst moments of this altered London life, Evelina learns just how much an address determines the behaviour of *others*. The dysfunctional family go to Vauxhall, and Evelina finds herself forced into the 'Dark Walks' with the Branghtons. They are suddenly (but not surprisingly) surrounded by 'a large party of gentlemen', all leering drunkenly at Evelina. When one of them seizes on her as 'a pretty little creature', Evelina violently breaks away, only to be caught by another set of lascivious gentlemen. When she cries for help, and is 'rescued' by Sir Clement, her admirer from better days, she finds herself 'surprised at a freedom so unexpected' when he passionately kisses her hands and tries to lead her back into the darkness. She exclaims indignantly: 'from you, who know me, I had a claim for protection, —not to such treatment as this' (p. 199). But he knew her in Queen-Ann-Street – not in the Dark Walks, and not in Holborn. His behaviour she contrasts with Lord Orville's, who also appears in a dubious park scene at Marylebone Gardens to come to her aid: 'But, whatever might be his doubts and suspicions, far from suffering them to influence his behaviour, he spoke, he looked, with the same politeness and attention with which he had always honoured me when countenanced by Mrs. Mirvan' (p. 239).

Through her experiences in all corners of London, Evelina ends up with an acknowledged father and an earl for a husband, as well as the ability, as Mr Villars had earlier counselled, 'not only to *judge*, but to *act*' for herself' (p. 166). London shapes Evelina as it helps destroy Clarissa, and as it shapes and entraps and reinvigorates Moll (who returns to London from transportation to America with best husband Jemy – she had five – and a satisfyingly great deal of wealth). The novel offered the time and space (hundreds of prose pages) for the reader to *live*, and not just visit, the spaces of eighteenth-century London.

There are many Londons, and they have demanded a great variety of narratives. London in the eighteenth century – the century that witnessed the generic explosions of topographies, travel narratives, newspapers, periodicals, biographies and autobiographies, and the novel – found itself rewritten in all those (and more) genres. London exerted itself not just in the imaginations but in the patterns of the prose of its many chroniclers. London in narrative *moves*; it offers itself to static capsules and walking tours and small daily moments and life-changing decisions. In all, the seventeenth- and eighteenth-century narrative accounts of the city overwhelmingly recognise London as a shaping force of experience and of prosal representation of that experience. London is narrated over and over again, given an endlessly fascinating local habitation and a name. The centre of these literary works *was* the centre of the eighteenth-century world. As Samuel Johnson noted, 'When a man is tired of London, he is tired of life; for there is in London all that life can afford.'[36]

Notes

1 Daniel Defoe, *A Tour thro' the Whole Island of Great Britain*, 3 vols. (London: printed and sold by G. Strahan, in Cornhill ..., 1724–6), Volume II, Letter 2, p. 94. Further references are to this edition and are cited in arabic numbers by volume, letter, page.

2 *Ibid.*, 2.2.96.

3 Samuel Pepys, *The Diary of Samuel Pepys*, 11 vols., ed. Robert Latham and William Matthews (Berkeley and Los Angeles: University of California Press, 1995), *passim*.

4 James Boswell, *London Journal 1762–63*, ed. Frederick A. Pottle, foreword by Peter Ackroyd (New Haven: Yale University Press, 2004), p. 130.

5 John Stow, *A Svrvay of London, Conteyning the Originall, Antiquity, Increase, Moderne estate, and description of that City, written in the yeare 1598, by Iohn*

Stow, Citizen of London (London: imprinted by Iohn Windet, printer to the honorable Citie of London, 1603), pp. 134–5.

6 John Strype, *A Survey of the Cities of London and Westminster*, 6th edn, 2 vols. (London, 1755), Vol. I, p. 436.

7 *Ibid.*, p. 683.

8 Celia Fiennes, *The Illustrated Journeys of Celia Fiennes 1685–c. 1712*, ed. Christopher Morris (Gloucester: Alan Sutton, 1995), p. 32.

9 Joanna Picciotto, 'Breaking through the Mode: The Exercise of Curiosity in Early Eighteenth-Century England,' *Literature Compass* 6.2 (2009), 291–303.

10 Fiennes, *Illustrated Journeys*, p. 222.

11 Mary Delany, *Mrs Delany at Court and among the Wits*, ed. R. Brimley Johnson (London: Stanley Paul, 1925), pp. 47–8.

12 Boswell, *London Journal*, pp. 53–4.

13 Pepys, *Diary*, Vol. VI, pp. 255–65 (August–September 1664).

14 *Ibid.*, Vol. V, p. 307 (October 1664).

15 *Ibid.*, Vol. X, p. 564 (31 May 1669).

16 *Spectator* 10 (12 March 1711), in Joseph Addison and Richard Steele, *The Spectator*, ed. Donald F. Bond, 5 vols. (Oxford: Clarendon Press, 1965), Vol. I, p. 44.

17 *Ibid.*, Vol. I, pp. 3–4.

18 *Ibid.*, p. 44.

19 *Ibid.*, Vol. IV, p. 98.

20 *Ibid.*, p. 99.

21 *Ibid.*, p. 101.

22 *Ibid.*, p. 102.

23 *Ibid.*, Vol. I, pp. 295–6.

24 Edward Ward, *The London-Spy, Compleat in Eighteen Parts*, 4th edn, 2 vols. (London, 1709), Vol. I, p. 2.

25 *Ibid.*, Vol. I, p. 2.

26 *Ibid.*, p. 26.

27 *Ibid.*, p. 5.

28 *Ibid.*, Vol. II, pp. 40, 41.

29 *Ibid.*, Vol. I, p. 100.

30 *Ibid.*, pp. 68–9.

31 *Ibid.*, pp. A2–A2v.

32 *Ibid.*, p. 65.

33 Daniel Defoe, *The Fortunes and Misfortunes of the Famous Moll Flanders, &c.*, ed. G. A. Starr (Oxford: Oxford University Press, 1987), p. 224.

34 Samuel Richardson, *Clarissa; or, The History of a Young Lady*, ed. Angus Ross (Harmondsworth: Penguin, 1985), p. 744.

35 Frances Burney, *Evelina; or, The History of a Young Lady's Entrance into the World*, ed. Edward A. Bloom, intro. Vivien Jones (Oxford: Oxford University Press, 2002), pp. 25–6.

36 James Boswell, *Life of Johnson*, ed. R. W. Chapman, intro. Pat Rogers (Oxford: Oxford University Press, 1980), p. 859 (20 September 1777).

7

WILLIAM SHARPE

London and nineteenth-century poetry

So he who wishes to see a Vision, a perfect Whole,
Must see it in its Minute Particulars ...
William Blake, *Jerusalem*[1]

I asked him whether there was a great fire anywhere? For the streets
were so full of dense brown smoke that scarcely anything was to be seen.
'Oh dear no, miss', he said. 'This is a London particular.'
Mr Guppy, explaining a London fog to Esther Summerson,
in Charles Dickens, *Bleak House*[2]

In the nineteenth century London became the greatest city in the world; it
also became largely invisible – at least for poets. The 'Minute Particulars'
that for Blake enabled vision had been buried under a grimy blizzard of
soot, smoke, and damp known as 'a London particular', a dense fog whose
persistence grew along with the city's population and pollution. While the
sun never set on the British empire, it sometimes never rose on its capital –
for a week at a time, as Ruskin noted in *The Storm Cloud of the Nineteenth
Century* (1884). Like Blake and many of his contemporaries, Ruskin placed
a premium on vision: 'To see clearly is poetry, prophecy, and religion, – all
in one', he memorably asserted in *Modern Painters* (1843).[3] But what to do
when circumstances – both cultural and climatic – hinder your taking a good
look at your subject? This essay suggests that Romantics and Victorians
struggled to represent the city for two interconnected reasons: a figurative,
'mind-forg'd' aversion and a literally obscured perspective.[4] For not only
was the city in its obstreperous plenitude and ceaseless mobility resistant to
efforts to view it poetically, it was also quite simply hard to see, thanks to
fog, smoke, and darkness.

In the decades after Wordsworth's extensive treatment in Book VII of *The
Prelude* (1805; published 1850), no poet successfully settled on contemporary London as the central topic of a major work. Not till the time of William

Ernest Henley's *London Voluntaries* (1892) do poets seem to recover from the urban blindness initiated by the 'damn your eyes!' that greets Byron's Don Juan when he enters the city *circa* 1800.[5] Ever more fully imaged in the novel, the poetic city becomes an elusive, insubstantial landscape of contamination (Clough), aggression and revulsion (E. B. Browning), or nightmare (Thomson). London is reduced to a closed door and a drizzly street in Tennyson's *In Memoriam*, and to a serpentine string of street-lamps in Rossetti's 'Jenny'.

Over the course of the century London's population expanded sevenfold, from one to seven million. As open ground was swallowed up by the spread of suburbs, the sheer physical size of city, covering hundreds of square miles, daunted would-be explorers. Eighteenth-century admirers of the city took stock of it from distant hilltop prospects, but already in the 1830s there were complaints that not even from the dome of St Paul's could one bring the whole into view. By Victorian times the standard trope of the modern city had become its unrepresentability. In sheer multitudinousness of lives, objects, events, and criss-crossings of people, capital, and ideas, it beggared description. Friedrich Engels opened the 'Great Towns' chapter of his *Condition of the Working Class in England* (1845) by noting, 'London is unique, because it is a city in which one can roam for hours without leaving the built-up area and without seeing the slightest sign of the approach of open country.'[6] It was not easier to conquer on paper: Thomas Carlyle wrote to his brother in 1824, 'Of this enormous Babel of a place I can give you no account in writing.'[7]

Hence poetic London seems to exist in figures and phrases: the 'midnight streets' of Blake, the 'mighty heart' of Wordsworth, the 'central roar' of Tennyson, the 'iron lilies of the Strand' of Le Gallienne.[8] Although poets often paused to stare at the city, whether from a window or in the midst of a crowded street, motion was what they saw; it was the city's key feature and its essential literary identity. Amid its excess of signs, London functioned as a sign of excess, never securely captured, ever evading closure. While novelists, prompted by the temporality of their genre, might revel in this dynamic, ever-changing environment, poets were mostly haunted by a fear of flux and the uncertainty about how to face it. For most of the century they preferred static topics and fixed points of view, projecting the city as an organic entity that could be momentarily stilled to ponder or dissect.

But as Byron remarked in *Don Juan*, London altered so fast that 'even / Change grows too changeable' (XI.82). Huge construction projects, unlinked by any overall plan, tore up and remade the landscape: Regent Street and Regent's Park, along with the installation of 40,000 gas-lamps, in the 1820s; the railway lines and stations in the 1830s and 1840s; the new Houses of

Parliament in the 1840s and 1850s, the Underground in the 1860s; the metropolitan drainage system and the Thames Embankment in the 1860s and 1870s; the Underground expansion and changeover to electric lighting in the 1880s and 1890s. Hence, one source of the city's elusive visual identity was its physical impermanence. The surging crowds in the streets – some half a million a day entering and leaving the city on omnibuses alone – echoed the ebbs and flows of the Thames. The economic life of the city – on ''Change', as the stock market was called – ebbed and flowed as well.

Moreover, visibility itself seemed in flux, owing to the instability of the light and atmosphere. In Victorian poetry, St Paul's dome, the reassuring constant by which Londoners judged the solidity of their city from the time of Wren to the Blitz, looms, hovers, and dissolves in the mist – it's a 'bubble' in Oscar Wilde's 'Impression du matin', an airborne floating shadow in John Davidson's 'London'.[9] Fog, night, and wavering gas-light produced a blurred city that would not come into focus or sit for its portrait. And after dark, the wilfully unseen prostitute roamed the streets, an unsettling form of sexual mobility that further undermined proper 'appearances'.

After considering assaults on vision in Blake, Wordsworth, and Byron, I will focus on poetic images of the city in mist and darkness as metaphors for the difficulty of envisioning nineteenth-century London. Moving from an anxious exploration of London's physical and metaphoric obscurity in the early- and mid-Victorian period, poets arrive at a celebratory acceptance of fog and night in the wake of Whistler's *Nocturnes* late in the century (see Figure 7.1). Along the way, gas-lamps emerge as a salient new feature of the poetic landscape, gradually changing from a symbol of iniquity to one of unconcealed delight. Scene of the first gas-lighting in 1807, the artificially lit city of London opened a new chapter in the history of representation, a chapter filled with exciting opportunities but also fraught, for poets, with unusual challenges.

Blind spots

Joanna Baillie's 'London' (1790) forecasts how the coming century will regard the city poetically. She begins by praising the sight of the city's skyline in the clear air – but finds the city more compellingly 'sublime' when it is less visibly arrayed in a 'grand panoply of smoke'. It becomes 'a curtain'd gloom' while the 'lurid dimness' of the streets appears through 'tinted vapours' and then at night a 'luminous canopy athwart the dark'. Finishing with the 'roar of many wheels' as the spectator approaches the town, the poem moves from a detailed eighteenth-century topographical view to Victorian obscurity, from clarity to smoke to glare, noise, and commotion. What holds the vision

Figure 7.1 James McNeill Whistler, *Nocturne in Blue and Gold – Old Battersea Bridge* (1872–5).

together is the poet's sense that each element is linked to the natural world: St Paul's is an alp emerging through the mist; the 'drizzly rain' becomes 'cataracts of tawny sheen', the street-lamps are stars, and the wagon wheels sound like the ocean.[10] In the eighteenth century poets and painters had developed the aesthetic category of the sublime, revelling in the description of natural forces that dwarfed human endeavour even as they provided an exhilarating revelation of divine and imaginative power. Baillie reveals the beginning of the process by which an *artificial* sublime emerged to confront the growing immensity of human constructs, infernally tinged with the fire and smoke of blast furnaces and gas-lamps. As Anne Janowitz remarks in a fine article on how shifting notions of the sublime helped sustain poetry of the city, 'the transmutation of natural light into artificial – the motif of stars and street lamp – carries across the whole of nineteenth-century London poetry from oil to gas to electric'.[11]

William Blake had no trouble seeing London as the intersection of natural and human powers, but his scale was as much spiritual as physical. 'I behold Babylon in the opening Streets of London. I behold / Jerusalem in ruins wandering about from house to house'.[12] While Baillie used a mixture of the natural and artificial sublime to portray the city, Blake reminds us that the biblically inflected ways of seeing cities, as versions of dark, fallen Babylons or shining, heavenly New Jerusalems, also continued to underpin how London was represented. In Plate 84 of *Jerusalem* he describes a scene he had already drawn in *Songs of Experience*: 'I see London, blind & age-bent, begging thro' the streets / Of Babylon, led by a child; his tears run down his beard.'[13] The illustration accompanies the poem 'London' (1794), which – because of the enormous compression with which it binds together individuals and institutions, nature and society, sexuality and death, writing and reading, hearing and seeing – has become the single most studied text of the modern city. As a microcosmic social tapestry of power and disease, 'London' looks ahead to Dickens's *Bleak House* (1853); as a peripatetic investigation of the hallucinatory unreal city of sexually tainted sounds and signs, it anticipates Eliot's *The Waste Land* (1922). The wandering poet launches the reader into a street-level investigation of urban misery, in a city where even the river is constrained by political force and the anguished, ban-ridden citizens are victims of their own 'mind forg'd' self-imprisonment. While Blake's imagery, as he indicts church, government, and family, seems strikingly visual, Blake shifts from seeing in the first stanza to hearing in the last three, stressing this with an acrostic HEAR in the first letters of Stanza 3.

London prostitutes stereotypically lurk 'near where the charter'd Thames does flow', but Blake's poem may have become the classic urban night text precisely because, while heard, the prostitute in 'London' remains threateningly unseen:

> But most thro' midnight streets I hear
> How the youthful Harlot's curse
> Blasts the newborn Infant's tear
> And blights with plagues the Marriage hearse.[14]

What we can't see can harm us. The young Harlot curses in multiple senses not only the institution of marriage but the child she still is, the child she bears, the child she will blind prenatally through venereal disease. No city can survive where sight, birth, marriage, labour, nature, and even the human voice are blighted. Blake spins the web of consequences so forcefully that his poem is like a winding sheet for a society.

A decade later, in Book VII of *The Prelude*, William Wordsworth wrote an extraordinary passage that has come to seem a counterpart to Blake's unseen but luminous experience. It describes the poet's sensations as he is carried along in the crowded streets. Basing the poem on his long stays in 1791 and 1795, Wordsworth wrote in 1804 as an enthralled former resident of London, not a tourist. His fascinated, often horrified account of London's heterogeneity and phantasmagoric spectacle sets him with Blake as co-founder of modern urban literature. For Wordsworth, what makes London unique is the disorienting, hallucinatory feeling that 'The face of every one / That passes by me is a mystery!'.[15] This sensation compels the poet into a trance-like journey in the crowd until

>   lost
> Amid the moving pageant, 'twas my chance
> Abruptly to be smitten with the view
> Of a blind Beggar, who, with upright face,
> Stood, propped against a wall, upon his chest
> Wearing a written paper, to explain
> The story of the man, and who he was.
> My mind did at this spectacle turn round
> As with the might of waters, and it seemed
> To me that in this label was a type,
> Or emblem, of the utmost that we know,
> Both of ourselves, and of the universe;
> And, on the shape of the unmoving man,
> His fixèd face and sightless eyes, I looked,
> As if admonished from another world.   (VII.609–23)

The blind beggar functions as the harlot does for Blake, a social reality become a symbolic, heaven-sent warning. Stopped in his tracks by a visual short-circuit, the poet is 'admonished from another world' for his inability to read past his own blindness, into the lives of others and into the story of the beggar. He is also chastised for his presumption in writing *The Prelude* itself, attempting to create his own 'written paper, to explain / The story of the man, and who he was'. The blind beggar is not only Wordsworth's figure for himself, but for Milton too, the old blind storyteller 'of the utmost that we know'. The passage functions as a brief résumé of the Bible, from fall into knowledge to deluge 'with the might of waters' to revelation, and the scandal that motivates this urban illegibility is partly sexual, paradise lost through harlotry.

The feeble salutation of 'some unhappy woman' heard in Wordsworth's next stanza leads straight to the infernal din of Bartholomew Fair, where the poet seeks out 'some showman's platform' to carry poet and reader safely 'Above the press and danger of the crowd'. But there is no perspective that can render the scene poetic: 'What a hell / For eyes and ears! What anarchy and din / Barbarian and infernal' (658–60). It is a sight 'that lays / If any spectacle on earth can do, / The whole creative powers of man asleep!' (652–4). What's missing is some form of deeper organisation, some Blakean or providential scheme that can speak what the babel-din cannot say for itself. Wordsworth decides that finally London is no more than this, a 'blank confusion' where the inhabitants are slaves to 'the same perpetual flow / Of trivial objects, melted and reduced / To one identity, by differences / That have no law, no meaning, and no end' (701–4). Blinded and weakened by the tumult that exceeds his power to detail a meaning for it, Wordsworth concludes the book by returning to the 'Spirit of Nature' that he claims has shone through 'self-destroying, transitory things' (735, 739). 'Composure and ennobling Harmony' are the final words of Book VII. Many readers believe that this is wishful thinking, and are glad of it. For Wordsworth's brave grappling with intransigent London – 'Thus have I looked, nor ceased to look, oppressed / By thoughts of what and whither, when and how' (598–9) – caused him to produce the greatest urban poetry of the century.

But the lessons of Wordsworth's *Prelude* were not available to readers until 1850, and by then his reputation as a poet of nature was so reverently established that Book VII seemed itself invisible to reviewers. Fortunately for London-lovers, 'Composed upon Westminster Bridge, Sept. 3, 1802' stepped in to fill its place. The sonnet is everything Book VII of *The Prelude* could not be: unified, tranquil, oriented toward heaven, sublimely and serenely visible. Perhaps for these reasons it became *the* poem of London for the nineteenth century. Balanced between conviction of London's greatness ('Earth hath not anything to show more fair') and joy at its stasis, it is the perfect poem for urbanites anxious to bask in the city's glory without being crushed by its juggernaut:

> This City now doth like a garment wear
> The beauty of the morning; silent, bare,
> Ships, towers, domes, theatres, and temples lie
> Open unto the fields, and to the sky;
> All bright and glittering in the smokeless air.[16]

For once the light is animated but the smoke is not. The poem's power stems from the clear sight it affords of the city's unexpected repose:

> Ne'er saw I, never felt, a calm so deep!
> The river glideth at his own sweet will:
> Dear God! The very houses seem asleep;
> And all that mighty heart is lying still! (11–14)

Taking us back to Spenser, the uncharter'd river enjoys its own sweet, prelapsarian will; the virginal purity of the scene suggests a vision of the New Jerusalem, 'adorned like a bride', rather than the familiar Harlot of modern Babylon. As a narrative stopped at the moment before the visionary city and poet awaken from their dream, the poem served as a nostalgic touchstone for Victorians. Like the sleeping houses, the stilled heart assuages the urbanite weary of motion, just as the 'smokeless air' grants respite from gloom and fog. Whenever the poem is read, the city becomes 'composed' once more, and the heart is 'lying still' – that is, still lying about the dynamic unsleeping city obscured by the poem. Lying still, the organic city takes on the body of an ideal woman, inert and pliable, a Sleeping Beauty ready to be kissed. If *The Prelude* in its honest fascination and repulsion shows how richly complex urban poetry would eventually become, 'Westminster Bridge' privileges a moment apart from the struggle, before the dream can be shattered or fulfilled, the last moment of sunlight for a long time.

Mighty Babylon

According to historian Donald Olsen, 'The ways in which people regarded London changed completely and permanently during the decade following 1825. London turned from being an object of pride to an object of shame, from a symbol of wealth to a symbol of poverty, from a vision of health to a vision of disease, from one of light to one of darkness.'[17] Olsen suggests that the 1832 and 1833 cholera epidemics that killed 6,800 were 'the shock that contributed most to the changed perception of London' from clean to 'dirty and deadly'. In fact, London had lower mortality rates and higher sanitary standards than leading Continental cities. Olsen believes that Dickens, who started writing at this time, reinforced this negative image 'by imposing his brilliant but perverse vision of London on the consciousness both of his contemporaries and of posterity'.[18]

Many Victorian poets, under the spell of Dickens's love of the lurid, feared there was nothing salutary left to versify in London. But the negative reaction is visible even earlier in the poetry of Keats, Shelley, and Byron. Keats's sonnet on escaping from London, 'To one who has been long in city pent' (1816), builds on Milton's description of Satan sallying forth from hell to see Eve in Eden: 'As one who long in populous city pent / Where houses thick and sewers annoy the air'.[19] While Keats only implies London's infernal nature and blackening skies as he seeks 'the fair / And open face of heaven' outside it, Shelley openly proclaims in 'Peter Bell the Third' (1819) that

> Hell is a city much like London–
> A populous and a smoky city;
> There are all sorts of people undone,
> And there is little or no fun done;
> Small justice shown and still less pity.[20]

In Cantos x and xi of *Don Juan* (1823) Byron describes Juan's entry into Regency London. Coming from the continent, he is at first awed by the sight: 'A mighty mass of brick and smoke and shipping, / Dirty and dusky, but as wide as eye / Could reach'. Size, obscurity, activity: Byron works through the conventions, then pronounces the smoke to be, not sublime, but a dingy dunce cap: 'A huge, dun cupola, like a foolscap crown / On a fool's head – and there is London town!' (x.82). As Juan contemplates the sunset city spread before him, 'he was interrupted by a knife, / With "Damn your eyes! Your money or your life!"' (xi.10). Unfazed, the ambushed hero draws a pistol and kills his man, then descends into the city, 'mighty Babylon', through endless suburbs and congested streets, drawing up in the lamplit heart of town near 'St. James's hells' (xi.23, 29). Byron comically undercuts the discourse of the urban sublime, even as he makes its infernal resonances clear.

Thus the worldly city of London carried well into the nineteenth century its biblical underpinnings of Babel, Babylon, and (occasionally) the New Jerusalem. Along with the biblical framework came the pervasive association of godliness with the country and evil with the city. The ideological fallout of Cowper's famous phrase, 'God made the country, and man made the town',[21] was felt to the very end of Victoria's reign. Of major long poems of the Victorian era only Barrett Browning's *Aurora Leigh* (1856) gives sustained attention to London. None of Tennyson or Browning's classic lyrics or dramatic monologues deals for more than a moment or two with contemporary London; ditto for Christina Rossetti, Morris, Swinburne, Hopkins, Emily Brontë, Meredith, Patmore, and others.

Why? As Charles Kingsley's protagonist, a 'poet of the people', shuddered in *Alton Locke* (1850): 'All this is so – so unpoetical.'[22] Try as they might, few early- or mid-Victorians found London attractive material for their art. 'Reflect', wrote Matthew Arnold in 1849, 'how deeply *unpoetical* the age and all one's surroundings are. Not unprofound, not ungrand, not unmoving; – but *unpoetical*.'[23] Leigh Hunt concurred: 'London ... is not a poetical place to look at.'[24] Or, as Arnold's disillusioned friend Arthur Hugh Clough, one poet who did consistently struggle with the issue, concluded in 'To the Great Metropolis' (1841): mercantile London is 'a huge Bazaar, / A railway terminus, a gay Hotel /Anything but a mighty Nation's heart'.[25]

Overwhelmed by London's commotion and obscurity, Victorian poets added fear of contamination to the list of elements impinging on their urban eyesight. By the 1850s the population of London was crossing the three million mark, and the gradual development of separate areas for living and working, along with expansion of the suburbs and public transport, had created a city increasingly segregated by class. Distance and unfamiliarity augmented fear of the poor, and the germ theory of the day, that disease was spread by airborne miasma, increased reluctance to breathe or touch anything 'foul', whether atmospheric or human. For Clough, to walk in London is to wonder how 'to escape / Contamination in the jostling street / And foul contagion from diseased base souls'.[26] The crowd ultimately represents violation: as Clough says in *Dipsychus* (1850), he dreads 'To enter the base crowd and bare one's flanks / To all ill voices of a blustering world'.[27]

Arnold summed up the general feeling: 'these are damned times ... everything is against one; the absence of great natures, the unavoidable contact with millions of small ones ...'.[28] 'Contact' is a key word. One could discuss all of London poetry in terms of distance and proximity, from Wordsworth's strategy of sanitising even 'city smoke, by distance ruralized' to Tennyson's presumption in 'Locksley Hall Sixty Years After' (1886) that close quarters breed sin on the 'crowded couch of incest in the warrens of the poor'.[29] Even as the crowd was becoming a central feature of the classic poetry of Paris and New York, written by Baudelaire and Whitman just at this time, for Victorians it spelled dread infection. Tennyson seemed to speak for the public when his misanthropic narrator in *Maud* (1855) declares: 'And I loathe the squares and streets, / And the faces that one meets'.[30]

Hence Arnold's 'Lines Written in Kensington Gardens' (1852) may well be the most typical of Victorian poems about the city, since it devotes itself to escaping London through an impassioned quest for rural repose. 'Screened' by foliage, hidden from 'the world that roars hard by', the poet finds 'peace forever new'. Echoing Wordsworth's 'Ne'er saw I, never felt, a calm so deep!' even to the exclamation point, Arnold finds his solace not in sight of the city, but shielded from it: 'Calm, calm me more! nor let me die

/ Before I have begun to live'.[31] Given these sentiments, it is not surprising that in 1855 Victorians shut down the turbulent Bartholomew Fair that had given Wordsworth so much trouble, or that the utopian William Morris would urge his readers to 'forget the spreading of the hideous town' in order to 'dream of London, small, and white, and clean'.[32]

But the Victorians themselves noticed their aversions. On a number of occasions they called for poetry, not of another world, but as Clough put it directly, 'what *is* here'.[33] F. G. Stephens wrote in 1850 that 'there is the poetry of the things about us; our railways, factories, mines, roaring cities ...'.[34] In his *London Poems* (1866), Robert Buchanan implored, 'Poesy O Poesy, / Stay in London lanes with me!'.[35] One indication of Victorians' self-consciousness appears in their celebration of the category 'city poet'. Charles Kingsley built a whole novel, *Alton Locke*, around the idea. Elizabeth Barrett Browning spent hundreds of lines in *Aurora Leigh* (1856) situating her heroine of that name, the first female writer-protagonist in English literature, as a poet working in London. Attacking Arnold's idea that poetry should deal with the great actions of the past, Barrett Browning asserts the duty of modern writers to deal with 'this live throbbing age' – even while recognising that 'Camelot to minstrels seemed as flat / As Fleet Street to our poets'.[36]

In 1973, critic Robert Stange was the first to try to pinpoint the causes for the Victorian poets' anti-urbanism, deciding that 'a strange mixture of Romantic gestures, aristocratic pastoralism, and middle-class prudery blinded poets to the grandeur and misery of their city' until the 1890s.[37] A decade later William B. Thesing showed in *The London Muse* how much more poetry of the city there was than had been thought, but his conclusions were similar: 'the dearth of truly first-rate poetic works between Blake's *Jerusalem* and Eliot's *The Waste Land* is explained by the traditions, partly inherited, and the conceptions, partly self-imposed, that most Victorian poets held concerning what a poet should be and what he should write about'.[38] More recently Alan Robinson has seen a version of these factors – aesthetic and moral aversion, pastoralism, and the lack of grand vistas – as limiting the painting of the Victorian city as well.[39] I want to suggest a further impediment: obscurity. The moral London – raw, rude, depraved – that one did not wish to see conditioned vision to the point that it seems to have dimmed actual perception of the physical London – dirty, ugly, endless – that loomed fitfully through the fog-bound atmosphere. As Clough wrote in 1850 of the vulgar sights in London streets, 'Shall they be daily, hourly seen / And not affect the eyes that see?'.[40] Not wanting to see the city, Victorians found that fog and night colluded to prevent them from doing so.

A 'sooty spectre'

> ... inanimate London was a sooty spectre, divided in purpose between being
> visible and being invisible, and so being wholly neither.
>
> Charles Dickens, *Our Mutual Friend*[41]

Julian Wolfreys notes that in opening *Sketches By Boz* (1836) with liminal images of morning and evening streets, the astute Dickens apparently overlooked 'the city of the daytime, the city in full view'.[42] For 'the city in full view' had become a scarce commodity since Wordsworth's time; as a concept it had little imaginative life. When Esther Summerson arrives in London at the start of *Bleak House*, she remarks, 'We drove slowly through the dirtiest and darkest streets that ever were seen in the world (I thought), and in such a distracting state of confusion that I wondered how the people kept their senses.'[43] Roden Noel complained that pestilential dimness blanketed the city like an admission of guilt and a conscious deprivation of the sight of heaven: 'But over all a brown Plutonian gloom / Of murk air dismal and defiled, the breath / Of our monstrous town – her visible sin'.[44] Back in 1837, Dr John Hogg had complained in *London as It Is* that his subject could not be seen from St Paul's because of the fog; while Nathaniel Hawthorne, visiting in 1857, commented on how the fog even crept indoors unbidden; and in 1886 *Punch* ran a cartoon showing patrons at an art exhibition groping blindly through fog in the gallery.[45] Arnold's 'Consolation' (1852) begins, 'Mist clogs the sunshine. / Smoky dwarf houses / Hem me round everywhere; / A vague dejection / Weighs down my soul'.[46]

The arch-text of Victorian fog is the first page of Dickens's *Bleak House*: 'Fog everywhere. Fog up the river ... Fog on the Essex Marshes, fog on the Kentish heights ...'.[47] Were it not that in poetry one cares where the lines end, this passage would long ago have been nominated one of the great poems of the era. In fact, Dickens has so thoroughly conditioned our eyes to view *his* London as *the* London, that readers eager to 'see' London in poetry have for over a century and a half had to wrestle with a further layer of obscurity, the all-enmeshing web of imagery he laid down over the city. But Barrett Browning's portrayal of what Aurora Leigh sees from her garret window is almost as memorable. While Dickens links the fog to the impenetrable windings of the Chancery Courts, the poet Aurora uses fog as a murder weapon:

> I saw
> Fog only, the great tawny weltering fog
> Involve the passive city, strangle it
> Alive, and draw it off into the void,

> Spires, bridges, streets, and squares, as if a sponge
> Had wiped out London, – or as noon and night
> Had clapped together and utterly struck out
> The intermediate time, undoing themselves
> In the act. Your city poets see such things
> Not despicable.   (III.178–87)

As in *Sketches* or *Bleak House*, fog collapses noon and night, wiping out the intervening time, assassinating the spires and bridges of the Wordsworthian city like the Thuggee-style garrotters that terrorised London in the 1850s. Then, the poet takes sublime pleasure watching nature drown her man-made adversary:

> sit in London at the day's decline
> And view the city perish in the mist
> Like Pharaoh's armaments in the deep Red Sea,
>
> ......
>
> You feel as conquerors though you did not fight,
> And you and Israel's other singing girls,
> Ay, Miriam with them, sing the song you choose.
>   (III.195–7, 201–3)

Turning the Pharaoh's destruction into feminist poetic liberation, Barrett Browning finds a way for woman poets to rise above the fray. Interestingly, both Wordsworth and Barrett Browning write compellingly of the city as they are carried into town by the momentum of their autobiographical, blank-verse narratives. Wordsworth floundered on his showman's platform at Bartholomew Fair, but Aurora, who is verbally assaulted when she ventures into the back streets, boldly obliterates the London she cannot see, turning it into a song she can sing, making fog a Jericho-razing instrument not only of violence, but 'of vision and of tune' (III.200).

With the fog, the power of darkness grew too. As the gas-lit city became ever more illuminated and lively, its image blackened in poetry. Like the fog, night-time illumination set London apart from the countryside, but paradoxically focused attention on the metaphoric and moral obscurity of the city. When Dickens published his very first account of the night he insisted, 'the streets of London, to be beheld in the very height of their glory, should be seen on a dark, dull, murky winter's night, when there is just enough damp gently stealing down to make the pavement greasy, *without cleansing it of any of its impurities ...*' (my italics).[48] In contrast to poets like Arnold, whose moonlit city appears in 'Plainness and clearness without shadow of stain', or Dante Gabriel Rossetti, who sees a belated prostitute caught out at dawn 'in London's smokeless resurrection light' as a sign of 'love deflowered',[49] Dickens chooses to accept without condemnation the 'impurities' of night, fog, and the city. Similarly revealing the sexually transformative power of the urban night time, Thomas Hood's 'The Bridge of Sighs' (1844) remakes an actual daytime Regent's Canal suicide attempt, in which a middle-aged mother tried to take her children with her, into a riveting nocturnal re-enactment of a beautiful young woman's last moments. The gas-light that illumines her plight signals her connection to women of the street: 'Where the lamps quiver / So far in the river, / ... / She stood, with amazement, / Houseless by night'. Unafraid of 'the black flowing river', she jumps:

> Mad from life's history,
> Glad to death's mystery,
> Swift to be hurl'd –
> Any where, any where
> Out of the world![50]

For James Thomson, author of *The City of Dreadful Night* (1874), life loomed through a dark 'impenetrable veil' for which the urban night was emblematic.[51] While the city of Thomson's poem is not explicitly London – and there are many symbolically weighted geographical features meant to universalise its reach – its allegorical intensity returns most readers to Babylon-on-the-Thames, even to the lack of daylight. An insomniac's nightmare, where 'street-lamps burn amidst the baleful glooms',[52] *The City of Dreadful Night* functions as something of a test poem for critics, by turns deeply psychological, radically political, or daringly modernist, but always profoundly murky. The city never rests, yet there is no meaning to any action:

> The City is of Night, but not of Sleep;
> There sweet sleep is not for the weary brain;
> The pitiless hours like years and ages creep,
> A night seems termless hell.   (lines 113–16)

Exploring the dark city, the poet desperately strives to make sense of the human condition and its terrible isolation. But Thomson's midnight wanderer discovers to his relief that he is not alone in his woe. As if responding to the curses of Blake's harlot, Thomson's poem is ultimately about talk: listening to each other, fellow sharers of the darkness take hope that

> Yes, here and there some weary wanderer
> In that same city of tremendous night,
> Will understand the speech, and feel a stir
> Of fellowship in all-disastrous fight.

(lines 29–32)

Figure 7.2 Gustave Doré, 'Hounsditch', from *London: A Pilgrimage* (1872).

Gustave Doré picked up on this collegiality of despair in his nocturnal illustrations to *London: A Pilgrimage* (1872), drawn as Thomson was writing;
the denizens of Houndsditch, Whitechapel, and Bluegate Fields lean and
lurk together in the solidarity of abject poverty (see Figure 7.2). While the
poem ends by asserting that 'none can pierce the vast black veil uncertain'
of life (line 1107), Thomson makes a case for learning to live with the veil,
and, to paraphrase Wordsworth, 'like a garment wear / The desolation of
the night'.

Fog, gaslight, and glory

Things are because we see them, and what we see, and how we see it, depends
on the Arts that have influenced us ... At present, people see fogs, not because
there are fogs, but because poets and painters have taught them the mysterious
loveliness of such effects.

Oscar Wilde, 'The Decay of Lying'[53]

Whistler is the turning point toward accepting and enjoying the urban night
time. While Wordsworth worried about perception in *The Prelude* ('things
that are, are not', VII.643), Whistler and his disciple Oscar Wilde proclaimed
that seeing the city as beautiful makes it so. Whistler presented his ideas
visually in his series of *Nocturnes*, begun in 1866, and verbally in his con-
troversial 'Ten O'Clock' lecture of 1885, a statement about urban aesthetics important enough to rival Burke's ideas of the sublime. Whistler shifted
emphasis from the observer's moral reaction to a scene toward the artist's
sensitive rendering of it. For Whistler darkness paradoxically illuminates the
allure of the dormant city's body:

when the evening mist clothes the riverside in poetry, as with a veil, and the
poor buildings lose themselves in the dim sky, and the tall chimneys become
campanili, and the warehouses are palaces in the night, and the whole city
hangs in the heavens, and fairy-land is before us – then ... Nature, who, for
once, has sung in tune, sings her exquisite song to the artist alone ...[54]

Night's arrival clothes the city in 'poetry', magically redeeming the look
of Babylonian London with a harmonious drapery of colour and form.
Wordsworth had realised how crucial the atmospheric garments of the city
were, and Whistler appreciatively employs Thomson's impenetrable veil as
a cloak that reveals rather than conceals urban beauty. On Whistler's thinly
painted canvases, surface becomes substance, and the veil itself becomes a
body of artistic knowledge.

Regarded as an avant-garde upstart in the 1870s, by the 1880s Whistler
represented an exemplary break from older Victorian ideas and forms.
Widely circulated, his ideas became the era's most popular lens for seeing
the city. Holbrook Jackson wrote, 'It was Whistler who taught the modern
world how to appreciate the beauty and wizardry of cities', while Arthur
Symons commented, 'English mist is always at work like a subtle painter,
and London is a vast canvas prepared for the mist to work on.'[55] Henry
James praised 'the friendly fog' that helped a writer concentrate: 'during the
lamplit days the white page he tries to blacken becomes, on his table, in the
circle of the lamp, with the screen of the climate folding him in, more vivid
and absorbent ... It is bad for the eyesight, but excellent for the image.'[56]

Poets found this out, as Whistler's *Nocturnes* transformed aesthetic perception. Under the combined spell of the French symbolists and Whistler, poets including Wilde, Alfred Douglas, Arthur Symons, and Richard Le Gallienne made the London nocturne one of the most characteristic expressions of the Aesthetic Movement. For them the city became a work of art, and they saw it through Whistler's eyes.[57] In Oscar Wilde's 'Impression du matin' (1881), this was literally the case: he depicts the coming dawn not as moving from dark to light, but from one Whistler canvas to another: 'The Thames nocturne of blue and gold / Changed to a Harmony in grey.'[58] Signalling the greater social freedom of the era, poets used the night to evoke the sense of escaping the high noon of Victorian inhibitions. Le Gallienne proclaimed in 'A Ballad of London' (1895): 'Ah, London, London, our delight, / Great flower that opens but at night'.[59] Revelling in 'The long embankment with its lights, / The pavement glittering with fallen rain', Symons wrote in 'Nocturne' (1892) that 'We were free, / Free of the day and all its cares.'[60]

The cover of night also helped put Victorian poetry on the road to Imagism and the elliptical styles to follow. Lionel Johnson sensed as much when he complained of Symons, 'a London fog, the blurred, tawny lamplight, the red omnibus, the dreary rain, the depressing mud, the glaring ginshops, the slatternly, shivering women: three dexterous stanzas, telling you that and nothing more'.[61] This was precisely the point. Just as Whistler had, the poets sought to eliminate superfluous narrative and commentary, presenting only the essence of the image. Pound regarded Whistler as a proto-Imagist, and as he launched the Imagist movement in 1912, he wrote that it was 'an endeavor to carry into our American poetry the same sort of life and intensity which he [Whistler] infused into modern painting'.[62]

As poets accepted the actual fog, the figurative fog lifted. In *A London Plane Tree* (1889), Amy Levy was among the first new-wave proponents of the virtues of town over country. She took the epigraph to her book from Austin Dobson's 'On London Stones' (1876): 'Mine is an urban Muse, and bound / By some strange law to paven ground'. The sentiment is illustrated by a picture of the woman poet bending over her desk, the London skyline visible out of her attic window (see Figure 7.3). Like Aurora Leigh, with whom she shared initials, Levy devoted herself to making herself a 'city poet', but without dissolving her subject in fog. In 'A March Day in London', the discouraged writer discovers that the beauty of the gas-lit city brings a peace that the day could not deliver:

> The gas-lamps gleam in a golden line;
> The ruby lights of the hansoms shine,
> Glance, and flicker like fire-flies bright;
> The wind has fallen with the night,

Figure 7.3 Illustration from Amy Levy, *A London Plane Tree* (1889).

> And once again the town seems fair
> Thwart the mist that hangs i' the air.[63]

Wordsworth's matinal adjective 'fair' now applies to the city night. Yet Levy, who committed suicide after correcting final proofs for her book of poems, was not a complete advertisement for the joys of London life. Radical, lesbian, and Jewish, she feminised the 'weary wanderer' of Thomson, with whom she felt she shared an outsider's view: 'Most of us at some time or other of our lives have wandered the City of Dreadful Night; the shadowy forms, the dim streets, the monotonous tones are familiar to us.'[64] But in her poems she identifies the city with love, promise, and beauty, while the countryside holds no lasting attractions. Deborah Parsons has proposed Levy as London's first *flâneuse*, but she seems to have been more comfortable painting the city from her apartment window, or from the top of a bus: 'A wandering minstrel, poor and free, / I am contented with my fate – / An omnibus suffices me.'[65]

Equally modern, Alice Meynell delighted in 'November Blue' (1898) to find that the cerulean colour banished by daytime fog returned at night under an electric glow:

Figure 7.4 William Hyde, 'The Embankment by Night', from Alice Meynell, *London Impressions* (1898).

> when the gold and silver lamps
> Colour the London dew,
> And, misted by the winter damps,
> The shops shine bright anew –
> Blue comes to earth, it walks the street,
> It dyes the wide air through ...[66]

Artifice restores what nature had lost; the pavement becomes a pathway through the sky. Meynell wrote the text for *London Impressions* (1898), where the Thames nocturne made an electric debut in an illustration by William Hyde, *The Embankment by Night* (see Figure 7.4). Widely known for her essays on London life, Meynell addressed 'Westminster Bridge' directly, finding London not inert but full of motion: 'On Westminster Bridge at early morning Wordsworth thought of the heart of London, but a view of London in the long day and night of movement, when the mystery of sleep is away, suggests not the involuntary heart of men, but their wilful feet.'[67]

The poetry of late Victorian London comes together in a grand flourish with William Ernest Henley's *London Voluntaries* (1892), a conscious recapitulation of the century's themes and images. Influenced by Whistler, Whitman, and the French Symbolists, Henley adopts a musical structure to his exuberant 350-line poem. The first, *Grave*, describes a peaceful sunset on a summer Sunday, while the second, *Andante con moto*, depicts a joyous night-time cab ride racing through the lamp-lit city till the day comes up. The central section, *Scherzando*, revels in the glow of a golden afternoon in October where even 'The very blind man pottering on the curb' enjoys 'the universal alms of light'.[68] In *The Prelude* the young Wordsworth had vainly hoped that actual London would match descriptions 'by pilgrim friars / Of golden cities' (VII.86–7). Henley fulfils the longing when the sun gilds his city: ''Tis

El Dorado – El Dorado plain, / The Golden City!'. Light is what paves the streets with gold; it becomes the substance that sustains the vision. In *Largo e mesto*, a wintry east wind reminiscent of *Bleak House* grimly 'sits him down / To the black job of burking London town'; shivering harlots retreat to bed while wind, rain, river, and dark sky reel beneath images of crime, disease, and blight. But in *Allegro maestoso* the poem concludes with the rejuvenating spring breeze, as the park's new leaves 'touch to an ecstasy the act of seeing' and 'the liberal and transfiguring air' makes men and women burst with sexuality, 'a tidal race of lust from shore to shore'. Tennyson's 'long unlovely street' of *In Memoriam* becomes 'this radiant and immortal street'.

While the preponderance of Victorian verse was engaged elsewhere, in the past and in the pastoral, the struggle with the city's visualisation, through aversion, fog, and darkness, gave London a uniquely tortured, tantalising, and finally triumphant poetry in the nineteenth century. Henley's city is paradise regained: an Edenic, 'shameless, elemental mirth' breaks out, revising Wordsworth one more time as 'The enormous heart of London joys to beat / ... / Wanton and wondrous and forever well'.

To conclude: if the approach sketched above sounds plausible – and I hope it does – we can't forget that poetry often baulks at any attempt to write it into a narrative. Regardless of shared reference to sublimity, fog, or Babylonian blindness, each poet's London is different. Each time we read 'London' we have to begin again. In Tennyson's *Idylls of the King*, for example, there is a shadowy, shrouded city called Camelot that just might represent the centre of the British empire, with its hazy hopes and dreams, and its all-too-vivid failures. When the aspiring knight Gareth remarks that the 'city moved so weirdly in the mist' that he doubts 'whether there be any city at all, / Or all a vision', he is told that he is in the presence of an unpredictable artistic construct. He will just have to live with it, if he wants to make something of himself:

> the city is built
> To music, therefore never built at all,
> And therefore built for ever.[69]

Notes

1 William Blake, *Jerusalem*, Plate 91, lines 21–2, in *Blake: Complete Writings*, ed. Geoffrey Keynes (Oxford: Oxford University Press, 1969), p. 738.
2 Charles Dickens, *Bleak House*, Chapter 3, 'A Progress' (Boston: Ticknor and Fields, 1867), p. 17.
3 John Ruskin, *The Works of John Ruskin*, ed. E. T. Cook and Alexander Wedderburn, 39 vols. (London: George Allen, 1903–12), Vol. III, 14.16.28.
4 Blake, 'London,' in *Complete Writings*, p. 216.

5 Byron, *Don Juan*, XI.10, ed. T. G. Steffan, E. Steffan, and W. W. Pratt (Harmondsworth: Penguin, 1973), p. 359.

6 Friedrich Engels, 'The Great Towns', from *The Condition of the Working Class in England in 1844*, in *The Longman Anthology of British Literature*, 4th edn, 6 vols. (New York: Longman, 2010), Vol. IIB, ed. William Sharpe and Heather Henderson, p. 1101.

7 Thomas Carlyle, cited in Julian Wolfreys, *Writing London: The Trace of the Urban Text from Blake to Dickens* (New York: St Martin's Press, 1998), p. 136.

8 Blake, 'London,' in *Complete Writings*, p. 216; William Wordsworth, 'Composed upon Westminster Bridge, Sept. 3, 1802', in *Longman Anthology*, Vol. IIA, ed. Susan Wolfson and Peter Manning, p. 436; Alfred, Lord Tennyson, 'Ode on the Death of the Duke of Wellington,' in *Tennyson's Poetry*, ed. Robert W. Hill, Jr. (New York: Norton, 1971), p. 200; Richard Le Gallienne, 'London', in Sharpe and Henderson, *Longman Anthology*, Vol. IIB, p. 1907.

9 Oscar Wilde, 'Impression du matin', in Sharpe and Henderson, *Longman Anthology*, Vol. IIB, p. 1821; John Davidson, 'London', in *A Victorian Anthology 1837–1895*, ed. E. C. Stedman (Cambridge: Riverside Press, 1895), p. 1038.

10 Joanna Baillie, 'London', in Wolfson and Manning, *Longman Anthology*, Vol. IIA, p. 345.

11 Anne Janowitz, 'The Artifactual Sublime: Making London Poetry', in *Romantic Metropolis: The Urban Scene of British Culture, 1780–1840*, ed. James Chandler and Kevin Gilmartin (Cambridge: Cambridge University Press, 2005), p. 254.

12 Blake, *Jerusalem*, Plate 74, in *Complete Writings*, p. 714.

13 *Ibid.*, p. 729.

14 *Ibid.*, p. 216.

15 William Wordsworth, *The Prelude: A Parallel Text*, ed. J. C. Maxwell (Harmondsworth: Penguin, 1971), VII.596–7, p. 286. The 1805 text is cited unless otherwise indicated.

16 Wordsworth, 'Westminster Bridge', lines 4–8, p. 436.

17 Donald J. Olsen, 'Introduction: Victorian London', in David Owen, *The Government of London, 1855–1889: The Metropolitan Board Of Works, the Vestries, and the City Corporation* (Cambridge, MA: Belknap, 1982), pp. 10–12.

18 Donald J. Olsen, *The City as a Work of Art* (New Haven: Yale University Press, 1986), p. 23.

19 John Milton, *Paradise Lost*, IX.445–6.

20 John Keats, 'To one who has been long in city pent', in Wolfson and Manning, *Longman Anthology*, Vol. IIA, p. 884; Percy Bysshe Shelley, 'Peter Bell the Third', in *Poetical Works*, ed. Thomas Hutchinson (Oxford: Oxford University Press, 1970), lines 147–51, p. 350.

21 William Cowper, *The Task* (1785), Book I, line 749, in *The Poems of William Cowper*, ed. John D. Baird and Charles Ryskamp, 3 vols. (Oxford: Clarendon Press, 1980–95), Vol. II, p. 136.

22 Charles Kingsley, *Alton Locke, Tailor and Poet*, 2 vols. (New York: J. F. Taylor, 1898), Vol. I, p. 251.

23 Matthew Arnold, *The Letters of Matthew Arnold to Arthur Hugh Clough*, ed. H. F. Lowry (Oxford: Oxford University Press, 1932), p. 99.

24 Leigh Hunt, 'London' (1851), in *Table Talk* (London: Smith, Elder, 1882), pp. 213–14.

25 Arthur Hugh Clough, *The Poems of Arthur Hugh Clough*, 2nd edn, ed. F. L. Mulhauser (Oxford: Clarendon Press, 1974), p. 157.

26 Clough, 'The Contradictions of the Expanding Soul', in *ibid.*, p. 307.

27 Clough, *Dipsychus*, VII.94–5, in *ibid.*, p. 258. See William Sharpe, 'Confronting the Unpoetical City: Arnold, Clough, and Baudelaire', *The Arnoldian* 13.1 (Winter 1985/6), 10–22.

28 Arnold, *Letters*, p. 111.

29 Wordsworth, *The Prelude* (1850), I.89; Tennyson, *Poetry*, p. 474.

30 Tennyson, *Maud*, Part II, lines 232–3, in *Poetry*, p. 244.

31 Matthew Arnold, *Poetical Works* (London: Macmillan, 1910), pp. 263–5.

32 William Morris, *The Earthly Paradise* (1868), in *News from Nowhere and Other Writings and Designs*, ed. Asa Briggs (New York: Penguin, 1984), p. 68.

33 Arthur Hugh Clough, 'Recent English Poetry', *North American Review* 77 (1853), 3.

34 F. G. Stephens, 'Modern Giants', *The Germ* 4 (1850), 170.

35 Robert Buchanan, 'Summer Song in the City', *Every Saturday* 6 (11 July 1868), p. 64.

36 Elizabeth Barrett Browning, *Aurora Leigh and Other Poems* (London: The Woman's Press, 1987), V.203, 212–13, p. 201.

37 Robert Stange, 'The Frightened Poets', in *The Victorian City: Images and Realities*, ed. H. J. Dyos and Michael Wolff, 2 vols. (London: Routledge and Kegan Paul, 1973), Vol. II, pp. 475–94.

38 William B. Thesing, *The London Muse: Victorian Poetic Responses to the City* (Athens: University of Georgia Press, 1982), p. xvii.

39 Alan Robinson, *Imagining London, 1770–1900* (London: Palgrave Macmillan, 2004), pp. 124–6.

40 Clough, 'These Vulgar Ways', in *Poems*, p. 303.

41 Charles Dickens, *Our Mutual Friend*, ed. Stephen Gill (Harmondsworth: Penguin, 1971), p. 479.

42 Wolfreys, *Writing London*, p. 166.

43 Dickens, *Bleak House*, Chapter 3, p. 17.

44 Roden Noel, 'A Lay of Civilization, or London' (1885), lines 84–6, in *Collected Poems of Roden Noel* (London: Kegan Paul, 1902), p. 300.

45 See 'Shadows and Fog: Impressionist London', in Nicholas Freeman, *Conceiving the City: London, Literature, and Art, 1870–1914* (Oxford: Oxford University Press, 2007), pp. 89–146.

46 Arnold, *Poetical Works*, p. 150.

47 Dickens, *Bleak House*, p. 1.

48 Charles Dickens, 'The Streets – Night' (January 1836), in *Sketches by Boz* (London: Chapman and Hall, 1850), p. 50.

49 Arnold, 'A Summer Night', in *Poetical Works*, p. 259; Dante Gabriel Rossetti, 'Found' (1881), in *Poetry of the Victorian Period*, 3rd edn, ed. Jerome Hamilton Buckley and George Benjamin Woods (Glenview, IL: Scott, Foresman, 1965), p. 553.

50 Thomas Hood, 'The Bridge of Sighs', in *The Oxford Book of English Verse*, ed. Arthur Quiller-Couch (Oxford: Clarendon Press, 1919), p. 654. See L. J. Nicoletti, 'Downward Mobility: Victorian Women, Suicide, and London's

"Bridge of Sighs"', http://homepages.gold.ac.uk/london_journal/nicoletti.html, for a fine reading of the poem.

51 Cited in Philip Tew, 'James Thomson's London: Beyond the Apocalyptic Vision of the City', in *A Mighty Mass of Brick and Smoke: Victorian and Edwardian Representations of London*, ed. Lawrence Phillips (Amsterdam: Rodopi, 2007), p. 113.

52 James Thomson, 'The City of Dreadful Night', line 85, in Buckley and Woods, *Poetry of the Victorian Period*, p. 586.

53 Oscar Wilde, 'The Decay of Lying', in *The Writings of Oscar Wilde*, 15 vols. (London: Keller, 1907), Vol. x, pp. 47–8.

54 James McNeill Whistler, 'Mr. Whistler's Ten O'Clock', in *The Gentle Art of Making Enemies* (New York: Dover, 1967), p. 144.

55 Holbrook Jackson, *The Eighteen Nineties* (London: Grant Richards, 1913), p 106; Arthur Symons, *London: A Book of Aspects* (London: private printing, 1909), p. 162.

56 Henry James, 'London', in *Essays in London and Elsewhere* (New York: Harper, 1893), pp. 30–1.

57 See Robert L. Peters, 'Whistler and the English Poets of the 1890's', *Modern Language Quarterly* 18 (1957), 251–61; and William Sharpe, *New York Nocturne: The City after Dark in Literature, Painting, and Photography, 1850–1950* (Princeton: Princeton University Press, 2008), pp. 105–131.

58 Wilde, 'Impression du matin', p. 1821.

59 Le Gallienne, 'London', p. 1907.

60 Arthur Symons, 'Nocturne', in *Silhouettes*, 2nd edn (London: Smithers, 1896), p. 63.

61 Lionel Johnson, quoted in William Butler Yeats, *The Autobiography of William Butler Yeats* (New York: Macmillan, 1965), p. 204.

62 Cited in Donald Holden, *Whistler: Landscapes and Seascapes* (New York: Watson-Gupthill, 1969), p. 84.

63 Amy Levy, *A London Plane-Tree and Other Verse* (London: Unwin, 1889), p. 20.

64 Amy Levy, *The Complete Novels and Selected Writings of Amy Levy*, ed. Melvyn New (Gainsville: University of Florida Press, 1993), p. 502.

65 Levy, 'Ballade of an Omnibus,' in *A London Plane-Tree*, p. 21. See Deborah Parsons, *Streetwalking the Metropolis: Women, the City, and Modernity* (Oxford: Oxford University Press, 2000), p. 92.

66 Alice Meynell, 'November Blue', in *Wayfaring* (London: J. Cape, 1929), p. 213.

67 Parejo Vadillo, *Women Poets and Urban Aestheticism: Passengers of Modernity* (London: Palgrave Macmillan, 2005), pp. 78, 98; and Alice Meynell, 'The Roads', in *London Impressions* (London: Constable, 1898), p. 26.

68 William Ernest Henley, *London Voluntaries*, in Buckley and Woods, *Poetry of the Victorian Period*, pp. 801–3.

69 Alfred Lord Tennyson, 'Gareth and Lynette', lines 272–4, in *Tennyson: Poems and Plays* (London: Oxford University Press, 1965), p. 300.

8

ROSEMARIE BODENHEIMER

London in the Victorian novel

Mid-nineteenth-century London acquired its breadth, depth, and density as a fictional space almost entirely through the work of Charles Dickens. Many of his contemporaries set their novels in London, of course, establishing networks of social and economic relationships that depend on the proximities afforded by a capital city. But it was Dickens who discovered how to blend his intimate walking knowledge of the city with fictional techniques that would create London on the page from a variety of perspectives. Although 'Dickens's London' may conjure up immediate images of dense, sooty fog, or labyrinthine courts and alleys, these features take their places in a far wider repertoire of imaginative strategies by which Dickens took hold of a vast, heterogeneous city with an evocative power that continued to influence fictive Londons well into the twentieth century.

The sheer scope of Dickensian London becomes clear when we glance at other mid-Victorian novels set in the metropolis. William Thackeray's *Vanity Fair* (1847), for instance, follows standard novelistic procedure in setting up a small number of households in which much of the London action will unfold. These households are class-coded through street names that 'everyone' in a middle-class readership could be supposed to recognise: the rich merchant Osborne and the wealthy old lady Miss Crawley live at Park Lane, while the bankrupt adventuress Becky Sharp takes a house nearby in Curzon Street, Mayfair. The economically waning Sedleys live in Russell Square – the Duke of Bedford's elegant eighteenth-century housing project, going middle class by the time Thackeray was writing – until their bankruptcy exiles them to suburban Fulham, entirely off the social map. Osborne's counting-house in Thames Street puts his office in the City of London, sensibly near the river and the wharves. A visit to the pleasure-ground at Vauxhall just across the river testifies to urban entertainment in the 1810s. Apart from such iconic names, the physical presence of a historical urban space is given slight notice. Although Thackeray was writing about a period during which George IV and his architect Thomas Nash were creating the parks, squares, and stucco-coated terraces of the elegant West End, the reader sees a stable West End with a City source of wealth: classic, recognisable, barely described.

Anthony Trollope follows similar street-coding conventions, though he is more interested in the London that surrounds and supports middle- and upper-class parliamentary life. In his financial novel *The Way We Live Now* (1875), main characters are given largely Mayfair addresses, and the social conquests of upstart speculator Melmotte are represented by his house in Grosvenor Square. When a character takes a cab from Pall Mall to a lodging house in Islington, the narrator evokes a stereotypical neighbourhood on the nether verge of gentility: 'We all know the garden; – twenty-four feet long, by twelve broad; – and an iron-gated door, with the landlady's name on a brass plate'.[1] The American woman lodging there is not quite respectable, of course, and we know it; the cab ride marks the social distance between Pall Mall and the unnamed streets of Islington.

In *Daniel Deronda* (1876), her single foray into fictional London, George Eliot expands the urban geography as far east as Whitechapel and St Mary Axe in the City – names coded Jewish by the 1870s – where Daniel wanders through barely realised streets in search of Mirah's family. Daniel's adoptive family is typically placed at Park Lane, while the thrifty middle-class Meyrick women inhabit a narrow row-house in Chelsea along the river – economically placed from the outside, though the wide and curious minds of its inhabitants redeem the narrowness of the house. The more arresting part of George Eliot's London takes place on the Thames, where Daniel rows innocently (and curiously serene amid river traffic) toward two meetings with destiny, in which he encounters his future wife Mirah and her proto-Zionist brother Mordecai. This is a Thames running in poetic space, where Daniel may encounter the Jewish part of himself that upper-class life onshore has kept hidden.

Dickens's work thoroughly undid the literary image of a 'known' London centred in the fashionable addresses of the West End. His success in doing so was not universally appreciated. In the October 1858 *National Review* we can hear the cultivated voice of Walter Bagehot as he politely condemns Dickens's city writing to the sphere of journalism:

> Mr. Dickens's genius is especially suited to the delineation of city life. London is like a newspaper. Everything is there, and everything is disconnected … His memory is full of instances, of old buildings and curious people, and he does not care to piece them together. On the contrary, each scene, to his mind, is a separate scene, – each street a separate street … He describes London like a special correspondent for posterity.[2]

The posterity in question has reason to thank Dickens more wholeheart-edly than Bagehot could. But his challenge to Dickens's artistic unity has persisted, in a critical heritage divided between those who celebrate the var-iety, accuracy, and imaginative play in Dickens's streetwise observations, and those who argue for more totalising views of the city by focusing on passages that seem to offer visionary panoramas of death, despair, disorien-tation, or apocalypse.[3] Such differences in emphasis are tied together by a fundamental question that comes into play whenever representations of the city are discussed: in what sense, if at all, can a metropolis like London – the first and the largest of the world cities in the nineteenth century – be known, understood, or viewed as a whole?[4]

In the case of Victorian London, it was not just that its population grew from just under a million in 1800 to 7 million by 1911, or that its geographi-cal limits expanded enormously during the same period. London's develop-ment into a modern urban space was singularly chaotic: building and civic improvement were haphazard, piecemeal, and controlled by no overarching administrative authority until late in the century.[5] Neighbourhoods, roads, bridges, railroads, and Thames docks were perpetually in process, with progress in one influencing the development of the others. Seeing London whole was impossible, despite the popularity of balloon rides that promised a panoramic view, and every part of the city was subject to physical trans-formation. Dickens was the only mid-Victorian novelist who took on the challenge of representing at least fragments of this historical process, at the same time as he connected the subjectivity of his characters with their daily negotiations of urban life.

In this chapter I consider Dickens and his late-nineteenth-century succes-sors as they map a concrete London of particular streets, walking routes, houses, and neighbourhoods. This, I will suggest, was the special contri-bution of Victorian realism to a fictional London that has had remarkable staying power. The history of criticism on this subject has had a tendency to turn melodramatic, whether the focus lands on the city as a figure of the unknowable, or on a gendered London centred on the prostitute and the detached (usually male) urban observer known as the *flâneur*. Such figures emphasise the ways that a city provides ample opportunity for the object-ification or appropriation of others in the gazes of passers-by; they stand in for the alienating and commodifying tendencies associated with modernity.[6] Yet Victorian novelists were equally concerned to make London familiar, representing its streets as identifiable, historically inflected, and well-used by their characters. My purpose is to suggest a range of ways that urban realism took shape in the novel, as well as some conflicts within particular writers' visions of the metropolis.

Dickens's London

To begin with, Dickens sewed different parts of London together simply by describing the walking routes his characters take. The naming of particular streets, bridges, and turnings creates London in space and suggests the time it takes to walk from one part of the city to another; streets become routes through the city rather than coded addresses. Criminally inclined characters know how to negotiate back streets, courts, and alleys so they remain hidden; thus Fagin in *Oliver Twist* walks between his two dens, at Field Lane and Whitechapel, on a route that conceals him from public view. Characters who commute daily from home to work, or who set forth on business with others, are seen to cover long distances as a matter of course. Kate Nickleby has to walk from Lower Thames Street east of London Bridge (a place to which Dickens's imagination frequently returns) to Mantalini's West End dressmaking shop in Cavendish Square. Wemmick's southward commute from the Criminal Courts near St Paul's through Southwark to Walworth is well known by all readers of *Great Expectations*, but the commuting life is shared by previous Dickens characters as well. In *Our Mutual Friend* Bradley Headstone and his pupil Charley Hexam walk the long distance from their school, deep in southeast London, to the Surrey side of Westminster Bridge. Crossing it, they turn west along the river to Smith Square, Millbank, in order to catch a glimpse of Lizzie Hexam at her lodging. These instances can only suggest how Dickens mapped the expanding city, and created the urban experience of people moving between home and work, home and encounters with others. His characters are examples of what Michel de Certeau calls the 'ordinary practitioners of the city', who 'live "down below", below the threshold at which visibility begins. They walk – an elementary form of the experience of the city; they are walkers.' The city comes into being (as it does in the everyday life of all urban dwellers) as an articulation of individual and intersecting paths through an unimaginable whole.[7]

Such purposeful and necessary walking does not come under the rubric of the *flâneur*, nor is it confined to male characters. As Lynda Nead has argued, the notion that the city's visual space was controlled by the voyeuristic male gaze, and that respectable women did not walk alone in the city, defies both common sense and journalistic evidence from the period. Of course it was necessary for a middle-class woman walker to observe discretion in dress and control over her own gaze to avoid being taken as a target for flirtation.[8] Dickens, hardly a radical in his treatment of proper feminine conduct, shows a number of female characters walking alone: Kate Nickleby walks across town to work; Ruth Pinch of *Martin Chuzzlewit* walks daily from her Islington lodgings to pick up her brother Tom from work at the Temple;

Bella Wilfer of *Our Mutual Friend* rushes alone from the West End to her father in the City after she has become disillusioned with Mr Boffin, and her father is only surprised that she has given up the show of wealth associated with arrival in a carriage. Esther Summerson, narrating her portion of *Bleak House*, is a keen-eyed observer of other people in the streets during her first London walk. Highly attuned to the possible dangers faced by walking women, Dickens sometimes shadows his characters with sexual threats: Kate Nickleby has to resist her wicked uncle's attempts to make her into a courtesan for boorish aristocrats, while Little Dorrit and her friend Maggie, locked out of their lodgings overnight and passing the time on London Bridge, are taken – by a shocked prostitute – for a mother selling her daughter on the street. The borderline between women walking in the city and streetwalking may sometimes blur, but it is not collapsed.

Streets and public buildings also provide places of encounter between characters, whether these are accidental or not. Quite often a character will deliberately intercept the known path of another, to create a scene (welcome or unwelcome) that may take place on the street or in a secluded square. Such techniques should not be dismissed as Dickens's manipulation of coincidence; they help create the city as a public space in which the network of intersecting streets provides an intermittent visibility that is open to exploitation by characters as well as authors. Numerous episodes in which detectives, spies, or other interested parties conceal themselves while following others through the streets attest to Dickens's special interest in London streets as spaces of hiding, secret knowledge, and unwitting self-revelation. His imagination of the urban gaze is as much about odd privacies enacted in public space as about gender or class difference.

In Raymond Williams's well-known formulation, Dickens's vision of urban modernity lies 'in the form of his novels … It does not matter which way we put it: the experience of the city is the fictional method; or the fictional method is the experience of the city.' Williams's way of imagining this comes in the familiar synecdoche of the city as crowd: in his view Dickens presents characters as isolated members of the crowd rushing past one another, seen fleetingly in a way 'that belongs to the street'. As the novels proceed, underlying relationships and commitments are 'forced into consciousness', providing a grid of connection beneath 'the sheer rush and noise and miscellaneity of this new and complex social order'.[9] The description endures as a powerfully evocative image of how Dickens's plotting gradually draws secret relationships into the light. It depends on a view of the overwhelming crowds of strangers frequently named by early-nineteenth-century newcomers to London, perhaps most famously as 'the Babel din / The endless stream of men and moving things' registered in Wordsworth's

1805 *Prelude*.[10] Early in his career, Dickens occasionally evokes such conventions as his characters enter London and perceive the city-as-crowd, or the city as a set of juxtaposed contrasts between rich and poor. In ordinary practice, however, his rendering of the crowd in the street, often expressed in the Wordsworthian terms *stream* and *roar*, more simply suggests the way Londoners walk (then as now): fast, oblivious of others, all through the day and night, making it potentially dangerous to be physically impaired, lost, or otherwise slowed down. When characters turn into secluded or sheltered spots – the Adelphi arches, a deserted City cemetery, a forgotten little square – the sudden quiet and peace is made palpable. Thus Dickens registers a new rhythm in the alternating sensations of urban street life: the fast-paced roar, and the momentary respite in quiet, deserted spots.

The conventional depiction of the street crowd as a fearsome or unruly mob also shows up in the early novels *Oliver Twist* and *Barnaby Rudge*, where Dickens displays his skill in evoking its excitement, as well as its destructive power. But crowdedness, rather than crowd psychology, was a more abiding social concern. His attention to the criminal and disease-breeding slums, or rookeries, nestled close to respectable areas of London, with their falling-down houses, sewage in the streets, and criminal hideouts, was historically well informed. In 1800 a good deal of the London housing stock was just over 100 years old, rebuilt after the Great Fire of 1666. Remaining pockets of Old London persisted as notorious slums threaded through the city. Slum clearance projects generally meant building new roads through decaying districts, leaving displaced residents nowhere to go. As a result, the small garden spaces behind old rotting houses in nearby slums were filled up during the 1830s and 1840s with new sub-par housing, crammed into tiny courts and alleys accessible through gateways from the outer street.[11] When Dickens writes about characters who know how to negotiate the 'mazes' or 'labyrinths' of slum areas, he points not only to unimproved seventeenth-century streets, but also to these newly packed and neglected pockets of poverty, unknown and barely visible to the eyes of middle-class passers-by.

The thieves' dens in *Oliver Twist* are accurately located in Saffron Hill, Whitechapel, Bethnal Green, and Jacob's Island, a falling-down slum surrounded by fetid ditches south of the river in Bermondsey. What Dickens wrote in 1839 spurred on the clearance of Jacob's Island, but the problem of self-enclosed rookeries persisted well into the late nineteenth century, and Dickens returned to it in the 1850s. Tom All Alone's, where the street urchin Jo finds minimal shelter in *Bleak House*, is not precisely located; Jo has to walk some distance to the Chancery Lane area where he sweeps the streets for pennies, and Mr Snagsby follows Detective Bucket on an undefined route as they approach Tom All Alone's in quest of Jo. Dickens famously writes a hellscape of filth, disease, drunkenness, and death when they enter the area, but he is also quite explicit about its status as illegally held and legally ignored property: 'It is a black, dilapidated street, avoided by all decent people, where the crazy houses were seized upon, when their decay was far advanced, by some bold vagrants, who, after establishing their own possession, took to letting them out as lodgings.' Houses have recently fallen, the narrator notes, and 'have made a paragraph in the newspapers, and have filled a bed or two in the nearest hospital. The gaps remain, and there are not unpopular lodgings among the rubbish.'[12]

Dickens's attention to the state of housing stock in London was not limited to rookeries and the failures of slum clearance. He took delight in looking down the back streets and around the corners of fashionable neighbourhoods, discerning there the prices people paid in comfort and space for the sake of maintaining West End addresses. The pathetically aspiring Miss Tox of *Dombey and Son* 'inhabited a dark little house that had been squeezed, at some remote period of English History, into a fashionable neighbourhood at the west end of the town, where it stood in the shade like a poor relation of the great street around the corner'.[13] This 'dingy tenement', like so much else in Dickens's city writing, suggests the historical patchwork of modern and old building in every part of town, as well as the old custom of building fancy streets backed by mews and courts intended for middle- and lower-class suppliers of services to the rich. Tite Barnacle, the powerful overlord of the Circumlocution Office in *Little Dorrit*, is similarly placed in a cramped and smelly little house on Mews Street, Grosvenor Square, a dead-end abode of coachmen and chimney-sweeps except for the houses located nearest the entrance to the Square; here Barnacle pays three times more than he would for a decent house with a different address.[14] Dickens is always keen to destabilise the class cachet of West End 'Stuccovia', where grand houses are generally on the dark side of the street, and 'to let' signs on neglected homes signal the constant mobility of urban dwellers and the frequent decay of neighbourhoods overbuilt for the class of tenants desired.[15]

He is also drawn to chaotic, unfinished borderland areas of every description. The ambiguous areas where expanding London trails off into suburb, leaving tracts of wasteland behind, stimulated some of his most imaginative writing. North London comes into play in *Dombey and Son*, where the poor side of the Carker family lives in a place 'neither of the town or country. The former, like a giant in his travelling boots, has made a stride and passed it, and has set his brick-and-mortar heel a long way in advance, but the intermediate space between the giant's feet, as yet, is only blighted country' (Chapter 33). It recurs in the Holloway neighbourhood of the Wilfers in *Our Mutual Friend*, 'a suburban Sahara, where tiles and bricks were burnt, bones were boiled, carpets were beat, rubbish was shot, dogs were fought, and dust was heaped by contractors'.[16] When he comes to Bradley Headstone's school in South London, 'where Kent and Surrey meet', Dickens emphasises the unfinished or abandoned building projects that were common sights in Victorian London: 'They were in a neighbourhood which looked like a toy neighbourhood taken in blocks out of a box by a child of particularly incoherent mind, and set up anyhow; here, one side of a new street; there, a large solitary public house facing nowhere; here, another unfinished street already in ruins.' The random mix of features includes kitchen gardens, a railway viaduct, and a canal; in the narrator's view it all suggests that 'the child had given the table a kick, and gone to sleep' (II.1). Are such passages harbingers of modernist despair? The playful images of the incoherent child and the urban giant suggest rather a particular blend of fantasy and realism, touching both on the lack of central urban planning in London and on the truth about the wastelands that great cities spawn on their outskirts.

Dickens's attitudes toward the modernisation of the city are complicated. His novels pull the reader simultaneously toward the energetic excitement of change and toward a nostalgic sense of an older London associated primarily with places in the City. His most direct fictional encounter with technological change appears in the passages about railway building in *Dombey and Son*, published during the railway boom of the 1840s. The railway works in Staggs's Gardens, Camden Town, are likened to natural disaster, 'the first shock of a great earthquake' that creates unnatural hills and ponds, shaking the foundations of nearby buildings. 'Everywhere were bridges that led nowhere; thoroughfares that were wholly impassable, Babel towers of chimneys, wanting half their height … and piles of scaffolding, and wildernesses of bricks, and giant forms of cranes, and tripods straddling above nothing.' And then, in an amusing shift of tone, the wonderfully observed performance of the chaos that precedes construction is downshifted to the official language of Victorian improvement: 'In short, the yet unfinished and unopened Railroad was in progress; and, from the very core of all this dire disorder, trailed smoothly away, upon its mighty course of civilization and improvement' (Chapter 6).

Dickens is just as interested in making fun of the human tendency to resist dramatic change as he is in suggesting the existential shock of the railway. Only a few 'bold speculators' have made efforts to attract railway workers by changing the names of their pubs; otherwise 'Staggs's Gardens was regarded by its population as a sacred grove not to be withered by railroads' (Chapter 6). Once the railway is complete, however, the old, frowzy, suburban borderland vanishes completely, even from the memories of its inhabitants. Improvement is palpable; the neighbourhood is well rebuilt, prosperous, and vitalised: 'Bridges that had led to nothing, led to villas, gardens, churches, healthy public walks', while the pulse of the railway's harnessed energy throbs in its citizens. It is odd, then, to hear Dickens finish the passage with a ritual bow toward his own resistance to unstoppable change: 'But Staggs's Gardens had been cut up root and branch. Oh woe the day when "not a rood of English ground" – laid out in Staggs's Gardens – is secure!' (Chapter 15). The bow toward popular nostalgia may well be a way of hedging his bets with his audience, or a sign of his own natural ambivalence. Dickens did not return to the railway, except as a normal form of conveyance, after *Dombey and Son*. As the major London termini gradually came into being, rail travel, along with its junctions, timetables, tearooms, and railway fiction, became ordinary facts of urban life that provided him with some amusing material for journalistic sketches.

The description of Todgers's boarding house in *Martin Chuzzlewit*, another of the most frequently discussed passages of city writing in Dickens, also displays a mixed set of tones. Critics have focused intently on Modernist or metaphysical readings of the 'labyrinthine' approach to the house and the visual nausea that comes over those who attempt to look at the London panorama from Todgers's rooftop, only to find themselves irrationally fixated on nearby details. But Todgers's, too, is an old bit of City undergoing and resisting change. Located in one of Dickens's favourite spots, somewhere in a tangle of passages off Thames Street near the Monument that commemorates the Great Fire of 1666, the neighbourhood is cluttered with ancient houses turned into warehouses, and tiny streets trying to bear the traffic of international commerce from nearby St Katherine's Dock, opened in 1828. 'All day long', Dickens writes, 'a stream of porters from the wharves beside the river, each bearing on his back a bursting chest of oranges, poured slowly through the narrow passages; while underneath the archway by the public house, the knots of those who rested and regaled within, were piled from morning until night'.[17] The old city is both deadened and enlivened by the influx of warehoused goods, trucks stopping up traffic, and miniature 'towns' of wholesale wine and groceries crammed into blind alleyways or the foundations of buildings. The old inhabitants of the area carry on obliviously, their belief in the superiority of old English ways gently mocked by the narrator.

The whole passage stunningly portrays the way expansionist Victorian London fits itself somehow into ancient, decaying neighbourhoods, which hover on the border between modernity and nostalgia. As a life-long London walker, Dickens registered each change in familiar neighbourhoods with a blending of the two responses, which meet in many other representations of the City. The beneficent Cheeryble brothers of *Nicholas Nickleby* are traders on the international scene, but their firm is quartered in a neglected, dusty, but somehow pastoral little square near St Mary Axe, where they dispense paternalistic favours in old-school forms. Sol Gill's nautical instrument shop, an old-fashioned offshoot of the shipping industry, is placed in the heart of the City, where it provides a haven for the good in *Dombey and Son*. As late as *Our Mutual Friend*, Dickens was imagining a pastoral haven on the rooftop of Pubsey and Co.'s bill-broking office in St Mary Axe, where the old Jew Riah entertains Lizzie Hexam and Jenny Wren. By this time Dickens had witnessed the transformation of the old City into a modern financial centre that emptied its population out at night, but he clung wistfully to imagined pockets of lingering, old-fashioned goodness surrounded by aggressive or dynamic commercialism.

In the desire to emphasise the concreteness, historicity, and scope of Dickens's London I have deliberately saved for last a mention of Dickens's more subjective, atmospheric city writing. He was perfectly aware that the city looks different to people in different moods, and often exploited weather writing for emotional effect or to set the scene for dramatic episodes. The great opening of *Bleak House* is an elaborately rhetorical example of a technique Dickens had been developing since *Oliver Twist*. As Oliver is led by his captors Sikes and Nancy past Smithfield Market and Newgate Prison, Dickens creates a murky light of thickening 'heavy mist' and rain impenetrable by the bright gas-light in shop windows, rendering 'the strange place still stranger in Oliver's eyes'. Passing a gas-lamp allows Oliver a momentary glimpse of the fearful pallor on Nancy's face.[18] Gas lighting had spread quickly in London since its introduction shortly after the turn of the century, and Dickens had his own ways of turning it to fictional purposes. The chiaroscuro effect of gas lighting helped him create what he called in his preface to *Bleak House* 'the romantic side of familiar things', often in scenes where lamp-light struggles helplessly against the darkness of fog, soot, and rain. This image returns in the opening paragraphs of *Bleak House*; here murky weather overspreads the city only to be turned into a metaphor for the obstructive, obsolete practices of the Court of Chancery:

> As much mud in the streets, as if the waters had newly retired from the face of the earth, and it would not be wonderful to meet a Megalosaurus, forty feet long or so, waddling like an elephantine lizard up Holborn Hill. Smoke lowering down from chimney-pots, making a soft black drizzle, with flakes of soot in it as big as full-grown snow-flakes – gone into mourning, one might imagine, for the death of the sun. (Chapter 1)

The passage also establishes what might be called the peculiar subjectivity of the omniscient narrator. What he sees at first – people slipping and sliding on muddy Holborn streets – could easily be witnessed from a nearby window. As he continues, however, the perspective rises above and beyond the human, discerning not only the geographical reach of the fog beyond London, but individual people hidden indoors, in ships' cabins, or – in a recursive image of his own panoramic vision – peeping over London bridges 'into a nether sky of fog … as if they were up in a balloon, and hanging in the misty clouds' (Chapter 1). The scene is brilliantly evoked, and as quickly left behind: we see the second narrator, Esther, observe the fog from street-level the same day, but the next day the weather is fine. The fog that seems to define London is, after all, a momentary narrative effect.

Dismal London is more directly linked with subjective vision in *Little Dorrit*, where the chronic depressiveness of its hero Arthur Clennam shapes occasional passages of rainy London gloom. Ships and shipping detritus looming through fog and rain are used to great effect in the melodramatic riverside scenes of *Our Mutual Friend*; the wind also gets its turn in that novel, where it is seen 'sawing' paper trash all about the city as if it were 'mysterious paper currency', turning the gritty city into a landscape of hopelessness. These descriptions are linked to the consciousnesses of the young lawyers Eugene Wrayburn and Mortimer Lightwood, and herald scenes that involve them in the criminal side of the riverside world (1.12). What's remarkable about Dickens's mood-setting cityscapes is their endless metaphorical inventiveness, which takes the edge off any attempt to fix the metropolis with stable meanings. As London iconography, however, Dickens's gas-lit fogs and muddy 'labyrinthine' streets were to become recognisable fixtures in late-nineteenth-century fiction.

After Dickens

By the last two decades of the nineteenth century, London had changed noticeably. Joseph Bazalgett's city-wide sewage system, built between 1863 and 1875, had cleaned up the filthy Thames, moving the city's wastes seaward in tunnels under the new public spaces of the Thames Embankments. The expansion of cheap public transportation – trams, omnibuses, underground railways – allowed both middle- and working-class people to move into suburban housing, setting off a predictable literary moan about creeping red-brick suburbia. In town, blocks of flats were beginning to replace the ubiquitous lodging house. Middle- and lower-middle-class women were working, walking, and living on their own in the capital. The West End had become a centre of commercial activity, including department stores, office buildings, hotels, and restaurants. Inner London manufacturing declined, as the city grew more fully into the political and financial centre of the British empire.

During this period, London's East End came into prominence as an unknown underworld of poverty, crime, degradation, and political threat. Journalists, sociologists, and middle-class do-gooders converged in a cultural fantasy of the East End as 'darkest London', sometimes imagining it as a savage colony simmering dangerously right next door, or a mysterious labyrinth that a West End cabbie might refuse to enter. The 'othering' of the East End can readily be analysed as a fearful and sensationalist cultural mood in which twin fears about poverty and immigrant groups flourished – and motivated liberal philanthropic projects like settlement houses or schemes of adult education. Yet despite its imaginative currency, most novelists did not actually set their work in the East End. The exception was Arthur Morrison, who grew up in Poplar, moved up into West End journalism, and made his reputation by writing knowledgeably about class codes of behaviour in the East End. *Mean Streets* (1894) brings a Kiplingesque voice of detachment to its depictions of daily violence and spiteful neighbours; *A Child of the Jago* (1896) brings *Oliver Twist* up to date as it describes the thieving life of the Old Nichol area in Bethnal Green, a notorious slum then on the verge of demolition.

Other types of popular fiction set their action in a London hardly distinguishable from that of Dickens. Robert Louis Stevenson's Gothic tale, *The Strange Case of Dr Jekyll and Mr Hyde* (1886), splits its protagonist into civilised and savage sides just as London was split in the popular imaginary of the 1880s and 1890s, but it is set in undesignated west or central portions of the city. As he evokes the spooky atmosphere of night-time London, Stevenson offers us Dickensian descriptions of fog striated by light, the sounds of footsteps on the streets, and empty gas-lit streets suddenly erupting into grotesque violence as Mr Hyde runs over a small girl or beats an old gentleman to death. The architectural variations of a many-layered city are used to good symbolic effect: Dr Jekyll's respectable house in a declining square has a mysterious back door in an ugly court that juts obtrusively into the neatly improved shopping street around the corner.

Arthur Conan Doyle's *The Sign of Four* (1890) offers another version of Dickensian London, complete with foggy, lamp-lit wet streets and an all-knowing detective who can, despite the fog, identify every street passed during a long cab ride from Baker Street into the labyrinthine district of Lambeth. Although Holmes is given a late-nineteenth-century character spiced with science and cocaine, his rapid movements in the murky city follow closely on the heels of Dickens's cheerful Detective Bucket of *Bleak House*. Holmes and Watson do a formidable amount of walking, their routes on both sides of the river implied or named, before they engage in a wild steamer-chase down the Thames to catch their prey. Much like Stevenson, Doyle capitalises on mappings, moods, and images made familiar by Dickens to ground his late-century tale of imperialist robbery and revenge. Such writers adapted to their own purposes Dickens's understanding of London as a detective's natural habitat: an extensive streetscape that allows for surprising encounters, invisibility, sudden visibility, and frantic chase scenes.

Literary mastery of a self-consciously post-Dickensian London arrived, however, in Joseph Conrad's *The Secret Agent* (1907). Set in the West End during the anarchistic decade of the 1880s, this novel evokes, mocks, and rewrites Dickens in an entirely original way. As double agent Verloc walks from sleazy Soho to the Russian Embassy in Belgravia, Conrad plays impressionistically, not with fog and labyrinth, but with the strange 'bloodshot' sunlight that erases the shadows of wealthy riders in Hyde Park's Rotten Row, and with the disorienting vagaries of addresses detached from the houses they sign. When the unnamed Assistant Commissioner of Police descends into the slimy, foggy atmosphere of nearby Soho, the shadowy shapes of vans and the brilliant colours of oranges and lemons on a fruit stand manage both to feel spooky and to make fun of the detective's desire to enter 'darkest London' as if he were back at his colonialist post in the jungle.[19] The boundaries of subjectivity are threatened by the city as a whole: London rain creates despair in characters who look out of windows onto a world that seems to be dissolving into chaos, while the complete indifference of the enormous city excites existential panic in others. The perpetual ironies in the narrator's voice surround each form of London rhetoric with invisible quotation marks; thus *The Secret Agent* may be understood as Conrad's wry marking of a balancing point between Dickens's substantially evoked London and a Modernist-subjectivist vision that dissolves the city into a metaphor for suicidal despair.

George Gissing was the only late-century novelist to take on London as a full-time job, turning his attention to different parts of the city in novel after novel. Like Dickens, Gissing was a constant walker whose novels were generated largely through responses to the city; he learned his trade by studying and revising Dickens's London. Although they did not venture into East End settings, Gissing's 1880s novels made a point of depicting in detail parts of the city that middle-class readers were not likely to frequent. *Thyrza* (1887) is primarily set south of the Thames in Lambeth; *The Nether World* (1889) in Clerkenwell and Islington. The central actions of both novels concern respectable working-class and lower-middle-class characters whose lives take shape on networks of named streets in small, closely observed neighbourhoods.

Gissing's idea of London is one thing; his representation of people in city streets is another. His narrator insists that London is a systematic killer of souls: a place where millions of people toil endlessly and hopelessly in an attempt, never realised, to achieve some sort of peace, relief, or pleasure. Whether their labour occurs in factories, millinery workshops, or in the lodgings of those who try to live by their pens, the relentlessness of labour in a commercial and industrial centre wears out the will to live. *The Nether World* frequently returns to such condemnations, sometimes through the jaded perspective of its heroine Clara Hewitt. Her view from an upper window in the Farringdon Buildings (an actual block of flats built for working-class tenancy in 1874) revises the opening of *Bleak House* with a decidedly Gissingesque twist: 'Down in Farringdon Street the carts, wagons, vans, cabs, omnibuses crossed and intermingled in a steaming splash-bath of mud; human beings, reduced to their due paltriness, seemed to toil in exasperation along the strips of pavement, bound on errands, which were a mockery, driven automaton-like by forces they neither understood nor could resist.'[20] It is common to understand the grim Gissing city in late-nineteenth-century terms, as a determining environment that cannot help but breed a trapped, stunted, or degenerate urban race. Yet it is also possible to appreciate the way each of Gissing's fictional groups creates a familiar locale through neighbourly and hostile relationships that make little communities within the greater anonymity of the metropolis. Like Dickens, Gissing makes London a place of ordinary encounter and usage, although he confines his characters within narrower ranges of motion.

Gissing regularly describes the walking routes his characters take, naming the streets they follow and precisely where they turn. His quite literal realism makes it easy to follow their movements on a modern map of London. In *Thyrza* and *The Nether World* workplaces are within easy walking distance of lodgings, and most of the walks so carefully detailed by the narrator can be accomplished within a few minutes. When characters go to more distant parts of the city, it is an event; they make plans to travel by omnibus or train from one named station to another. Thus Gissing suggests a London fragmented into a series of localities. His characters move from one cheap lodging to another as their incomes rise and fall by shillings and pence; the address – usually within walking distance of the previous one – invariably tells the tale of their fortunes. If Dickens brings London together by weaving connections among characters scattered all over the city, Gissing's London looks like an area map of cheap lodgings and free public spaces in which characters manage to sustain their domestic and social existences.[21]

A turning from one street to another brings us to houses of greater or lesser decency and respectability; each street, sometimes each end of the same street, has its own delicately calibrated status level. Gissing's characters, also calibrated by status level, become involved with one another because they are neighbours; they might share the same lodging house, or walk the same network of streets. Physical fights, often between women, occur in public alleyways; the dying infants of the poor are displayed on doorsteps. Characters who are romantically – or more insidiously – involved can often see each other privately only by walking each other part-way home; public streets and buildings, parks and embankments are the drawing rooms of the poor and the lonely. If they are trying to avoid notice, such characters might rendezvous in a cheap café or at a railway station a few minutes' walk away from their normal routes. Gissing's streets are social opportunities, possibilities for dialogues hurriedly snatched, sandwiched between the places characters have just left, and where they are expected to return. Even as his narrator bemoans the unrelenting ugliness of grimy brick row houses, Gissing is busy creating a public metropolis that his characters know how to use.

The sociological observation of lives on the brink of poverty connects Gissing's style and perspective with contemporary investigations of conditions in the East End. But the East End appears, in *The Nether World*, only as a depth of unimaginable horror, a sight briefly glimpsed from a train window as some Clerkenwell characters travel eastward for a brief country holiday. They pass 'across miles of a city of the damned, such as thought never conceived before this age of ours; above streets swarming with a nameless populace, cruelly exposed by the unwonted light of heaven; stopping at stations which it crushes the heart to think should be the destination of any mortal' (Chapter 19). Gissing's sensibility recoiled from the aesthetic deprivation he saw in lower-middle-class lives and streets; he was content to leave the East End alone in its otherness.

Near the end of *The Nether World*, the surviving characters are placed in a new sort of hell: the northern suburb of Crouch End. Protagonist Sidney Kirkwood, now burdened with the care of the whole Hewitt family, can just afford to keep them in one of the pretentious, shoddily built 'villas' where 'poverty tries to hide itself with venetian blinds, until the time when an advanced guard of houses shall justify the existence of the slum' (Chapter 39). This grim bow to the rapid development of working-class suburbia was followed by Gissing's turn in the 1890s to more middle-class – if equally restless and struggling – segments of the London populace. *In the Year of Jubilee* (1894) takes us into the south-of-Thames suburb of Camberwell, regularly figured in earlier novels as a sign of genteel respectability. As

Gissing characteristically puts it, 'Each house seems to remind its neighbour, with all the complacence expressible in buff brick, that in this locality lodgings are *not* to let.'²² The characters that inhabit the houses belie this old-fashioned respectability through their slovenly ways or their modern hatred of its stifling requirements. The restless protagonist Nancy Lord escapes from her father's house by flinging herself into the crowd celebrating Victoria's Jubilee (1887) in the West End streets, where she is carried along by the exhilarating crush of moving bodies. It is a scene of mass cultural frenzy that Gissing officially hates and deplores, though he depicts its course, with its accidental losses and meetings of acquaintances, in vivid detail. He can offer Nancy Lord nothing satisfactory between the dull pretensions of suburbia and the opportunistic, rapid-fire entrepreneurship of the modern city.

Like Dickens, Gissing depicted a historically inflected London in ways both intimate and panoramic, but his ways of knowing mixed ethnographic observation with a *fin de siècle* sense of hopeless decline, unadorned by imaginative play. Quite deliberately, Gissing stripped London down to its brick-and-mortar substrate, eliminating the romantic projections that his predecessor thrived on. Both writers understood the social injustices created by the structure of the urban metropolis, and both thrust them energetically into their readers' imaginations. But London was for Dickens a place of plenitude, mystery, dark connection, and nostalgia; for Gissing a place of deprivation, ugliness, weary work, and degrading mass culture. Over the course of the nineteenth century, these two writers between them largely carried the literary burden of making a Victorian London and taking it to the brink of modernity.

Notes

1 Anthony Trollope, *The Way We Live Now* (New York: Modern Library, 1977), Chapter 39. Because there are many editions of the texts discussed in this chapter, subsequent quotations from novels will be cited parenthetically in the text by title and chapter number.

2 Walter Bagehot, 'Charles Dickens,' *National Review* 2 (October 1858), 458–86, reprinted in *The Collected Works of Walter Bagehot*, ed. Norman St John-Stevas, 15 vols. (London: The Economist, 1965), Vol. II, p. 87.

3 Dorothy van Ghent's famous 1950 essay, 'The Dickens World: A View from Todgers's', *The Sewanee Review* 58 (1950), 419–38, might stand as an early example of the desire for a totalising view of the city; her discussion of the dizzying view from Todgers's boarding house in *Martin Chuzzlewit* offers the passage as a synecdoche for Dickens's hallucinatory London as a whole. Many critics have followed in her wake; for a recent example see Robert Alter, *Imagined Cities: Urban Experience and the Language of the Novel* (New Haven and London:

Yale University Press, 2005), pp. 43–81. At the other end of the spectrum, Julian Wolfreys celebrates the fragmented, decentralised writing, 'where the knowable is constantly displaced' and the city is defined as what cannot be seen whole; see *Writing London: The Trace of the Urban Text from Blake to Dickens* (New York: St Martin's Press, 1998), pp. 141–78 (p. 143).

4 For different angles on the problem of knowledge see Richard Maxwell's discussion of allegorical models for writing the city, in *The Mysteries of Paris and London* (Charlottesville: University of Virginia Press, 1992), pp. 14–20; and Michel de Certeau, 'Walking in the City', in *The Practice of Everyday Life*, trans. Steven Rendall (Berkeley: University of California Press, 1984), pp. 91–110.

5 Roy Porter, *London: A Social History* (Cambridge, MA: Harvard University Press, 1994), pp. 205–9.

6 For sophisticated discussions of the *flâneur* and the woman in the street, see Deborah Nord, *Walking the Victorian Streets: Women, Representation, and the City* (Ithaca, NY: Cornell University Press, 1995); and Judith Walkowitz, *City of Dreadful Delight: Narratives of Sexual Danger in Late-Victorian London* (Chicago: University of Chicago Press, 1992).

7 De Certeau, *The Practice of Everyday Life*, p. 93.

8 Lynda Nead, *Victorian Babylon: People, Streets and Images in Nineteenth-Century London* (New Haven and London: Yale University Press, 2000), pp. 62–73.

9 Raymond Williams, *The City and the Country* (New York: Oxford University Press, 1973), pp. 154–5.

10 William Wordsworth, *The Prelude: A Parallel Text*, ed. J. C. Maxwell (Harmondsworth: Penguin, 1971), VII.158–9.

11 Jerry White, *London in the Nineteenth Century: A Human Awful Wonder of God* (London: Vintage, 2007), pp. 9–12, 29–35.

12 Charles Dickens, *Bleak House*, ed. Nicola Bradbury (London: Penguin, 1996), Chapter 16.

13 Charles Dickens, *Dombey and Son*, ed. Alan Horsman (Oxford: Oxford World's Classics, 2008), Chapter 7.

14 Charles Dickens, *Little Dorrit*, ed. Stephen Wall and Helen Small (London: Penguin, 1998), Book 1, Chapter 10.

15 Roy Porter discusses the phenomenon of overbuilding and class decline in neighbourhoods built on speculation under the system of ninety-nine-year leases on property: see Porter, *London: A Social History*, pp. 207–8.

16 Charles Dickens, *Our Mutual Friend*, ed. Adrian Poole (London: Penguin Classics, 1997), Book 1, Chapter 4.

17 Charles Dickens, *Martin Chuzzlewit*, ed. Patricia Ingham (London: Penguin, 1999), Chapter 9.

18 Charles Dickens, *Oliver Twist*, ed. Philip Horne (London: Penguin, 2003), Chapter 16.

19 Joseph Conrad, *The Secret Agent*, ed. Michael Newton (London: Penguin, 2007), Chapters 2, 7.

20 George Gissing, *The Nether World*, ed. Stephen Gill (Oxford: Oxford World's Classics, 1999), Chapter 31.

21 John Goode's analysis of the differences between Dickens's London and Gissing's emphasises the way Gissing's localisation 'is partly organized to keep class relationships to an abstraction'. See John Goode, *George Gissing: Ideology and Fiction* (London: Vision Press, 1978), pp. 90–108 (p. 100).

22 George Gissing, *In The Year of Jubilee* (London: J. M. Dent, 1994), Chapter 1.

9

SHEARER WEST

London in Victorian visual culture

Over 150 years separate Hogarth's etching and engraving of *Gin Lane* (see Figure 9.1) from Walter Richard Sickert's painting *The Camden Town Murder; or, What Shall We Do about the Rent?* (Figure 9.2). However, a particular view of London, one that is geographically and socially specific, as well as morally charged, envelops both of these representations. *Gin Lane*, normally paired with the more prosperous and cheerful London of *Beer Street*, was Hogarth's attempt to influence the passage of the Gin Act to regulate the sale of spirits that was driving the London poor to theft, murder, and suicidal despair. His grim satirical engraving, set in the notorious district of St Giles, with Hawksmoor's St George's Church peeping up behind the decrepit scrim of tenements, reduces social life to the pawn shop, the distillers, and the undertakers. The gin-sodden poor gnaw bones with the animals, while the negligent mother at the perspectival heart of the composition commits careless infanticide.

Sickert eschews the legibility of Hogarth's moralistic engraving. His painting was retrospectively titled in an attempt to erect a narrative around the scene of desolation that it represents. The painting depicts the interior of a flat in the north London suburb of Camden Town, where Sickert and his colleagues lived and painted in the early years of the twentieth century, drawing much of their subject matter from the predominantly drab and depressed working-class culture of that district. The reference to the Camden Town murders gives the work an association with notorious events of 1907, in which the underbelly of suburban life in Camden Town was exposed in a series of highly publicised murder trials. However, unlike Hogarth, Sickert does not preach here, nor does he provide the viewer with a readily accessible story. Instead, he focuses his attention on a painterly technique of heavy impasto and a limited palette of dirty earth colours to evoke the grim scene of misery. Despite the indistinct image, a number of details here offer a clue to the setting: the iron bedstead, the woman's overly coiffed hair and saggy body, ugly patterned wallpaper that has the aura of mildew, the man's plain

Figure 9.1 William Hogarth, *Gin Lane* (1751).

working clothes and rough beard. The man sits with his hands folded in prayer or despondency, while the nude woman turns her head away, possibly in depression or shame. The psychological disconnection between the two figures, despite their physical proximity, enhances the sense of quiet catastrophe, just as the clipped composition, which condenses both figures to partial bodies compressed uncomfortably together in the corner of the room, engulfs the image with a sense of claustrophobia.

Both Hogarth's and Sickert's representations provide potent visual myths of London. Both dwell on poverty, degradation, despair, and crime. Both take as their setting specific parts of London that would have been meaningful to their contemporary audiences. Both of them tell

Figure 9.2 Walter Sickert, *The Camden Town Murder* (also known as *What Shall We Do about the Rent?*) (c. 1908).

stories, or allow for stories to be told about them. Where they differ is in terms of their legibility and the way in which the moral geography of the city is used. Hogarth's work is visual satire, drawing on the methods of Swift or Pope, and he employs a semiotic catalogue of observed detail to ensure the efficacy of his narrative. His message is clear, and the setting of St Giles provides a commentary on the behaviour of the poor who inhabit it. Sickert's painting has no moral message, but dwells on the despair of the characters just as Zola's naturalist novels wallowed in the degradation of his urban protagonists. Sickert reduces Hogarth's expansive urban public space to a tiny corner of a dimly lit private bedroom, where social life is swallowed up in domestic misery. Despite the differences in their approaches to London, Sickert was the last in a long line of Victorians who admired Hogarth and whose images of London owe much to his legacy. In the wake of Hogarth's moral mapping of Georgian London, these artists depicted a rapidly changing Victorian London through highly charged representations, endowing the real landmarks and boroughs of the city with poetic resonance.

London underwent dramatic physical and social changes in the 150 years between Hogarth and Sickert. While Georgian London consisted largely of three discrete areas – the courtly West End, the mercantile City and the East End manufacturing and port district, the extensive campaign of slum clearances, railway construction, urban redevelopment, and the erection of both modern sewerage systems and embankments along the Thames transformed medieval and Georgian London into a nineteenth-century city with a multiplicity of new spaces, functions, and communities. Traces of the old city lingered both physically and in the imagination of Victorian Londoners, but for much of the nineteenth century, large parts of London were effectively building sites. The physical changes in the city precipitated social changes as well. Slum clearances drove the poor out of their traditional neighbourhoods, and they became itinerant inhabitants of an East End where industry was declining while its immigrant population was growing exponentially, first with an influx of Irish in the early part of the century, and then of Russian and East European Jews escaping pogroms in the latter decades of Victoria's reign. New bridges built across the Thames during the Regency enabled a freer flow of urban traffic, and with the expansion of the railways, more of the middle class decamped to the suburban developments of north, south, and west London. A plethora of service industries such as hotels, restaurants, theatres, music halls, shops, and pleasure gardens created novel opportunities for Londoners, and by the end of the nineteenth century, women as well as men were taking regular advantage of the consumer possibilities of fashionable shopping districts such as Regent Street.

This sketchy overview of architectural and social change in Victorian London provides some context for understanding the visual culture of the period, but it does not offer an explanation for it. The way artists engaged with the new Victorian London owed more to the legacy of predecessors like Hogarth, and to London as conceived by novelists like Charles Dickens and social campaigners such as Henry Mayhew. This London was one that was often represented with a misleading photographic accuracy, designed to evoke an effect of visual precision, but the way in which writers and artists wallowed in the physical details of urban modernity, such as trains, omnibuses, crowded shopping streets, and urban types, from the East End poor to the new suburban middle class, was always overlaid by a sense of London as a city that was as much imaginary as real. Even photographs of the period that document the changes in the urban space have something of the unreal about them. Photographs showing the piles of wreckage that accompanied railway construction frequently encompass the London landmarks of the past that were allowed to remain amidst the debris (see Figure 9.3). These nostalgic references amidst the unpicturesque effects of urban change stimulate in the viewer what Roland Barthes has called the *punctum* – a deep and piercing sensation, both nostalgic and ineffable.[1] Although Victorian

Figure 9.3 Clearing the site opposite Broad Sanctuary for construction
of the District Railway (*c.* 1867).

representations of London varied enormously in approach and vision, they
shared this same ambivalent engagement with fact and fiction, prose and
poetry, modernity and the past.

Another dichotomy underlay Victorian depictions of London. Recent
scholarship on representations of the city builds on Michel de Certeau's
distinction between two approaches to the urban environment: the rational,
ordered topographical city, observed from a panoptic bird's-eye view; and

the city as experienced from the street, which is ambiguous, dangerous, and unsettled.[2] The former represents a geography that can notionally be controlled, ordered, and described; the latter is experiential and sensory and therefore impervious to rational construction. Although, in de Certeau's formulation, there is a disjunction between the city as it is mapped and ordered, and the city as it is experienced and imagined, in visual representations of Victorian London the persistence of a Hogarthian moral geography, even in the least legible representations of the city, suggests that artists endeavoured to reconcile the known and the experienced city through their work. While visual artists could draw on the techniques and approaches of their literary counterparts – whether novelists or social reformers – the envisioning of London that appears in their prints, paintings, and photographs offers a particular take on urban change, from the iconic spaces and places of London, to the Thames and its bridges and the looming significance of the East End in popular imagination. De Certeau's ordered, rational city is one that is visualised, while his experienced, irrational one can also be heard, felt, tasted, and smelled. The penchant for various manifestations of realism and impressionism among London artists notionally supported the rational ordering of space and place, but the mysterious, unknowable, or desired city was present just underneath the familiarity and exactitude of represented urban spaces.

With this in mind, it is worth considering which parts of London Victorian artists chose to depict and how these relate to the legacy of Hogarth's moral geography. Hogarth deliberately selected specific districts, streets, or squares of London – recognisable through iconic buildings, or signalled through the texts that accompanied his prints – and in doing so, he was providing his audiences with an unambiguous context for his protagonists' behaviour. So *A Rake's Progress* (1735) takes Tom Rakewell from a licentious orgy in Covent Garden's Rose Tavern, to the fashionable St James, and subjects him to the indignity of both Fleet debtors' prison and Bethlem Hospital, as his profligate life catches up with him. Hogarth's *Four Times of Day* (1738) pokes fun at characteristic London types in the identifiable settings of Covent Garden piazza, the French quarter of St Giles, Islington, and Charing Cross, while his idle apprentice (1747) stands trial at the Old Bailey before spending his final moments on the gibbet at Tyburn. Temple Bar, the Guildhall, Tottenham Court Road, and many other London landmarks, all appear in Hogarth's various prints. However, while the specificity of London settings in Hogarth's work was designed to guide viewers to adopt a particular attitude toward his corrupt characters, his representations of iconic London buildings such as St Paul's or London Bridge were never wholly architecturally accurate.

An echo of Hogarth's place-specific approach can be seen throughout the art of the nineteenth century, but the physical properties of the locations and their social and moral associations had in many cases changed in the meantime. William Holman Hunt set his *Awakening Conscience* (1853), an image of a fallen woman, in the fashionable St John's Wood, a district notorious for middle-class sexual liaison; Ford Madox Brown's *Work* (1852–65) was located in the working-class suburb of Hampstead. William Powell Frith's *Morning, Noon and Night* trilogy of sketches (1862) paid tribute to Hogarth's *Times of Day*, by setting one of its narrative incidents in Covent Garden (echoing Hogarth's *Morning*), while the other two paintings in the series added the modern shopping district of Regent Street, and the Haymarket, the latter a well-known hang out for prostitutes since the eighteenth century, but an area that Hogarth never represented himself.

Of all Victorian artists, Frith quoted Hogarth more directly and more frequently than his contemporaries did. Although in his autobiography Frith declared that his two moral series, *The Road to Ruin* (1878) and *The Race for Wealth* (1880) 'avoid[ed] the satirical vein of Hogarth, for which I knew myself to be unfitted',[3] the very conception of a series of works that told a story was drawn from Hogarth's example. The place of London in both of these series is particularly telling. In *The Road to Ruin*, Frith's dissolute anti-hero discovers a taste for gambling while an undergraduate at Cambridge, squanders his funds at Ascot, faces the consequences of his extravagance when bailiffs visit his ancestral home, and tries to recoup himself by writing plays in France, but finally ends his life in a garret in London, locking the door while he reaches for his gun. London then is absent from the series until the denouement, when it represents the ultimate decline of the modern rake. In *Race for Wealth* again London is invisible until the last two paintings in the series, in which a fraudulent financier gets his comeuppance at the Old Bailey (not unlike Hogarth's idle apprentice), and then is consigned to Millbank prison. Frith studied both of these locations first-hand, and he photographed the interior of the Old Bailey to ensure a faithful rendering. In Frith's moral series, then, London becomes the context for crime and punishment, rather than prosperity and happiness. In works such as these, it is noteworthy that the city represented is London. Although London to a certain extent is a cipher for the dangers of urban modernity, as in the last scene of *The Road to Ruin*, the studied specificity of artists like Frith suggest that the real spaces and places of London were also significant in and of themselves.

However, the putative objectivity that underlay representations of such architectural features and carefully observed urban topography masks a less orderly and even imaginary London under the surface. A number of nineteenth-century artists saw their purpose as close observation and re-production of what was before them, and to achieve this end, they would go to great lengths to choose locations, models, and props that they represented with as much fidelity as possible, often with the aid of photographs, as Frith did with the Old Bailey. This appears to be the case in William Logsdail's painting of *St Martin-in-the-Fields* (see Figure 9.4), which was exhibited at the Royal Academy of Arts in 1888. Logsdail established a temporary studio inside a Pickford's removal van that he parked in Trafalgar Square,[4] where he observed the bustle of the street and endeavoured to reproduce with utmost accuracy the detailed features of the classical portico of St Martin-in-the-Fields and the dreary grey atmosphere of a winter day. Yet however objectively rendered it appears, the work possesses nostalgic undercurrents. The young flower-seller in the foreground draws the viewer into the painting by offering up her basket with a winsome expression on her face. She, like the news vendor and orange-seller in the far background, is a character lifted out of the eighteenth-century 'Cries of London' prints, which represented itinerant street-traders in London as part of a typology of London life. By the late nineteenth century, the 'Cries of London' was part of the mythology of old London, with the criers' roles being more thoroughly subsumed into a general notion of the trades of the London poor. So in Logsdail's work there is a disconnection between the flower-seller's picturesque presence and the objective envisioning of a busy modern metropolis.

There were numerous works of art like Logsdail's that purported to represent London as it was, but such 'realism' often relied implicitly or explicitly on the techniques of journalists or social observers. London appeared prominently in published writing of the nineteenth century, from Rudolf Ackermann's *Microcosm of London* (1808), to Pierce Egan's *Life in London* (1821–3), and any number of guidebooks that walked the reader through the city, such as John Murray Fisher's *The World of London* (1843) or Pete Cunningham's *Handbook to London* (1849). Many of these works were illustrated with engraved vignettes of urban scenes. Augustus Sala's *Twice round the Clock*, a collection of essays first published in the journal *Welcome Guest* in 1858, claimed to give the reader a true slice of London life: 'I wish you to see the monster LONDON in the varied phases of its outer and inner life, at every hour of the day-season and the night-season.'[5] Sala's vivid, highly personal, rhetorically ornamental account of London life inspired George Elgar Hicks to produce a series of works he exhibited at the Royal Academy, including *Billingsgate Fish Market* of 1861 (see Figure 9.5). Hicks's crowded composition, filled with a diverse collection of poor and dazed urban types jostling each other for the best place in the early morning

Figure 9.4 William Logsdail, *St Martin-in-the-Fields* (1888).

scramble for fresh fish, undoubtedly owed much to Sala's description of the
same market before dawn:

> Upon my word, the clock has struck five, and the great gong of Billingsgate
> booms forth market-time. Uprouse ye, then, my merry, merry fishmongers,
> for this is your opening day! And the merry fishmongers uprouse themselves
> with a vengeance ... A rush hither and thither at helter-skelter speed, appar-
> ently blindly, apparently without motive, but really with a business-like and
> engrossing pre-occupation, for fish and all things fishy ... An eager crowd of
> purchasers hedge in the scaly merchandise.[6]

Figure 9.5 George Elgar Hicks, *Billingsgate Fish Market* (1861).

While Hicks's work captures the general bustle of Billingsgate, Sala goes much further in providing a full history of the fish market as well as a minutely detailed catalogue of the produce available there, specific features of the detritus scattered on the wharfside, and a thorough analysis of the process followed by the auctioneers. This proliferation of detail, underpinned by personal memoranda and deictic address to the reader, gave a richness to Sala's work that Hicks was unable to capture in his busy scene. Nevertheless, the viewers of Hicks's painting were the same class who read Sala's journalism, and the relationship between the two works was noted by contemporary observers. Hicks's seemingly documentary analysis of the fish market would therefore have been viewed with the meanderings and editorialising of Sala in mind.

The literary references that underpin many representations of Victorian London were not far from the thoughts of the journalist Tom Taylor, when he wrote a narrative commentary on Frith's *Railway Station* (1862). Frith had built his early career on producing paintings based on the novels and plays of Goldsmith, Sterne, and Shakespeare, and for many years he avoided what he called 'hat and trousers pictures',[7] as he found representations of modern life ugly. His great admiration for Dickens, however, led him to depict the character of Dolly Varden in *Barnaby Rudge*, and afterwards he turned his attention to making modern life as picturesque as possible. *The Railway Station* was a dramatic diagonal view of the interior of the Great Western Station (Paddington), with a crowd of people rushing to catch a train that is about to depart. In his autobiography, Frith claimed rather disingenuously, 'I don't think the station at Paddington can be called picturesque, nor can the clothes of the ordinary traveller be said to offer much attraction to the painter',[8] but this was nevertheless one of his most popular works, exhibited in a private gallery to record-breaking crowds. The faithful architectural detail of the Great Western Station (opened only ten years before Frith's work) served as a backdrop for a range of stories about departures that Taylor lavishly embellished in his pamphlet on the painting. Taylor declared Frith's work to be a piece of 'prose' in contrast to the poetry of the railway that Turner had discovered in his *Rain, Steam and Speed*, but to Taylor, the story told here was not about London but about 'joys and sorrows ... to be found in contrast and combination at every railway platform'.[9] However, while the title of the painting suggests a generic scene, the specificity with which Frith reproduced the architectural features of the station made it instantly recognisable as a London setting. Although Taylor claimed that *The Railway Station* represented a prose genre, rather than a slice of London life, he wove stories about the small boy going off to school, the wedding party, a man being arrested by two plain-clothes London detectives, that called upon the precise London setting and London types represented. While Taylor's rhetoric was very different from that of Sala, he nevertheless, like Sala, dwelt on specific detail in order to reinforce the authority of his narrative.

This mixture of specificity and fantasy in so-called 'realist' painting was in part due to the proliferation of views of London available to Victorian audiences. London was represented everywhere: in prints in the *Illustrated London News*, front covers of song sheets, 'realisations' of urban scenes in the theatre,[10] and through increasingly sophisticated landscape and architectural photography. The abundance of available views of London did not lessen demand, although they did collectively reinforce expectations and prejudices about London as a geographical space as well as a social one. Photography had a particular role to play here. While ostensibly reinforcing the objectivity of modern London scenes, photography reified the objects and settings of London in such a way as to make them strange and fascinating, even while they were familiar and routine.

However, the specificity of setting that made Victorian 'realist' paintings analogous to photography only rarely represented the kind of panoptic view that de Certeau identified as one of the two modes of conceiving of the city. In the cases already discussed, segments of the city were selected and tailored to meet the needs of the artist. However, Victorian audiences were aware of the eighteenth-century example of Canaletto, whose paintings of the Thames (which Hogarth never represented) employed a bird's eye perspective to depict a city that is knowable and seemingly orderly. However, a closer look at Canaletto's topographical depictions begins to undermine the

Figure 9.6 Canaletto, *London: Westminster Bridge from the North
on Lord Mayor's Day* (1747).

seeming clarity of his viewpoint. His *London: Westminster Bridge from the
North on Lord Mayor's Day* (see Figure 9.6) was specifically commissioned
to commemorate the building of Westminster Bridge, which Canaletto represents in full in his painting. The painting takes an imaginary aerial view
of the Thames, and Canaletto litters the river with recognisable barges of
the city guilds, such as the Fishmongers and Merchant Taylors, which had
an established place in the Lord Mayor's procession. These boats surround
the dominant Lord Mayor's barge, which looks not unlike an oversized gon-
dola, with its eighteen oarsmen throwing up spray as they cut across the
river. Canaletto's painting was produced over 100 years before the construction of the Victoria and Albert Embankments, so at this time, the Thames
could only be seen fully from the river itself and not from the banks, and
certainly not from above. Canaletto, like Hogarth, employed iconic objects
to signal the setting – in this case the newly erected Westminster bridge,
as well as St Margaret's Church and Westminster Abbey on the left; and
also like Hogarth, Canaletto's topography was distorted to suit his purpose. While his image provides an authoritative representation of a London
festival, the full expanse of the bridge is given excessive prominence, while
the haphazard disorder of pleasure boats on the river, and the chaos of the

procession itself, confer a sense of uncontrolled profusion, rather than orderly authority.

It was Canaletto who provided Victorian artists with the template for representing the Thames, but his successors chose to tackle their representations of the river very differently. The Thames itself, its bridges and its effect on London life and health, were an obsession of both Regency and Victorian society. No less than three new bridges were built across the Thames in the nineteenth century – Vauxhall (1816), Waterloo (1817), and Southwark (1819) – and others, such as Battersea and Blackfriars, were reconstructed later in the century. A number of artists followed in Canaletto's wake by commemorating the erection of new bridges, including Constable, whose *Opening of Waterloo Bridge (Whitehall Stairs June 18, 1817)* was exhibited at the Royal Academy in 1832, and George Chambers, who painted the opening of the new Blackfriars Bridge by Queen Victoria in 1869. The construction of the new embankments under the auspices of the Metropolitan Board of Works (founded in 1855) offered artists further access to the Thames, and in the last decades of the nineteenth century, literal renderings of iconic bridges were replaced by works that engaged with the poetry of the river itself.

The artist whose work epitomises the evocative qualities of the Thames was James McNeill Whistler. Whistler's fascination with the Thames appeared early in his career in a series of etchings he produced between 1859 and 1861 representing the banks of the river near Rotherhithe and Wapping, and in 1864 he exhibited an oil painting of *Wapping* at the Royal Academy. It was not coincidence that Whistler, a declared admirer of Hogarth, selected a section of the river that had particular associations – in this case, with what remained of London's industrial port. Whistler's painting of *Wapping* was criticised for its vulgarity, as it appeared to represent a prostitute cavorting with a port labourer in a part of London that was alien to the largely middle-class visitors to Royal Academy exhibitions. The Thames itself was also replete with associations of corruption, decay, and illness. The cholera epidemics of 1832, 1848–9, and 1853–4 were eventually traced to water supplies that were contaminated by untreated sewage pouring into the river. The so-called 'Great Stink' of 1858, the result of an excessively hot summer infecting the whole of London with pernicious odours from the river, was the final straw that stimulated the construction of embankments and sewers to clean up the Thames. It is significant that Whistler's Thames etching series was begun the year following the 'Great Stink', at a time when the river was seen by all as a source of disease and what one colourful commentator later referred to as 'urbo-morbus'.[11]

Whistler returned frequently to the Thames as a subject in paintings that were as evocative as they were indistinct (see Figure 7.1). The negative criticism of Whistler's Thames scenes was in no small part due to the perceived vulgarity of his choice of subject matter, as well as to his idiosyncratic style of representation. The terms critics used to condemn Whistler's Thames scenes were revealing: they were 'pictile nightmares', 'occult', 'freaks and fancies', and his painting style was said to consist of 'mud-colours', 'dirty black', 'dinginess', 'smears', and 'blotches'.[12] The language chosen by critics shows that the Thames as a repository of sewage and a stimulus for aberrant imagination was rarely far from the minds of Whistler's audiences. It was a Thames scene – *Nocturne in Black and Gold – The Falling Rocket* (1877) – that provoked John Ruskin to a criticism of Whistler that resulted in the artist taking out a libel action against the famous critic and engaging in a public trial in which he defended his idiosyncratic approach to art.[13] However, despite, or perhaps because of, the river's historic association with miasma and disease, Whistler clearly found beauty in the Thames, which he described vividly in his 'Ten O'clock Lecture' of 1885: 'And when the evening mist clothes the riverside with poetry, as with a veil, and the poor buildings lose themselves in the dim sky, and the tall chimneys become campanili, and the warehouses are palaces in the night ...'.[14] Following Whistler's poetic approach, Oscar Wilde, in his dialogue 'The Decay of Lying' (1891), was undoubtedly referring to Whistler when he argued that art had altered how people saw the world. Like Whistler, Wilde saw the beauty of the river as enhanced by the smog, the modern bridges, and the signs of waterway commerce:

> CYRIL.... you must show that Nature, no less than Life, is an imitation of Art. Are you prepared to prove that?
>
> VIVIAN. Certainly. Where, if not from the Impressionists, do we get those wonderful brown fogs that come creeping down our streets, blurring the gas-lamps and changing the houses into monstrous shadows? To whom, if not to them and their master, do we owe the lovely silver mists that brood over our river, and turn to faint forms of fading grace curved bridge and swaying barge? The extraordinary change that has taken place in the climate of London during the last ten years is entirely due to a particular school of Art ... To look at a thing is different from seeing a thing. Then, and then only, does it come into existence. At present, people see fogs, not because there are fogs, but because poets and painters have taught them the mysterious loveliness of such effects.[15]

Whistler's passion for representing the poetry of the Thames inspired many subsequent representations of the river, especially those by the French Impressionist artists, Claude Monet and Camille Pissarro, who both came to London in 1870–1 to avoid conscription into the Franco-Prussian War. Over the next few years, following several more trips to the city, Monet produced about 100 paintings of the Thames at different times of day.[16]

Sharing the sentiments of Wilde, Monet wrote to his art dealer, René Gimpel, 'I adore London ... But what I love more than anything is the fog.'[17] As Impressionists, Monet and Pissarro were committed to representing the world as the eye saw it, and the so-called 'London Impressionists' – a group of Whistler's admirers, led by Sickert – followed their French counterparts in claiming that their goal was to render modern urban life as faithfully as possible. Indeed, when a critic maligned Sickert for merely copying Degas in his depictions of East End music-hall interiors, Sickert responded contemptuously: 'It is surely unnecessary to go so far afield as Paris to find an explanation of the fact that a Londoner should seek to render on canvas a familiar and striking scene in the midst of the town in which he lives.'[18] Sickert's 'London Impressionist' colleagues, including Sidney Starr, Philip Wilson Steer, Theodore Roussel, and Paul Maitland, spent their time scouring London through the windows of hansom cabs for motifs that they could include in their art. Starr revisited Frith's Paddington Station in 1889, but his representation diverged sharply from Frith's in its avoidance of anecdote, and in the way in which its use of occluded perspective and feathery brushwork gave a sense of the momentary, quotidian quality of life as it passed on the railway platform. Starr was no doubt paying homage to the ideas of Baudelaire, whose *Le Peintre de la vie moderne* (1863) was well-known in Sickert's circle and challenged artists to seek the subject matter of modernity and to render it in a way that captured the pace and vigour of the contemporary world. Sickert's exclusively male group was adopting the position of Baudelairean *flâneurs* – visual consumers of the city who took pleasure in looking – and this position was one in which women tended to have an ambivalent position as objects of the gaze, rather than observers themselves. However, it is worth noting that in the representations of the London Impressionists, as well as those of many other artists who depicted London, women's presence in public life was acknowledged and depicted, if sometimes in a way that indicated ambivalence about their increasing visibility in urban public spaces.

But Sickert and his circle did not explicitly concern themselves with the gender dimensions of modern life. In a published dialogue between a 'Philistine' and 'Two Impressionists', Sickert provided a flavour of the type of modernity that his group sought and contrasted Frith's approach to London life with that of Whistler and the London Impressionists. Referring to a series of etchings Whistler produced of the streets near his Chelsea home, Sickert wrote: 'Whistler's Chelsea shops will tell the discoverers [1000 years hence] exactly what London was like at the end of the nineteenth century. You ask how Frith's "Derby Day" differs from our pictures. Simply because it is panorama. The eye could not possibly see all he depicts. We only paint that which we actually see.'[19] Sickert notably conceives of Frith's *Derby Day* – a forerunner to *The Railway Station* – as 'panoramic', providing the authoritative yet overly determined view that de Certeau saw as characteristic of a panoptic position. While Sickert and his followers claimed that their approach to London was experiential and sensitive to the nuances of modern life, this group also owed inspiration to writers such as Arthur Symons, Ernest Dowson, and Lionel Johnson, who themselves were avid followers of French Symbolism. Therefore, while these artists laid claim to the most accurate representations of London modernity, they also were aware of how much of this modernity was beneath the surface, rather than in the observable details of everyday life.

As Whistler's Thames scenes and Sickert's views of Camden Town and London music halls show, the pose of objectivity adopted by many artists during the Victorian period was frequently undermined by their choice of subject matter and by the means by which they chose to represent it. While Frith or Logsdail sanitised their views of London life, other artists wallowed in the darker side of the city. This propensity was fuelled by the exposés of the life of the London poor initiated by Henry Mayhew in his *London Labour and the London Poor* (first three volumes 1851; fourth volume 1861–2) and carried forward by other social reformers and a range of fiction writers from Dickens to George Sims. The latter's various novels of London life, including his most popular, *How the Poor Live* (1883), identify the city as a 'Povertyopolis',[20] filled with misery, starvation, and good people corrupted by a bad environment.

Following directly in the wake of Mayhew's work was the founding of the journal *The Graphic* by William Luson Thomas in 1869. *The Graphic* was a direct challenge to pictorial journals such as the *Illustrated London News*, which Thomas felt was riddled with second-rate illustrations produced by hack engravers. The very first issue of *The Graphic* (4 December 1869) included Luke Fildes's *Houseless and Hungry*, showing poverty-stricken men, women, and children huddling in a snowstorm outside a casual ward. The appearance of this illustration in a journal launched just before Christmas was no doubt intended to provoke the philanthropic instincts of the journal's readers. *The Graphic*'s illustrations were richly delineated and designed for discerning connoisseurs, and although their subject matter dwelt more on the brutal side of poverty than that of some contemporaneous journals, the beauty of the large, often double-page illustrations gave them a visual elegance that countered the repellent nature of some of their themes.

The same monochromatic approach to depicting London, and a similar engagement with the problematic aesthetics of poverty, were adopted by the French illustrator, Gustave Doré, when he teamed up with the journalist

Figure 9.7 Gustave Doré, 'Over London – By Rail', from *London: A Pilgrimage* (1872).

Blanchard Jerrold, to produce a series of scenes in *London: A Pilgrimage* (see Figure 9.7). This was first published in 12 individual instalments and then printed as a single volume with 180 engravings in 1872, and it served to update Ackermann's *Microcosm of London* of 1808, which had included voluminous illustrations by Thomas Rowlandson. To a certain extent, *London: A Pilgrimage* also followed the precedent of journalists such as George Sala in its engagement with a range of settings of London life. However, while Sala's work provided a positive spin on the variegated quality of London life, in *London: A Pilgrimage*, there was a disparity between Jerrold's buoyant text and many of Doré's sinister and gloomy illustrations. Jerrold began *London: A Pilgrimage* by declaring that he and Doré had scoured the corners of London 'in search of the Picturesque', and that they were not disappointed:

> It is impossible, indeed, to travel about London in search of the picturesque, and not accumulate a bulky store of matter after only a few mornings. The entrance to Doctor's Commons; Paternoster Row; the drinking fountain in the Minories surrounded with ragged urchins; the prodigious beadle at the Bank; the cows in the Mall, with the nurses and children round about … a London

cab stand; a pawnbroker's shop on Saturday; the turning out of the police at night; the hospital waiting room for outpatients: outside the casual ward ... London an ugly place indeed! We soon discovered that it abounded in delightful nooks and corners: in picturesque scenes and groups; in light and shade of the most attractive character.[21]

Jerrold's Sala-like proliferation of detail and eager tone suggest a London that was replete with visual excitement, but the 'casual ward' and pawn shop in his description lack the 'picturesque' implications contained in references to 'ragged urchins' and nurses with their charges. Jerrold's insistence that London is a picturesque place is redolent of the approach of artists like Logsdail, with his charming flower-girl, or Frith, with his crowded but mostly happy narrative incidents. This tone and manner contrast strongly with some of Doré's illustrations, many set at night and lingering on the gloom of decrepit London streets and the desperate underclass who inhabit them. Given that Doré and Jerrold were accompanied by policemen during their ramblings in the East End, they were not in a position to assume the insouciant invisibility of the *flâneur*, and Doré apparently made most of his engravings from memory, rather than from sketches. The eighteenth-century British artistic tradition of representing the poor as dishevelled, rather than filthy; rural, rather than urban; and contented, rather than despondent, was reversed here by Doré, whose illustrations of London are aesthetically pleasing but hardly picturesque. George Sims also struggled with the expectations that picturesque traditions would be followed in his various novels of the life of the London poor. In *How the Poor Live*, he addressed the question directly:

> The difficulty of getting that element of picturesqueness into these chapters which is so essential to success with a large class of English readers, becomes more and more apparent ... Rags, dirt, filth, wretchedness, the same figures, the same faces, the same old story of one room unfit for habitation, yet inhabited by eight or nine people, the same complaint of a ruinous rent, absorbing three-fourths of the toiler's weekly wage, the same shameful neglect by the owner of the property of all sanitary precautions, rotten floors, oozing walls, broken windows, crazy staircases, tileless roofs, and in and around the dwelling-place of hundreds of honest citizens the nameless abominations which could only be set forth were we contributing to the *Lancet* instead of the *Pictorial World*.[22]

The 'beauty' of scenes of poverty in illustrations by Doré and the *Graphic* artists, like the poetry of the stinking Thames, as depicted by Whistler; or the often unpicturesque modernity of urban streets as realised by Frith and his followers such as Hicks, on the one hand, and Sickert and his

Impressionist circle on the other; provide a multifarious and diverse set of visual responses to London during the Victorian period. Despite the radical difference in their approaches, all of these artists were attempting to engage with the real London but were doing so through its many imaginary manifestations. All of these artists also owed a debt to Hogarth, but they cast aside his satirical and moralising view, while drawing upon his use of specific London places and spaces for their modernity, lyrical resonance, and evocative visuality.

Notes

1 Roland Barthes, *Camera Lucida: Reflections on Photography*, trans. Richard Howard (London: Cape, 1982).
2 Michel de Certeau, *The Practice of Everyday Life*, trans. Steven Rendall (Berkeley: University of California Press, 1984).
3 William Powell Frith, *My Autobiography and Reminiscences*, 3 vols. (London: Richard Bentley and Son, 1887), Vol. II, pp. 121–2.
4 Anna Gruetzner Robins, *A Fragile Modernism: Whistler and His Impressionist Followers* (New Haven: Yale University Press, 2007), p. 152.
5 George Augustus Sala, *Twice round the Clock; or, The Hours of the Day and Night in London* (Leicester: Leicester University Press, 1971), p. 9.
6 *Ibid.*, p. 18.
7 Frith, *My Autobiography and Reminiscences*, Vol. I, p. 185.
8 *Ibid.*, p. 327.
9 Tom Taylor, *The Railway Station* (London: Henry Graves, 1865), p. 4.
10 Martin Meisel, *Realizations: Narrative, Pictorial, and Theatrical Arts in Nineteenth-Century England* (Princeton: Princeton University Press, 1983).
11 James Cantlie, *Degeneration amongst Londoners* (London: Field and Tuer, 1885), p. 24.
12 See the range of reviews quoted by James McNeill Whistler, *The Gentle Art of Making Enemies* (New York: Dover, 1967), pp. 299–323.
13 See Linda Merrill, *A Pot of Paint: Aesthetics on Trial in Whistler v. Ruskin* (Washington: Smithsonian Institution, 1992); and Shearer West, 'Laughter and the Whistler/Ruskin Trial', *Journal of Victorian Culture* 12.1 (Spring 2007), 42–63.
14 Whistler, *Gentle Art*, p. 144.
15 Oscar Wilde, 'The Decay of Lying', in *The Complete Works of Oscar Wilde* (Glasgow: HarperCollins, 2003), p. 1086.
16 John House, Petra ten-Doesschate Chu, and Jennifer Hardin, *Monet's London: Artist's Reflections on the Thames 1859–1914* (St Petersburg, FL: Museum of Fine Arts, 2005).
17 René Gimpel, *Diary of an Art Dealer*, trans. John Rosenberg (New York: Farrar, Straus, and Giroux, 1966), p. 73.
18 Walter Richard Sickert, 'The New English Art Club Exhibition', *The Scotsman* (24 April 1889), in *The Complete Writings on Art*, ed. Anna Gruetzner Robins (Oxford: Oxford University Press, 2000), p. 4.

19 Walter Richard Sickert, 'The Gospel of Impressionism', *Pall Mall Gazette* (21 July 1890), in *Complete Writings*, p. 76.
20 George R. Sims, *How the Poor Live* (London: Chatto and Windus, 1883), p. 14.
21 Gustave Doré and Blanchard Jerrold, *London: A Pilgrimage* (London: Grant, 1872), pp. viii–ix.
22 Sims, *How the Poor Live*, p. 29.

10

PETER BARRY

London in poetry since 1900

A novel or a play has to have a setting, but the same is not quite true of a poem. In a poem, the 'setting' may be little more than an implicit extrapolation from content. Where, for instance, is the speaker in Hopkins's anguished sonnet 'No worst, there is none'? We know that he wrote it in Dublin, but it contains no identifiable reference to the city, so it is not in any meaningful sense a 'Dublin' poem. At the opposite extreme are intensely localised poems, like Wordsworth's 'Tintern Abbey', Coleridge's 'Frost at Midnight', and Arnold's 'Rugby Chapel', which vicariously situate the reader in the precise locale in which the poetic meditation purports to be happening. A poem thus 'localised' is in every sense a 'London' (or wherever) poem. Between these two extremes are poems in which places in London are mentioned explicitly, but in a less sustained or interiorised way. This gives us a 'London' spectrum that runs from the implicit, through the explicit, to the fully 'localised'. The present chapter leaves aside the first category and focuses on the second and third. The topic might be treated in several different ways – generic and thematic approaches are possible, and traces of these will be evident in what follows, but a broadly chronological approach to London in post-1900 poetry has been adopted, as this foregrounds the pattern of successive shifts and developments in poetic technique – from Aestheticism to Imagism to Modernism and beyond – and at the same time shows the direct relationship between London poetry and London history (such as the presence in the poetry of the developing suburbs early in the century, the impact of the two world wars, and the effects of postwar patterns of immigration).

Early Modernist London

In Modernist writing a certain effect of 'blurring' is often crucial, including the blurring of one scene into another, of one historical time into another, of myth into history, and of history into myth. T. S. Eliot's *The Waste Land* and

Four Quartets, discussed later in this chapter, provide definitive examples of these techniques. In the age of 'proto-Modernism', however, during the decade before the First World War, when Yeats was living at 18 Woburn Buildings, and Pound in his Kensington bedsitter, London is often merely a repressed or implicit location in British poetry, for the poets usually seem to want to be somewhere else. Thus, in the poems of Pound's early collection *Lustra* (1916), the speaker, in his imagination, is usually anywhere but here and now – Thrace, Cana, Provence, China, for example. Though a more place-specific, Imagist aesthetic was already emergent, the dominant note was from way back in the Aestheticism of the 1890s, almost as if Ford Madox Ford's famous 1911 roll on the floor (in suppressed mirth at Pound's poetic archaisms) had never happened.

But the here-and-now of London is occasionally glimpsed in that early Poundian verse, sometimes as a deliberately bathetic descent from 'higher' things, as in 'Amities', where a friend is praised because 'You once discovered a moderate chop-house' – it was Bellotti's in Old Compton Street, Richard Aldington believed, which Pound thought 'the cheapest clean restaurant [in London] with a real cook'.[1] In this phase of Pound's work many of the London references concern women glimpsed in the street, in shops, in restaurants, or cafés: in 'The Garden', it is a woman seen walking in Kensington Gardens, 'Like a skein of loose silk blown against a wall' (p. 92); in 'Simulacra', it is a 'horse-faced lady of just the unmentionable age / [who] Walk[s] down Longacre reciting Swinburne to herself' (p. 117); and in 'Black Slippers: Bellotti', it is a closely observed lady at another table in the restaurant who has 'her little suede slippers off / with her white-stocking'd feet / Carefully kept from the floor by a napkin' (p. 115). The early Poundian London, then, is the locale of Hardyesque glimpses of intriguing but unattainable women, each represented by a single impressionistic trait that conjures up a version of the male-imagined feminine (the blue-stocking, the flirt, the middle-aged spinster, and so on). The minimalist poetic technique obviates subtlety or individualisation, but these figures are intended as indicative attributes of the locale – they embody 'Kensington' – rather than as fully interiorised or novelised human beings.

The 'London' a tourist might recognise tends not to feature prominently in twentieth-century London poetry, though there are a few exceptions, such as the Imagist John Gould Fletcher's poem 'The Unquiet Street' (1914), where the 'Omnibuses with red tail-lamps, / Taxicabs with shiny eyes' evoke an image reminiscent of the London Underground travel posters of the 1920s. The 'Imagist' element is intensified to provide the ending:

On rainy nights
It dully gleams
Like the cold tarnished scales of a snake:
And over it hang arc-lamps
Blue-white death-lilies on black stems.[2]

For another of the Imagists, F. S. Flint, in his poem 'London' (1914), the city is personified as a female figure of the dreamy pre-Raphaelite kind, 'shimmering through the curtain / of the silver birch' in the 'pale green sky' at sunset. Moon-glow moves across suburban lawns, the stars are glimpsed above the treetops, and the viewer longs to 'climb / into the branches / to the moonlit tree-tops' to cool his fevered imagination.[3] This has that same *fin de siècle* atmospheric air, and again, the highly coloured tonalities are reminiscent of contemporary posters encouraging the middle classes to buy mock-Tudor houses on the outer reaches of the Underground lines. But Flint is undeniably good at this kind of urban Georgianism; his props are London's characteristic trees – ash, poplar, silver birch, and the London plane – set among red chimney-pots, and the 'blue mist of after-rain'. Even when registering London's early experience of aerial bombardment in the Zeppelin raids (in 'Searchlight' of 1917), the threat seems curiously unthreatening. Thus, the searchlight, when the wakened sleeper looks out into the darkness, seems just one more element in an English scene that might have been painted by Paul Nash or Eric Ravilious, as 'The houses and gardens beneath / lie under snow / quiet and tinged with purple'.[4]

The black-out conditions imposed in London for the first time from autumn 1914, and the collective sense of trauma that grew as the war went on, are seen in Section VI of Ford Madox Ford's *Antwerp* (1914), which presents a radically altered atmosphere, as anxious crowds await the arrival of a troop train bringing back soldiers and wounded:

This is Charing Cross;
It is midnight;
There is a great crowd
And no light.
...
These are the women of Flanders.
They await the lost.
...
This is Charing Cross; it is past one of the clock;
There is very little light.
There is so much pain.[5]

The dreary flatness of pace and diction conveys its sense of despairing resignation, and this is unmistakably the poetry of Modernism, as the push against the pentameter gets underway, and the necessary job of bringing poetry closer to prose has begun to take effect.

London from armistice to war

The three-stage model described at the start can be extended by suggesting that 'London' poems, whether in the 'explicit' or 'localised' modes, often combine 'seeing' London and 'visioning' it. The former mode incorporates a documentary registering of the here-and-now, including actual street names and other local features, whereas the 'visioning' mode presents a historical or even mythological 'London' that tends to eclipse the present. The London of *The Waste Land*, for instance, frequently juxtaposes London seen and London visioned, and much of its power derives from this 'over-mapping' process. Hence, the poem incorporates what might be called Eliot's personal geography. At the time of writing, he was working in the Foreign and Colonial Department of Lloyds Bank, then situated behind the church of St Mary Woolnoth in Lombard Street. Each morning he arrived at London Bridge Station, and walked across the Bridge into the City among thousands of other commuters, feeling that he was entering a city of the dead:

> Unreal city,
> Under the brown fog of a winter dawn,
> A crowd flowed over London Bridge, so many,
> I had not thought death had undone so many.[6]

The passage continues by tracing his journey 'up the hill and down King William Street, / To where St Mary Woolnoth kept the hours / With a dead sound on the final stroke of nine' (lines 66–8). All the streets mentioned in *The Waste Land* radiate from Lombard Street, where Eliot spent his working days from 1917 to 1925. In the era of steam and coal, the light was often murky or lurid, and references such as 'the brown fog of a winter dawn' and 'the violet hour' are frequent, and reinforce the air of Dantesque gloom. The poem also embodies knowledge of the minutely stratified social-class geography of London, such as the precise social status of Thames-side towns like Richmond and Kew, which the Metropolitan Underground Railway had made an affordable day-trip for shop assistants or clerks. Likewise, the social difference between the Cannon Street Hotel and, say, the Dorchester underpins the poem's pervasive awareness of London's social geography.

Eliot's only escape from the commercial 'unreal city' of the present is via the 'visioned' London of the past – a cerebral, partly imaginary place overlaid onto the present-day cityscape – he *looks at* the Thames, for instance, but *sees* 'Elizabeth and Leicester beating oars' (lines 279–80). This other

London is centred upon the many post-Reformation churches in the City of London. Few medieval London churches survived the Great Fire of 1666, so fifty were rebuilt by Christopher Wren, and for Eliot, these 'new' churches of the seventeenth century embodied the humanist Anglican theocracy of John Donne and Lancelot Andrewes, representatives of Eliot's period of ideal integration between intellect, emotion, and the senses, before the 'dissociation of sensibility set in', as described in his 1921 essay 'The Metaphysical Poets'. Many of these churches were on restricted sites, with large, clear-glass windows and white-painted walls to avoid perpetual semi-darkness. With the pulpit as main focus, enlightening discourse – rather than mysterious ritual – is emphasised, characteristics seen in Wren's church on Lower Thames Street, 'where the walls / Of Magnus Martyr hold / Inexplicable splendour of Ionian white and gold' (lines 263–5). Eliot's note adds that this 'is to my mind one of the finest among Wren's interiors', indicating that he is in the habit of visiting these churches, presumably in his lunch hours. *The Waste Land*, then, is a sustained example of a poem that combines the two modes of 'London-seen' and 'London-visioned' writing.

The supreme example of a 'London-seen' poem, on the other hand, is Louis MacNeice's *Autumn Journal* (1939). The urge behind this work, and sometimes even the tone, is similar to that of the 'Mass Observation' movement of the late 1930s, for a 'journal' is not so private and purely personal a document as a diary.[7] The sequence was written in the build-up to and aftermath of the Munich Crisis (the agreement was signed on 30 September 1938); the speaker returns to London after the holidays: 'And so to London and down the ever-moving / Stairs / Where a warm wind blows the bodies of men together / And blows apart their complexes and cares'.[8] The neon whisky advert in which 'Johnny Walker moves his / Legs like a cretin' seems like the only escape, and in the Lyons Corner House 'the carpet-sweepers / Advance between the tables after crumbs / Inexorably, like a tank battalion'. Arriving at Parliament Hill Fields the speaker notes with foreboding preparations for the building of anti-aircraft batteries. This is the spot from which the whole of London seems spread before the viewer, with St Paul's visible in the distance, the place where you are most likely to be struck with a sense of the vulnerability of the city to air attack – here the narrator in Wells's *The War of the Worlds* (1898) gazes out across the ruins of London, and notices 'a huge gaping cavity' in the western side of the dome of St Paul's.[9] Such are the speaker's fears as:

> Hitler yells on the wireless,
> The night is damp and still
> And I hear dull blows on wood outside my window;

> They are cutting down the trees on Primrose Hill.
> The wood is white like the roast flesh of chicken,
> Each tree falling like a closing fan;
> ...
> They want the crest of this hill for anti-aircraft,
> The guns will take the view
> And searchlights probe the heavens for bacilli
> With narrow wands of blue.   (p. 113)

The sequence ends with a Christmas visit to Barcelona, a city that shows London its future, already enduring black-out and bombing, with people sleeping in the Metro. 'Tonight we sleep / On the banks of the Rubicon – the die is cast' (p. 153).

In contrast to the secular and demotic tone of the Mass Observation data and MacNeice's *Autumn Journal*, much of the writing that portrays aspects of wartime London uses the highly coloured Christian apocalyptic rhetoric that became one of the dominant strains of 1940s poetry. Thus, David Gascoyne's 'Ecce homo' (*c.* 1943) evokes a blitzed city in terms of the crucifed Christ: 'Behind His lolling head the sky / Glares like a fiery cataract',[10] and Edith Sitwell's 'Still Falls the Rain (The Raids, 1940. Night and Dawn)' begins:

> Still falls the Rain –
> Dark as the world of man, black as our loss –
> Blind as the nineteen hundred and forty nails
> Upon the Cross.[11]

By contrast, J. F. Hendry's 'London before Invasion: 1940' is one of many poems that seem to be a kind of prospective 'After London', imagining the city's long history finally ended; the poem begins:

> Walls and buildings stand here still, like shells.
> Hold them to the ear. There are no echoes even
> Of the seas that once were.[12]

T. S. Eliot's London Blitz episode in Part 2 of 'Little Gidding', the last of the *Four Quartets* (1943), his four-part philosophical and religious sequence, supremely exemplifies the 'localised' London poem of the 'visioned' rather than the 'seen' kind. The effect, again, is overtly Christianised, for example in the description of a bomber as the 'dark dove with a flickering tongue', identified by Martin Scofield as a kind of negative version of the Holy Spirit.[13] The vividness of the wartime scene – the 'disfigured street', 'between three districts whence the smoke arose' – is overlain with the Dantesque scenario of the 'familiar compound ghost' who falls into step and walks with the speaker in the eerie light of the burning city, one of several urban moments

in Eliot's work when a half-recognised, supernumerary presence material-
ises. London, for Eliot, was always a city of such ghostly *flâneurs*, like the
figure encountered outside the church of Saint Mary Woolnoth – 'There I
saw one I knew, and stopped him, crying: "Stetson! / You who were with me
in the ships at Mylae!"' (lines 69–70).

Between *The Waste Land* and *Four Quartets* Eliot had moved further
away from 'seeing' London towards 'visioning' it: in the former we have
geography – named streets, and buildings like St Mary Woolnoth, London
Bridge, King William Street, and so on, counterbalanced by the moments
when the 'unreal city' intervenes (visionary episodes like Elizabeth and
Leicester beating oars). In the later text, by contrast, there are residual
glimpses of 'the driven wind that sweeps the gloomy hills of London' ('Burnt
Norton', III), and of the anxious-making moment when 'an underground
train, in the tube, stops too long between stations' ('East Coker', III), but
mostly, London is implicit or 'unreal', so that when the 'dead patrol' passage
begins 'amid three districts whence the smoke arose', we are not told which
three districts they are, or in what direction the trodden pavement takes
them. Of course, we are not meant to ask, for the passage intends to come
out of the loco-specific and into a wider philosophical space.

This is also true of H. D.'s London wartime sequence *Trilogy* (1944–6).
The first part, 'The Walls Do Not Fall', uses (like Hendry's poem, quoted
earlier) the image of bombed-out buildings whose outer walls remain standing around an empty shell within, beginning with a segment that vividly
delineates the effects of the London Blitz, in which emergencies or explosions in particular streets were referred to in news bulletins as 'incidents':

> An incident here and there,
> and rails gone (for guns)
> from your (and my) old town square:
> …
> The shrine lies open to the sky,
> the rain falls, here, there …
> …
> – we pass on
> to another cellar, to another sliced wall,
> where poor utensils show
> like rare objects in a museum
> …
> Over us, Apocryphal fire[14]

This is Section 1, and the image of the unfallen walls returns in Section 43 at
the end of this first part of the trilogy, but the forty-one sections in between
are entirely concerned with H.D.'s personal psychodrama, which seems to

carry on regardless of the war, and she comes close to welcoming the outer turmoil as an emblem of, or spur to, the longed-for transformation from within. The temptation to see fire and destruction as 'apocryphal' seems irresistible to the poets of the day – 'what is War', she asks in the second part, 'to Birth, to Change, to Death?' (p. 550).

However, when a dream is recorded in the second part, 'Tribute to the Angels', we perhaps see the impinging of the threat of destruction within which Londoners then led their daily lives:

> I was talking casually
> with friends in the other room,
> when we saw the outer hall
> grow lighter – then we saw where the door was,
> there was no door
> (this was a dream, of course)   (p. 562)

The dream is triggered by 'the phosphorescent face / of my little clock' by the bedside.

Near the beginning of the final part of the trilogy, 'The Flowering of the Rod', local reality is abandoned altogether – 'leave the smouldering cities below / (we have done all we could) / ... and mount higher / to love – resurrection' (p. 578).

London 'now in the mind indestructible': the 1940s and 1950s

London is also 'visioned' more than 'seen' in such key twentieth-century Modernist texts of the postwar period as Ezra Pound's *Pisan Cantos* (1948) and David Jones's *The Anathemata* (1952). In the *Pisan Cantos* we are given a kaleidoscopic reprise of the London of *Lustra* in a series of emblematic glimpses of the writers of that period – in Canto LXXIV the illustrious dead, the 'Lordly men to the earth o'ergiven', as 'Fordie', 'Bill', and 'Jim' (that is, Ford Madox Ford, W. B. Yeats, and James Joyce) are recollected.[15] The recalled *mots justes* tossed out by an idealised community hammering out an aesthetic are a kind of challenge to the shallower sensibilities of the present. In Canto LXXXI, the heady days are recalled when the shock-troops of Modernism went over the top to break the pentameter ('that was the first heave', p. 518). But these moments float in air, and seem rooted to no palpable urban or social specificities. There are just the briefest of moments when London is seen rather than visioned, as at the end of LXXX:

> And the Serpentine will look just the same
> and the gulls be as neat on the pond
> and the sunken garden unchanged   (p. 516)

But as if to emphasise that the survival of this 'seen' fabric is not the point, the text continues 'and God knows what else is left of our London / my London, your London'. Even when an address is mentioned ('18 Woburn Buildings', Yeats's address for twenty-four years, in Canto LXXXII, for example) it is merely to crystallise the moment of a visionary remark, for London merges into an amalgam of several different vital and idealised city spaces. Wagadu and the city of Dioce in Canto LXXIV, for instance, coalesce into a single essence as the city 'now in the mind indestructible':

> 4 times was the city rebuilded, Hooo Fasa
> Gassir, Hooo Fasa dell' Italia tradita
> now in the mind indestructible, Gassir, Hooo Fasa
> With the four giants at the four corners
> and four gates mid-wall Hooo Fasa
> and a terrace the colour of stars   (p. 430)

A similarly 'visioned' version of London is presented in David Jones's epic *The Anathemata*, especially in Parts IV and V, 'Redriff' and 'The Lady of the Pool', where we see a 'London-of-the-mind' portrayed with vigour in two sustained dramatic monologues. In the first, the speaker is a Rotherhithe ('Redriff') shipwright who is asked by a captain to do a rushed repair job, so that he can get out of port fast and save on harbour dues. The time seems to be some point in the nineteenth century when Jones's maternal grandfather, Eb(enezer) Bradshaw, was in business as a 'mast maker', and the section is loosely based on family anecdotes about such an incident.[16] The shipwright goes mental (as the phrase is) at the idea that he would rush or skimp any job, and the three-and-a-half pages of 'Redriff' are his shocked tirade at politely being asked 'would he expedite' the job 'for a tidy consideration' (that is, for a generous tip).[17] The answer is that he would never do such a thing, 'Not for a gratis load of the sound teak in / Breaker's Yard ... Not if the Trinity Brethren ... / stood caps in hand for a month of Sundays' (pp. 118–19). His job is to make joints 'as smooth as a *peach* of a cheek' (p. 120). If the job was to mend the 'Rootless Tree' of the world, 'I'ld take m'time' and do the job properly. He ends with a resounding message to the captain: 'tell him – tell the old Jason ... he's got / till the Day o' Doom / to sail the bitter seas o' the world!' (p. 121). The sense of place is vivid throughout, and what Gerard Manley Hopkins called 'the gear and tackle' of trade is solidly and accurately rendered.

In the following section, 'The Lady of the Pool', the monologue is spoken by a lavender-seller along the wharves to another incoming captain, but this time, though the locale is the same, the scene has jumped back to the Middle Ages. Again, though, the germ of the passage – a much longer episode of forty pages – is a family anecdote. The time is late summer, and as Jones's own note explains 'When, in August, lavender was cried in the street, my maternal grandmother was saddened by the call, because she said it meant that summer was almost gone' (p. 125). The opening rhetorical question firmly sets the piece in quantifiable London geography – 'Did ever he walk the twenty-six wards of the city, within and extra [inside and outside the walls]?' (p. 124), and the female 'voice-over' launches into a sustained monologue, the voice being that of a figure like Joyce's Anna Livia Plurabelle, who embodies the Liffey in *Finnegans Wake*, or the Wagnerian Rhine-daughters, who are transformed in *The Waste Land* into the Thames-daughters. The writing has Jones's typically dense, multilayered historical and mythological referencing, many of the pages half filled or more with his meticulous annotation. Unlike those of *The Waste Land*, these notes are an integral part of the poem, not an afterthought, and text and notes work as a composite, two rivers flowing in parallel to the same destination. The effect is exhilarating, and the world evoked is that of the street-wise Jacobean city comedies of Jonson, Marston, and Middleton. Yet it is all, it must be said, far more of a visionary construct than a representation of a mundane day-to-day place seen and recorded.

Psychogeographical London

Under this category we can place a number of big-scale London texts originating from the 1970s, like Iain Sinclair's *Lud Heat* (1975), Allen Fisher's *Place* (1976), and Aidan Dun's *Vale Royal* (1995). The smaller-scale prototype of that kind of writing is perhaps Lee Harwood's 'Cable Street', which appeared in his early Fulcrum Press book *The White Room* in 1968. Though it is not on the scale of later works in the genre (it prints at eight or nine pages) this poem is the pioneer work of psychogeography, dated 1964, when Harwood was living in the East End, near Cable Street in the heart of the Jewish (and later Bangladeshi) East End, and scene of the infamous 'Battle of Cable Street' in October 1936, when a consortium of left-wing protesters prevented a Police-assisted Fascist march along Cable Street. The poem contains a mixture of elements that became familiar in the 1970s, including loose, diary-style jottings, the incorporation of 'extra-textual' documentation, and the *vérité* scenes of the inner city reminiscent of the style of the Beat and New York poets:

> Walk down nearby alley Sunday afternoon. Hardcase men in blue suits and white shirts. Ford Zephyrs and Zodiacs round the corner. all standing round in the sun, outside jukebox cafés. smell of stuff hits you one end and by the time you're half way down you're high too.[18]

That verse paragraph could have been Allen Ginsberg or Frank O'Hara, but after a number of these, the piece moves into a phase in which the past is overlaid on the present, especially the recent past of 'Hunger marchers, mid '30s, columns of grim pale men silent' and 'May 1926. General Strike. armed food convoy moving up East India Dock Road and Commercial Road' (p. 143). Interwoven is a lyrical account of a gay love affair, the contrasts in tone within the poem deliberately bizarre and extreme:

> Sea noises outside
> and you in my arms
> among the cool milk sheets
> distant car lights sliding across the room
> high tide and the moon boats
> swaying in the night
> wind   (p. 145)

There is much historical material, yet a sense of the lived present moment is also vivid – 'standing grey faced at the window – no flowers, no blue skies. Peeling off my overalls after the night-shift of cleaning out office blocks' (p.147). This is a remarkable poem, both for the then novelty of its methods, and because of the progeny it would beget in the 1970s.

Iain Sinclair includes 'Cable Street' as one of the two Harwood poems in his *Conductors of Chaos* anthology (1996), and this may be taken as a kind of tribute to Harwood's precedence in the psychogeographical method. This is not the place to try to define psychogeography in detail: Merlin Coverley quotes Guy Debord's 'oft-repeated "definition"', and that must suffice here; it is the 'study of the specific effects of the geographical environment, consciously organised or not, on the emotions and behaviours of individuals'.[19] In his *Lud Heat* of 1975 Sinclair produced its definitive text, so far as poetry is concerned, rendering his section of the London East End as both 'visioned' and 'seen', both 'historicised' and 'mythologised', both realised and fantasised. The mix is like a scaling up of 'Cable Street'; there are the documentary denotations, the personalised lyric fragments, the scientific bits, the musings and the wry observations of the university graduate doing menial work. What Sinclair adds is the occult and the more remote histories (both have Blake, but Harwood goes back no further than that).

Another major work in the psychogeographical mode is Allen Fisher's *Place* sequence (which is about South London), where the technological materials are much emphasised, and the incorporation of documentary extra-textual elements (letters, extracts from historical documents, etc.) is very marked. Personalised lyric observations are incorporated, and the ambulatory emphasis is taken over from the Situationists – movement across the city in Fisher's sequence is not exactly random, but it is directed by a 'drift' or *dérive* ('a technique of transient passage through varied ambiances')[20] which takes it across the usual flows of commerce or traffic, according to the self-conscious purposelessness of the *flâneur*, the private obsessions of the 'walker-stalker', the agenda of the visionist, who is (for instance) following the track of an underground river via streets that ignore its presence, or tracing the line of a long-buried field, whose original contours are still marked by the contours of the street pattern.

A final work in this psychogeographical category is Aidan Dun's sequence *Vale Royal* (1995), the author's name for the valley of the Fleet River, which runs down from Highgate ponds in North London, through Camden Town, and into the Thames, for the most part buried underground. Dun sees the district of King's Cross as the focus of poetic lives and energies, with its epicentre in St Pancras Old Church, built on the site of the oldest Christian church in Britain, supposedly dating from the third century. The church is situated behind St Pancras Station, close to the British Library. Dun's 'Sun Child' persona sees neither, for he resolutely prefers the 'visioned' London to the seen:

> I passed through a more fluid city.
> I broke up the imprint of all familiar places,
> shutting my eyes to the boredom of modern contours.[21]

Postcolonial London

The London poetry of postwar writers of Afro-Caribbean origin offers a unique insider–outsider view of the place. London makes fleeting appearances in two of the major works of the older generation, Edward Brathwaite's *The Arrivants: A New World Trilogy* (1973), and Derek Walcott's *Omeros* (1990). Brathwaite's epic considers the whole phenomenon of Caribbean diaspora in a vast kaleidoscopic text. The evocations are impressionistic with a minimum of scene-setting: 'In London, Undergrounds are cold. / The train rolls in from darkness / with our fears // and leaves a lonely soft metallic clanking / in our ears', but the growth of racial antagonism as the 1950s progress is noted with quiet precision; there is prejudice against letting rooms to the recent arrivants, and in this period many London buses had white drivers and black conductors, but:

> The chaps who drive the City buses
> don't like us clipping for them much;
> in fact, make quite a fuss.
> Bus strikes loom soon.

The men who lever ale
in stuffy woodbine pubs
don't like us much.
No drinks there soon.

Or broken bottles.
The women who come down
to open doors a crack
will sometimes crack

your fingers if you don't
watch out. Sorry!
Full! Not even Bread
And breakfast soon[22]

Walcott's *Omeros* is a modern, postcolonial Homeric epic of global reach, the first two and last two of its seven books set in St Lucia, the third in Africa, and the fourth in the USA. In the fifth book the itinerant narrator reaches London from Lisbon, both cities seen as former imperial capitals. A battered ancient 'in a bargeman's black greatcoat', he passes the imperial statuary of Trafalgar Square in a London still insistent on its role as the centre of empire ('It was summer. London rustled with pride'). Walcott's wanderer/seafarer figure gravitates toward the river and has 'curled up on a bench beneath the Embankment wall'. The imperial history on view seems like a curse over the city, which is seen as shackled and yoked by its own empire, the Thames like a slave-collar round the city's neck:

> He saw London gliding with the Thames around its neck
> like a barge which an old brown horse draws up a canal
> if its yoke is time. From here he could see the dreck
> under the scrolled skirts of statues, the grit in the stone lions'
> eyes; he saw under everything an underlying grime
> that itched in the balls of rearing bronze stallions,
> how the stare of somnolent sphinxes closed in time
> to the swelling bells of 'cities all the floure'
> petalling the spear-railed park where a couple suns
> near the angled shade of All-Hallows by the Tower,
> as the tinkling Thames drags by in its ankle-irons[23]

The passage ends with 'black iron trees' and 'a gliding fog hides the empires: London, Rome, Greece' (p. 196). Walcott's Thames may be linked with the visionary Thames that tops and tails Conrad's *Heart of Darkness*.[24] But there are many other echoes too, and the whole passage is an ironic counterpart to William Dunbar's 'In Honour of the City of London', with its refrain 'London, thou art the flour of Cities all'.[25] Walcott's speaker, like

Dunbar, notes the swans and their gracefulness ('the sinuous swans on the Serpentine'), but only to make a despairing point about his people – 'The swans are royally protected, but in whose hands / are the black crusts of our children?' (p. 197). For them he sees only 'Dark future down darker street'.

The London scene is less bleakly rendered in the work of another poet of the older generation, James Berry, in *Lucy's Letters and Loving* (1982). Berry writes these two sequences of poems in the persona of 'Lucy', who has emigrated to London from the West Indies and writes home a series of letters to her friend Leela; the tone is lively and there are plenty of regrets: 'Things harness me here. I long / for we labrish bad. Doors / not fixed open here' ('labrish' is a Jamaican word for chat or gossip). Their way of life is changing; her husband gets into the car to go for a newspaper, and hardly ever goes for a walk, and they never look at the sea or up at the moon. When he glimpses the moon his sarcastic response is 'Good Laad, you sure / it not Flyin' Saucer?'. On the other hand, sexist role-stereotyping is reduced, and though he's as mad as ever about cricket, 'he wash a dirty dish now, me dear'. The sense of the self changing in the new environment is vividly conveyed – there is nostalgic regret for the old self lost, and curiosity about the new self forming, and the result is that when she goes home for a visit 'I'm here an' not here.'[26]

A similar sense of bi-culturality and transition is crucial in the work of John Agard, a Guyanese poet of a younger generation (born 1949) who came to Britain in 1977. In Agard's postcolonial London, the cultural divide seems more of a gulf, but the tone is witty and upbeat, as in his well-known 'Listen Mr Oxford Don', which begins:

> Me not no Oxford don
> me a simple immigrant
> from Clapham Common
> I didn't graduate
> I immigrate.[27]

The immigrant asserts his rights over the Standard English that contributes to his social disadvantage ('I don't need no axe / to split/ up yu syntax / I don't need no hammer / to mash / up yu grammar'). But linguistic war is not the same as real war, and the poem makes its point about the social divide primarily through humour, as does 'Finders Keepers', which again uses the naïve persona (like Berry's Lucy) that is common in West Indian satirical forms:

> This morning on the way to Charing Cross
> I found a stiff upper lip
> lying there on the train seat

Rather than handing it in to the lost-and-found he decides 'Come with me to the Third World / You go thaw off' (p. 45).

The London social and racial divide is treated much more uncompromisingly in the early work of Linton Kwesi Johnson (born in Jamaica, 1952) in lyrics like 'Five Nights of Bleeding', which record 'five nights of horror an of bleeding / broke glass / cold blades as sharp as the eyes of hate'.[28] Published originally in his collection *Inglan is a Bitch* (1980) is 'Sonny's Lettah (Anti-Sus Poem)', probably Linton Kwesi Johnson's best-known piece. Instead of the easy-going musings of Berry's *Lucy's Letters*, this is a letter home addressed from 'Brixtan Prison / Jebb Avenue / Landan south-west two / Inglan' (p. 25), to 'Dear mama' and telling her that her son Jim, whom he'd promised to look out for, had been stopped by the police at a bus-stop (on 'Sus' or suspicion, as the much-hated law of the day allowed), and that the speaker, intervening as they beat him up, had killed a policeman and is now serving a life sentence in jail. Other poems commemorate the New Cross Fire of January 1981, when thirteen black youths at a party were killed in a suspected racially motivated arson attack ('New Craas Massahkah', p. 38), and the Brixton riots, in April of the same year ('Di Great Insohreckshan', p. 43), the latter said to have been the most violent disturbances in London in the century, and sparked by several days of relentless operation of 'Sus' laws. Inevitably, then, London in poetry at the height of the Thatcher era reflected the social polarisation and confrontation that were so much the climate of those times.

London *noir*

Something reminiscent of the film *noir* atmosphere of the psychogeographers is seen in an important large-scale work with a London setting: Val Warner's 1998 Carcanet collection *Tooting Idyll*, containing the sequence 'Mary Chay', which is about seventy pages long. It tells the story (the back cover tells us) of 'a murder in Victoria [London] in 1994, seen from many viewpoints and deploying a variety of forms'. The victim had bought a novel in Waterstone's bookshop, then walked to the tube station, wearing the white scarf with which she was shortly to be strangled. In the re-enactment of her last journey, and employing the *noir*-ish motif of doubling, the victim's role is played by a Woman Police Officer, who walks through London streets now transformed from the mundane into the nightmarish terrain in which a killer's eye selects its victim:

> Walk out of Waterstone's, still
> on stage, a copy of
> Carey's *Oscar and Lucinda* under my arm,

like her. Neutral eyes gun for me –
...
I'm her
to a T in the November evening's
all-consuming murk
...
Last night, I dreamed this
bleeding walk
...
Charing Cross Road, where they watch me – duck
And weave across Cambridge Circus, anonymous. Silver Moon
Bookshop, where she maybe window-shopped
...
sucked underground down Leicester Square tube,
with one more safe exit before the last[29]

The murdered Mary Chay, eventually traced by dental records back to her Manchester home town, lives an unattached metropolitan life; nobody has reported her missing (like the unidentified victims of the 1987 King's Cross fire, the last of whom was not identified until 2004). The police appeal for information produces nothing, and the *Sun* newspaper sets up a 'Murdered Mary Hotline' (p. 101) so that anyone with information can call in: the 'dead ash blonde' is thirty, 'workless', and 'from Wembley Park'. Mary Chay, en route to her soirée, evokes Eliot's Prufrock, walking 'Streets that follow like a tedious argument / Of insidious intent'.[30] The poem registers the lure of London, a place that people move away from but never really go beyond – 'From where I never leave, I walk away' – as the beautiful end-line of this poem puts it. The poem embodies a notion of 'place' expanded to include ambience, mind-set, situation, and culture, rolled into one and considered as an entity that is more than just the wrap-around or starting context of a poem. *Tooting Idyll* is a masterpiece of contemporary London writing deserving of wider recognition.

Liquid London

A marked tendency in London poetry is its long-standing gravitational pull toward the Thames – many 'London' poems are actually 'Thames' poems, and many of these have been collected in Anna Adams's anthology *Thames: An Anthology of River Poems* (1999). There is a powerful fusion of identity between a city and the river that flows right through it (Dublin and the Liffey, Paris and the Seine, Budapest and the Danube). Such rivers become both a major barrier (creating distinct identities and communities on either bank), and a major highway, and hence a formative influence on industry and commerce. In such cities, the river is the most evident natural force in the urban environment, and the misty Thames is irresistible to writers of all kinds, if only as a frame for other themes (social, political, personal, and so on): George Barker opens 'Battersea Park' (1940) with this stanza:

> Now it is November and mist wreathes the trees,
> The horses cough their white blooms in the street,
> Dogs shiver and boys run; the barges on the Thames
> Lie like Leviathans in the fog; and I meet
> A world of lost wonders as I loiter in the haze
> Where fog and sorrow cross my April days.[31]

Here the 'locative' elements are just the prelude to the more personal content of the poem, and it never quite lives up to the unforgettable loco-specificity of its opening scenic panorama. For Barker the London details are just 'setting' – he is thinking *within*, but not *with* London. Contrast that with Thomas Hardy's 1911 London poem 'Beyond the Last Lamp (near Tooting Common)', where 'two linked loiterers', 'walking slowly, whispering sadly' are encountered 'beyond the last lamp', as the rain 'descended darkly, drip, drip, drip'. The dreariness of the scene, and the despondent couple who 'seemed lovers', stick in his memory for thirty years (its original title when first published in *Harper's* in December 1911 was 'Night in a Suburb'). Hardy's poem works because the misery depicted is not his own but others', so it can only be rendered externally, and this means that the 'watery way' and the 'lamplight's yellow glance' are not just setting or ground – they are what the poem is.[32]

A similar balance is aimed for in Andrew Motion's four-part poem 'Fresh Water – In Memory of Ruth Haddon'. The dedicatee was one of the victims in the August 1989 Thames disaster when the pleasure-boat *Marchioness* sank after colliding with the dredger *Bowbelle* near the Canon Street Railway Bridge. In a series of episodes, the poem traces the Thames from its source to Tower Bridge, where the context of a family visit enables him to explain, to the reader by proxy, and to his children within the simulacrum of the poem, that 'the river starts many miles inland / and changes and grows, changes and grows, until it arrives here, / London, where we live, then winds past Canary Wharf // (which they've done in school) and out to sea'. It continues:

> Afterwards we lean on the railings outside a café. It's autumn.
> The water is speckled with leaves, and a complicated tangle of junk
> bumps against the embankment wall: a hank of bright grass,
> a rotten bulrush stem, a fragment of dark polished wood.

> One of the children asks if people drown in the river, and I think
> of Ruth, who was on the *Marchioness*.[33]

He recalls a survivor's account, and the detail that bursting at last into the air 'he felt that he was a baby again', and then imagines 'Ruth swimming back upstream, her red velvet party dress / flickering around her heels as she twists through the locks / and dreams round the slow curves, slithering on for miles', and eventually, passing the 'plastic wrecks and weedy trolleys', reaching the 'small wet mouth of the earth' that is the source of the Thames (pp. 150–1). The underlying images of 'change and growth', birth and death, seem to map naturally onto the idea of rivers, so much so as to risk descent into cliché, but the poem avoids the drop, so to speak, because, again, the setting is as much subject as background.

The Adams anthology also contains U. A. Fanthorpe's notable 'Rising Damp', a prize-winning poem in the Arvon International Poetry Competition of 1980 and included in her *Standing To* (1982). The poem is not about the Thames, but about London's many 'lost rivers' – that is, tributaries like the Fleet and the Walbrook, now buried beneath the streets. The poem sees these rivers as the buried subconscious of the city, 'the currents that chiselled the city', now forgotten, except when 'They return spectrally after heavy rain', in a kind of return of the repressed. In some places above their courses there is an increase in bronchitis statistics and paranormal sightings ('A silken / Slur haunts dwellings by shrouded / Watercourses, and is taken for the footing of the dead').[34] The line just quoted refers to a detail in the poem's sourcebook, Nicholas Barton's *The Lost Rivers of London* (1992), which records that the sound of nearby underground movements of water, sometimes described as being like the swishing of a lady's long gown along the floor, results in legends of hauntings.

A short 'Thames' lyric that exemplifies what can be called 'urban double visioning' is Jeremy Hooker's 'City Walking, 1', part of a longer work called *Groundwork*, and reprinted in the Adams anthology. In the poem, the speaker is in Battersea, just south of the river, visiting St Mary's Church, where Blake was married to Catherine Boucher, and where Turner came to paint the riverside scene at Chelsea on the opposite bank. The poet is shown round by one of the local parishioners, his own life deeply entwined with this church. 'The old man / is full of stories'; the poem continues:

> And here (our guide shows us
> the vestry window) Turner
> sat to paint clouds
> and sunsets over the water –
> where we can see tower blocks,

> luxury flats, a marina,
> a power station
> that drives the Underground. (pp. 68–9)

In the 'double visioning' of this poem, past and present terrain are viewed simultaneously, like superimposed photographs, as poet and guide look out of the vestry window together, and see both the clouds and sunsets that Turner saw, and the tower blocks, marina, and power station that now occupy the ground. The best loco-specific writing often seems to do this, combining the modes described earlier as 'seeing' and 'visioning'.

It is worth asking, in conclusion, whether there is any quantitative difference between studying 'London in poetry' and studying any other city. Would all such studies merely be facets of a broader field entitled, say, 'Poetry and the City'? Further, is that topic itself just a sub-branch of a yet broader stratum called 'The Poetry of Place', or 'Poetry and Place', or (more recently) 'Poetry and Space' or 'Poetry and Spatiality'? Certainly, from about 1995 onward, there has been an enormous growth in the academic field now usually called 'Literary London' or 'London in Literature'. It is strongly interdisciplinary in character, closely affiliated to the fields of 'area studies' or literary 'place' studies, and to that theorisation of notions of the city and urban space that has been a phenomenon of the past two decades.[35] A range of London books of the anthology or survey type is beginning to emerge,[36] there are MA and undergraduate courses on the topic, as well as specialised journals and conferences and the growth of a new interdisciplinary outlook and methodology that derives from recent theorisations of urban space.[37] Few other places show evidence of a growth in academic infrastructure comparable to London's, and the cultural resonances and deposits of London undoubtedly give it a unique national and international standing and a unique hold on our cultural imagination.

Notes

1 Ezra Pound, *Selected Poems* (London: Faber, 1959), p. 106; further references to Pound's shorter poems are to this edition. On the identification of the chophouse, see Peter Brooker, *A Student's Guide to the Selected Poems of Ezra Pound* (London: Faber, 1979), p. 99.
2 John Gould Fletcher, 'The Unquiet Street', in *Imagist Poetry*, ed. Peter Jones (Harmondsworth: Penguin, 1972), p. 70.
3 F. S. Flint, 'London', in *ibid.*, p. 75.
4 F. S. Flint, 'Searchlight', in *ibid.*, p. 77.
5 Ford Madox Ford, *Antwerp*, in *ibid.*, pp. 81–2.
6 T. S. Eliot, *The Waste Land*, lines 60–3, in *Collected Poems 1909–1962* (London: Faber, 1963), p. 55.

7   For a sample of Mass Observation material, see Sandra Koa Wing, ed., *Our Longest Days* (London: Profile Books, 2008).

8   Louis MacNeice, *The Collected Poems of Louis MacNeice* (London: Faber, 1966), p. 10; subsequent references are to this edition.

9   H. G. Wells, *The War of the Worlds*, ed. Patrick Parrinder (London: Penguin, 2005), p. 170.

10 David Gascoyne, 'Ecce homo', in *Collected Poems* (Oxford: Oxford University Press, 1965), p. 45.

11 Edith Sitwell, 'Still Falls the Rain (The Raids, 1940. Night and Dawn)', in *Collected Poems* (London: Sinclar-Stevens, 1993), pp. 272–3.

12 In Iain Sinclair, ed., *Conductors of Chaos: A Poetry Anthology* (London: Picador, 1996), p. 74.

13 Martin Scofield, *T. S. Eliot: The Poems* (Cambridge: Cambridge University Press, 1988), p. 233.

14 H. D., *H. D. Collected Poems, 1912–1944*, ed. Louis Martz (Manchester: Carcanet Press, 1984), p. 509.

15 Ezra Pound, *The Cantos* (London: Faber, 1975), pp. 432, 74.

16 René Hague, *Commentary on the Anathemata of David Jones* (Wellingborough: C. Skelton, 1977), p. 147.

17 David Jones, *The Anathemata* (London: Faber, 1972), p. 118; subsequent references are to this edition.

18 In Sinclair, *Conductors of Chaos*, p. 142.

19 Merlin Coverley, *Psychology* (Harpenden: Pocket Essentials, 2006), p. 10.

20 *Ibid.*, p. 93.

21 I have written extensively about *Lud Heat*, *Place*, and *Vale Royal* elsewhere (see Peter Barry, *Contemporary British Poetry and the City* (Manchester: Manchester University Press, 2000), Chapter 7.

22 Edward Brathwaite, *The Arrivants: A New World Trilogy* (Oxford: Oxford University Press, 1973), pp. 54–6.

23 Derek Walcott, *Omeros* (London: Faber, 1990), p. 195.

24 See Robert D. Hammer, *Epic of the Dispossessed: Derek Walcott's* Omeros (Columbia: University of Missouri Press, 1997), p. 110.

25 William Dunbar, 'In Honour of the City of London', in *The Oxford Book of English Verse*, ed. Arthur Quiller-Couch (London: Oxford University Press, 1919), no. 19.

26 James Berry, *Lucy's Letters and Loving* (London: New Beacon Books, 1982), pp. 39, 48, 40, 42.

27 John Agard, *Mangoes and Bullets* (London: Serpent's Tale, 1990), p. 44.

28 In Linton Kwesi Johnson, *Tings and Times: Selected Poems* (Newcastle upon Tyne: Bloodaxe, 1997), pp. 10–12.

29 Val Warner, *Tooting Idyll* (Manchester: Carcanet, 1998), pp. 84–5.

30 T. S. Eliot, 'The Love Song of J. Alfred Prufrock', lines 8–9, in *Selected Poems* (London: Faber, 1974), p. 13.

31 George Barker, 'Battersea Park', in *Thames: An Anthology of River Poems*, ed. Anna Adams (London: Enitharmon, 1999), p. 45.

32 Thomas Hardy, *The Complete Poems*, ed. James Gibson (London: Palgrave, 2001), pp. 314, 961n.

33 In Andrew Motion, *Selected Poems 1976–1997* (London: Faber, 1998), pp. 149–50.
34 U. A. Fanthorpe, *Selected Poems: U. A. Fanthorpe* (Harmondsworth: Penguin, 1986), pp. 42–3.
35 The books of Edward Soja, such as *Postmetropolis* (Oxford: Blackwell, 2000), make an excellent starting-point in this area.
36 I have found the following very useful: Anna Adams, *London in Poetry and Prose* (London: Enitharmon, 2002); Adams, *Thames*; Joe Kerr and Andrew Gibson, eds., *London from Punk to Blair* (London: Reaktion Books, 2004); Lawrence Phillips, ed., *The Swarming Streets: Twentieth-Century Literary Representations of London* (Amderdam: Rodopi, 2004); Nick Rennison, ed., *Waterstone's Guide to London Writing* (London: Waterstone's, 1999); Barnaby Rogerson, ed., *London: A Collection of Poetry of Place* (London: Elan Press, 2004); and Sinclair, *Conductors of Chaos*.
37 Covering such concepts as *flâneurie*, situationism, psychogeography, and heterotopia; see Jenny Bavidge, *Theorists of the City: Walter Benjamin, Henri Lefebvre and Michel de Certeau* (London: Routledge, 2009).

11

LEO MELLOR

London and modern prose, 1900–1950

Having completed five books of city exploration in the 1920s, each with 'London' in the title, the journalist H. V. Morton went out *In Search of England* (1927). He started from the capital again – but now with a realisation: 'no man living has seen London'.[1] This was because there was no single vantage-point over the modern metropolis, but also – implicitly and more interestingly – because the city was a myriad of conflicting impressions that could not be unified. Ford Madox Ford had made a similar point in his *The Soul of London* (1905). His introduction carries a disavowal of the systematic: 'I have tried to make it anything rather than encyclopaedic, topographical, or archaeological'; his tour of London proceeds instead through impressionistic detail. The accretion of textured observations and anecdote is set against the fear of entropic anonymity, of modern London as unknowable: 'how little of a town, how much of an abstraction'.[2] This tendency in both writers – one a blunt, bestselling populist, one a key force in British literary experimentation – is characteristic of many others across genres; it also marks the fault line between twentieth-century London writing and its predecessors, for while Victorian London could be infinitely rich, bewildering, and despair-inducing it was, ultimately, knowable through texts. This was not the case for the literature of modernity; it rather faced simultaneously acknowledging the importance *and* apparent impossibility of depicting, and thus understanding, modern London.

However, twentieth-century writers did find ways of successfully experiencing and representing versions of London; of grasping essences, details, codes – or shuddering in awe of its totality. These included the well-trodden routes of the *flâneur*, the model of an attentive (male) walker whose progress through the city could be refracted and reflected into literature. The veneration of the pedestrian as key to accessing the city, and to 'reading' it, has been a mainstay of critical commentary – exemplified by theoretical insights such as Michel de Certeau's in *The Practice of Everyday Life*:

> the ordinary practitioners of the city live 'down below', below the threshold at which visibility begins. They walk – an elementary form of this experience of the city; they are the walkers, *Wandersmänner*, whose bodies follow the thicks and thins of an urban text they write about without being able to read it.[3]

Yet while foot-slogging through the streets was still important – as a plot device or narrative model – it was complemented and counterpointed in the early twentieth century by two radically different ways, or rather perspectives, for knowing the city. The aerial view from above brought the threat of the bomber, the lure of totality, and the promise of the sublime in flight. From below, the subterranean world of the ever-expanding underground railway offered rapidity, discombobulation, and multiple metaphorical fears. The implications of understanding such new vistas meant the modern literature of the city had to deal with aspects of its inheritance. For despite the anxiety, expressed by both contemporary writers and critics, of the mismatch between the stimuli of urban experience and the inheritance of Victorian literary forms, London's literature of the period *is* modern. It represents multiple attempts to write from, and about, the position of *being* modern: a position that, for most of the twentieth century, is synonymous with being urban. This does not however represent the emergence of coterie or 'high' literary modernism opposed to the established traditions of realism, but rather a plurality of 'modernisms', each locating city characters as subject to modernity within rooms, streets, districts – and vocabularies. These texts are consequently concerned with the arrangement of fragments – of experience, consciousness, and topography – into narratives. They thus also involve the recognition of sedimented pasts, both recent and dimly prehistoric. But prose that pertains to London, even if it avails itself of the new aerial or subterranean perspectives, is ultimately created through the layering of the authors' imagination onto physicality, the transformation of the actual city into one representable in language.

Darkness underground

The literal London Underground in the twentieth century is the underground railway, a network where perception triumphed over reality in the business of representation. For Harry Beck's iconic tube map of 1931, based on drawings of electrical circuits, is a spatial fiction – offering an abstract narrative of inner London rather than actual topography. H. G. Wells's version of the Underground also did not conform to the literally mappable; it is proleptic of an electrified, organised world – like the one in his *Anticipations* (1902), where a reader is asked to imagine 'that black and sulphurous tunnel, swept and garnished, lit and sweet'.[4] Subterranean fears animate *The Time Machine* (1895) with the possibilities of a future that might involve the degeneration of humanity into the Morlocks, 'undergrounder' cannibals who commute to the surface to feast on the fey Eloi. The London thriller's use of artificial caverns is typified by Geoffrey Household's *Rogue Male* (1939), in which the violent fight with a Nazi agent in the dead-end tube station at Aldwych, involving the claustrophobia of close-quarters combat, prefigures the hero's *finale* in a burrowed hideout deep in Dorset.

Yet attempts to portray London in the early twentieth century returned repeatedly to ideas of the subterranean in a broader sense, with the unearthing of hidden lives and their poverty as a theme for political, aesthetic, and moral writings. Depictions of what was concealed in the slums, especially those of the East End, built on reformist tracts of the nineteenth century – but they adopted divergent fictional and nonfictional forms. Fictional excursions included Somerset Maugham's first major novel, *Liza of Lambeth* (1897), with its voyeuristic depiction of a young woman's decline and death; and Israel Zangwill's *Children of the Ghetto: A Study of a Peculiar People* (1892), an ethnic romance that 'introduces' a mass readership to the traditions of the East End Jews. The politicisation of the reportage-based narrative reached an apogee in George Orwell's *Down and Out in Paris and London* (1933). Yet Orwell owed much, as he acknowledged, to Jack London's *People of the Abyss* (1903) – a walking tour that takes place in London slums and an incendiary tract calling for political change. It indicts all: from the airless fug and lightless life to 'the slops and water-witcheries of the coffee-houses'.[5] This rendering of the city as an 'abscess, a great putrescent sore' (p. 31), calls into question, among many things, the achievements of empire: '[i]f this is the best that civilisation can do for the human, then give us howling and naked savagery' (p. 153).

Joseph Conrad's *Heart of Darkness* (1897) opens with imperial London at dusk providing the setting for the telling of a story, and the tale that is told of the voyage to find Kurtz shows the link between the capital and the colonies it exploits. The connection is confirmed at the close of the novella, where the river described as leading into darkness is the river of the frame-narrative – not the Congo but again the Thames. Concepts of the dark as subterranean, overtly political, and filled with the betrayals and urgency of revolutionary fervour, impel the narrator of Conrad's 'The Informer' (1906) to characterise his agent by a simple sentence: 'He had had what I may call his underground life.'[6] Conrad's London is developed to the greatest extent in *The Secret Agent* (1907); here it is a place where characters actually desire the invisibility the city can offer. It is a maze, a 'cold, black, wet, muddy, inhospitable accumulation of bricks, slates, and stones, things in themselves unlovely and unfriendly to man'.[7] But through it slip those coming to buy pornography in Verloc's Soho shop; Inspector Heat flits through the streets (equating himself with the criminals); and, most sinisterly, the Professor – a member of the Anarchist gang – at the close vanishes into the metropolis, a potential suicide-bomber: 'unsuspected and deadly, like a pest in the street of men' (p. 227). Verloc is the titular, anti-heroic, agent/informer; and the novel is driven by his attempts to remain in employment at the nameless embassy. He does this through attempts to provoke the complacent British – and so have the conspirators caught. The moral darkness of the agent-provocateur who uses a handicapped child in his scheme (and thus kills him) is apparent; but then so too is that of the self-righteous police, and the degenerately compromised Anarchists.

The pattern of enmeshing continues with the complicity of the reader in Conrad's work; the free indirect narrative allows no moral purchase or standpoint: for we are, like the characters, in darkness – and can only perceive London through *their* impressions and the stories they tell. Elements of local life abound, and street names are real, as are the details of the attempt to blow up Greenwich Observatory. Yet the names, sensations, and individual characters give only fragments of specificity; although *The Secret Agent* is the only one of Conrad's novels to stay with a unity of place, London remains a dark and unknowable maze. Its oppressive inescapability is visited on the heroine at the close, where darkness and physical depths converge: 'She was alone in London: and the whole town of marvels and mud, with its maze of streets and its mass of lights, was sunk into a hopeless night, rested at the bottom of a black abyss from which no unaided woman could hope to scramble out' (p. 198).

Making stories from the city

Against such darkness, the interwar years saw the emergence of an illuminated city that could be 'read' in the most literal way, as in Gerald Kersh's thriller *Night and the City* (1938):

> Ping went the clock, on the first stroke of eight. Up and down the streets the shops began to close. West Central started to flare and squirm in a blazing vein-work of neon tubes. Bursting like inexhaustible fireworks the million coloured bulbs of the electric signs blazed in a perpetual recurrence over the face of the West End.[8]

London's lights and advertising hoardings give visual proof in *Murder Must Advertise* (1933) that the hard work of the sloganeers has not been in vain: 'SOPO SAVES SCRUBBING – NUTRAX FOR NERVES – CRUNCHLETS ARE CRISPER'.[9] But the inclusion of these signs in popular plot-driven fiction glosses over a more deep-rooted reading of the sensations of the city as a means to construct narratives. That comes, however, in the preoccupations of two divergent authors, Katherine Mansfield and Evelyn Waugh, both of whom transform inchoate urban sensations into stories.

Mansfield, though born in New Zealand, is a writer whose short stories in the 1920s are both a reflection on London and an attempt to construct narratives from its ephemera. She writes of different social classes and different situations, but the perceptiveness of Mansfield's prose comes in the obliqueness of her characters' own attempts at making a story. The 'Life of Ma Parker' (1921) uses the feeling of the elderly protagonist who has just watched her grandson die, and who has to deal with the insults of the 'literary gentleman' she cleans for – and with the leavings of his casual sordidness, 'toast crusts, envelopes, cigarette ends'.[10] Amid it all she suddenly desires 'a good cry'. The sensation here implied by the narrator is inchoate sorrow, a grief that has been internalised for years. But while all the protagonist wants is 'a cry', London's class-stratified spaces do not allow this: 'Ma Parker stood, looking up and down. The icy wind blew out her apron into a balloon. And now it began to rain. There was nowhere' (p. 288).

In the final version of Mansfield's 'Pictures' (1920)[11] this desire to show how desperation might be narratable is more complex – and more successful. In the story, a failed actress called Ada Moss spends a day failing in a variety of ways (not paying the rent to a rapacious landlady, not getting a job, being insulted, crying in a park) before convincing herself, in a tour de force of self-deception, that she is only going to the Café de Madrid for a coffee. The downward slide to prostitution is made absurdly poignant by her attempts continually to tell her own story through the generic template of film – the very medium in which she is refused work. These attempts to project a story of success allow her to wander London and transcend the clutter she encounters. Strewn debris is there from the start: 'her room, a Bloomsbury top-floor back, smelled of soot and face powder and the paper of fried potatoes she brought in for supper the night before' – but so is the desire to see what she *wants*: 'A pageant of Good Hot Dinners passed across the ceiling, each of them accompanied by a bottle of Nourishing Stout' (p. 133). Out in the London morning Miss Moss is patronised or ignored; she is, obviously, merely part of urban detritus herself. Indeed she is not only a bad presence, but a bad odour: '"Can I see the producer, please?" said Miss Moss pleasantly. [...] The girl not only frowned; she seemed to smell something vaguely unpleasant; she sniffed.' The storyline provided by the application form – '"Can you aviate – high-dive – drive a car – buckjump – shoot?" read Miss Moss' (p. 140) – is one she cannot be part of; but she, unlike Ma Parker, sits on the street and tries to compose another:

Café de Madrid. 'I could just go in and sit there and have a coffee, that's all', thought Miss Moss. 'It's such a place for artists too. I might just have a stroke of luck ... A dark handsome gentleman in a fur coat comes in with a friend, and sits at my table, perhaps.' [...] 'Excuse me, I happen to be a contralto, and I have sung that part many times ... Extraordinary!' 'Come back to my studio and I'll try your voice now.' (p. 140)

One of Mansfield's final stories, 'A Cup of Tea' (1922), has the heroine's Londonness assured by the fact that her 'parties were the most delicious mix of the really important people and ... artists' (p. 345). Parties – and life despite parties – preoccupied Evelyn Waugh. In *Vile Bodies* (1930) London is the setting for the stop-go courtship of the insouciant Nina by the incompetent Adam Fenwick-Smythe (a writer whose own novel is burnt by customs men at the start). Their romance provides a connective thread running through multiple escapades, yet neither love nor lust makes the city narratable. Rather the urge to drink and the attempt to have fun drive this novel of brittle restlessness. At a soirée in a tethered balloon a weariness comes over Adam: 'Oh Nina, what a lot of parties'.[12] The social round is then listed, and peopled, as if seen in the vista:

Masked parties, Savage parties, Victorian parties, Greek parties, Wild West parties, Russian parties, Circus parties, parties where one had to dress as somebody else, almost naked parties in St John's Wood, parties in flats and studios and houses and ships and hotels and night clubs, in windmills and swimming-baths [...] all that succession and repetition of massed humanity ... Those vile bodies ...   (p. 123)

Waugh's ellipsis at the end of this phobic list offers both a point of empathetic vantage – and a decisive retort to any idea of pleasure. For London has become the setting for disordered sensations, and is furthermore itself only ultimately understandable *as* a sensation, one apprehended in hyper-sensitised and maudlin ways. Waugh's overt derision toward experimental possibilities for prose, which hardened into his carapace of clerico-reactionary disdain, can obscure the shock of the new that he himself creates. Among his instruments for doing this is the telephone, a signifier of modernity and an apparatus filled with comic potential; it is also the harbinger of virtual interaction in the city through simultaneity and abstraction. The potential is exploited tersely:

Adam rang up Nina.
'Darling, I've been so happy about your telegram. Is it really true?'
'No, I'm afraid not.'
'The Major *is* bogus?'
'Yes.'

'You haven't got any money?'

'No.'

'We aren't going to be married today?'

'No.'

'I see.'

'Well?'

'I said, I see.'

'Is that all?'

'Yes, that's all, Adam.'

'I'm sorry.'

'I'm sorry, too. Goodbye.'

'Goodbye, Nina.' (pp. 183–4)

Sensations – of shock and desire – are converted into updated stichomythia, Greek tragedy's form of quickfire riposte. There is also a minimalist absurdity where 'to see' becomes a deeply problematic metaphor – as on a telephone nobody actually 'sees' at all. But the sensations – in both senses – of the parties, and the inconsequential connections, are mythologised in a gossip column: with the columnist being – at various points – nearly every character in the novel. Here the city is categorised in terms of the latest styles – but '[a]s the days passed Mr Chatterbox's page became almost wholly misleading [...] he announced that the buffet at Sloane Square tube station had become the haunt of the most modern artistic coterie' (p. 116).

Being modern: mapping, walking, flying

One way of comprehending the space of a changing London meant finding literary forms that were analogous to maps, or could incorporate characters' encounters with vistas or directions. Yet charting the city in words is also a moment of realising the limits of mapping: the knowing title of Patrick Hamilton's trilogy *Twenty Thousand Streets under the Sky* (1935), with its nod to both Jules Verne and city plans, demonstrates the near unknowability of metropolis when its true scale was appreciated (for example, the first edition of the *A–Z Atlas and Guide to London and Suburbs* in 1936 had required the compiler Phyllis Pearsall to walk 3,000 miles along the 23,000 streets of 1930s London). Other texts attempted to indicate the expansiveness of the city through subtle means: Jean Rhys's fatalistic novella *After Leaving Mr Mackenzie* (1930) depends upon having each chapter of the London section named after a specific location with its own history: 'Acton', 'Notting Hill', 'Golders Green' – but then goes on to undercut such precision with generic misery in Chapter 11, 'It Might Have Been Anywhere'. James Bone's anti-guidebook *The London Perambulator* (1925), lacking all tourist sites or a hierarchy of sights, stresses the virtue of walking as a mode of continual discovery – and has been remembered where others, such as Paul Pry's *For Your Convenience* (1937), have been forgotten. Written under a pseudonym, the mock-Platonic dialogue details the locations of public lavatories – but in fact represents the first modern gay guide to London.[13] Yet while walking could act as an index for the gap between actual human experience and its cartographic simulacra there was another, more estrangingly potent, perspective becoming available: the aerial view.

Aircraft offered compelling vistas for the consciousness – or even the sub-consciousness – of both characters and writers. Virginia Woolf's interest in new perspectives that could expose the actuality of thought itself, with all attendant partiality, estrangement, and doubt, meant that attempts to render a stream of consciousness became a favoured mode. And her attempts to show how sensations were reordered by an individual's mental state also used the literal new vistas only knowable from the air, from the perspective of the 'aeronaut' in *Orlando* (1928) to the word-breaking zoom of fighters that closes *Between the Acts* (1941). It is a product of 'airmindness', the interwar fascination and dread engendered by flight. Woolf's interwar essay 'Flying over London' (only published in 1950) initially appears to be the record of a day-trip to see the capital from above. Life below the putative observer as they escape cloud-ward is both aestheticised – and revelatory:

> Houses, streets, banks, public buildings, and habits and mutton and Brussels sprouts had been swept into long spirals and curves of pink and purple like that a wet brush makes when it sweeps mounds of paint together. One could see through the Bank of England; all the business houses were transparent; the river Thames was as the Romans saw it, as paleolithic man saw it, at dawn from a hill shaggy with wood.[14]

Then, with the aid of binoculars, a focus emerges – tracking in on a house, a door, a person: 'then it was a woman's face, young perhaps, in any case in a black cloak and a red hat'. Such an empathetic leap in perspective destabilises the position of the narrator: '[e]verything had changed its value when seen from the air. Personality was outside the body, abstract' (p. 211). Yet the whole trip, and the doubts that it raises, are ultimately themselves framed as fictitious – merely a flight of the imagination.

Seeing how the self would alter through both the possibilities of aeriality *and* the more earth-bound apprehension of the city drives *Mrs. Dalloway* (1925). This novel gives a day in the life of Clarissa Dalloway, society hostess and wife, as she prepares for a party. Her movements around London and her fleeting encounters, criss-crossing with other characters and invaded by memories of her past, attempt to portray a totality – in a manner analogous to the European city-symphony films of the period, with their attempts to incorporate the quotidian and discontinuous stories that compose the whole of urban life. But whereas films such as *Berlin: Die Sinfonie der Großstadt* (1927) attempt a synoptic view of classes and industry, the intensity of the focus on Mrs Dalloway herself means that insight forms through tranches of personal reverie. Yet her individual consciousness, altering on every street corner, presages the possibility of a collective unconscious in the city.

Reading the habits of everyday life as collectively diagnostic of modernity was the project of the anthropological/political organisation Mass Observation. Founded in 1937 by Tom Harrisson, Charles Madge, and Humphrey Jennings, Mass Observation used volunteer observers to record life in Britain and thereby create an 'anthropology of ourselves'.[15] Owing much to Surrealism for their veneration of dreams, their interest in coincidence and their disavowal of direct narration, the group compiled books from the records of observers, the most famous of these being *May 12 1937* (1937) – a documentation of everyday London, and the minutiae of experience, on the day of George VI's coronation. The masses have no such consciousness in *Mrs. Dalloway*, indeed a beggar is more animal than human; yet aeriality does bring connectivity to the larger whole. When 'the sound of an aeroplane bored ominously into the ears of the crowd',[16] they are cast as vulnerable, the adverb 'ominously' converting them to potential victims, although what they see is merely a piece of sky-writing:

> Dropping dead down the aeroplane soared straight up, curved in a loop, raced, sank, rose, and whatever it did, wherever it went, out fluttered behind it a thick ruffled bar of white smoke which curled and wreathed upon the sky in letters. But what letters? A C was it? an E, then an L? [...]
> 'Glaxo', said Mrs. Coates in a strained, awe-stricken voice, gazing straight up, and her baby, lying stiff and white in her arms, gazed straight up.
> 'Kreemo', murmured Mrs Bletchley, like a sleep-walker. (p. 17)

The banality of whatever product is being spelt out does not eclipse the power of the airborne medium; indeed ominousness leaks through in the writing: in the aircraft's 'dropping dead down', and in the baby's 'lying stiff and white'. But the acrobatic play of the plane – as it shoots in and out above the crowds, beyond the limits of description: 'whatever it did, wherever it went' – foreshadows a synoptic vista in fiction that approaches the sublime.[17]

But Woolf also used another new spatial sensation of modernity in London – a sensation engendered by the Underground. In *The Waves* (1931) the experiences of all the major characters are remade by the practices of tube travel, presenting them with a discontinuous city analogous to their

lives – and the episodic nature of such travel brings both intimacy and alienation. But for one character especially, Jinny, the potentiality of movement
brings power, as when she pauses in Piccadilly Circus station: 'to stand for
a moment under the pavement in the heart of London', where she then feels
'I am in the heart of life.'[18] But it is as early as 1917, in her short story 'The
Mark on the Wall', that the metaphorical potential of the Underground for
Woolf is obvious:

> Why, if one wants to compare life to anything, one must liken it to being
> blown through the Tube at fifty miles an hour – landing at the other end with-
> out a single hairpin in one's hair! Shot out at the feet of God entirely naked!
> [...] Yes, that seems to express the rapidity of life, the perpetual waste and
> repair; all so casual, all so haphazard ...[19]

Yet to set against such traumatic case studies of being above and below
London another, more earthbound, way toward the sublime is proposed
both in Mrs Dalloway's walks and in some other of Woolf's essays. In
'Street Haunting: A London Adventure' (1930) she leads the perambula-
tory mode into the realms of the subconscious – where walking can reveal
desires otherwise suppressed. The apparent desire to possess a lead pencil
gives 'an excuse for walking half across London between tea and dinner',
but the desire to understand the city – and the self – through perambula-
tion remains half-suppressed: 'as if under cover of this excuse we could
indulge safely in the greatest pleasures of town life in Winter – rambling
the streets of London. [...] The evening hour gives us the irresponsibility
that darkness and lamplight bestow. We are no longer quite ourselves.'[20]
Along with what is being searched for here, implicitly and explicitly, and
beyond the pleasurable alienation that wandering brings, the writer's 'we'
matters – and it has to do with class. For this *flâneuse*, a female equivalent
of Bauadelaire's *flâneur*, is problematic, partly owing to the contemporary
expectation that streetwalking women could be equated to low-class prostitutes, and partly because the time for the pleasurable activity enjoyed in
this essay, like the shopping of Mrs Dalloway, is dependent on unexamined
wealth and privilege.

An important London novel of the period by Patrick Hamilton moves,
like Woolf, between the aerial and the pedestrian, while illuminating the sexual negotiations that mark out city existence. Yet *Hangover Square* (1941)
is not a London locale but a state of mind; and it involves a very different
social milieu from Woolf's Bond Street, tracking the last desperate months of
George Harvey Bone, a clumsily awkward alcoholic, as Britain slides toward
war. Bone, helplessly in love with the disdainful Netta, wanders London's
pubs, cheap hotels, and cinemas: alternating between resigned acceptance of

his fate – and the 'dead moods' that come over him with a 'click', like that in a telephone exchange, transforming him into a killer. This is a walking (or somnambulating) novel, with added demi-Conradian gloom par excellence, as Bone's tramping progresses around an area of London explicated in the subtitle: 'A Story of Darkest Earl's Court'.

A wretched *flâneur*, and obsessive supplicant to Netta, Bone cannot gaze on her for long before she inverts or defeats his gaze. Rather, she dominates – and does so aerially: 'sending out a ray, a wave from herself, which seemed to affect his whole being, to go through him like a faint vibration'.[21] The anti-narrative of Bone's wanderings counterpoints these signals that travel, with menace, through the air. Indeed the repeated naming of streets that Bone walks along, and the listing of cinema times (pp. 66–7) seem compensatory, gratuitous in their excess – as if they were merely delaying something. As Bone himself thinks, 'You couldn't believe that it would ever break, that the bombs had to fall' (p. 101). The certainty of that 'had' could be due to the savant qualities of Bone or to Hamilton's composition of the novel after the war started. Or the conviction could have just been in the air, as it was in Orwell's *Coming up for Air* (1939): 'below us you could see the roofs of the houses stretching on and on, the little red roofs where the bombs are going to drop';[22] or in the remark made by one guest to another in Henry Green's *Party Going* (1939) as they survey a crowd at a London terminus: '"What targets", one by him remarked, "what targets for a bomb"'.[23]

Narrative fascination with London's interwar airspace can be found in Mr Kelly's tantalising kite-tail over Kensington Gardens in Samuel Beckett's *Murphy* (1938) – but also in the hysteria of both pulp fiction and military planning, areas whose symbiotic connection is now acknowledged. J. F. C. Fuller, tank-commander, friend of Aleister Crowley and expert on yoga, wrote: 'in future warfare, great cities, such as London, will be attacked from the air', and prophesied the result: 'London for several days will be one vast raving Bedlam, the hospitals will be stormed, traffic will cease, the homeless will shriek for help, the city will be in pandemonium.'[24] London as an over-tempting target resonates throughout much popular literature of the inter-war period: Anderson Graham's *The Collapse of Homo Sapiens* (1923) has it levelled; in Stephen Southwold's *The Gas War of 1940* (1931) it is 'blotted out'; while in Shaw Desmond's *Ragnarok* (1926) fire-bombs are merely the prelude to the slaughter of its fleeing inhabitants. The hyper-extrapolation of destruction from the First World War and the first aerial bombardment of London by zeppelins in 1915 produced imagined post-assault cityscapes marked by absolute devastation. Ladbroke Black's *The Poison War* (1933) turns a mannered hero into a survivor prepared to pillage as he encounters local warlords, and it couples lists of streets with names of the dead. These works still fascinate, despite being 'appalling and dreadful in both the original and modern senses of the word';[25] they encode 'airminded' fears while hyperbolically predicting the fate of the city. But they also repeatedly utilise the subterranean as a space for action, shelter, and brutal death. From William Le Queux's vision in *The Invasion of 1910* (1906) of the panicking East Enders trapped 'like rats in a hole' on the Underground, to the descriptions in *The Poison War* of tube stations packed with bodies of those who had failed to escape the gas attacks, these works once more place the aerial in a dialectical relationship with the Underground – and again presage the reality, of tube-shelterers and the politics of refuge, that was about to fall from the sky.

The Second World War: bombs, ghosts, spies

The 1940–1 Blitz on London, while not on the scale predicted by inter-war fiction or military planners, altered forever the cityscape and its literature. Among many Henry Green and William Sansom portrayed the attacks themselves, and also the inherent problems of writing about them. Both were volunteer firefighters, and both were keen to show the limits of realism. Sansom's short stories fracture temporality, focusing, for example, on the 'timeless second' in 'The Wall' (1941) when a fireman's newly awakened perception transforms him. The title of Henry Green's *Caught* (1943) plays with unstable meanings – referring both to the peril of fire and to the socio-sexual entanglements in which the characters find themselves. Green implicitly places his full-time fireman Pye and the new volunteer Roe together to form *pyro* – the stem-word for fire – as they begin to comprehend the task ahead. At the close of the novel Roe realises how all experience of fire is inevitably altered by description, and in the final sequence some parentheses (akin to the ones used for the intensification of Mrs Dalloway's musings) become a marker for the gap between reality and its mental reconstruction. Roe says overtly that fire in the Docks made it look like a giant hearth. But then: '(It had not been like that at all. What he had seen was a broken, torn-up dark mosaic aglow with rose where square after square of timber had been burned down to embers, while beyond the distant yellow flames toyed joyfully with the next black stacks which softly merged into the pink of that night.)'.[26] Knowing what you've seen, or what you think you've seen, is a problem as well for the amnesiac protagonist of Graham Greene's *The Ministry of Fear* (1943). The novel loots from prewar thrillers and spy-stories, animating them with an irrationally riddling plot and a phantasmagoric sensibility. Through guessing the right (and wrong) weight of a cake at a shabby summer fête the protagonist Rowe is mistaken for a spy – and thus launched into a life that, as he recognises, appears to owe much to the books of his childhood. Greene's city is also regressing: 'London was no longer one great city: it was a collection of small towns',[27] as it also was, owing to the blackout, for Evelyn Waugh's characters, who 'set out into the baffling midnight void. Time might have gone back two thousand years to the time when London was a stockaded cluster of huts down the river, and the streets through which they walked, empty sedge and swamp.'[28]

But Rowe's progression across London, as he is both hunted and haunted, brings the subterranean world of the tube-shelterers to life, counterpointing the contemporary shelter-drawings of Henry Moore. Trying to sleep in a tube station, one of the many converted to offer protection as a shelter, '[h]e woke up to a dim lurid underground place [...] all along the walls the bodies lay two deep, while outside the raid rumbled and receded [...] I'm hiding underground, and up above the Germans are methodically smashing London to bits all round me' (pp. 64–5). Even the climactic moment of menace, when the police corner the head of a spy-ring (and ghastly clairvoyant) in her rooms, depends on multiple concepts of needing to go beneath the surface to find truths well hidden in wartime London:

'Is this your best tea-service, ma'am?' wincing ever so slightly at the gaudy Prussian blue.

'Put it down', Mrs Bellairs implored, but he had already smashed the cup against the wall. He explained to his man, 'The handles are hollow. We don't know how small these films are. You've got to skin the place.'

'You'll suffer for this', Mrs Bellairs said tritely.

'Oh no ma'am, it's you who'll suffer. Giving information to the enemy is a hanging offence.'

'They don't hang women. Not in this war.'

'We may hang more people, ma'am', Mr Prentice said, speaking back at her from the passage, 'than the papers tell you about' (pp. 175–6)

Secret London also emerges in Elizabeth Bowen's 'Postscript' to the American edition of her collection of short stories *The Demon Lover* (1945), where she explains the return again and again to disturbed notions of selfhood and the uncanny.[29] Her oblique version of the uncanny figures it as a new sensibility, one of being individually, physically changed – and becoming receptive: '[w]alls went down; and we felt, if not knew, each other' (p. 95). She locates this sense of change in the pressures of the wartime cityscape: '[w]alking in the darkness of the nights of six years (darkness which transformed a capital city into a network of inscrutable canyons) one developed new bare alert senses, with their own savage warnings and notations' (p. 99). Ultimately Bowen suggests that the mode of survival for understanding the contingency of London during the bombing was a kind of physical and mental *bricolage*: 'People whose homes had been blown up went to infinite lengths to assemble bits of themselves – broken ornaments, odd shoes, torn scraps of the curtains that had hung in a room – from the wreckage. In the same way, they assembled and checked themselves from stories and poems, from their memories, from one another's talk' (p. 97). Yet to assemble and check yourself from the fragments of other texts can release unexpected results; and this is what occurs in two of Bowen's most famous stories. In 'The Demon Lover', which takes its ominous title from a ballad concerning an inconstant woman, the chic Mrs Drover returns to her London house – but her visit heralds a vertiginous fall into the uncanny. First comes the dust, not in the air suspended as for T. S. Eliot in 'Little Gidding' (1942), but present as index to destruction elsewhere, for even in the street 'an unfamiliar queerness has silted up'.[30] Inside the house 'her former habit of life' is menacingly present in the 'bruise' of a handle and the traceable 'claw-marks' of removed furniture. A letter is waiting for her – stating how her now-forgotten soldier lover, assumed dead, is still intending to keep his rendezvous. The denouement of the story comes with the clichéd appearance, and thus the apparent reassurance, of a black London taxi-cab. But at the wheel of the taxi is the returned ghost of the past – the demon lover – and Mrs Drover now unwillingly becomes the driven. Silently screaming she is pressed against the partition glass as the taxi, without mercy, made off with her into the hinterland of deserted streets' (p. 666).

Bowen's 'Mysterious Kôr' (1944) opens with an estrangingly aerial view of more streets: 'Full moonlight drenched the city and searched it; there was not a niche left to stand in. The effect was remorseless: London looked like the moon's capital – shallow, cratered, extinct' (p. 728). Yet the whole experience is understood through a past literary text reanimated. The central couple, Pepita and Arthur, roam the illuminated city at night, until she starts to quote a sonnet, the poem that gave Rider Haggard the images for his novel *She* (1887). The city summoned through her incantational recitation '*Mysterious Kôr thy walls forsaken stand*' is a ghostly double of London – and, echoed by Arthur, it becomes enchantingly infectious. As he later recalls:

> 'So we began to play – we were off in Kôr.'
> 'Core of what?'
> 'Mysterious Kôr. Kôr – ghost city.'
> 'Where?'
> 'You may ask. But I could have sworn she saw it, and from the way she saw it I saw it too. A game's a game, but what's a hallucination? You begin by laughing, then it gets into you, and you can't laugh it off.' (p. 738)

Indeed deciding upon the real in wartime London becomes problematic when, as Pepita says, 'if you can blow whole places out of existence, you can blow whole places into it' (p. 730).[31] The potency of apparitions continued in Bowen's later *The Heat of the Day* (1949): 'Most of the dead, from mortuaries, from under cataracts of rubble, made their anonymous presence – not as today's dead but as yesterday's living – felt throughout London. Uncounted they continued to move in shoals through the city day, pervading everything to be seen or heard or felt with their torn-off senses...'.[32] The deferral of the verb in the first sentence makes this passage particularly unsettling; what the dead will do is itself unknown until their 'presence' in the text, as well as within London, is unambiguously 'felt'. *The Heat of the Day* knows a lot about the uncanny and its shifting presence in the cityscape, which is now itself apparitional. Yet fears are held taut as the web of relationships within the novel works out the balancing acts of intelligencing and counter-intelligencing, surmising clues and remaining obliviously naïve. Such complexities, used as a way to capture a city transformed by war, allow readings where the central love-triangle is metaphoric for British relations with Ireland (Bowen spied, or at least reported, from there herself) as well as those where the novel maps out the spatiality of the blackout.[33] But it is a work set in 1942 where emotions and sensations are already in retrospect, as a character realises 'that psychic London was to be gone forever; more bombs would fall but not on the same city' (p. 92).

The new London jungle

In 'Miss Anstruther's Letters' (1942) Rose Macaulay fictionalises her own despair when, at the height of the Blitz, her flat was burnt down – and with it all her possessions and the cache of her lover's letters that she failed to save. Aimed squarely at Americans – it was published only in the USA in a volume titled *London Calling* in order to raise awareness of Britain's survival and endurance – this is a short story about an act of salvage that did not take place and about the remorse that followed amid the irredeemable ashy ruins. But throughout the war – and after it – London's bombsites were colonised by plants and animals, becoming luxuriant spaces where ruins were shaded by leaves and flowers. The symbolic value of such survival became central to Macaulay's *The World My Wilderness* (1950), where it was entwined with questions of literary salvage. In this novel, a seventeen-year-old girl called Barbary arrives in London with her half-brother, and they take refuge in the 'green world' of the bombsites.[34] These sites were extensive, truly verdant – and culturally significant. When the director of Kew Gardens lectured on bombsite flowers, *The Times* published his lyrical litany: '[w]ildflowers had spread over the bombsites: rose-bay willowherb, coltsfoot, groundsel, Oxford ragwort, Canadian fleabane and thornapple, Thanet cress'.[35] For just as both Modernism and pulp fiction had presented the city as a zone of fragmented destruction, so other writers had long proleptically envisaged the return of the wild.

The figure of a visitor from the future encountering London as an unkempt pile of ruins – for example, 'The New Zealander' engraved by Gustave Doré for *London: A Pilgrimage* (1873; see Figure 11.1) – haunted the late-Victorian pessimistic-futuristic imagination. Notable for using a native British character in excursions into a proto-future is Richard Jefferies in *After London; or, Wild England* (1885). The title itself gives the plot, and the narrative illustrates the lowlands of the Thames valley through the prism of the Arts and Crafts Movement; the new sea that covers London leads to a reversion to demi-chivalric subsistence farming. What has happened to London is retold with pleasure by the narrator: '[f]or this marvellous city, of which such legends are related, was after all only of brick, and when the ivy grew over and trees and shrubs sprang up, and, lastly, the waters underneath burst in, this huge metropolis was soon overthrown'.[36] Jefferies inspired many, including his biographer the poet and walker Edward Thomas, whose nonfictional *The South Country* (1909) included a revenge fantasy for his beloved 'Nature':

> I like to think how easily Nature will absorb London as she absorbed the mastodon, setting her spiders to spin the winding-sheet and her worms to fill in the grave, and her grass to cover it pitifully up, adding flowers – as an unknown hand added them to the grave of Nero. I like to see the preliminaries of this toil where Nature tries her hand at mossing the factory roof, rusting the deserted railway metals, sowing grass over the deserted platforms and flowers of rose-bay on ruinous hearths and walls.[37]

In this passage pleasurable contemplation of the end of a city moves from metaphor to the specifics of change; but Thomas was not to know that rose-bay – the only species he specifically names – would become talismanic. For this plant, with its pink flowers and down-coated leaves, commonly known as rose-bay willowherb, recurs more than any other in writings about the bombsites. Thomas himself had pressed it into literature before, in his poem 'Adlestrop', but after the bombings it became emblematic and ubiquitous, with its plethora of seeds per plant and its liking for burnt soil. Even its nickname – 'Fireweed' – is worthy of elucidation. The name is a basic descriptive compound: this plant comes after fire and it is a weed. But the flowers also resemble fire still burning, with drifts of red and pink, offering a seeming after-image of destruction in the actuality of rebirth.[38]

Figure 11.1 Gustave Doré, 'The New Zealander', from *London: A Pilgrimage* (1872).

In *The World My Wilderness* the main locales of the novel – the bombsites around St Paul's (see Figure 11.2) – are accurately described, with actual streets and actual damage, including named churches, buildings, and even windows. Barbary, as a damaged but resilient *flâneuse*, traverses these streets to lose herself in the enfolding verdancy of the bombsites. But this jungle is composed of a very specific collection of flowers that Macaulay portrays in multi-clausal, labyrinthine descriptions. The vantage-point gained by Barbary, from the top of a ruin, offers 'a wilderness of little streets, caves and cellars, the foundation of a wrecked merchant city, grown over by green and golden fennel and ragwort, coltsfoot, purple loosestrife, rosebay willow

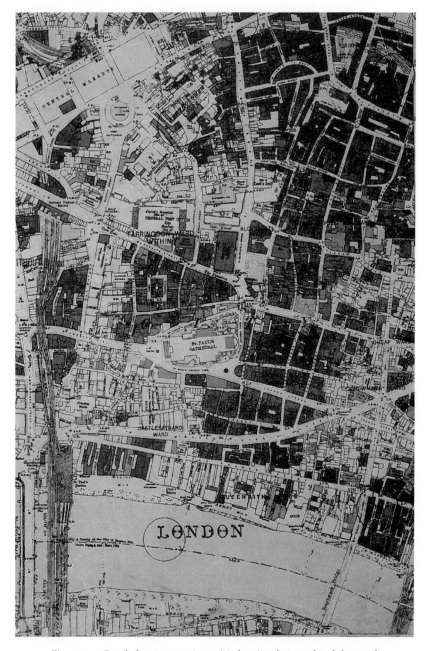

Figure 11.2 Bomb damage map (1946/7) showing destroyed and damaged
buildings around St Paul's Cathedral.

herb' (p. 53). The tangled spaces of the sites are mimetically reproduced by prose that withholds final meaning until the close:

> Summer slipped on; a few blazing days when London and its deserts burned beneath a golden sun, and the flowering weeds and green bracken hummed with insects, and the deep underground cells were cool like churches, and the long grass wilted, drooped and turned to hay; then a number of cool wet days, when the wilderness was sodden and wet and smelt of decay, and the paths ran like streams, and the ravines were deep in dripping greenery that grew high and rank, running over the ruins as the jungle runs over Mayan temples, hiding them from prying eyes. (p. 79)

These ruins cloaked in vegetation offer an analogy for the fragments of many other texts embedded in Macaulay's work. The significance of Eliot's *The Waste Land*, both for characters within the novel, who cite it freely, and for the novelist herself, who employs it to shape the text, shows her reimagining of Modernism as actuality in the city. Direct quotations include a reworking of 'Where are the roots that clutch, what branches grow, out of this stony rubble?' with an answer – 'But you can say, you can guess, that it is yourself, your own roots ... the branches of your own being that grow from this and nowhere else' (p. 129). A lamentation is thus spun into an affirmation. Nevertheless, adrift in London, Barbary's place as true inhabitant of the ruins frightens her father: 'would the daughter eventually qualify as salvage, or would [she] remain drifting with the wreckage' (p. 139). Macaulay thus typifies 'salvage' as a potent literary trope, forerunner of city-as-a-text theories, and also a moral question.

Indeed Macaulay's *The Pleasure of Ruins* (1953), a languorous guide to ruins-in-history, has the recent bombsites as corollary of historic destruction; and as personal justification for her intellectual project. Sometimes this is subtle: the ghost of Marie Lloyd is here again with her music-hall song: 'I am very, very fond of ruins, ruins I love to scan', which is also sung in *The World My Wilderness*. But London's position in the lineage of ruins is only fully explicit at the close; for the capital of empire, home of decadence, Victoriana, spies, ghosts, and the seething stuff of life entered the second half of the twentieth century as a city of ruins. These ruins foretell the fate of all cities – and all of their writers – and thus need a mantle of green so their pain will be 'enjungled and engulfed'.[39]

Notes

1 H. V. Morton, *In Search of England* (London: Methuen, 1927), p. 4.
2 Ford Madox Ford, *The Soul of London: A Survey of a Modern City* (1905), ed. Alan G. Hill (London: J. M. Dent, 1995), pp. 3, 7.

3 Michel de Certeau, *The Practice of Everyday Life*, trans. Steven Rendall (Berkeley: University of California Press, 1988), p. 93.

4 H. G. Wells, *Anticipations of the Reactions of Mechanical and Scientific Progress upon Human Life and Thought* (London: Chapman and Hall, 1902), p. 29.

5 Jack London, *People of the Abyss* (1903), ed. Brigitte Koenig (London: Pluto Press, 2001), p. 126. Further references cited parenthetically.

6 Joseph Conrad, *Selected Short Stories* (London: Wordsworth, 1997), p. 140.

7 Joseph Conrad, *The Secret Agent* (1907), ed. John Lyon (Oxford: Oxford World's Classics, 2008), p. 42. Further references cited parenthetically.

8 Gerald Kersh, *Night and the City* (1938) (London: London Books, 2007), p. 15.

9 Dorothy L. Sayers, *Murder Must Advertise* (London: Hodder and Stoughton, 2003), p. 98.

10 Katherine Mansfield, *Selected Stories*, ed. D. M. Davin (Oxford: Oxford World's Classics, 1981), p. 283. Further references cited parenthetically.

11 'Pictures' developed through three different versions from 1917 to 1920, moving from being a dialogue or script to a rather more artful story.

12 Evelyn Waugh, *Vile Bodies* (1930) (Harmondsworth: Penguin, 1979), p. 123. Further references cited parenthetically.

13 The full title being *For Your Convenience: A Learned Dialogue, Instructive to All Londoners & London Visitors, Overheard in the Thélème Club and Taken Down Verbatim* (London: Routledge, 1937).

14 Virginia Woolf, *Selected Essays*, ed. David Bradshaw (Oxford: Oxford World's Classics, 2008), p. 208. Further references cited parenthetically.

15 See Nick Hubble, *Mass-Observation and Everyday Life* (Basingstoke: Palgrave, 2006).

16 Virginia Woolf, *Mrs. Dalloway* (1925), ed. David Bradshaw (Oxford: Oxford University Press, 1992), p. 17. Further references cited parenthetically.

17 Other attempts in *Mrs. Dalloway* to understand London from new vantage points include the radiating ripples of sound: 'Remember my party, remember my party, said Peter Walsh as he stepped down the street, speaking to himself rhythmically, in time with the flow of the sound, the direct downright sound of Big Ben striking the half-hour. (The leaden circles dissolved in the air.)'; *ibid.*, p. 41.

18 Virginia Woolf, *The Waves* (1931) (Harmondsworth: Penguin, 1951), p. 165.

19 Virginia Woolf, *The Complete Shorter Fiction of Virginia Woolf*, 2nd edn, ed. Susan Dicks (London/New York: Harcourt, 1989), p. 84.

20 Woolf, *Essays*, p. 177.

21 Patrick Hamilton, *Hangover Square* (Harmondsworth: Penguin, 1974), p. 50. Further references cited parenthetically.

22 George Orwell, *Coming up for Air* (1939) (Harmondsworth: Penguin, 1990), p. 19.

23 Henry Green, *Party Going* (1939) (London: Harvill, 1996), p. 154.

24 J. F. C. Fuller, *The Reformation of War* (London: Hutchinson, 1923), p. 150.

25 Martin Ceadel, 'Popular Fiction and the Next War', in *Class Culture and Social Change: A New View of the 1930s*, ed. Frank Gloversmith (Brighton: Harvester, 1980), p. 161.

26 Henry Green, *Caught* (London: Harvill, 2001), p. 181.

27 Graham Greene, *The Ministry of Fear* (London: Penguin, 1973), p. 69.
28 Evelyn Waugh, *Men at Arms* (Harmondsworth: Penguin, 1971), p. 23.
29 Elizabeth Bowen, 'Postscript', in *The Mulberry Tree: Writings of Elizabeth Bowen*, ed. and intro. Hermione Lee (London: Virago, 1986), p. 95. Further references cited parenthetically.
30 Elizabeth Bowen, *Collected Stories* (London: Vintage, 1999), p. 661. Further references cited parenthetically.
31 Other works of the period also populate London with apparitions – such as those in G. W. Stonier's *Memoirs of a Ghost* (1947) or Charles Williams's *All Hallows' Eve* (1945).
32 Elizabeth Bowen, *The Heat of the Day* (Harmondsworth: Penguin, 1962), p. 91. Further references cited parenthetically.
33 Recent useful readings of wartime Bowen include: Maud Ellman, *Elizabeth Bowen: The Shadow across the Page* (Edinburgh: Edinburgh University Press, 2003); and Neil Corcoran, *Elizabeth Bowen: The Enforced Return* (Oxford: Oxford University Press, 2004).
34 Rose Macaulay, *The World My Wilderness* (London: Virago, 1983), p. 181. Further references cited parenthetically.
35 *The Times* (3 May 1945), p. 2.
36 Richard Jefferies, *After London; or, Wild England* (1885), ed. and intro. John Fowles (Oxford: Oxford University Press, 1980), p. 36.
37 Edward Thomas, *The South Country* (London: Dent, 1993), pp. 75–6.
38 See also Geoffrey Hill's poem 'Churchill's Funeral IV', in which he memorialises the churches lost in the Blitz – 'St Mary Abchurch, St Mary Alderbury, St Mary-le-Bow' – through glimpses of 'the ragwort / and the willow-herb / as edifiers / of ruined things', in *Canaan* (Harmondsworth: Penguin, 1996), p. 48.
39 Rose Macaulay, *The Pleasure of Ruins* (London: Weidenfield and Nicolson, 1953), p. 453.

12

JOHN CLEMENT BALL

Immigration and postwar London literature

In an article published in the *Guardian* in 2004, the West Indian-born, British-raised novelist Caryl Phillips remarked on the curious absence in 1950s British literature of a phenomenon that was visibly transforming the nation throughout that decade. Immigration from the far-flung possessions of an empire that had begun decolonising in earnest after the war burgeoned in the 1950s, with the West Indies and Africa especially supplying hundreds of thousands of new residents to Britain (and to London in particular). Yet despite what Phillips calls 'the daily presence of these new people on the streets, on the buses, and working in hospitals and factories all over the country' at the time, leading British-born writers such as Kingsley Amis and John Osborne displayed a general – and perhaps, Phillips suggests, even a wilful – blindness to the nation's emerging multiracial and multicultural reality.[1] The key exception, he notes, was Colin MacInnes, who was born in London in 1914, grew up in Australia, eventually moved back to London, and, in the late 1950s, wrote three important novels that feature multiracial groups of protagonists and vividly depict a city in flux. Of the three, Phillips gives pride of place to MacInnes's first, *City of Spades*, published in 1957.

For its time *City of Spades* is indeed remarkable – a novel of unusual racial balance that unfolds, in alternating chapters, the parallel first-person narratives of two young metropolitan greenhorns. Montgomery Pew is an English welfare officer whose first day on the job introduces him to Johnny Fortune, a Nigerian immigrant navigating his own first day in London – straight off the boat, as it were. Immediately captivated by Johnny's self-confidence and energy, the liberal-minded Pew is drawn into a kinetic subculture of African and West Indian 'Spades', from which experience he, as what Fortune calls a white 'Jumble' (i.e. 'johnbull'), soon comes to 'thank goodness they've come into our midst … Because they bring an element of joy and fantasy and violence into our cautious, ordered lives'.[2] Even at this early stage of 'New Commonwealth' immigration, English spaces have been transformed and reterritorialised; Pew, though 'not a lover of that gloomiest of English institutions – the public house', finds himself in one pub 'where dark skins outnumbered white by something like twenty to one' and where 'there was a prodigious bubble and clatter of sound, and what is rare in purely English gatherings – a constant movement of person to person, and group to group, as though some great invisible spoon were perpetually stirring a hot human soup' (pp. 42, 43). The novel may end on a note of racist injustice perpetrated on a newly 'sour' Johnny forced to question his metropolitan belonging (p. 238), but with its (literally and figuratively) colourful cast of characters, its intricately interracial plot, and its sharing of narrative authority between a white Londoner and a black one, *City of Spades* stirs the racial 'soup' much more than other British novels of its time. In doing so, it represents a London in which West Indians, Africans, and born-and-bred Britons have (or at least deserve) a more-or-less equal stake in and claim on the imperial heartland. Not only were MacInnes's fellow white writers not doing that, but it would take the migrant and expatriate authors of the Commonwealth who wrote almost all the other postwar novels of London immigration several decades to produce fictions as committed to representing both sides of London's (post)imperial racial divide.

Cities have always been places of mixture, of the commingling of differences across the borders that otherwise separate people into cultures, races, ethnicities, classes, religions, generations, and nations. In his influential book *The Uses of Disorder*, the urban theorist Richard Sennett celebrates this aspect of cities: their creative, heterogeneous 'disorder', which combats impulses toward segregation, 'purity', and the erection of spatial or psychological boundaries.[3] With a kind of evangelical verve Sennett endorses the city's capacity – from street-level physical encounters to its gathering of varied worldviews and ideologies – to break down 'the self-contained qualities of the various ethnic groups' that inhabit it (p. 56). While *City of Spades* implicitly shares this vision of city-space, it does so not in a naïve or utopian way. Indeed, Montgomery loses his welfare-officer job for being 'a little too familiar with the coloured races' (p. 109); he later questions his involvement with black Londoners because, 'exhilarating' as their company is, 'if you stole some of their physical vitality, you found the price was that they began to invade your soul: or rather, they did not, but your own idea of them did – for they were sublimely indifferent to anything outside themselves!' (pp. 152–3). In various ways, MacInnes's narrative of transcultural interaction (despite or perhaps because of its inclination to exoticise the black 'other') is alive to the limitations of the mutual involvements of peoples that the city promotes – a cosmopolitan world city like London in particular.

Mutual involvement – a concept Zadie Smith would later make much of in her lively novel of multicultural London *White Teeth* (2000)[4] – is a recurring theme in postwar London literature, with a direct causal line often drawn between, on the one hand, Britain's historical decision to get involved in the lives of Africans, South Asians, and the indigenous peoples of the Americas and antipodes, and on the other, the presence of Commonwealth subjects in the metropolitan centre. The Jamaican poet Louise Bennett famously described what West Indians were doing in postwar England as 'Colonization in Reverse';[5] as the black British cultural critic Kobena Mercer has succinctly put it, 'We are here because you were there.'[6] In a similar spirit, MacInnes's Montgomery offers a contextualising retort to his boss's complaint that 'Thousands, you see, have come here in the last few years from Africa and the Caribbean, and given us what we never had before – a colour problem'; 'Could it not be', Montgomery dares to say, 'that we have given them just that in their own countries?' (p. 10). That perception of 'colour' as a 'problem' – ubiquitous in the postwar decades – engendered barriers between races that led early immigrant writers such as George Lamming (Barbados) and Samuel Selvon (Trinidad) to write London novels almost exclusively populated by West Indians. In Lamming's *The Emigrants* and especially Selvon's *The Lonely Londoners*, published in the mid 1950s, the city's aforementioned role as gatherer of differences is primarily enacted in relation to the people (mostly men) from various West Indian islands, normally separated by hundreds of miles, who came together – became *involved* with each other – in the imperial centre based on their shared blackness, West Indianness, and use of the coloniser's language. The white Londoners who dominated the city at the time are rarely seen in these novels. The involvement of blacks with whites that is imperial history's legacy is apparent not through the kinds of reciprocity and mutuality represented in MacInnes's novel, but rather through the continuation of hierarchies of power, and barriers of isolation and marginalisation, of the sort that colonial power arrangements and discourses perpetuated.

Reasons for Lamming and Selvon's narrative choices can be found in the history of postwar London immigration and settlement. The two writers arrived in England in 1950 on the same boat; two years earlier, on 22 June 1948, the SS *Empire Windrush* had arrived in Tilbury with 492 West Indians, an event commonly seen as ushering in the mass Commonwealth migration of subsequent decades. Though initially welcomed as imperial brethren (albeit 'dusky' ones), as this small first wave of immigrants was followed by successive ones, the burgeoning black- and brown-skinned population was increasingly seen to be undermining and diluting traditional notions of Britishness, as well as threatening the white working classes through competition for jobs. The 1948 Nationality Bill that conferred British Citizenship on all Commonwealth peoples the year *Windrush* arrived turned out to be, in Ian Baucom's words, 'the last major piece of legislation that sought to assert the global dimensions of Britishness'.[7] It was followed in later decades by increasingly restrictive legislative measures culminating in the 1981 Nationality Act, which substituted a concept of 'patriality' (or family heritage and, implicitly, race) for the time-honoured principle of *ius soli*, or citizenship by place of birth. To be recognised as British, it was no longer enough to have been born on British soil (which included the imperial territories); one now had to have had a parent or grandparent born in Britain. The effect was to exclude the vast majority of Commonwealth subjects from citizenship. As Harry Goulbourne has written, 'the most powerful and influential of the attempts to redefine the post-imperial British national community is such that membership excludes non-white minorities who have settled on these shores since the Second World War'.[8]

But it was not only legal restrictions that undermined the initial welcome extended to Commonwealth subjects; a preferential 'colour bar' affected many immigrants' access to housing, employment, schooling, and fair treatment by police. The appearance during the 1950s and 1960s of discriminatory signs on flats for rent (e.g. 'No Blacks No Dogs No Irish'), along with events such as the 1958 Notting Hill Riots, the racist speeches of Conservative MP Enoch Powell a decade later, and the emergence of the right-wing National Front, all contributed to a climate in which dark-skinned immigrants were forced to confront the precariousness of their claims to belong. What is remarkable, then, in the literature that imaginatively records such experiences from the 1950s to 1970s, is the range of attitudes to metropolitan life they convey toward the city, given their protagonists' isolation from mainstream society. In key novels such as those by Lamming and Selvon mentioned above, and by Andrew Salkey (Jamaica), V. S. Naipaul (Trinidad), Buchi Emecheta (Nigeria), Kamala Markandaya (India), and Anita Desai (India), there is bitterness and anger and frustration, but there is also fascination and curiosity and even, at times, delight with what the heart of the erstwhile empire has to offer. The metropolis is both resisted and revered, a prison that can be a playground, a place of exclusions but also of expansive embrace. The composite portrait these diverse works create is an ambivalent one: as a symbol of and metonym for the historical empire and present-day nation of which it is the centre, London was a natural object for postcolonial resistance of the 'Empire Writes Back' sort; it was also, however, a world city that increasingly, in the postwar period, could be seen as a microcosm of the decolonising societies whose members were sailing in to take possession of the metropolis and begin remaking it in their own images.

The earliest novel, Lamming's *The Emigrants* (1954), is telling in what it chooses not to do: namely, represent the urban landscape in which its almost exclusively West Indian characters were living. With no outdoor scenes and few place names – indeed, with every scene in its 150 pages of London narrative taking place in a room (typically a basement one) – the effect of its rather ponderous, fragmentary, and disorienting narrative is of people barred entry to the very city they have crossed the Atlantic to inhabit. Visible minorities, in Lamming's book, inhabit a virtually invisible city; they are cut off from it, from all but a few of its white residents, and often from each other – the fellow islanders with whom they were thrown together on the long sea journey that brought them there in the novel's first section. The contrast between London's constraints and their lives back home is revealing:

> In another climate, at another time, they would ramble the streets yarning and singing, or sit at the street corners throwing dice as they talked aimlessly about everything and nothing. Life was leisurely. But this room was different. Its immediacy forced them to see that each was caught in it. There was no escape from it until the morning came with its uncertain offer of another day's work. Alone, circumscribed by the night and the neutral staring walls, each felt himself pushed to the limit of his thinking.[9]

This bleak novel's dominant images are of blindness, closed doors, immobility, and fractured interpersonal relations. The small spaces the characters are given to inhabit – rooms, clubs, and shops – come across as consolation prizes they are claiming in lieu of a city that is not yet theirs. Lamming may be resisting the metropolis by refusing to represent it; alternatively, he may be holding back from the arrogant, quasi-imperialist presumption that he can competently represent a place he and his fellow West Indians have just begun to inhabit. Either way, this first London novel by a postwar immigrant conveys radically curtailed lives in a city that seems out of reach and out of sight.

In contrast to the static entrapment of Lamming's subterranean subjects is the mobile connoisseurship of the narrative in *The Lonely Londoners* (1956). One of several London fictions by Selvon – others include the novels *An Island Is a World* (1955), *The Housing Lark* (1965), and *Moses Ascending* (1975), and short stories published in *Ways of Sunlight* (1961) – it has emerged by scholarly consensus as the quintessential postcolonial account of postwar immigration to London. Selvon, like Lamming, places his mostly male West Indians in isolating rooms: 'It have people living in London who don't know what happening in the room next to them, far more the street, or how other people living. London is a place like that. It divide up in little worlds.'[10] He shows almost no interactions between white-skinned and dark-skinned Londoners, and his characters struggle with poverty, hunger (one kills a seagull a day for food), and the vertiginous marginality of their perches on the labour market. But Selvon's dialect-flavoured, episodic narrative of immigrant misadventures is lighter and more inclined to gentle comedy than Lamming's. It is more upbeat and optimistic in its vision of an incipient community of West Indians coalescing over time through shared hardship in and affection for their new home. Its visual, picaresque, *flâneur*-like narrative roams about a London it, unlike Lamming's, sees vividly and takes pleasure in representing; the storied city of Shakespeare and Dickens and Woolf, with its famous landmarks, is romanced in a new, at times even euphoric, West Indian voice:

> Oh what it is and where it is and why it is, no one knows, but to have said: 'I walked on Waterloo Bridge', 'I rendezvoused at Charing Cross', 'Piccadilly Circus is my playground', to say these things, to have lived these things, to have lived in the great city of London, centre of the world. To one day lean against the wind walking up the Bayswater Road (destination unknown), to see the leaves swirl and dance and spin on the pavement (sight unseeing), to write a casual letter home beginning: 'Last night, in Trafalgar Square ...' (p. 121; ellipsis in original)

With passages like this – and a ten-page, single-sentence reverie on summer – offsetting the bleaker experiences telegraphed by its title, *The Lonely Londoners* achieves a delicate balance between London as a place that constrains and defeats its black immigrants and as a place that stimulates liberating, pleasurable feelings of access to and inclusion within a desirable metropolitan world. The narrative's easy movement between indoor and outdoor spaces – metonymically, the basement and the street – reinforces its critical but affectionate vision of a city that West Indians are creatively inhabiting, carefully observing, and coming to know as theirs. *Moses Ascending*, published nineteen years later as a kind of sequel, extends Selvon's earlier themes of immigrant struggle in a more satiric direction signalled by an early passage celebrating the unique opportunities London's labour market supposedly offers its black residents:

> The alarms of all the black people in Brit'n are timed to ring before the rest of the population. It is their destiny to be up and about at the crack o'dawn ... [The black worker] does not know how privileged he is to be in charge of the city whilst the rest of Brit'n is still abed. He strides the streets, he is Manager of all the offices in *Threadaneedle* street, he is Chief Executive of London Transport and British Railways, he is Superintendent of all the hospitals, he is Landlord of all the mansions in Park Lane and Hampstead, he is Head Gourmet and Master Chef of all the restaurants ... He holds the keys of the city, and he will unlock the doors and tidy the papers on the desk, flush the loo, straighten the chairs, hoover the carpet ... Here he is, monarch of all he surveys ... Oh, the ingratitude, the unreasonableness of those who only

see one side of the coin, and complain that he is given only menial tasks to perform![11]

Another target of Selvon's satire in *Moses* is the Black Power movement that had crossed the Atlantic from the USA and gained a foothold among London's black communities in the late 1960s and early 1970s; Lamming's second London novel, *Water with Berries* (1971), also engages critically with Black Power, as does Andrew Salkey in *Come Home, Malcolm Heartland* (1976).

Salkey's first London novel, *Escape to an Autumn Pavement* (1960), is set in the late 1950s and complements Lamming's in its general confinement to indoor spaces such as flats, stairwells, and clubs. Its protagonist, a young Jamaican named Johnny, has an ambivalent attachment to London, and he and his friend Larry do not seem at home in a city that is still a place of division. Interracial relations – whether sexual with a white woman or nextdoor-neighbourly with an Indian one – are invariably fractious, and the backlash against black immigrants that marked the period is reflected in a racist pamphlet Johnny and Larry are handed on the street: 'Keep w.11 white – keep Notting Hill white', it reads: 'it is no good bringing coloured people who are very different to ourselves. Oil and water will not mix.'[12] Johnny may be a young man on the make and on the move – not unlike MacInnes's Johnny – but his London is a gloomier, less enthralling place than the Londons of MacInnes or Selvon.

The disappointments and (dis)illusions of the first decade of postwar, post-*Windrush* London inhabitation were fictionally rendered from a largely West Indian and almost exclusively male point of view.[13] But as the period recedes into increasingly distant (and much-mythologised) history, it has attracted contemporary novelists eager to rethink its meaning and add women's experiences to our understanding of it – even when the novelists in question are male. Caryl Phillips's Leila in *The Final Passage* (1985) sails in 1958 from her Caribbean home, accompanied by her husband Michael and baby boy, to reunite with her mother, who went to London for medical treatment. After they arrive, difficulties finding suitable accommodation and work are compounded when the wayward Michael drifts away in pursuit of white women. With her mother having died and a new baby on the way, Leila gives up on Michael and a London whose negatives are anticipated by her first impressions of the English coast: 'Leila looked at England, but everything seemed bleak. She quickly realized she would have to learn a new word; overcast. There were no green mountains, there were no colourful women with baskets on their heads selling peanuts or bananas or mangoes, there were no trees, no white houses on the hills, no hills', and so the litany of negation continues.[14] The Trinidadian-Canadian writer Neil Bissoondath, a nephew of V. S. Naipaul, includes a year in the life of a West Indian diplomat's wife in 1950s London in *The Worlds within Her* (1998). While, like Leila, Shakti has disappointments in both her husband and her environment, in her privileged position these are lower-stakes matters: her workaholic husband misses promised walks on the Thames and doesn't apologise; 'my biggest disappointment with London', Shakti says, 'was those tiny backyard gardens' in a city where 'I had expected to find only grandeur everywhere'.[15] The ambivalence with which she arrives reflects that of many West Indian migrants toward the imperial 'mother country': 'England was a fantasy for us in the island. We loved it, loved belonging to the majesty of it – and we hated it, because that very majesty was what kept us, in their eyes and ours, childlike' (p. 175). Most recently, the West Indian experience of 1950s London has been fictionally revisited in Andrea Levy's Orange Prize-winning novel *Small Island* (2004).[16]

Lamming, Salkey, and Selvon were leading figures in a generation of male West Indian writers – others included Edgar Mittelholzer and Wilson Harris from Guyana, and V. S. Naipaul from Trinidad – that came to London in the 1950s to establish careers not possible at home. With no literary book publishers in the region and only a fledgling literary culture, they journeyed to the imperial centre, which soon became, in Kenneth Ramchand's words, 'indisputably the West Indian literary capital'.[17] Indeed, writers and other West Indians could form communities in London that weren't possible among their scattered island homes; in one of the many fascinating writers' memoirs of this time, Sam Selvon writes that 'my life in London taught me about people from the Caribbean, and it was here that I found my identity'.[18] Writers' building of communities and finding of identity was helped immeasurably by the BBC radio programme *Caribbean Voices*, which also helped get them established and developed audiences for their work. From 1945 to 1958 this weekly London-based programme broadcast writing by West Indians – solicited from across the region and substantially from the London-based writers – to listeners throughout the British Caribbean. Their work was introduced and discussed (respectfully if at times rather patronisingly) by the British host Henry Swanzy and guest commentators such as Arthur Calder-Marshall. Authors were paid for their work, which was a boost psychologically and financially, and they formed panels to discuss literary topics. Although the programme replicated a colonial economic model whereby resources are gathered from far-flung colonies for processing at the centre and export back, the enabling role *Caribbean Voices* played was crucial to the development of the region's literature. As Lamming wrote in *The Pleasures of Exile* (1960), writers in the region would look forward to that Sunday evening at half-past seven. It was their reprieve. Moreover, 'Caribbean Voices' enabled writers in one island to keep in touch with the latest work of writers in another island … From Barbados, Trinidad, Jamaica, and other islands, poems and short stories were sent to England; and from a London studio in Oxford Street, the curriculum for a serious all-night argument was being prepared.[19]

V. S. Naipaul hosted *Caribbean Voices* in the mid 1950s after Swanzy left, but hosting wasn't all he did at the BBC. In his memoir 'Prologue to an Autobiography' (1984), Naipaul tells the story of how 'in a BBC room in London, on an old BBC typewriter … I wrote the first sentence of my first publishable book'.[20] That book, *Miguel Street* (1959), was, like Naipaul's other early fiction, set in Trinidad, but by the mid 1960s Naipaul had begun writing about London – in some of the short stories collected in *A Flag on the Island* (1967) and, most notably, in the novels *Mr Stone and the Knights Companion* (1963) and *The Mimic Men* (1967). *Mr Stone*'s eponymous protagonist is not an immigrant, but the novel does, in John McLeod's view, capture something of the immigrant Naipaul's 'conflicting perceptions of London: the fantasy of reassuring metropolitan purpose when seen from afar, and its betrayal both in and by the postwar city'.[21] *The Mimic Men* offers Naipaul's most extended early exploration in fiction of an immigrant's experience of London, including its own idiosyncratic version of that sense of betrayed metropolitan fantasy.[22] Ralph Singh, a former politician from a Trinidad-like island called Isabella, is living in exile in London and writing the memoirs of his various London and Isabella adventures. Introspective, cerebral, and something of a loner, Singh is more detached observer than community-builder – though as a young man he has a turbulent relationship with a white British woman named Sandra. In his mordantly ironic reflections on urban life and light – he is fascinated by the different qualities of temperate London's light compared to tropical Isabella's – he expresses disappointment at finding the very 'disorder' that Richard Sennett values in urban life:

> So quickly had London gone sour on me. The great city, centre of the world, in which, fleeing [Isabella's] disorder, I had hoped to find the beginning of order … Here was the city, the world. I waited for the flowering to come to me. The trams on the Embankment sparked blue. The river was edged and pierced with reflections of light, blue and red and yellow. Excitement! Its heart must have lain somewhere. But the god of the city was elusive … In the great city, so solid in its light … in this solid city life was two-dimensional.[23]

A tone of world-weariness and fastidious disgust prevails, but the isolation of Singh is a function of his character as much as his place and race. It seems at least partly chosen, given his view of migrancy as self-reinvention: 'In London I had no guide. There was no one to link my present with my past, no one to note my consistencies or inconsistencies. It was up to me to choose my character, and I chose the character that was easiest and most attractive. I was the dandy, the extravagant colonial' (p. 20). Even so, 'It is with cities as it is with sex. We seek the physical city and find only a conglomeration of private cells. In the city as nowhere else we are reminded that we are individuals, units' (p. 18). Singh, hailing from a region of 'transitional or makeshift societies' depicted through a controlling image of 'shipwreck', realises he has simply found another kind of shipwreck in 'the greater disorder, the final emptiness: London and the home counties' (p. 8).

A less abstract and intellectualised, more quotidian bleakness besets the first-person immigrants in the novels of Buchi Emecheta, the most important African writer to write regularly of London in the postwar period. Her first, the semi-autobiographical *In the Ditch* (1972), relates the struggles of a Nigerian single mother with five children to survive and find adequate housing in Britain's welfare state. Life on the dole for a black family involves constant compromise and disappointment, especially for Adah, who will bend over backwards (almost literally) to keep her dignity even if it means offering to do an exploitative, back-breaking cleaning job so she can make £2 more a week and buy Christmas gifts. Leaky ceilings and walls, tense relations with white working-class neighbours, casually inflicted humiliations by agents of various institutional powers (and, unwittingly, by the interracial community of working-class women who support Adah but sometimes remain blinkered to their own racism): Emecheta's novel offers an unvarnished portrait of poverty, marginalisation, and struggle in a London that still offers only a begrudging, discouraging welcome to new black residents.

As in most of the male-authored West Indian texts that preceded it, the early-1960s London of *In the Ditch* is a London lived primarily behind walls and doors, a city whose urban landscape is largely unobserved and unindividualised. Save a few landmarks identifying her North London neighbourhood, Adah could be living in any number of British cities of the time. Almost twenty years after Lamming's new arrivals were virtually imprisoned indoors by their author, Emecheta's heroine is portrayed mostly in the domestic environment – what Susan Yearwood calls the 'feminized space' of 'the ditch'[24] – to which her gender, parental responsibilities, and poverty tie her. Although she makes much of the image of the dwelling-place that so many postcolonial authors emphasise in narrating imperial (and reverse-imperial) occupation, displacement, and migration, Emecheta's London, like Lamming's, has little of what Kevin Lynch calls 'imageability'.

In *The Image of the City*, Lynch defines imageability as the visual coherence that can 'invite the eye and the ear to greater attention and participation' – a combination of 'shape, colour, or arrangement which facilitates the making of vividly identified, powerfully structured, highly useful mental images of the environment' and helps city-dwellers orient themselves.[25] Lamming's London's lack of imageability reflected his characters' disorientation and non-participation in the urban milieu; Adah, too, presents a severely curtailed image of her metropolitan world.

Emecheta's follow-up novel, *Second-Class Citizen* (1974), is a prequel that explains how Adah, a well-educated, well-employed young Nigerian woman, came to be on her own with five children in the metropolis. Fiercely independent, she leaves a good job with the American embassy in Lagos to follow her husband, Francis, a feckless student and, it becomes increasingly clear, a myopic, negligent, and abusive partner. Adah's struggle, as more children join the two she came with, is as much against the (patriarchal, chauvinist) baggage of 'Nigerianness' represented by her husband and other unsavoury male migrants as with London and 'Britishness'. Indeed, she finds more support and understanding among the English co-workers at her library job than among her own people:

> Thinking about her first year in Britain, Adah could not help wondering whether the real discrimination ... was not more the work of her fellow countrymen than of the whites. Maybe if the blacks could learn to live harmoniously with one another, maybe if a West Indian landlord could learn not to look down on the African ... there would be fewer inferiority feelings among the blacks.[26]

A complex set of contexts influences Adah's identity and conflicted relations in London – race, class, culture, nation, family, education, work, and of course gender. Because she can be seen as 'second class' in most of these contexts, her freedom, safety, and hopes for her children and herself are undermined in every metropolitan space she can inhabit – home, street, daycare, hospital, and even (since Francis stymies her attempts at birth control) her own body. An exception is the library where, among fellow book-lovers, she nurtures the ambition to write her first novel; outside that supportive multiracial world, she remains imperilled, as does the precious manuscript of the novel, which Francis callously burns in a horrific scene that feels, to Adah, like the murder of 'my child' (p. 181). In Emecheta's documentary-realist vision, not even the imagined, self-created space of the fictional text provides an ameliorating alternative to quotidian suffering – though the manuscript burning is the final straw that prompts Adah to leave her ne'er-do-well, abusive husband.

Emecheta is the only major postcolonial novelist of the immediate post-war decades to offer a sustained portrait of immigration to London from a woman's point of view. The West Indians Joan Riley (Jamaica) and Beryl Gilroy (Guyana) would do so beginning in the mid 1980s, and Ama Ata Aidoo of Ghana has a caustic London section in *Our Sister Killjoy* (1977), in which she writes, 'the story is as old as empires. Oppressed multitudes from the provinces rush to the imperial seat because that is where they know all salvation comes from. But as other imperial subjects in other times and other places have discovered, for the slave, there is nothing at the centre but worse slavery.'[27] Two leading female novelists from India – Kamala Markandaya and Anita Desai – wrote significant London novels in the 1960s and early 1970s; however, their Indian-immigrant protagonists are all male. Markandaya's *Possession* (1963) brings a young man from the obscurity of his South India village to 1950s London under the patronage of an imperious, wealthy British woman who sees the metropolis as the ideal spot to cultivate his talent for painting, and to exhibit both the artworks and the 'exotic' painter himself to metropolitan society. Valmiki's privileged, performative experience of London is thus hardly typical of postwar immigrants', though his ultimate resistance to his patron and return to a kind of Gandhian austerity and authenticity in his village serves Markandaya's primarily allegorical drive. Lady Caroline signifies imperial England presuming to know what's best for (and thus to take command of) an 'undeveloped' India (Valmiki) that will nonetheless elude its full control. London in this novel becomes a site where old tensions can be played out on an intriguing new stage – where, *pace* Kipling, 'East' and 'West' can meet but, in the end, recognise the different worldviews and goals that divide the 'twain'.[28]

The Nowhere Man (1972), also by Markandaya, portrays a more characteristic, grittier experience of immigrant un-housing. Its protagonist, an elderly Indian named Srinivas, has lived in London for fifty years, but a concatenation of events forces him to question his claim to belong. A homeowner there since the 1930s, he becomes a victim of the ramped-up racism of the 1960s after years of peaceful relations with British neighbours. His house, where he sheltered grateful Londoners in his basement during wartime air raids, becomes a contentious site when his leprosy (which he keeps secret) forces him to evict his tenants at a time of housing shortages. When an ousted tenant's mother rails at Srinivas for 'coming to this country … acting as if you owned it, oppressing *us*', his son defends him by invoking colonial history: 'if we do, we have learned from our masters, madam'. The tenant's father replies, 'That's the gratitude we get … after all we've done for them.'[29] In this unfortunate climate of binary 'us and them' thinking, itself a legacy of colonialist discourse, an angry racist named Fred Fletcher makes it his mission to burn down the house, which in his mind has come to represent a contaminated nation-space that he must heroically purge and purify. At the novel's denouement, however, some ironic reversals powerfully challenge the too-easy equation of racial groups with the spaces to which they are seen to properly belong.

In *The Nowhere Man*, as in most novels discussed so far, metropolitan domestic spaces and acts of dwelling readily point to larger questions of racial-ethnic entitlement, power, and purchase on the wary British nation that are encoded with the messy histories of imperial invasion and inhabitation. Later novels by Riley (*Waiting for the Twilight*, 1987) and Gilroy (*Boy-Sandwich*, 1989) also depict elderly, homeowning, long-time London residents becoming unhoused by forces beyond their control. As James Procter notes in *Dwelling Places*, his fine study of postwar 'black British' writing, the conditions of inhabitation may change over the decades – from the marginal foothold of Lamming's basement bedsit, through the home-ownership schemes of Selvon's *Housing Lark* gang and post-1950s Moses, to the secure homes from which young second-generation immigrants simply want to escape in late-twentieth-century novels by Hanif Kureishi, Diran Adebayo, and Meera Syal. But dwelling 'as both a noun (a house, a home, a territory) and a verb (to linger, to settle, to stay)'[30] is a constant preoccupation and point of reference. For Procter, this literary fixation on the local forces us to recognise emplacement, location, and inhabitation as viable alternative frames to postcolonial theory's dominant emphasis on global displacement, mobility, and diaspora.

For the protagonists of Desai's *Bye-Bye Blackbird* (1971), young male Indians rambling around London in 1965, the emphasis is less on dwelling(s) than on the immigrant's psychological and emotional responses to public space, particularly monuments. The British exported Gothic architecture to nineteenth-century India, the vaunted 'jewel in the crown' of empire, influenced by Ruskin's view of English architecture's 'identity-forming and reforming power'.[31] Architecture could both support the Englishness of colonisers abroad and impress it upon colonial subjects, and Desai's Dev finds the Albert Memorial reminiscent of 'similar nightmares of stone and marble in India' such as Bombay's Victoria railway terminus and Calcutta's Victoria Memorial.[32] Dev's besotted affection for metropolitan scenes familiar from 'the pages of Dickens and Lamb, Addison and Boswell' to which his colonial education exposed him (p. 10) – and whose built space raises persistent questions of authenticity and imitation – is offset by his friend Adit's sudden turn against a London life that feels 'unreal'. Adit vows to return to India to 'start living a real life' (p. 204), while Dev is happy to stay. Both men are prone to imaginary geographies and fantasies of place-identity, a sign perhaps of their insecure hold on the metropolis. One of the novel's most memorable images is Dev's fancy of the Battersea Power Station, which he sees as a shrine to Britain's power, as site of an Indian *puja* that includes a ceremonial fire from which 'the electricity of London is generated' (p. 54). This is a playful acknowledgment of the ways the imperial might encoded in the capital's spatial monumentality is derived from the energy and resources of the colonies that supported it.

Indeed, as Roy Porter writes in his social history of London, the city grew and prospered in tandem with imperial involvements: 'The key to the capital', he says, 'is the British Empire'.[33] The debt Britain's economy and culture owe to its empire has been playfully and memorably conveyed by the Jamaican-born cultural theorist Stuart Hall:

> People like me who came to England in the 1950s have been there for centuries … I am the sugar at the bottom of the English cup of tea. I am the sweet tooth, the sugar plantations that rotted generations of English children's teeth. There are thousands of others beside me that are, you know, the cup of tea itself. Because they don't grow it in Lancashire, you know … Where does it come from? Ceylon – Sri Lanka, India. That is the outside history that is inside the history of the English.[34]

That shared history is also a shared – albeit unevenly shared – geography; London was a place that colonised subjects imaginatively, and often quite affectionately, shared with their English masters. As the Indian novelist R. K. Narayan once wrote, 'Through books alone we learnt to love the London of English literature',[35] and Desai's Dev repeatedly conveys this sense of both love and intimate knowledge. Earlier in the essay quoted above, Hall stresses the specialness of London as a destination in ways that echo Selvon's *Lonely Londoners* narrator: 'You have to live in London', Hall writes: 'If you come from the sticks, the colonial sticks, where you really want to live is right on Eros Statue in Piccadilly Circus … You want to go right to the centre of the hub of the world. You might as well. You have been hearing about that ever since you were one month old' (p. 24).

Just as one can't actually live on a statue in Piccadilly Circus, the reality on the ground is inevitably more prosaic than the imagined one – less idealised, less 'central', less loveable. A recurrent imagery of downsizing and rhetoric of disappointment pervade postcolonial London literature, and the city that was the heart of empire becomes an object of resistance – both indirectly to the history of imperial subjugation that it metonymically represents, and directly to the present-day perpetuation of empire's racially hierarchical, marginalising power structures in the realms of housing, employment, and the like. As the English language is, in the words of the pioneering theorists of *The Empire Writes Back*, subject to 'simultaneous processes of abrogation and appropriation' by postcolonial writers, so is the city at the heart of imperial power both appropriated (inhabited, inscribed) and abrogated (resisted, refashioned) by those writers who represent the post-war immigrant's experience there.[36] Their literary works, including many of those discussed above, contain an ambivalent mixture of commitment to and critique of London, both of which are evident in the ways immigrants struggle not just to live in the city but, in the spirit of reverse colonisation, to reterritorialise it, to transform it, to remake it in their own images.

This is usually achieved through the small, everyday ways that migrants dwell in and use a city – as with the English pub where patterns of social interaction change as the dominant colour of skin changes in MacInnes's *City of Spades*. It can happen in larger ways when neighbourhoods such as Notting Hill (through its famous carnival) or Brick Lane (through Bangladeshi settlement) become demographically transformed. Gibreel Farishta imagines himself transforming the metropolis in an extreme, top-down way in Salman Rushdie's *The Satanic Verses* (1988), the most important novel of London immigration from what we might call the post-postwar period. Gibreel's delusional vision is both literally and metaphorically over the top, as he believes himself to be an angel on high with the power unilaterally to transform 'London into a tropical city'.[37] Rushdie's humorous catalogue of benefits a 'tropicalized' (and essentially Indianised) London would possess recalls Dev's fancy of a *puja*-infused Battersea Power Station. But while Desai's mid-1960s immigrants seem, at that early stage of postcolonial settlement, merely idiosyncratic – without social or political valence in a city still dominantly white and English and where Indians, like West Indians and Africans, still have a slender purchase – Rushdie's mid-1980s setting offers more possibilities for empowering agency in the city. Nonetheless, Gibreel fails spectacularly; it is his friend and nemesis Saladin Chamcha who, through street-level rather than top-down activities, has the more realistic (however magically brought about) transformative effect on metropolitan life.

The urban street is a multivalent space representing, variously, purposive mobility; leisurely strolling; pleasurable consumption; mingling with and spectatorship of others; and collective, carnivalesque celebration. Less positively, the street invokes images of the alienating crowd, the perils and pathos of homelessness, the fear of getting lost, and dangers from hostile others. While some of the fictions discussed here are more inclined than others to venture into the street, all of them in their *use* of the metropolis – characters inhabiting it, writers writing it – are like the urban pedestrians of Michel de Certeau's famous essay 'Walking in the City'. By using and representing the city in ways that reflect their cultures, histories, and personal goals, they are resisting the power symbolised in its spatial structures, just as an individual walker inventing a unique, street-level itinerary relates to the city differently than a planner or map-maker or aerial viewer. For de Certeau, 'The act of walking is to the urban system what the speech act is to language',[38] and as the city is used, the proper names associated with it lose their traditional or official significations. They 'detach themselves from the places they were supposed to define' and 'make themselves available to the diverse meanings given them by passers-by' (p. 104) – and, for our purposes, by writers. Another way of putting this is to say that postcolonial writers and their migrant characters do for London what Homi K. Bhabha, in his influential essay 'DissemiNation', argues 'the people' do for the nation: counter its fixed, official, historically rooted 'pedagogical' version of its identity with a mutable, constantly renewed 'performative' version that they collectively create.[39] When Selvon's lonely Londoners, who are regularly shown walking, bandy about the names of London landmarks with easy familiarity – even nicknaming some of them, so Bayswater Road becomes 'the Water' and Marble Arch 'the Arch' (pp. 9, 82) – they are, through the smallest of acts, symbolically repossessing, re-signifying, and performing the metropolis.

London has always been a world city, a cosmopolitan place containing a mixture of national and racial others, but it became more and more visibly so over the postwar decades. As empire gave way to decolonisation and 'New Commonwealth' immigration and, through the 1980s and 1990s, globalisation, London increasingly became (and was seen and represented as) a transnational space related in intricate, web-like ways to the countless elsewheres from which its residents came. Going to London had long been seen as accessing 'the world' (or at least, a bigger 'world' of opportunity and experience than was available at home), but increasingly it really was a microcosm of the world. As a result, the identities formed and re-formed there are, particularly for postcolonial migrants, relational identities. Novels of London immigrants are never simply about London: they are also about the homeland that connects to, contrasts with, or otherwise frames the new metropolitan world. The earliest West Indian fiction of London, Jean Rhys's prewar *Voyage in the Dark* (1934), does this as the drab, disorienting, lookalike London streets contrast starkly and unfavourably with the narrator's memories of her colourful, comprehensible, highly differentiated West Indian island environment. The most recent (and final) novel to be discussed here, Amitav Ghosh's *The Shadow Lines* (1988), does so too, but in a way that quite radically globalises and internationalises London.

Ghosh's young Bengali narrator finds his postcolonial identity and political vision in and among three distant cities, London, Calcutta, and Dhaka. As his

fluid, nonlinear narrative oscillates back and forth across four decades beginning in 1939, and as it meditates on memories and events in all three places
and involving two extended families, the cities and their people (whether
English or South Asian) mirror each other in complex ways that emphasise
their transnational relatedness over their differences. The novel's levelling,
dematerialising, border-hopping vision has been criticised for its seeming
'wishing away of troublesome realities' such as national borders from a position of privileged, middle-class mobility,[40] but distinctions between here and
there don't entirely evaporate. Ghosh commits to both the specificity of the
local and the transcendence of the global, negotiating between them as he
draws intricate vectors of connection – the shadow lines of his title – between
times, places, and peoples. His novel is as comfortable and interested in
dwelling-places as airport lounges, in imagined places as experienced ones,
and in a wartime London bombsite as in the Taj Travel Agency that stands
there forty years later. There is something in his synchronic, all-encompass-
ing, somewhat untidy vision that is definitive of London itself.

At one point Ghosh's narrator marvels at 'the experience of hearing Bengali
dialects which I had never heard in Calcutta being spoken in the streets of
London'.[41] Unique things can indeed happen in the metropolis. Because of
the city's special place in imperial history, the global economy, and the cultural and literary imaginations of England's once-colonised subjects, writers
of the postwar decolonising era have set narratives in the streets of London
that could not have taken place anywhere else.

Notes

1 Caryl Phillips, 'Kingdom of the Blind', www.guardian.co.uk/books/2004/jul/17/
   featuresreviews.guardianreview1 (accessed 5 August 2010).
2 Colin MacInnes, *City of Spades* (London: Allison and Busby, 1980), p. 66. Further
   references are parenthesised within the text.
3 Richard Sennett, *The Uses of Disorder: Personal Identity and City Life* (New
   York: Knopf, 1970), p. xviii. Further references are parenthesised within the
   text.
4 Zadie Smith, *White Teeth* (London: Hamish Hamilton, 2000), p. 376.
5 Louise Bennett, 'Colonization in Reverse', http://louisebennett.com/newsdetails.
   asp?NewsID=8 (accessed 5 August 2010).
6 Kobena Mercer, *Welcome to the Jungle: New Positions in Black Cultural Studies*
   (London/New York: Routledge, 1994), p. 7.
7 Ian Baucom, *Out of Place: Englishness, Empire, and the Locations of Identity*
   (Princeton: Princeton University Press, 1999), p. 9.
8 Harry Goulbourne, *Ethnicity and Nationalism in Post-Imperial Britain*
   (Cambridge: Cambridge University Press, 1991), p. 1.
9 George Lamming, *The Emigrants* (Ann Arbor: University of Michigan Press,
   1994), p. 192.

10 Sam Selvon, *The Lonely Londoners* (Toronto: TSAR, 1991), p. 58.

11 Sam Selvon, *Moses Ascending* (Oxford: Heinemann, 1984), pp. 5–7.

12 Andrew Salkey, *Escape to an Autumn Pavement* (London: Hutchinson, 1960), p. 118.

13 For an important prewar West Indian woman's perspective on London, see Jean Rhys, *Voyage in the Dark* (London: Constable, 1934).

14 Caryl Phillips, *The Final Passage* (London: Faber, 1999), p. 142.

15 Neil Bissoondath, *The Worlds within Her* (Toronto: Knopf Canada, 1998), p. 183.

16 See John McLeod's chapter in this volume (pp. 241–260) for a discussion of *Small Island*.

17 Kenneth Ramchand, *The West Indian Novel and Its Background* (London: Faber, 1970), p. 63.

18 Samuel Selvon, 'Finding West Indian Identity in London', *Kunapipi* 9.3 (1987), 37.

19 George Lamming, *The Pleasures of Exile* (London: Michael Joseph, 1960), pp. 65–6.

20 V. S. Naipaul, 'Prologue to an Autobiography', in *Finding the Centre: Two Narratives* (Harmondsworth: Penguin, 1985), p. 15.

21 John McLeod, *Postcolonial London: Rewriting the Metropolis* (London/New York: Routledge, 2004), p. 68.

22 Naipaul did go on to write of his 1950s experiences in London in later books such as the memoir disguised as a novel, *The Enigma of Arrival* (1987; discussed in James Donald's chapter in this volume, pp. 261–278), and the fictional Willie Chandran's experiences during the same period in his novel *Half a Life* (2001).

23 V. S. Naipaul, *The Mimic Men* (Harmondsworth: Penguin, 1969), pp. 18–19.

24 Susan Yearwood, 'The Sociopolitics of Black Britain in the Work of Buchi Emecheta', in *Black British Writing*, ed. R. Victoria Arana and Lauri Ramey (New York/Basingstoke: Palgrave, 2004), p. 138.

25 Kevin Lynch, *The Image of the City* (Cambridge, MA: MIT Press, 1960), pp. 10, 9.

26 Buchi Emecheta, *Second-Class Citizen* (Oxford: Heinemann, 1994), p. 70.

27 Ama Ata Aidoo, *Our Sister Killjoy; or, Reflections from a Black-Eyed Squint* (London: Longman, 1988), pp. 87–8.

28 See Rudyard Kipling's poem 'The Ballad of East and West': 'Oh, East is East, and West is West, and never the twain shall meet', in Rudyard Kipling, *Complete Verse* (New York: Anchor Books, 1988), p. 233.

29 Kamala Markandaya, *The Nowhere Man* (New York: John Day, 1972), pp. 273–4.

30 James Procter, *Dwelling Places: Postwar Black British Writing* (Manchester: Manchester University Press, 2003), p. 14.

31 Baucom, *Out of Place*, p. 20.

32 Anita Desai, *Bye-Bye Blackbird* (New Delhi: Orient, 1985), p. 83.

33 Roy Porter, *London: A Social History* (London: Hamish Hamilton, 1994), p. 2.

34 Stuart Hall, 'The Local and the Global: Globalization and Ethnicity', in *Culture, Globalization and the World-System: Contemporary Conditions for the Representation of Identity*, ed. A. D. King (Minneapolis: University of Minnesota Press, 1991), pp. 48–9.

35 R. K. Narayan, 'English in India', in *A Story-Teller's World: Stories, Essays, Sketches* (New Delhi: Penguin India, 1989), p. 21.

36 Bill Ashcroft, Gareth Evans and Helen Tiffin, *The Empire Writes Back: Theory and Practice in Post Colonial Literatures* (London/New York: Routledge, 1989), pp. 38–39.

37 Salman Rushdie, *The Satanic Verses* (New York: Viking Penguin, 1989), p. 365.

38 Michel de Certeau, 'Walking in the City', in *The Practice of Everyday Life*, trans. Steven Rendall (Berkeley: University of California Press, 1984), p. 97.

39 Homi K. Bhabha, 'DissemiNation: Time, Narrative and the Margins of the Modern Nation', in *The Location of Culture* (London/New York: Routledge, 1994), p. 146.

40 A. N. Kaul, 'A Reading of *The Shadow Lines*', in Amitav Ghosh, *The Shadow Lines* (Delhi: Oxford University Press, 1995), p. 303.

41 Amitav Ghosh, *The Shadow Lines* (New York: Penguin, 1990), p. 236.

13

JOHN MCLEOD

Writing London in the twenty-first century

On the evening of Wednesday 6 July 2005, when London was celebrating the news announced that day that the city had won the bid for the 2012 Olympic Games, a fledgling novelist, Chris Cleave, attended the launch party of his first novel, *Incendiary*, which was to be published the following morning. His book was resolutely concerned with life in London in the shadow of the atrocities of 9/11, the US-led invasion of Iraq and Afghanistan, the bombings of trains in Madrid on 11 March 2004, and the infamous events at Abu Ghraib prison. As Cleave subsequently explained, 'The airwaves were filled with body counts and brutish ideologies, and I needed to write something to remind myself of the simple human cost of this folly. And I think I wanted my son, when he was older, to understand something of the febrile nature of the times he was born into.'[1] In the novel, Cleave depicted London struggling to cope in the wake of a genocidal terrorist attack on a Premier League soccer match attended by thousands of fans between two major clubs, Arsenal and Chelsea, at which the unnamed narrator loses her husband and son amidst the carnage. Penned as an extended letter from the narrator to Osama Bin Laden, Cleave's ambitious and often remarkable debut novel explored the imagined social and psychological consequences of a city lost to terror. *Incendiary* was toasted long into the night of 6 July.

Hours later, on the following morning, 52 Londoners were killed and at least 770 injured by 4 suicide bombers in central London who had travelled from Leeds and attacked the Underground railway and bus network. As a mark of sensitivity and respect for the dead and injured of '7/7', as it has come to be known, *Incendiary* was temporarily withdrawn from sale, and the advertising campaign and book tour were cancelled. Such a chilling coming-together of London and literature that day 'made fiction unimportant', recalled Cleave. 'What use is there in fiction in times like these?'[2] This comment, ostensibly a way of displaying commendable compassion to those who suffered the attacks on London, phrases an ongoing and important challenge to those concerned with the business of representing London today. In an age when the city's local fortunes are ever more subject to the travails of global happenings – armed conflicts, poverty and refugeeism, the 'war on terror' – writers' contemporary visions of the city (of its past as well as its present) cannot remain immune from the changed atmosphere and conditions of a new, already embattled century. Yet many depictions of contemporary London refuse to give up hope in the city's potential to broker new cultural relations amidst tension and terror, and they frequently value the resilience often associated with the city's chameleon and heteroglot Londoners.

London's new century began with a spectacular display of cheerfulness and delight, epitomised by the evocative sight of people eagerly gathering on the Embankment as midnight approached on 31 December 1999 to watch the dramatic New Year's Eve light show that illuminated the London Eye and Houses of Parliament on the banks of the Thames (see Figure 13.1). Sadly, too soon was this vivid vision of festivity and fireworks gazumped by another now-famous image of twenty-first-century London that signified carnage rather than collectivity: the wreck of a red double-decker London bus that was detonated on 7 July 2005 in Tavistock Square, just yards from the graceful statue of Mahatma Gandhi, the Indian nationalist leader and advocate of non-violence whose life also met a murderous end (see Figure 13.2). These two contrasting images may help us mark out the terrain of London's literary imagining in recent years, which has given attention to the city's vernacular conviviality on the one hand and to incendiary prejudices and global cultural tensions on the other. As I intend to show in this chapter, even before 7/7 many twenty-first-century representations of London negotiated between an optimistic vision of a city deemed to be leaving behind some of the social and cultural conflicts of the twentieth century and witnessing (in Salman Rushdie's marvellous phrase) how *'newness enters the world'*,[3] and a more sobering encounter with the city's latest problems, born from the global conflicts of the age and which manifest themselves in London's society and culture. In order to insist upon a sense of the visionary qualities of contemporary London writing, I shall make figurative use of one of the city's most recently erected famous landmarks by considering the texts below as collectively constituting new 'London eyes' that espy and envision the complex fortunes of an ever-changing metropolis.

My exploration of twenty-first-century visions of London is inevitably selective and concise, but intends to give a sense of the range of representations of the city in recent years. As London is one of the globe's major world cities, it should be no surprise that the predominant tenor of much contemporary writing is culturally diverse and hybrid. It is no longer the case that,

Figure 13.1 Fireworks above the London Eye on 1 January 2000.

Figure 13.2 Wreck of the no. 30 double-decker bus in Tavistock Square, 8 July 2005.

as in the 1950s and 1960s, multicultural representations of the city constitute a minority or marginal strand in a wider literary landscape. These days
London writing is much more consistently and recurrently reflective of a
city in which over 300 languages are spoken daily, to the extent that those
writers or historians who do have little or nothing to say about London's

humdrum diversity seem increasingly out of touch with the city's history and fortunes.

With all of this in mind, I want to offer three ways of regarding London writing since 2000 in terms of this pervading negotiation. First, I will examine the ways in which many writers have excavated a polycultural and multiracial vision of London's problems and possibilities. This vision is significantly different from those migrant and diasporic representations of London in the twentieth century that tended to prioritise one kind of displaced cultural experience in the city – Caribbean, South Asian, Chinese etc. – and neglect social and cultural engagements (other than crudely prejudicial or spectacularly violent ones) between new and established Londoners. Polycultural narratives afford an alternative to older diasporic models of urban and individual identity (majority–minority, native–foreigner, black–white), and they also attest to an optimistic sense of London as a site of transformative social and cultural encounter *for all* amidst the new prejudices of the twenty-first century. Against this polycultural background, a second strand of writing offers alternative mappings of the city's social geographies. As London has shifted from imperial metropolis to world city in recent decades, many writers have focused on the difficult lives of those – asylum-seekers, undocumented refugees, menial labourers – often pushed to the side in official views of London as a vibrant centre of world capital and global culture. Third, in the wake of 9/11 and 7/7, the so-called 'War on Terror' has led writers to explore the psychological and moral consequences as well as the social impact of contemporary change. For such writers, the act of re-envisioning London has led them to ponder at length the significance and necessity of writing during challenging times. Throughout what follows, I want to maintain a crucial sense of urban representation as simultaneously a creative act and a means of bearing witness – *visionary* as well as mimetic – while insisting ultimately with the convivial, hopeful sense of London conjured by that image of the celebrating crowds gathered underneath the London Eye, illuminated by lasers and fireworks, as midnight struck on 1 January 2000.

Polycultural insights

For many, the first major event for literary London in the twenty-first century was the publication of Zadie Smith's *White Teeth* (2000). Reviewing the book in the *Observer*, the novelist Caryl Phillips praised its depiction of the 'dazzlingly complex world of cross-cultural fusion in modern-day London',[4] and his review in many ways summarised the critical mood. Here, at last, was a novel that seemed to relish riding the rapids of contemporary London, envisioning the city through a primarily comic and upbeat vista of the fun, frustrations, coincidences, and challenges of living between and beyond distinct cultures. Smith's polycultural cast of characters, struggling cheerfully to contend with life in the urban environ of Willesden, indexed the melting-pot city that many readers assumed was enthusiastically advocated by the novel. Smith's vision of contemporary London maintains a sense of the pain of migration and survival, of the 'cold arrivals' that have facilitated this polycultural metropolis. Yet more often than not her emphasis falls on the new friendships and allegiances struck between people from linked yet divergent histories, whose hybridised lives are marked but not conclusively moulded by the generations that begat them. As Laura Moss puts it, Smith's novel celebrates hybridity not as exceptional but 'as part of the practice of everyday life'.[5]

Smith's cheery novelist style – mingling streetwise skaz, Salman Rushdie's hyperbolic adventurousness and E. M. Forster's acute social sensibility – agreeably captures the absurdities wrought from polycultural contact, in which even the most challenging elements of living in a culturally diverse location are narrated with a wry smile. Such is the portrayal of Samad Iqbal, a Bangladeshi migrant, struggling to live as a good Muslim in a profane city that offers a frightening array of temptations and terrors. London's excitements are embodied by the figure of Miss Poppy Burt-Jones, a teacher at his sons' school, with whom he struggles to conduct an affair, while terror attaches to the fortunes of his sons, whom Samad is anxious to protect from the new identities being moulded amidst the latest generation of youthful Londoners. While Smith attends with moderate sobriety to the emotional turmoil in which Samad finds himself, the consequences of each predicament are played for laughs. This is especially true regarding his sons, one of whom (Magid) he sends to be raised in Bangladesh against the knowledge and wishes of his wife, Alsana, while the other, Millat, remains in London. Contrary to expectations, the Bangladeshi-educated Magid returns to London impeccably suited and speaking the Queen's English, every inch a South Asian Anglophile, while Millat's adventures in pop-cultural London lead him eventually to join the Keepers of the Eternal and Victorious Islamic Nation (or KEVIN, for short) and to become involved in seemingly fundamentalist activities as the novel heads toward its droll conclusion. Laughter attaches to virtually every cultural predicament or potentially painful encounter in *White Teeth*, as Smith makes sure that the harshness of life in London does not overwhelm the novel's witty tone.

Given the novel's predominantly satirical engagement with London and Londoners, it could be said that Smith's writing fails adequately to convey, in Homi K. Bhabha's oft-cited words, the gravitas of 'postcolonial migration, the narratives of cultural political and diaspora, the major social displacements of peasant and aboriginal communities, the poetics of exile, the grim prose of political and economic refugees'.[6] But such a reading of *White Teeth* misses the point of the novel's ebullient vision of London and the politics of its optimistic articulation of a polycultural city. Writing in the wake of 9/11 and the hardening of prejudicial attitudes it has stimulated, Paul Gilroy suggests that if we 'work toward creative possibilities that are too easily dismissed as utopian, our moral and political compass might profitably be reset by acts of imagination and invention that are adequate to the depth of the postcolonial predicament [of building new consciousness]'.[7] *White Teeth* can certainly be read as a utopian novel keen to endorse the creative power of the polycultural. It is a *strategically* hopeful imagining of London that endearingly and inventively envisions a cosmopolitan city whose diverse population, despite its formidable problems, cheerfully articulate both creativity and possibility to the last.

For these reasons, *White Teeth* seemed to offer something new in its vital exploration of the interactions of a range of London cultures that significantly includes so-called white Londoners as part of a wider polycultural neighbourhood rather than a remote or 'native' community. While subsequent representations of London as a polycultural city have not always sounded the same hopeful and buoyant note as *White Teeth*, several have also tried to depict Londoners, both past and present, moving beyond more exclusive or separatist models of migrant and host. In the latter decades of the twentieth century, migrant and diasporic representations of London tended to deal in the main with one migratory sphere.[8] These texts inducted the reader into a diasporic community or consciousness struggling to live 'out of place' but rarely depicted at length the responses of the so-called white 'host' community or indeed prolonged relations between communities (partly because such cross-cultural engagements were not always forthcoming at the time). This tradition has continued into the twenty-first century in novels such as Monica Ali's *Brick Lane* (2003), in which readers are invited into the Bangladeshi enclave of London's East End. However, and recalling the impulse of Smith's work perhaps, other writers have attempted a more culturally wide-ranging engagement with the difficult encounters between communities, or with the diasporic fortunes of those who historically have thought of themselves as native, as in Maggie Gee's depiction of a family of white Londoners in her novel *The White Family* (2002).

An important text that brings together the older model of migratory narrative and the new model of polycultural encounter is Andrea Levy's *Small Island* (2004). The novel's subject matter is familiar in London writing: the impact of the historic arrival of the SS *Empire Windrush* on 22 June 1948 at Tilbury docks, carrying 492 Caribbean migrants, whose disembarkation is seen as inaugurating the commencement of a busy period of postwar migration to London from so-called 'New Commonwealth' countries (in the Caribbean, Africa, and South and Southeast Asia). Yet Levy's approach is distinctly twenty-first century. The British-born daughter of Jamaican migrants, Levy casts a critical eye over the conduct and accounts of the 'Windrush generation' from the position of a later generation, and she effectively rewrites received images of these times. Whereas the migrants of the 1950s and 1960s (Sam Selvon, V. S. Naipaul, George Lamming, Andrew Salkey) tended to write about coming to London with little meaningful reference to women's experiences or to the complex responses of the white host community, Levy's depiction of migrant London in 1948 focuses on the lives of women and the cross-racial cultural contacts forged at the beginning of this seminal period of the city's polycultural history. Featuring multiple narrators, the novel concerns the fortunes of a migrant Jamaican couple, Gilbert and Hortense Joseph, who lodge with Queenie Bligh, also something of a newcomer to London as she was raised on a farm in the Midlands as a girl. Both Queenie's and Hortense's husbands have fought in the Second World War (Queenie's husband Bernard, who is missing at the novel's beginning, saw action in Asia). Rather than stage the encounter of the Josephs and the Blighs reductively as one between migrants and hosts, Levy presents instead their common contours of experience; indeed, the movement between different narrators underlines the events of the novel as a shared happening, a gathering of overlapping, intertwining voices into a choral but not necessarily concordant narrative. We are invited to consider not just the parallel war experiences that impact on each couple, but also the possible points of connection created by migration and gender. Queenie's journey from the English countryside to the metropolis resonates with Hortense's migration to London to join her husband, while the points of contact between these women open thresholds of concern and compassion that transgress, if not fully escape, racial divisions.

The 'small island' of the novel's title might be considered an apt description for the city that Levy describes, which is best epitomised by Queenie's boarding house: a diverse, polyvocal, and crowded space where different people must find ways of living and communicating together. Instead of treating the Windrush moment in terms of a racially exclusive black British history, Levy revisions it as the birth of a new yet challenging multiculturalism in which all are implicated. Small Island's denouement, which hinges on Bernard's unexpected return and Queenie's developing relationship with Gilbert, captures both challenge and hope in the figure of the child that Queenie conceives with another Jamaican migrant, Michael, having presumed Bernard to be dead. In considering what might constitute the best

interests of a mixed-race child in a racist, ruined city, Levy looks forward
with sobriety to the challenges that await the London-born children of
migrants in the postwar decades, well-documented in London writing since
1948 of course. Yet the child also embodies the fertility, fecundity, and inev-
itability of change – cultural, emotional, demographic – wrought by the
possibilities of everyday, convivial cultural encounters. Although its tone is
predominantly solemn, *Small Island* makes a vital genealogical connection
between the distinctly polycultural character of London in 1948 and the
twenty-first-century city of the present, eschewing the temptation to write
exclusively about a black or diasporic city.

London's past is also firmly interpreted within the concerns of the contemporary in the work of Bernardine Evaristo. Her 2001 novel-in-verse, *The
Emperor's Babe*, imagines the Roman city of Londinium in AD 211 and is
narrated by Zuleika, the daughter of Sudanese immigrants to the city, who
is married off to a Roman nobleman, Felix, at the age of eleven. Zuleika is
a feisty and vigorous figure whose excited portrayal of the city focuses on
the energies unleashed by its many different peoples, from England, Africa,
Scotland, Rome, Gaul, and China. A city populated by soldiers and slaves,
poets and prostitutes, Londinium emerges as an adventure playground for
Zuleika's adolescence as well as for the imagination of Evaristo, who was
Writer in Residence at the Museum of London in 1999. Evaristo's command
of poetic language and form allows her to combine contemporary street-
wise skaz with suitably arcane and Latinate diction, producing a vivid and
endlessly inventive novel that is perpetually playful and entertaining as we
follow Zuleika through Londinium's ribald streets. The novel's underlying
theme is that contemporary London is only the latest incarnation of a city
eternally characterised by its polycultural energies: bawdy yet often brutal,
a centre of commerce and exchange, and an ambivalent refuge for those fleeing conflicts in other lands.

Evaristo defiantly projects the quintessential admixture of the city that
makes a nonsense of inflexible notions of native and foreigner, resident and
stranger. Yet the presence of slavery casts a shadow over the novel, while
Zuleika's difficult relationship with her husband – as well as her affair with
the Roman emperor, Septimius Severus – reminds us that passion can lead
fatally to the cruellest suffering, especially for women in the city. For all
of her narrative exuberance and wit, Evaristo powerfully delivers a darker
articulation of London's enduring legacies of prejudice and pain that have
endured in various guises. Dave Gunning suggestively argues that 'in contra-
distinction to more utopian theorists of the fate of race in the (post)modern
city environment, [Evaristo] demonstrates how the cultural plurality of the
contemporary urban habitas is not sufficient on its own to annihilate racial

oppression'.[9] Unsurprisingly perhaps, Evaristo's most recent novel, *Blonde Roots* (2008), continues her investment in wildly transformative yet sobering visions of London's history, this time by reimaging the city as at the heart of a rich African empire in which white people find themselves miserably enslaved.

One of the most incisive and thought-provoking representations of London's polycultural transformation is Gautum Malkani's debut novel *Londonstani* (2006), which focuses on the influence of South Asian-influenced youth cultures in west London. The narrator, Jas, takes us into the teenage terrains of street credibility and cool via a narrative voice built from British Asian vernacular English and the newly emerging vocabularies of mobile telephone text messaging. 'Londonstani' names both an emerging youthful style of language and a particular stylisation of the self. Previously an awkward teenager with few friends, Jas, with his enthusiastic membership in a predominantly British Asian peer group – he adopts their clothes, their language, their attitude to sex and race – takes the reader into the bluster and frustrations of being a youthful member of a so-called ethnic minority, caught between the neon-tinted allure of London commerce and communerism and the obligations of tradition and family. Yet *Londonstani* ends with a significant revelation concerning Jas's background that (without wishing to spoil things for those yet to read the novel) shockingly compels us to look back at his narrative as about a distinctly polycultural London rather than a British Asian one, and to think about the attraction of so-called 'ethnic' forms of youth identity for those of all ethnicities outside diasporic communities. In Malkani's vision of London, an emerging process of identity transformation inverts the older 'native' demands that newcomers to the city integrate into the cultural practices and values of the host community and leave their cultural baggage behind. In plotting this new phenomenon Malkani joins other writers in exploring how Londoners (including so-called white ones) are absolutely embroiled in, and not detached from, the polycultural fate of the metropolis where divisive notions of native and foreigner, of who legitimately belongs and who doesn't, seem ever more inappropriate and unwieldy in the twenty-first century.

Unseen lives

In the climactic scene of Stephen Frears's 2002 film *Dirty Pretty Things*, an illegal immigrant, Okwe, meets with an unnamed English businessman who has come to collect a human kidney that he is unlawfully buying for the purposes of transplantation. When the businessman asks Okwe why he has not seen him before, Okwe replies bluntly: 'Because we are the people you do not see. We are the ones who drive your cabs. We clean your rooms, and suck your cocks.'[10] Okwe's words, like Frears's film, take us into the ghostly realm of those Londoners without whom the city could not function but whose presence is either shunned, barely noticed, or deliberately hidden from view: illegal workers, asylum seekers, prostitutes, London's poor. Secreted in the city's many subterranean sites or concealed inside innocuous-looking buildings and rooms, there exists a twenty-first-century London distinct from the heady street life of the city articulated in Malkani's and Smith's work, one that deliberately tries to keep far out of sight of London's officious eye.

In *Dirty Pretty Things* Okwe is a qualified doctor who has fled his home and family, having angered the Nigerian authorities for refusing to comply with their corruption. In London he works by day as a taxi driver and by night as a receptionist and porter at the exclusive Baltic Hotel, and must take stimulants to help him stay awake. The film's plot turns on Okwe's relationship with a Turkish immigrant, Shenay, and their uncovering of an illegal trade in human organs at the hotel masterminded by a fellow Spanish employee, Sneaky, who convinces illegal immigrants to sacrifice an internal organ in exchange for a fake passport that will secure a legitimate life in London. Frears's cinematic depiction of the city is scarcely recognisable from the touristic vista of London with its clichés of red London buses, the statue of Eros in Piccadilly Circus, or the fountains in Trafalgar Square. Much of the action takes place at night and in basement enclosures (an underground car park, a hospital morgue), in illegal sweatshops lurking within anonymous derelict buildings, or cramped and crumbling flats. When London is glimpsed out of doors, we see either a grey and indistinct industrial milieu or we witness the film's main characters as they hurry uncomfortably through humdrum, unattractive streets, keen to avoid the sinister attention of immigration officers who often appear unannounced. Frears's characters live spectral lives, lurking in the city's shadows and only coming out at night. As Juliette, a prostitute, smilingly tells Okwe one evening as she leaves the Baltic Hotel having visited a client: 'I don't exist, do I?'. Frears's characters are bound up in lives held in suspension, and whose ghostly existence is a measure of their immiseration and pain.

At one level, *Dirty Pretty Things* articulates a vision of the city as an infernal and dread location – Frears makes much use of the hellish colour of red in the scenes in the Baltic Hotel – which underlines a sense of the contemporary city as a locale of 'discipline, control and terror',[11] especially for those reduced to the most desperate conditions of bare life. Yet within the nightmarish London of the film, Frears also attends to the fragile, fleeting, yet firmly supportive new networks of the city's shadow

peoples, who come together to find a way to survive and potentially transform their existence, even if their tribulations are not over by the film's
ambivalent end.

The often gruesome history of the hidden histories of London have
been well-pursued in twenty-first-century writing. Iain Sinclair's *London
Orbital* (2002) uses a walk around the city's orbital motorway, the
M25, to circumnavigate the city's secreted and sinister pasts; while Peter
Ackroyd's *Thames: Sacred River* (2007) excavates the spectral remains
of London's sedimented centuries also by focusing on one of the city's
major passageways. In a similar spirit, a contemporary phantom London
preoccupies Tarquin Hall in his illuminating memoir *Salaam Brick Lane:
A Year in the New East End* (2005). Hall first glimpses a hidden world
during a meeting with his landlord, Mr Ali, a Bangladeshi Londoner, who
owns a clothing shop:

> quite suddenly, a secret door concealed in the wall to my left opened and the
> sounds of thumping machinery and raised voices spilled into the room. They
> were followed by a young Bangladeshi man in oil-stained clothes, his face
> hot and sweaty. In one hand he carried a red, lacy bra. This he handed to
> Mr Ali and, after a brief exchange between the two men, the worker withdrew
> through the door, closing it behind him.[12]

The concealed door acts as a passageway into another London, scarcely
acknowledged at large. Mr Ali defends the cottage clothing industry he is
illegally running in his basement as best he can: 'I'm creating jobs, contrib-
uting to the economy, innit. But there's people 'oo don't see it that way. Like
the coppers, yeah. They'd have a go at me, innit.'[13] While Hall depicts this
scene in a comical fashion, inspired no doubt by the likeable figure of Mr Ali,
much of *Salaam Brick Lane* unveils more gravely the clandestine lives that
many contemporary Londoners pursue in the city's shadows, anxious to
remain unobserved by the intolerant eyes of police officers and customs officials – and in some instances the cloistering surveillance of diasporic families
and fathers. Returning to London having worked as a journalist in India,
Hall is forced to rent a room from Mr Ali in Brick Lane for financial reasons. During the year he subsequently spends in the heart of London's East
End he uncovers a complex network of peoples scratching a living amidst
the sobering poverty of the locality. These include an aged and disappearing
generation of Jewish Londoners descended from those refugees who fled the
horrors of mid-twentieth-century Europe; the Bangladeshi communities that
have established themselves in the later twentieth century, running a number of often clandestine 'sweatshop' businesses in the area; white working-
class young men fencing goods in the local markets; and people like Naz, a

former gang member, ex-convict and son of a strict Bangladeshi father, who spends most of his free time reading Russian novels in Whitechapel's library or on the Circle Line trains of the London Underground.

Hall's immediate neighbours are three refugees and include Gul Muhammad, an Afghani who had fled the Taliban and spends much of his time in London searching for his brother, Hamidullah, who had been brought to London three years previously by a people smuggler but has since disappeared. Gul's co-tenants are Kosovar Albanians who had barely escaped a mass execution in their home village during the 1990s Serbian 'ethnic cleansing' programme of Slobodan Milošović. The lives of these three men index an overlooked underclass of contemporary Londoners, living in Britain illegally, cut off from and unable to return to their native lands, and living in dire poverty with little hope of change. 'If I return to my country', says Big Sasa, one of the Kosovar Albanians, 'I will be killed also. So I must be a refugee. This is not my choice. To be a refugee is the worst thing. No one like refugee … If I can do the work, I can make future for myself. Then I will not be the refugee. I will be the human being again.'[14] Yet the chances for building a future are limited in the London of *Salaam Brick Lane*, and for many a new life proves as impossible to find as Gul Muhammad's missing brother.

Hall is not the only writer to be preoccupied with the dubious reputation of London as a place of refuge and asylum. Parallel and probing representations can be found in Manzu Islam's novel *Burrow* (2004), which concerns the fate of an illegal immigrant in London's East End, and in Iqbal Ahmed's *Sorrows of the Moon: In Search of London* (2004), which like Hall's book is also something of a travelogue through the metropolis. Ahmed's stoical account of the city's down-at-heel enclaves considers the impoverished lives of Bengali migrants in Tower Hamlets and throughout the East End, and reminds us that it was 'in Brick Lane that the distressing word "refugee" had entered the English vocabulary, when French Protestants settled here after fleeing Catholic France towards the end of the seventeenth century'.[15] Yet a sense of London as refuge is quickly challenged in Ahmed's writing. A chance meeting with a hotel doorman, Solomon, enables Ahmed to learn of the harsh working and living conditions that are the norm for the thousands of people who contribute their labour and service while failing to reap the rewards of one of the world's major centres of international finance. As Solomon explains, those forced to live meagrely and to pursue menial jobs in London – as waiters, vendors, doormen, taxi drivers, cleaners, drug-dealers – exist cheek-by-jowl with the wealthy who scarcely acknowledge their existence. The psychological and emotional costs are as great as the economic ones, as Solomon explains in his account of surviving in London:

I saw the frightening faces of Africans selling marijuana at street corners, living on the fringes of society. Their only dealings with that society were to supply its misfits with narcotics to render them insensible. [...] I feared for my mental health if I didn't go to church regularly. I had left a family behind in Abuja, and I had no one to talk to in London. The bleakness of winter in London filled me with despair. I had enjoyed going to a park in summer to fill my spare time, but I longed to go back to Abuja during the winter. My father had suffered losses in his business, and he had fallen on hard times. I thought that it was better to bear cold than to be a coward. I spent my first winter in an unheated room.[16]

Ahmed's rendering of those 'living on the fringes' brings into view an array of fascinating and stalwart individuals whose existence is undercut by a chilling, spectral sense of temporariness that attaches itself to their lives. One such figure is Kasim, who works in a kiosk in Charing Cross Road amidst the tourists, theatre-goers, and pickpockets of central London, and who possesses a network of regular customers and friends. Raised in Egypt and having arrived as a young man in London unable to read and write English, Kasim has worked extremely hard to make a success of the kiosk, despite being assaulted by customers and threatened with closure by Westminster Council. Kasim is portrayed as a vibrant and likeable character with endearing degrees of fortitude and good cheer. But just as suddenly as he appears in Ahmed's book, Kasim is spirited away: the kiosk is closed, leaving Ahmed to wonder what had happened to him. In *Sorrows of the Moon*, Kasim exists for no more than a chapter, and his temporariness in the text powerfully conveys the unstable and overlooked existence of London's poorest inhabitants who are glimpsed only for a moment and who seem to leave only the faintest trace amongst the metropolitan *mélange* of twenty-first-century London.

Ahmed's means of portraying London – through a series of vivid characters who come into view only for a few pages, before disappearing never to return – is a particularly apt way of rendering urban experience in terms of aesthetic form. But it also reminds us that there are hundreds of thousands like Solomon and Kasim, or Mr Ali and Big Sasa in *Salaam Brick Lane*, whose lives are little known but without whom – as Frears's character Okwe also reminds us so vocally – today's London plainly cannot work.

Terror vision

Iain Banks's novel *Dead Air* (2002) opens with the narrator, Ken Knott, attending one September afternoon a house-cooling function at his friends' apartment in London's East End, where guests amuse themselves by throwing fruit, food, and other objects out of the eighth-storey window and watching with amusement as they burst on the pavement below. Unexpectedly, several of the guests' mobile phones begin to ring, and as the calls are answered and the news of 9/11 gets through, 'faces started to look puzzled and the atmosphere began to change and chill around us'.[17] Similarly, after the 7/7 bombings, Jamal, the narrator of Hanif Kureishi's novel *Something to Tell You* (2008) walks with his friend Henry 'about the chaotic, almost apocalyptical capital, taking pictures and looking at others who were frightened, dismayed, angry. Police cars and ambulances rushed about; the sound of sirens was abysmal. All day and night police helicopters thrashed above the damaged metropolis.'[18] In the light of these two events, some London writing of the twenty-first century has become embroiled in a reappraisal of the city as a place of possibility and hope, as well as a re-examination of the significance of art and literature in troubled times.

Literary responses to the impact of 9/11 on London have tended to engage, as does Banks, with the changed 'atmosphere' created in its wake. At large, there has been the heightening of prejudicial attitudes toward British Muslims worryingly perceived as a recalcitrant threat to the health of the nation and its myths of tolerance and openness, and the rearticulation of those shrill responses to the so-called '*Satanic Verses* affair' of 1989, which similarly condemned Islam in its entirety rather than the political activities of a particular section of British Muslims. Some texts have directly critiqued these alarming changes, such as Cleave's *Incendiary* and Monica Ali's aforementioned novel of London's Bangladeshi East End community, *Brick Lane*. Second, writers like Ian McEwan have envisioned 9/11 as a global event beckoning a distinctly local crisis for the prospect of democratic politics and protest in the UK at large in the wake of President Bush's 'War on Terror' supported by Blair's New Labour government, and for the significance of art and culture in current global dispensation. And while literary responses to 7/7 are still being formulated, it has been interesting to discern how some writers have been keen to rearticulate with urgency a sense of the city's multifarious cultural condition in the face of a divisive, and fatally explosive, logic of exclusion and purity. Indeed, and as with the '*Satanic Verses* affair', one wider consequence of 7/7 has been to sharpen the worrying (and highly questionable) sense of disjunction between the polycultural capital and the parochial British regions where multiculturalism is considered by its opponents largely to have failed. Those Britons who famously burned Rushdie's novel in 1989 were based in the West Yorkshire city of Bradford; the 7/7 bombers hailed from nearby Leeds. It will be interesting to see in the years to come the extent this sense of 'North–South' divide, which has its own long history of course, will play its part in representations of 7/7.

The London of Chris Cleave's *Incendiary* certainly succumbs to the changed atmosphere after 9/11 in its dramatic imagining of a similar attack in the UK. Cleave's capital is an apocalyptic realm of fear and loathing, a sinister necropolis where the images of the dead literally haunt the anxious lives of the living. As a response to the bombing of the soccer match by terrorists, and to prevent a further attack from the skies, the authorities launch a series of barrage balloons, on which are depicted the faces of the thousand people killed at the match, including the narrator's young son. London becomes a 'misty floating city with the thousand thick cables of the balloons lifting it into the sky'.[19] Amidst the outrage of London after the attack, new prejudices and hatreds form, something the narrator learns from a Muslim called Mena as both recover from their injuries in a London hospital:

> I have become enemy number one. There's one caff I walk past on my way to get here. The builders and the market traders go there. This morning I saw this old man in there. He must have been about 80. He was reading the paper and the headline was THE CRUELTY OF ISLAM. He looked up when I walked past and he sneered at me. He actually curled his lips. That is the nature of this madness. It fills the sky with barrage balloons and people's eyes with hate.[20]

The reference to the newspaper headline is Cleave's way of indicting the British media for the blanket condemnation of Islam in general as opposed to singling out the minority of violent Islamists in particular.[21] The ruinous predicament of London is only made worse by a lack of subtlety on all sides, it seems. Yet Cleave goes further than this in his dissection of the terrorised contemporary city by focusing on the themes of hypocrisy and infidelity: the novel's narrator learns of the attack on the soccer match, which her husband and son have attended, while having sex with a neighbour, Jasper Black. Cleave's London is a moral vacuum rather than an ideological battleground: a place where the exploitation of others is the norm, and where the claim that the West is fighting a just war against the opponents of civilisation is contradicted. Jasper and his partner, Petra, are journalists, and Cleave explores the ways in which those in the media abuse and exploit those caught up in tragedies for their own morally dubious ends. Later in the novel, the narrator develops a relationship with Terence Butcher, a police officer, and comes to learn that the authorities had a forewarning of the attack but chose not to act. In attempting to bring to light the perceived injustice of this revelation with the help of Jasper and Petra, the narrator's unhappy experiences invite us to contemplate the difficulty of distinguishing between truth and lies, right and wrong, and innocence and guilt in a terrorised city. Cleave's novel ultimately asks searching questions about the seeming moral bankruptcy of contemporary life in the wake of 9/11 (and now, chillingly in *Incendiary*'s case, 7/7).

The moral and philosophical, as opposed to narrowly ideological, impact of terrorism and the West's responses to it are also the preoccupation of Ian McEwan's outstanding novel *Saturday* (2005). Set on 15 February 2003, a day on which hundreds of thousands of people protested in London against British support for the impending US-led war in Iraq, the novel concerns one day in the life of a neurosurgeon, Henry Perowne. An atmosphere of terror pervades the novel throughout, and is linked explicitly to the aftermath of 9/11 in the opening pages as Perowne, waking at dawn, watches a burning aircraft pass over his house attempting to approach Heathrow Airport. The incident leads Perowne to contemplate all manner of issues: the impact of prayer during a catastrophe, religious fundamentalism, his medical career, science and reason, human morality. *Saturday* perceives of both the terrorist attacks and the western responses to them as posing a challenge to received ideas about reason, scientific progress, and art. For McEwan, this challenge is as much a part of the aftermath of 9/11 as the so-called 'War on Terror'; an epistemological and moral dispute has been engaged, not solely an ideological or political one. Like Virginia Woolf's influential novel of London, *Mrs. Dalloway* (1925), also set on one day, *Saturday* is concerned with the twists and turns of consciousness linked to a distinct historical context. During the events of this particular Saturday, Perowne turns over in his mind everything he deems valuable, from his love of music and fascination with neurosurgery to his passion for his wife. Later in the morning, while driving, Perowne has a contretemps with a sinister figure called Baxter, and he plays a game of squash with an American friend Jay that soon becomes unhealthily competitive. Later that evening, during a family dinner, Baxter forces his way into Perowne's home and threatens his family with a knife; the tremulous atmosphere of violence that has hung over London all day invades the seemingly cloistered world of Perowne's domestic environment.

A key element of McEwan's exploration of the consequences of 9/11 concerns the function of the creative arts. Perowne's son, Theo, is a musician and enthusiast of popular music, while his daughter Daisy is an up-and-coming poet. Perowne has little enthusiasm for literature. He has struggled to read classic literary works recommended to him by Daisy, but sees little immediate point in writing: 'The times are strange enough. Why make things up?'.[22] Coupled with his career as a neurosurgeon, Perowne's attitude invites us to think about the value of literature as constituting, or even usefully transforming, forms of consciousness, and asks us to reappraise the value of culture in the current 'strange' times. Significantly, when Baxter threatens Perowne's family later that evening, he orders Daisy to strip naked and recite one of her poems. She chooses instead to recite the Victorian poet Matthew Arnold's 'Dover Beach' (1867), and is made to repeat her performance by Baxter. Its impact is profound: Baxter's violent intentions are changed by the recital, while Perowne's consciousness is meaningfully altered too. At first the poem leads to him 'slipping through the words into the things they describe'[23] as he imagines Daisy happy in the arms of her lover. The poem gives him a way of thinking tenderly about his daughter's love for her partner as well as her burgeoning pregnancy, the evidence of which he has just seen owing to Baxter's brutal request that she take off her clothes. On second reading, Perowne finds himself contemplating issues of faith, pain, and armed conflict, as the poem offers a way of framing a perception on the current global conflicts in the wake of 9/11. As Dominic Head argues in his reading of this critical scene in the novel, this scene 'is not, of course, a simple celebration of the "power" of poetry, though the emotional impact of poetry is strongly registered. The scene also emphasizes the unpredictability and subjectivity of the aesthetic response, as well as the contingency of life.'[24] The scene is one of the major moments in the novel in which McEwan restates the case for the urgency and necessity of literature during trying times as brokering new forms of consciousness that might help us contest and think through the human capacity for violence and cruelty. Perowne's ongoing scepticism about literature and his investment in science mean that *Saturday* is by no means a simplistic or utopian endorsement of literature in a dangerous world. Instead, McEwan retains a vital faith in the necessity of literature as a means of making sense of the present, one that contributes to other important ways of exploring consciousness to be found in science, medicine, and philosophy.

Tellingly, one of Perowne's most epiphanic moments in *Saturday* is linked to music when he watches his son's blues band rehearse a song about London that contains the lyrics, 'Baby, you can choose despair, / or you can be happy if you dare. / So let me take you there, / My city square, city square.'[25] Musicians, he subsequently reflects, can

> give us a glimpse of what we might be, of our best selves, and of an impossible world in which you give everything you have to others, but lose nothing of yourself. Out in the real world there exist detailed plans, visionary for peaceable realms, all conflicts resolved, happiness for everyone for ever – mirages for which people are prepared to die and kill. Christ's kingdom on earth, the workers' paradise, the ideal Islamic state. But only in music, and only on rare occasions, does the curtain actually lift on this dream of community, and it's tantalisingly conjured, before fading away with the last notes.[26]

Perowne's delight in his son's music might be borrowed to answer Chris Cleave's gloomy question concerning the point of writing in a time of violence, specifically the investment in creativity as fashioning alternative visions of the world – convivial, cordial, communal – which can challenge the dogmatic pursuit of illiberal states. Theo and his band express this attitude with the eloquent simplicity of a blues song and significantly link it to the 'city square'. The suggestion here is that such alternative ways of thinking, brokered creatively by literature and music, ultimately must be discovered and made concrete in the contemporary urban milieu, hopefully challenging the otherwise anxious and hostile atmosphere of post-9/11 London that is witnessed with such sharpness in the novel.

Twenty-first-century representations of London have retained a fundamentally essential role in our encounters with the city, and they continue to remind us (often starkly, but always unequivocally) of the vital 'use' of art in negotiating with – perhaps even forging – the city's possible futures. In her recent exploration of contemporary Britishness, Vron Ware notes how one London schoolteacher, Martin Spafford, has attempted to tackle racism in the city by teaching a sense of the city's history as a collective, shared experience that can bring together different kinds of Londoners. 'We looked at the contributions of all the communities in the Second World War', he explains: 'We had people who lived through the Blitz in the East End, and old guys who had been firemen coming in [to class] with Somali seamen who'd been in the merchant navy, Pakistanis, and a Sikh who was a Battle of Britain pilot. We were looking at a shared experience through a piece of history.'[27] As we have seen, literary representations of twenty-first-century London have turned to the city's polycultural past as a way of reshaping an inclusive vision of its present and future. Others have attended to the spectral communities of undocumented Londoners whose conditions of bare life ensure both the city's survival and shame. And in the moral and philosophical questioning that follows from the new century's global circumstances of conflict and terror, creative artists seem keen to challenge the atmosphere of 'fright, dismay and anger' that Kureishi records in his aforementioned novel.

We might conclude, then, that twenty-first-century representations of London often refuse the divisive logic of prejudice and do not give up on those ghostly figures who walk through the city's walls or stir beneath its streets. These are rarely naïve or glibly celebratory visions, of course; but they can be hopeful in the best sense, in that they do not despair of representation's power to alter vision. And they retain a battered and bruised faith in the city's capacity to show that there is another way to be amidst the turmoil of the twenty-first century.

Notes

1 Chris Cleave, 'The Story behind *Incendiary*', www.chriscleave.com/main/?p=28 (accessed 24 October 2008).

2 *Ibid.*

3 Salman Rushdie, 'In Good Faith' (1990), in *Imaginary Homelands: Essays and Criticism, 1981–1991* (London: Granta, 1991), pp. 393–414 (p. 394). (Italics in the original.) This phrase also often resounds in Rushdie's London-concerned novel *The Satanic Verses* (London: Viking, 1988).

4 Caryl Phillips, '*White Teeth* by Zadie Smith' (2000), in *A New World Order: Selected Essays* (London: Secker and Warburg, 2001), p. 283.

5 Laura Moss, 'The Politics of Everyday Hybridity: Zadie Smith's *White Teeth*', *Wasafiri* 39 (2003), 11–17 (p. 11).

6 Homi K. Bhabha, *The Location of Culture* (London/New York: Routledge, 1994), p. 5.

7 Paul Gilroy, *After Empire: Melancholia or Convivial Culture?* (London/New York: Routledge, 2004), p. 58.

8 Relevant fictional examples include Caribbean-London, as in Sam Selvon's *The Lonely Londoners* (London: Allen Wingate, 1956); Nigeria-London, as in Buchi Emecheta's *Second-Class Citizen* (London: Allison and Busby, 1974); or Hong Kong-London, as in Timothy Mo's *Sour Sweet* (London: Deutsch, 1982).

9 Dave Gunning, 'Cosmopolitanism and Marginalisation in Bernardine Evaristo's *The Emperor's Babe*', in *Write Black, Write British: From Post Colonial to Black British Literature*, ed. Kadija Sesay (Hertford: Hansib, 2005), p. 165.

10 Stephen Frears, dir., *Dirty Pretty Things* (Miramax Films, 2002). All subsequent dialogue is quoted from this DVD-release edition of the film.

11 Büllen Diken and Carsten Bagge Laustsen, 'Zones of Indistinction: Security, Terror and Bare Life', *Space and Culture* 5.3 (2002), 290–307 (p. 294).

12 Tarquin Hall, *Salaam Brick Lane: A Year in the New East End* (London: John Murray, 2005), p. 17.

13 *Ibid.*, p. 17.

14 *Ibid.*, p. 88.

15 Iqbal Ahmed, *Sorrows of the Moon: In Search of London* (London: Constable, 2007), p. 17.

16 Ahmed, *Sorrows of the Moon*, p. 55.

17 Iain Banks, *Dead Air* (London: Abacus, 2003), p. 25.

18 Hanif Kureishi, *Something to Tell You* (London: Faber, 2008), p. 314.

19 Chris Cleave, *Incendiary* (London: Vintage, 2006), p. 65.

20 *Ibid.*, p. 65.

21 For a provocative insight into the emergence of Islamism as a contemporary ideology, as distinct from Islam as a world faith, see Ed Hussain, *The Islamist: Why I Joined Radical Islam in Britain, what I Saw Inside and why I Left* (London: Penguin, 2007).

22 Ian McEwan, *Saturday* (London: Jonathan Cape, 2005), p. 66.

23 *Ibid.*, p. 220.

24 Dominic Head, *Ian McEwan* (Manchester: Manchester University Press, 2007), p. 189.
25 McEwan, *Saturday*, p. 170.
26 *Ibid.*, pp. 171–2.
27 Vron Ware, *Who Cares about Britishness? A Global View of the National Identity Debate* (London: Arcadia, 2007), p. 100.

14

JAMES DONALD

Inner London

London was where I grew up, and I lived half my adult life there.

It is almost twenty years since I moved away from the city, and a dozen years since I left England for Australia. As I started work on this chapter, despite that long separation, I found that the place still has a hold on me. My attempts to shape an argument about London kept being interrupted by unbidden recollections and apparently random associations. Then I got it. These distractions were bringing into focus the question I want to address. That is, where, and how, does London exist?

The premise of the present volume is that, as well as being a physical city in the bottom right-hand corner of England, 'London' also has an existence of some sort 'in literature' and, beyond literature, in a variety of other cultural forms. It exists as an archive-city, an immaterial London, built of words, images, and stories.

This other, archival London is the London constructed in literary texts from Chaucer, through Dickens, to Iain Sinclair and Zadie Smith, and the London that I watch in movies. It is the London depicted in the images of Canaletto in the eighteenth century, Gustave Doré in the nineteenth century, or Christopher Nevinson and Gilbert and George at different ends of the twentieth century. It is the London reported daily on worldwide television news, or London as the dramatic backdrop for television fictions. It is also the London, observed and analysed, that I read about in academic monographs, sociological theorising, and government investigations.

This London takes on a meaningful existence, and begins to have consequences, as it is incorporated into a subjective, inner reality. Each of us builds up our own idiosyncratic storehouse of London images and London narratives, as a subset of the larger archive. Our own private London mediates our experience of being in the place, and shapes the act of thinking about London from afar. This, then, is the London that exists, for me, in memories of childhood, but that also has a symbolic and affective reality for millions of others, in a million individual acts of imagination, or anticipation, or fantasy.

The challenge is to draw the connections between place, archive, and imagination, not only by tracing those links in literary representations of London, but also by observing and describing the social, cultural, and subjective functions of London literature and London imagery.

London mummified

Although I have returned to London regularly since I left England, all too often, as time goes by, I feel emotionally short-changed by my visits. Now neither Londoner nor tourist, it is hard for me to craft a satisfactory relationship to the place. Increasingly, I am left with memories, which match the landscape and rhythm of the present city less and less. As I admitted this to myself, grappling with my first draft, one of my involuntary memories of London came to mind.

What flashed up was an image of the bombsites that had littered the London landscape of my 1950s childhood.

It surprises me, looking back, how much I took them for granted. Bombsites were scars left by 'The War', an overwhelming event that, however historically recent, was, in my child's mind, inscribed less in time than in mythology. Although part of a familiar and mundane landscape, these accidental memorials, like all ruins, had something of the sacred about them. Maybe that is why they signified, for me, less destruction and loss, than mystery and possibility. In my unreliable memory, I recall, especially, one bombsite on the corner of Queen's Gate Terrace and Prince Consort Road in Kensington, which my classmates and I would pass a couple of times a week, as we walked in crocodile formation from my junior school to do 'games' in Kensington Gardens. It provoked fantasies about what lurked there, and about the adventures that could happen there, but also speculation about what would eventually be built there. This was an early Ozymandias moment: a lesson about how easily apparently solid structures, social as well as architectural, can be destroyed; about the inherent link between destruction and creation; and about the fact that London, both real and imagined, exists in a temporal dimension.

Like much of my imaginative life, this memory of London's bombsites and their strange enchantment has been spiced by cinema.

Although I cannot recall when I first saw it, the film that joins the dots between a postwar, rubble-strewn London and my fantasy of childhood is, without question, *Hue and Cry*. Directed in 1946 by Charles Crichton, written by T. E. B. Clarke, and produced by Michael Balcon, this was the first in a series of much-loved comedies made in the 1940s and 1950s by the Ealing Studios production company. It is a story about a group of East

End lads. (There is one just-about-tolerated girl member, and a Scottish boy and a ring-in from Camberwell are as multicultural as it gets.) These kids stumble across a plot by a gang of thieves to use their favourite comic, *The Trump*, to disseminate secret messages and instructions about their robberies.

In another knowing reference to the public function of mass media, toward the end of the film, a cheeky messenger boy hijacks a solemn BBC weather forecast, slipping an unofficial note to be read by a sepulchrally voiced announcer. This alerts all the boys of London to head for the bombed-out Ballard's Wharf, beside the Thames in the East End docks, where the climactic battle with the crooks is to take place. 'Make it snappy', pipes in the messenger.

Among *Hue and Cry*'s incidental pleasures are watching Alistair Sim doing his eccentric turn as the ineffectually sinister author of the boys' favourite Selwyn Pike stories, and seeing Jack Warner – later the avuncular television policeman, Dixon of Dock Green – portray a sleek and plausible villain. Central to the film's appeal is the fantasy of children outwitting the forces of adult cynicism and corruption. Psychologically, this is a standard daydream of omnipotence. But the fantasy also has a social dimension. Michael Balcon had produced morale-boosting movies during the war. Now, in a period of tense peacetime austerity, his Ealing comedies were designed to celebrate the pluck and ingenuity of eccentric but self-sustaining British communities, as a conservative alternative to the social-democratic reformism of the postwar Labour government.

In *Hue and Cry*, the supposed virtues of London's working-class East End community – resilience, mutual support, a lack of social deference underlain by respect for legitimate authority – are projected onto the resourceful, if naïve, youngsters.

The social imagery of *Hue and Cry*, as well as its urban landscape, trades on the ethos of Humphrey Jennings's poetic wartime documentaries. Films like *London Can Take It* (1940) and *Fires Were Started* (1943) had bolstered the myth of the 'people's war' by showing stoical, good-humoured working-class East-Enders, making do during the Blitz, amid the flames of Stepney and Wapping. Further in the background is the perspective on East End community offered by the pioneering documentary, *Housing Problems* (1935), directed by Edgar Anstey and Arthur Elton, and produced by John Grierson. *Housing Problems* had defined a cinematic iconography of East End poverty and unemployment. Also, apparently for the first time, it had presented East End slum-dwellers speaking on film in their own voices, however stiltedly, about their problems. In *Hue and Cry*, the adult East-Enders are, for the most part, reduced to stock comic types, mouthing stock comic lines. In this context, the later film comes across as a manipulative, albeit beguilingly self-ironising, myth of postwar rebirth and regeneration.

Through such observations, I take a critical distance from the film. Why, then, does the landscape of *Hue and Cry* still resonate so disconcertingly with my affective relationship to London?

There is, certainly, the uncanny pleasure of seeing familiar places as they were, at a moment over sixty years ago. In a jumble of scenes in the cinema of my mind, some from *Hue and Cry* and some remembered or mis-remembered from other films of the period, the Tate Modern still appears, on the horizon, as a power station, at least two makeovers back. St Paul's Cathedral stands intact, in contrast to the devastation of the City, before the hubristic towers of postwar capitalism sprang up. The Thames bustles with tugs and commercial traffic, as it had for a century and more, bordered by an East End wasteland that would be remade as Docklands, in the Thatcherite 1980s.

Linked to the fascination of this familiar, but transformed, London, is the way that, in *Hue and Cry*, the uncanniness of an animate past, experienced in the present, is anchored and doubled by the fact of the bombsites. Their photographed images confront us with 'change mummified', to use a phrase coined by the film theorist André Bazin.[1] By 'mummified', Bazin meant that the automatic capture, on film, of events taking place, embalms both event and place, keeping them virtually alive at the same time as exposing, starkly, their irredeemable pastness.

Gashes in the skin of the city, the bombsites signify more than the vulnerability of London's physical fabric. Their destruction also reveals the temporality of the city. As change is mummified, mutability is exposed. The rubble brought to light is that of London in centuries past, not just of the destroyed building that stood most recently in that place. For me, looking at these images not only conjures up where I come from, but also brings home the impossibility of recovering that place; to be exact, that place at that time. I confront, on film, a symbolic London, which is lived, over and again, as irretrievably lost.

Representational space

In *The Production of Space*, first published in 1974, the French sociologist Henri Lefebvre explored how the real and the imagined blur together in the everyday experience of the city. Lefebvre distinguished 'three moments' in the creation and experience of 'social space': first, space as it is *perceived*; second, space as it is *conceived* (or conceptualised); and, third, space as it is *lived*.

In the register of the perceived, *spatial practice* translates human activities and social relations into material form. Waterloo Station, Heathrow Airport, St Paul's Cathedral, Norman Foster's 'Gherkin' building in the City (nicknamed for its pickle-like shape and London's most distinctive new building of the twenty-first century), Nine Elms Market (the dilapidated industrial site on the south bank of the Thames, to which the old Covent Garden fruit, vegetable, and flower market depicted in *Hue and Cry* moved in the 1980s), a high-rise tower of public housing in the East End, London's network of primary schools: all are designed, in one way or another, to meet identified human needs; to sustain the business of trade, travel, communication, and social reproduction; and to prescribe certain ways of acting and moving for the people using their spaces.

Representations of space refer to *conceptual* abstractions used by architects, planners, and designers, and that inform such spatial practices and their embodiments: Cartesian geometry and linear perspective, for example, but, equally, utopian schemes and reformist plans for the good city, the efficient city, the healthy city, or the sustainable city.

Most important for the argument here is Lefebvre's third dimension, which refers to the way that space is 'lived'. This he terms *representational space*. Grounded in individual and collective histories, and especially in their imaginary and symbolic elements, representational space is:

> space as directly *lived* through its associated images and symbols, and hence the space of 'inhabitants' and 'users', but also of some artists and perhaps of those, such as a few writers and philosophers, who *describe* and aspire to do no more than describe. This is the dominated – and hence passively experienced – space which the imagination seeks to change and appropriate. It overlays physical space, making symbolic use of its objects.[2]

Although the material city embodies a set of possible, preferred, or even normative scenarios, people negotiate these coercive stories in inventive, recalcitrant, and certainly less than wholly predictable ways. They ascribe their own arbitrary and inventive meanings to places: 'I had a girlfriend who lived there' – 'That used to be the best butcher's in North London' – 'That's where they filmed *Peeping Tom*.'

To take an example from London literature, no one conveys the texture of this *lived* or *representational space* better than Doris Lessing, in her novel, *The Four-Gated City* (1969). In 1950, Martha Quest, a Marxist émigré from Rhodesia, arrives in the London landscape of *Hue and Cry*. She discovers the local bombsite. 'The place had a fence and a sign which said under crossbones and skull: *Danger. No children*. Behind the ruin of the house a group of children squatted, spinning marbles off their thumbs across yellow earth.'³ Martha observes the ruined street with an intellectual stranger's critical eye. Iris, the local fish-and-chip shop owner with whom Martha is lodging, sees the neighbourhood quite differently. For Iris, her street is a palimpsest, a space animated by memory and history.

> Iris, Joe's mother, knew … about the houses which had been bombed, about the people who had lived in the houses, and the people who now lived in the houses of the part of the street which stood intact: some of them were from the site of rubble and dust and mud. She knew everything about this area, half a dozen streets for about half a mile or a mile of their length; and she knew it all in such detail that when with her, Martha walked in a double vision, as if she were two people: herself and Iris, one eye stating, denying, warding off the total hideousness of the whole area, the other, with Iris, knowing it in love. With Iris, one moved here, in a state of love, if love is the delicate but total acknowledgement of what is … (p. 18)

Iris not only perceives, but also inhabits, her street as representational space, in Lefebvre's sense, as 'space directly *lived* through its associated images and symbols'.

> Iris, Joe's mother, had lived in this street since she was born. Put her brain, together with the other million brains, women's brains, that recorded in such tiny loving anxious detail the histories of windowsills, skins of paint, replaced curtains and salvaged baulks of timber, there would be a recording instrument, a sort of six-dimensional map which included the histories and lives and loves of people, London – a section map in depth. This is where London exists, in the minds of people who have lived in such and such a street since they were born … (p. 18)

Lessing conjures up a *representational London*, a physical London overlaid by the symbolic patina of Iris's loving knowledge, a knowledge that is (for her) uniquely local and feminine.

What Lessing's account underestimates, perhaps, is the cultural mediation of the London that exists thus in 'women's brains'. The 'section map' achieves its depth through the interaction of empirical observation and memory with another coordinate. That is, the circulation of *representations of London*, which have the power to inform perception and shape experience – as I have tried to show in my description of the place of *Hue and Cry* in my own memories.

An example that is alert to the way this process works can be found in V. S. Naipaul's novel, *The Enigma of Arrival* (1987).

Like *The Four-Gated City*, *The Enigma of Arrival* tells of a young colonial arriving in London in 1950. Naipaul's aspiring Indian novelist from Trinidad is met by the same landscape as Lessing's Rhodesian, Martha

Quest. Looking back from anxious middle age, in the 1970s, he recalls how his loneliness had rendered his exploratory walks around London 'ignorant and joyless'. Even the signs of wartime destruction lost their power to affect him.

> Two doors away from my boarding house in Earls Court there was a bomb site, a gap in the road, with neat rubble where the basement should have been, the dining room of a house like the one in which I lived. Such sites were all over the city. I saw them in the beginning; then I stopped seeing them.[4]

The Enigma of Arrival is a sustained meditation on the role of place and time in the making of a self and, more precisely, in Naipaul's self-creation, and self-*re*creation, as a novelist. Sedimented into the novel's structure (another palimpsest) is the defining motif of the *Bildungsroman* – a young hero's sentimental education through the move from country to city – but here the motif is given a twentieth-century twist. Rather than a rustic Tom Jones seeking fame and fortune in eighteenth-century London society, Naipaul's colonial newcomer arrives at mid twentieth century, in the postwar twilight of empire. Soon, he grows to feel 'that I had come to England at the wrong time; that I had come too late to find the England, the heart of empire, which (like a provincial, from a far corner of the empire) I had created in my fantasy' (p. 120).

For Naipaul, the road to modern maturity runs from the fantasy of anticipation and through the disenchantment of arrival. *The Enigma of Arrival* explores the mediated nature, and complicated rhythm, of this process. At the moment of his first arrival, Naipaul's protagonist is struck by the artifice and spectacle of London.

> After the grey of the Atlantic, there was colour. Bright colour seen from the train that went to London. Late afternoon light. An extended dusk: new, enchanting to someone used to the more or less equal division of day and night in the tropics. Light, dusk, at an hour which would have been night at home.
>
> But it was night when we arrived at Waterloo station. I liked the size, the many platforms, the big, high roof. I liked the lights. Used at home to public places – or those I knew, schools, stores, offices – working only in natural light, I liked this excitement of a railway station busy at night, and brightly lit up. I saw the station people working in electric light, and the travellers as dramatic figures. The station gave a suggestion ... of a canopied world, a vast home interior.
> (pp. 117–18)

Here the iconography is very much that of first-half-of-the-twentieth-century urban Modernism: the liner, the train, electricity, the city as interior, cinema. But the hero's reaction is both surprising and telling: 'After five days on the liner, I wanted to go out. I wanted especially to go to a cinema'. Beyond historically anchoring imagery, what is the narrative function of the reference to cinema here? Why should arriving in London prompt the desire for cinema?

Naipaul's point, it seems, is that living in the present – being here and being now – is always mediated through anticipation and memory. For his young hero, this disjunctive temporality of fantasy had been both manifested, and managed, primarily, through movies. He had learned about London, as a place supposedly good to grow up in, in the cinemas of Trinidad, long before he arrived in the city.

> At home I had lived most intensely in the cinema ... In those dark halls I had dreamt of a life elsewhere. Now, in the place that for all those years had been the 'elsewhere', no further dream was possible ... I had thought of the cinema pleasure as a foretaste of my adult life. Now, with all kinds of shame in many recesses of my mind, I felt it to be fantasy. I hadn't read *Hangover Square*, didn't even know of it as a book; but I had seen the film. Its Hollywood London had merged in my mind (perhaps because of the association of the titles) into the London of *The Lodger*. Now I knew that London to be fantasy, worthless to me. (p. 124)

The melodramatic, studio-constructed London of John Brahm's *The Lodger* (1944) and *Hangover Square* (1945), consumed wide-eyed in the cinemas of Trinidad, prepared Naipaul's protagonist for the experience of the actual city, even if the artifice of the cinematic experience made the 'reality' of London initially a letdown. Bricks-and-mortar London, especially cheerless postwar London, simply could not live up to its representation on screen. He feels out of place, where he had hoped, and expected, to feel most at home. The depth of his disappointment reflects the scale of his imaginative investment in London: 'I had expected the great city to leap out at me and possess me; I had longed so much to be in it' (p. 121).

Naipaul interprets the disappointment of his first days in London as a particular kind of loss: 'I lost a faculty that had been part of me and precious to me for years. I lost the gift of fantasy, the dream of the future, the far-off place where I was going' (p. 124). London was 'the place that for all those years had been the "elsewhere"', but when he finally gets there, 'no further dream was possible' (p. 124). Cinema, as his primary medium for fantasising about London, is therefore spurned, collateral damage from his broader disillusionment. When the narrator starts watching films again, a decade later, he pointedly observes that it is no longer as 'a dreamer or a fantast but as a critic'.

'Disillusionment' may be too coarse-grained a description of the young author's metropolitan *Bildung*. Although he loses the capacity for the fantasies of childhood, he does retain an acute awareness of the process of symbolic projection onto other places, and grasps how past, present, and future intertwine in the life of the imagination.

> So I was ready to imagine that the world in which I found myself in London was something less than the perfect world I had striven towards. As a child in Trinidad I had put this world at a far distance, in London perhaps. In London now I was able to put this perfect world at another time, an earlier time. The mental or emotional processes were the same. (p. 121)

Although this projection across space and over time had been achieved primarily through cinema, the narrator, as a child in Trinidad, had also devoured literature, transposing everything he read onto the Trinidad landscape: 'Even Dickens and London I incorporated into the streets of Port of Spain.' This capacity was lost, along with cinema, with the move to London. 'That ability to project what I read on to Trinidad, the colonial, tropical, multi-racial world which was the only world I knew, that ability diminished as I grew older. It was partly as a result of my increasing knowledge, self-awareness, and my embarrassment at the workings of my fantasy' (p. 155). As soon as he comes to London in 1950, 'that gift of fantasy became inoperable ... When I was surrounded by the reality, English literature ceased to be universal, since it ceased to be the subject of fantasy' (p. 155). It is during the decade he spends in the Wiltshire countryside, in the 1970s, that the author learns to distinguish between, on the one hand, the child's projection of desire onto imagined places, and, on the other hand, the novelist's disciplined need to derive emotional and ethical significance from place. He also learns to convey those place-derived insights to his readers by describing landscape in accurate, yet also affective, prose.

The writer arrives in the countryside around Salisbury still with a residue of the child's capacity for fantasy, acknowledging how literature had planted a certain prevision of the place. 'So much of this I saw with the literary eye, or with the aid of literature. A stranger here, with the nerves of the stranger, and yet with a knowledge of the language and the history of the language and the writing, I could find a special kind of past in what I saw; with a part of my mind I could admit to fantasy' (p. 22). He admits to fantasy, but only in order to transcend fantasy, and to claim the salvation of experience. In his rural solitude, at first unwittingly, he transmutes the trauma of his arrival in London into a story about a 'fairytale landscape' of Africa: 'Now, in Wiltshire in winter, a writer now rather than a reader, I worked the child's fantasy the other way' (p. 155). For Naipaul, maturity turns out to be pretty much the same thing as becoming a writer, and embracing the aesthetic and ethical values of a certain realism. When he becomes a man, he puts childish

ways behind him – including his childish enthusiasm for literary and cinematic representations of London.

> The man who went walking past Jack's cottage saw things as if for the first
> time. Literary allusions came naturally to him, but he had grown to see with
> his own eyes. He could not have seen like that, so clearly, twenty years before.
> And having seen, he might not have found the words or the tone. The simpli-
> city and directness had taken a long time to get to him; it was necessary for
> him to have gone through a lot.   (p. 157)

A state of mind

In 1903, the German sociologist, Georg Simmel, published his lecture, 'The
Metropolis and Mental Life'. It remains a defining text for understanding
how modern experience and modern selfhood have been shaped by the modern city. Simmel's emphasis is less on symbolic projections onto the city, or
the subjective affect of representations of the city, than on the ways in which
the 'outside' of a great metropolis, like Berlin or London, gets translated into
the 'inside' of subjective life.

> An enquiry into the inner meaning of specifically modern life and its products,
> into the soul of the cultural body, so to speak, must seek to solve the equation
> which structures like the metropolis set up between the individual and the
> supra-individual contents of life. Such an enquiry must answer the question of
> how the personality accommodates itself in the adjustments to social forces.[5]

Simmel was writing at a time of huge internal migration to the great
European cities, and he framed his answer in terms of how, mentally, such
provincial newcomers might cope with the city's accelerated tempo and
its unprecedented abstraction. Compared to 'the pettiness and prejudices
which hem in the small-town man', the big city offered people an unprecedented degree of freedom and scope for self-invention.[6] At the same time,
that freedom produced a countervailing sense of loneliness, alienation, and
emotional discomfort. The external culture of the city gnawed away at the
existential integrity of subjective life.

This is what Simmel meant by the 'personality' accommodating itself to
social forces. It is the modern precursor to the experience of Naipaul's postcolonial 'provincial', half a century later, as he struggled to cope with the
scale and anonymity of postwar London.

'The individual,' wrote Simmel, 'has become a mere cog in an enormous
organisation of things and powers which tear from his hands all progress,
spirituality, and value in order to transform them from their subjective form
into the form of a purely objective life'. Changes in the scale and complexity

of metropolitan culture had become qualitative, and not just quantitative. It was the *'intensification of nervous stimulation'* that produced new forms of subjective being for metropolitan city-dwellers.[7] 'Here in buildings and educational institutions, in the wonders and comforts of space-conquering technology, in the formations of community life, and in the visible institutions of the state, is offered such an overwhelming fullness of crystallised and impersonalised spirit that the personality, so to speak, cannot maintain itself under its impact.'[8] Simmel observed how, in response to the weight and complexity of this experience, modern citizens, especially the newcomers amongst them, developed techniques for self-defence. Some would emanate a 'blasé reserve', a self-protective instrumentalism and an apparent indifference to others. Others (or the same citizens at other times) would adopt a mask of conspicuous, even excessive, idiosyncrasy in manner. As a substitute for the disciplines of maturity, they performed a pantomime of individuality.

In 'The Metropolis and Mental Life', Simmel suggests that 'personality', in the sense of stable and knowable characteristics unique to an individual, is rendered well nigh impossible in the modern city.

In his novel, *The Man without Qualities*, Robert Musil, too, was concerned with the hollowing out of experience by what Simmel called the 'overwhelming fullness of crystallised and impersonalised spirit'. Musil writes about Vienna, not Berlin, and he animates the sociologist's analytical categories with a sensual, almost synaesthetic immediacy. To convey what the implosion of 'personality' felt like, the novelist conflates social forces with vision, hearing, and movement.

> So let us not place any particular value on the city's name. Like all big cities it was made up of irregularity, change, forward spurts, failures to keep step, collisions of objects and interests, punctuated by unfathomable silences; made up of pathways and untrodden ways, of one great rhythmic beat as well as the chronic discord and mutual displacement of its contending rhythms. All in all, it was like a boiling bubble inside a pot made of the durable stuff of buildings, laws, regulations, and historical traditions.[9]

For Musil, the modernity of Vienna was experienced as cacophony and syncopation, as 'the chronic discord and mutual displacement of its contending rhythms'.

Walter Benjamin was just as concerned with the subjective impact of the modern metropolis as Simmel and Musil. Whereas they described an etiolation of selfhood, however, Benjamin picked up on the way that the city *changed* patterns of sensory experience, and so produced new forms of behaviour and being. Just as Musil refers to the *discord* and *rhythm* of the city, so, in 'The Metropolis and Mental Life', Simmel had already described the bewildered urban pedestrian's perception of the city in strikingly, although apparently unconsciously, cinematic terms: 'the rapid crowding of changing images, the sharp discontinuity in the grasp of a single glance, and the unexpectedness of onrushing impressions'.[10] Benjamin went further, linking the visual experience of the twentieth-century city as a series of 'shocks' explicitly to the spread of new media (photography, the telephone, the advertising pages of newspapers) as well as to 'the traffic of a big city'. He contrasts this sensory overload with Edgar Allan Poe's description of London pedestrians in the story, 'The Man of the Crowd'.

> Moving through this traffic involves the individual in a series of shocks and collisions. At dangerous crossings, nervous impulses flow through him in rapid succession, like the energy from a battery ... Whereas Poe's passers-by cast glances in all directions which still appeared to be aimless, today's pedestrians are obliged to do so in order to keep abreast of traffic signals. *Thus technology has subjected the human sensorium to a complex kind of training.*[11]

Benjamin is thus explicit about the *pedagogic* function of the city. The new technologies and traffic in a city like modern London teach us, not only how to move through the streets without getting knocked over, but also how to negotiate the discordant and syncopated rhythms of social life, how to process a blizzard of visual information, and perhaps how to understand and manage ourselves as subjective beings.

That experience, as Simmel had noted, produced new kinds of freedom, and these were further expanded by the ability of new urban media, like radio and cinema, to transcend the constraints of physical space and time.

In a famous passage about the liberating potential of cinema, Benjamin might be describing how Naipaul's hero was taught about a virtual London in the cinemas of Trinidad. 'Our bars and our city streets, our offices and furnished rooms, our railroad stations and our factories seemed to close relentlessly around us. Then came film and exploded this prison-world with the dynamite of the split second, so that now we can set off calmly on journeys of adventure among its far-flung-debris.'[12] A different potential for experimentation opened up by the modern city was identified by another of Simmel's students, Robert Park, founder of the Chicago school of urban sociology. In a 1916 essay, he sees the city as a social scientist's ideal *laboratory*:

> [A] great city tends to spread out and lay bare to the public view in a massive manner all the characters and traits which are ordinarily obscured and suppressed in smaller communities. The city, in short, shows the good and evil in human nature in excess. It is this fact, more than any other, which justifies the

view that would make of the city a laboratory or clinic in which human nature and social processes may be most conveniently and profitably studied.[13]

Like Benjamin and Simmel, however, Park was also alert to the subjective consequences of external urban change. Modern transportation and modern media of communication – 'the electric railway, the automobile, the telephone, and the radio' – had realigned both the industrial geography of the city and the distribution of the population. This was leading, in turn, to 'corresponding changes in the habits, sentiments, and character of the urban population'.[14] The city, says Park, has become *a state of mind*.

That formulation places Park four-square in the line of Modernist sociologists, along with Simmel, Benjamin, Kracauer, and others. Yet the empiricist Park's 'state of mind' implies a more radical proposition than the impressionist Simmel's image of the personality's 'accommodation' to modern urban culture. The inference is that the outside of the city had *become* inner life. A literary analogy might be with the way that in *Ulysses*, for all the precision of Joyce's observations and descriptions, Dublin functions primarily as a subjective landscape. 'The forces of action have become internal,' as Raymond Williams observed of the novel, 'and in a way there is no longer a city, there is only a man walking through it'.[15]

Or, perhaps, there is no longer a city, but only the crowd flowing across London Bridge in Eliot's 'unreal city'. The 'high-Modernist' London of *The Waste Land*, like the London of Woolf's *Mrs. Dalloway* or Dorothy Richardson's *Pilgrimage*, is, in its own way, as much a laboratory as Park's Chicago. But it is a laboratory for experiments in matching literary style to unheard-of modes of experience and being, to strange new states of mind. The dense language of the anglophone Modernists, layered with complex meanings and allusive references, was a response to an external metropolitan reality that was opaque, affectively overwhelming, and increasingly – in conventional terms – unrepresentable. As a counter to the supposed hollowing-out of authentic being in this alien new environment – the theme of Simmel and Musil – the Modernist alternative was the cultivation of a pedagogically or therapeutically *difficult* relationship to both literature and the metropolis.

Pedagogic, in the sense that an attuned reader could supposedly learn this skill from a critical engagement with modernist urban literature.

Therapeutic, in the sense that reading the literature critically was invested with the power to re-authenticate experience, and so to develop the skilled reader's resistance to conventional representations of the city, and the packaging of an imaginary 'London' for easy consumption in the newspaper, the detective story, or the movie in the corner cinema.

Reading the city

In 1968, Tony Elliott, an ambitious young entrepreneur with a feel for the counter-cultural times, set up a new magazine in, and for, London. These days, *Time Out* is an established franchise in the global leisure industry, with listings magazines in New York, Beijing, Barcelona, and over twenty other cities as well as in London; city guides for tourists; plus an annual film guide. In the beginning, in its distinctive and long-gone pocket-sized format, *Time Out* was designed to serve an 'alternative' audience that was young, hedonistic, sexually libertarian, a little bit underground, and, probably, more consumerist than they (we) liked to imagine. It mixed news about London not to be found in the mainstream press with listings of events. In 1976, it published the names of sixty people it claimed were London-based CIA agents.

The smart thing about the young *Time Out* was its focus on providing resources to enable its readers to *use* London in new ways. As a hoped-for side-effect, it sometimes seemed to have a broader social aim: that was, to create, less a new public *à la* Habermas, than what might then have been thought of as a new London *tribe*. By 1980, the magazine's (or Elliott's) radical aspirations had given way to the dull compulsion of a competitive marketplace. For a while, a breakaway group of journalists sustained *City Limits* as an alternative, harking back to *Time Out*'s founding principles of collective decision-making and equal pay, but that folded in the early 1990s. By then, most of the 'tribe' were paying off mortgages.

I mention *Time Out* to make a simple point, about the *function* of London literature. Although it is a *textual* representation of London, *Time Out* has never pretended to present a rounded *literary* portrait of London, mediated through a distinctive authorial voice, and encapsulating a society made up of identifiable groups and complex individuals, a polity, or even, in any anthropological sense, a culture. The purpose of *Time Out* is modestly pragmatic. It is designed for use as an aid to living reasonably well in London, and so also, to some extent, as a guide to ways in which one might choose to conduct one's life.

That pedagogic goal of training people to use the city was certainly not new in the press. In his book, *Reading Berlin 1900*, Peter Fritzsche has shown how provincial newcomers to Simmel's rapidly growing Berlin used newspapers to help them negotiate the disorienting new environment. In a very practical way, the papers advertised jobs new Berliners could go for, and listed entertainment and sporting events they could enjoy. At another level, the papers' collage of fragmentary stories packaged a 'word city' that Berliners, new and old, could read, distractedly, at home, in the workplace, or hurrying between the two. 'The city', observes Fritzsche, 'simply could not be used without the guidance of newspapers'.[16]

In comparison with novels, newspapers and listings magazines are exceptionally frank about their *utility* to city-dwellers. My argument is that novels and films have also provided an indispensable guide, if not to using London, then at least to the possibility of living in London. This is the pedagogic function of London in literature. London novels depict models for behaviour, and they enact, for citizen-readers, different scenarios for perceiving, experiencing, understanding, and being in the modern city.

London, virtually

As so often, the paradigm case is Dickens. As the architect and urban theorist, Kevin Lynch, once put it: 'Dickens helped to create the London we experience as surely as its actual builders did.'[17]

In part, Lynch was making the important point that Dickens, quite literally, taught a Victorian public how to live in a rapidly expanding and changing London. His novels were read as guides to London's complex, and often subterranean, relationships and interactions. They provided a record of the intricate relations between different dialects, different accents, and different registers of speech, which made up London as a linguistic city. They packaged emerging ways of conceptualising social issues. Dickens drew on the work of the social explorers for his portraits of London's slum districts, like Jacob's Island, in *Oliver Twist*; or Tom-all-Alone's, in *Bleak House*; and his cast of low-lifes has much in common with the journalist Henry Mayhew's obsessively detailed taxonomy of beggars, prostitutes, thieves, and swindlers in *London Labour and the London Poor* (1851). When he tackled 'the sanitary question' in *Our Mutual Friend* – the scandal of poor families living in filth – Dickens creatively recycled Edwin Chadwick's report on *The Sanitary Conditions of the Labouring Poor in Great Britain*. As well as repackaging social discourses about the city, Dickens also prefigured Simmel, insofar as he presents London as a stage, on which characters played out the narratives of their lives or executed their eccentric turns as personalities.

If Dickens taught his contemporaries new ways of understanding and negotiating London, to later generations he taught ways of imagining London. To the youthful hero of *The Enigma of Arrival*, in Trinidad, he provided an education in fantasy.

> I felt that when as a child far away I read the early Dickens and was able with him to enter the dark city of London, it was partly because I was taking my

own simplicity to his, fitting my fantasy to his ... Using, Dickens, only simple words, simple concepts, to create simple volumes and surfaces and lights and shadows: creating thereby a city or fantasy which everyone could reconstruct out of his own materials, using the things he knew to re-create the described things he didn't know. (p. 123)

Later, confronted with the reality of London, Naipaul notes how that 'gift of fantasy became inoperable', as he lost the ability to suspend his disbelief in 'the universal child's eye of Dickens' (p. 155). This was an equally important lesson. It constituted, one might say, Naipaul's Modernist conversion. He too learned to distrust the Dickens who believed that the detective, the social explorer or the novelist could still ultimately decipher the city. Although he eschewed the stylistic experimentation of high literary Modernism, Naipaul's writing about London in *The Enigma of Arrival* clearly 'comes after' Eliot's 'unreal city'.

One version of the transition from the Dickensian paradigm of London to a Modernist paradigm is captured, with exquisite precision, in an episode in J.-K. Huysmans's *A Rebours* (*Against Nature*), published in 1884. Its hero, Des Esseintes, is a late-nineteenth-century dandy, and the novel dissects his love of artifice, his fetishistic obsession with material objects, his often perverse pleasures, and his retreat from the hurly-burly of Paris into a private, interior reality. As Des Esseintes teeters toward nervous collapse, he turns from his usual literary taste for obscure Latin authors to – surprisingly, perhaps – the novels of Dickens. They fail to soothe him as he had hoped. Gradually, however, 'an idea insinuated itself in his mind – the idea of turning dream into reality, of travelling to England in the flesh as well as in the spirit, of checking the accuracy of his visions'.[18] Impulsively, Des Esseintes packs a trunk, takes a train into central Paris and, in weather foul enough for England, hails a cab.

... his mind conjured up a picture of London as an immense, sprawling, rain-drenched metropolis, stinking of soot and hot iron, and wrapped in a perpetual mantle of smoke and fog. He could see in imagination a line of dockyards stretching away into the distance, full of cranes, capstans, and bales of merchandise ... Up above, trains raced by at full speed; and down in the underground sewers, others rumbled along, occasionally emitting ghastly screams or vomiting floods of smoke through the gaping mouths of air-shafts. And meanwhile, along every street, big or small, in an eternal twilight relieved only by the glaring infamies of modern advertising, there flowed an endless stream of traffic between two columns of earnest, silent Londoners, marching along with eyes fixed ahead and elbows glued to their sides. (pp. 133–4)

Having bought a guidebook to London, Des Esseintes seeks refuge from the rain and cold in the Bodega, a cellar in one of Benjamin's arcades. It is full of English customers, drinking port and sherry.

> His senses dulled by the monotonous chatter of these English people talking to one another, he drifted into a daydream, calling to mind some of Dickens' characters, who were so partial to the rich red port he saw in glasses all about him, and peopling the cellar in fancy with a new set of customers ... He settled down comfortably in this London of the imagination, happy to be indoors, and believing for a moment that the dismal hootings of the tugs by the bridge behind the Tuileries were coming from boats on the Thames.   (p. 138)

From the cellar Des Esseintes moves on to a tavern where, despite months of near fasting, he indulges in what he imagines to be an English meal: oxtail soup, smoked haddock, roast beef and potatoes accompanied by pints of pale ale, stilton cheese, and rhubarb tart (with porter) rounded off by coffee laced with gin. When the time comes to catch his train, he cannot bring himself to move. 'When you come to think of it, I've seen and felt all that I wanted to see and feel. I've been steeped in English life ever since I left home, and it would be madness to risk spoiling such unforgettable experiences by a clumsy change of locality' (p. 143). Having experienced London, imaginatively, through a set of icons – 'smells, weather, citizens, food, and even cutlery' (p. 143) – and through London's virtual iterations in Dickens, in city guides and in the precursors of themed bars and restaurants, Des Esseintes gathers together his luggage, his packages, his rugs, and his umbrellas, and he takes the cab and the train back home.

An extreme case, for his times, Des Esseintes sees no need to be in London. As a prefiguratively modern man, he has learned to experience London virtually. For V. S. Naipaul, who did make the journey, the inner existence of a fantasy London set him up for what felt at the time like a loss. In time, however, he came to understand that the real but manageable trauma of his arrival in London was a decisive step in his journey to experience and maturity. And then there's me, who felt the place, however fretfully, in my bones, and then left. The task of having to think about that relationship, in a sustained and self-conscious way, triggered the itch of melancholy, the images and residues of things not worked through. Maybe the bombsites were less arbitrary than I first thought.

So, again, reflecting on London in literature and cinema serves its pedagogic turn. My fantasy of a lost London has been exploded. I have to acknowledge the loss of that London and all it embodies. Migration. Maturity. The necessary work of mourning.

Notes

1　André Bazin, 'The Ontology of the Photographic Image', in *What is Cinema?*, ed. and trans. Hugh Gray, 2 vols., Vol. II (Berkeley: University of California Press, 1967), p. 15.

2　Henri Lefebvre, *The Production of Space*, trans. Donald Nicholson-Smith (Oxford: Blackwell, 1991), p. 39.

3　Doris Lessing, *The Four-Gated City* (London: Macgibbon and Kee, 1969), p. 20. Further page references are given in the text.

4　V. S. Naipaul, *The Enigma of Arrival* (London: Penguin, 1987), p. 121. Further page references are given in the text.

5　Georg Simmel, 'The Metropolis and Mental Life', in *Simmel on Culture: Selected Writings*, ed. D. Frisby and M. Featherstone (London: Sage, 1997), p. 175.

6　*Ibid.*, p. 181.

7　*Ibid.*, p. 175.

8　*Ibid.*, p. 184.

9　Robert Musil, *The Man without Qualities*, trans. Sophie Wilkins (New York: Alfred A. Knopf, 1985), p. 4.

10　Simmel, 'The Metropolis and Mental Life', p. 175.

11　Walter Benjamin, *Charles Baudelaire: A Lyric Poet in the Era of High Capitalism*, trans. Harry Zohn (London: New Left Books, 1973), p. 132 (my italics).

12　Walter Benjamin, 'The Work of Art in the Age of Its Technological Reproducibility', in *Selected Writings*, 4 vols., Vol. III, *1935–1938*, ed. Howard Eiland and Michael W. Jennings (Cambridge: Harvard University Press, 2002), p. 117.

13　Robert Park, 'The City: Suggestions for the Investigation of Human Behaviour in the Urban Environment', in *Classic Essays on the Culture of Cities*, ed. R. Sennett (Englewood Cliffs, NJ: Prentice-Hall, 1969), p. 130.

14　*Ibid.*, p. 10.

15　Raymond Williams, *The Country and the City* (London: Chatto and Windus, 1973), p. 243.

16　Peter Fritzsche, *Reading Berlin 1900* (Cambridge, MA: Harvard University Press, 1996), p. 18.

17　Kevin Lynch, *Good City Form* (Cambridge, MA: MIT Press, 1981), p. 147.

18　J.-K. Huysmans, *Against Nature*, trans. R. Baldick (Harmondsworth: Penguin, 1959), p. 132. Further page references are given in the text.

GUIDE TO FURTHER READING

Introduction

Theory

Bridge, G. and S. Watson (eds.). *A Companion to the City*, Oxford, Blackwell, 2000.

de Certeau, M. *The Practice of Everyday Life*, trans. S. Rendall, Berkeley, University of California Press, 1984.

Lefebvre, H. *The Production of Space*, trans. D. Nicholson-Smith, Oxford, Blackwell, 1991.

LeGates, R. T. and F. Stout. *The City Reader*, 2nd edn, London, Routledge, 2000.

Sennet, R. (ed.). *Classic Essays on the Culture of Cities*, Englewood Cliffs, NJ, Prentice-Hall, 1969.

History and reference

Ackroyd, P. *London: The Biography*, New York, Anchor Books, 2003.

Inwood, S. *A History of London*, London, Macmillan, 2000.

Porter, R. *London: A Social History*, Cambridge, MA, Harvard University Press, 1995.

Weinreb, B., C. Hibbert, J. Keay, and J. Keay. *The London Encyclopedia*, 3rd edn, London, Macmillan, 2008.

Literature

Bradbury, M. (ed.). *The Atlas of Literature*, London, De Agostini Editions, 1996.

Moretti, F. *Atlas of the European Novel, 1800–1900*, London, Verso, 1998.

Williams, R. *The Country and the City*, Oxford, Oxford University Press, 1973.

Wolfreys, J. *Writing London*, 3 vols. London, Palgrave, 1998–2007.

1   Images of London in medieval English literature

Barron, C. M. 'London 1300–1540', in *The Cambridge Urban History of Britain: i. 600–1540*, ed. D. M. Palliser, Cambridge, Cambridge University Press, 2000, pp. 395–440.

Benson, C. D. 'Civic Lydgate: The Poet and London', in *John Lydgate: Poetry, Culture, and Lancastrian England*, ed. L. Scanlon and J. Simpson, Notre Dame, IN, University of Notre Dame Press, 2006, pp. 147–68.

Bird, R. *The Turbulent London of Richard II* London, Longman, 1949.

Boffey, J. and C. M. Meale. 'Selecting the text: Rawlinson C. 86 and some other books for London readers', in *Regionalism in Late Medieval Manuscripts and Texts: Essays Celebrating the Publication of A Linguistic Atlas of Late Medieval English*, ed. Felicity Riddy (Cambridge: Brewer, 1991), pp. 143–69.

Butterfield, A. (ed.). *Chaucer and the City*, Cambridge, Brewer, 2006.

Clark, J. 'Trinovantum: The Evolution of a Legend', *Journal of Medieval History* 7 (1981), 135–51.

Doyle, A. I. 'English Books in and out of Court from Edward III to Henry VIII', in *English Court Culture in the Later Middle Ages*, ed. V. J. Scattergood and J. W. Sherborne, London, Duckworth, 1983, pp. 164–81.

Doyle, A. I. and M. B. Parkes. 'The Production of Copies of the *Canterbury Tales* and the *Confessio Amantis* in the Early Fifteenth Century', in *Medieval Scribes, Manuscripts and Libraries: Essays Presented to N. R. Ker*, ed. M. B. Parkes and Andrew G. Watson, London, Scolar, 1978, pp. 163–210.

Epstein, R. 'London, Southwark, Westminster: Gower's Urban Contexts', in *A Companion to Gower*, ed. S. Echard, Cambridge, Brewer, 2004, pp. 43–60.

Fulton, H. 'Cheapside in the Age of Chaucer', in *Medieval Cultural Studies: Essays in Honour of Stephen Knight*, ed. R. Evans, H. Fulton, and D. Matthews, Cardiff, University of Wales Press, 2006, pp. 138–51.

Hanna, R. *London Literature, 1300–1380*, Cambridge, Cambridge University Press, 2005.

Keene, D. 'Medieval London and Its Region', *London Journal* 14 (1989), 99–111.

Kekewich, M. L., C. Richmond, A. F. Sutton, L. Visser-Fuchs, and J. L. Watts (eds.). *The Politics of Fifteenth-Century England: John Vale's Book*, Stroud, Sutton, 1995.

Kellaway, W. 'John Carpenter's *Liber Albus*', *Guildhall Studies in London History* 3 (1978), 67–84.

Kipling, G. *Enter the King: Theatre, Liturgy, and Ritual in the Medieval Civic Triumph*, Oxford, Oxford University Press, 1998.

Lindenbaum, S. 'London Texts and Literate Practice', in *The Cambridge History of Medieval English Literature*, ed. D. Wallace, Cambridge, Cambridge University Press, 1999, pp. 284–309.

Nightingale, P. *A Medieval Mercantile Community: The Grocers' Company and the Politics and Trade of London 1000–1485*, New Haven, Yale University Press, 1995.

Patterson, L. 'Chaucerian Commerce: Bourgeois Ideology and Poetic Exchange in the Merchant's and Shipman's Tales', in *Chaucer and the Subject of History*, Madison, University of Wisconsin Press, 1991, pp. 17–148.

Pearsall, D. 'Langland's London', in *Written Work: Langland, Labor, and Authorship*, ed. S. Justice and K. Kerby-Fulton, Philadelphia, University of Pennsylvania Press, 1997, pp. 185–207.

Richmond, C. 'The Pastons and London', in *Courts and Regions in Medieval Europe*, ed. S. Rees Jones, R. Marks, and A. J. Minnis, York, York Medieval Press, 2000, pp. 211–26.

Simpson, J. '"After Craftes Conseil Clotheth Yow and Fede": Langland and London City Politics', in *England in the Fourteenth Century*, ed. N. Rogers, Stamford, Watkins, 1993, pp. 109–27.

Staley, L. 'The Man in Foul Clothes and a Late Fourteenth-Century Conversation about Sin', *Studies in the Age of Chaucer* 24 (2002), 1–47.

Thrupp, S. *The Merchant Class of Medieval London*, Chicago, University of Chicago Press, 1948.

Wallace, D. 'Chaucer and the Absent City', in *Chaucer's England: Literature in Historical Context*, ed. B. A. Hanawalt, Minneapolis, University of Minnesota Press, 1992, pp. 59–91.

Williams, G. A. *Medieval London: From Commune to Capital*, London, Athlone Press, 1963.

2 London and the early modern stage

Agnew, J.-C. *Worlds Apart: The Market and the Theater in Anglo-American Thought, 1550–1750*. Cambridge, Cambridge University Press, 1986.

Archer, I. *The Pursuit of Stability: Social Relations in Elizabethan London*, Cambridge, Cambridge University Press, 1991.

Bailey, A. *Flaunting: Style and the Subversive Male Body in Renaissance England*. Toronto, University of Toronto Press, 2007.

Bruster, D. *Drama and the Market in the Age of Shakespeare*. Cambridge, Cambridge University Press, 1992.

Butler, M. *Theatre and Crisis 1632–1642*, Cambridge, Cambridge University Press, 1984.

Cox, J. D. and D. Kastan (eds.). *A New History of Early English Drama*, New York, Columbia University Press, 1997.

Dillon, J. *Theatre, Court and City, 1595–1610: Drama and Social Space in London*, Cambridge, Cambridge University Press, 1999.

Finlay, R. *Population and Metropolis: The Demography of London, 1580–1650*, Cambridge, Cambridge University Press, 1981.

Griffiths, P. *Lost Londons: Change, Crime, and Control in the Capital City, 1550–1660*, Cambridge, Cambridge University Press, 2008.

Howard, J. *Theater of a City: The Places of London Comedy, 1598–1642*, Philadelphia, University of Pennsylvania Press, 2007.

Knights, L. C. *Drama and Society in the Age of Jonson*, London, George W. Stewart, 1951.

Leinwand, T. *Theatre, Finance, and Society in Early Modern England*. Cambridge, Cambridge University Press, 1999.

Manley, L. *Literature and Culture in Early Modern London*, Cambridge, Cambridge University Press, 1995.

Muldrew, C. *The Economy of Obligation: The Culture of Credit and Social Relations in Early Modern England*, London, St Martin's Press, 1998.

Paster, G. *The Body Embarrassed: Drama and the Disciplines of Shame in Early Modern England*, Ithaca, NY, Cornell University Press, 1993.

3 London and the early modern book

Barnard, J. and McKenzie, D. F. (eds.). *The Cambridge History of the Book in Britain: iv. 1557–1695*, Cambridge, Cambridge University Press, 2002.

Blayney, P. *The Bookshops in Paul's Cross Churchyard*, Bibliographical Society Occasional Papers 5, London, 1990.

Eliot, S. and Rose, J. (eds.). *A Companion to the History of the Book*, Oxford, Blackwell, 2007.

Harkness, D. *The Jewel House: Elizabethan London and the Scientific Revolution*, New Haven, Yale University Press, 2007.

Johns, A. *The Nature of the Book: Print and Knowledge in the Making*, Chicago, University of Chicago Press, 1998.

Knights, M. *Representation and Misrepresentation in Later Stuart Britain: Partisanship and Political Culture*, Oxford, Oxford University Press, 2005.

Lake, P. *The Boxmaker's Revenge: 'Orthodoxy', 'Heterodoxy' and the Politics of the Parish in Early Stuart London*, Stanford, Stanford University Press, 2001.

Lake, P. and S. Pincus. 'Rethinking the Public Sphere in Early Modern England', *Journal of British Studies* 45 (2006), 270–92.

McDowell, P. *The Women of Grub Street: Press, Politics, and Gender in the London Literary Marketplace 1678–1730*, Oxford, Clarendon Press, 1998.

McKenzie, D. F. *Making Meaning: 'Printers of the Mind' and Other Essays*, ed. P. D. McDonald and M. F. Suarez, Amherst, University of Massachusetts Press, 2002.

McKenzie, D. F. and M. Bell. *A Chronology and Calendar of Documents Relating to the London Book Trade 1641–1700*, 3 vols. Oxford, Oxford University Press, 2005.

Pelling, M. *Medical Conflicts in Early Modern London: Patronage, Physicians, and Irregular Practitioners, 1550–1640*, Oxford, Clarendon Press, 2003.

Raven, J. *The Business of Books: Booksellers and the English Book Trade 1450–1850*, New Haven, Yale University Press, 2007.

'Constructing Bookscapes: Experiments in Mapping the Sites and Activities of the London Book Trades of the Eighteenth Century', in Mappa mundi: *Mapping Culture/Mapping the World*, ed. J. Murray, University of Windsor Working Papers in the Humanities, Windsor, 2001, pp. 35–59.

Raymond, J. *The Invention of the Newspaper: English Newsbooks 1641–1649*, Oxford, Oxford University Press, 1996.

Rogers, P. *Grub Street: Studies in a Subculture*, London, Methuen, 1972.

Watt, T. *Cheap Print and Popular Piety 1550–1640*, Cambridge, Cambridge University Press, 1991.

4   London and poetry to 1750

Archer, I. 'Shakespeare's London', in *A Companion to Shakespeare*, ed. D. S. Kastan, Oxford, Blackwell, 1999, pp. 43–56.

Bond, E. 'Historicizing the "New Normal": London's Great Fire and the Genres of Urban Destruction', *Restoration: Studies in English Literary Culture, 1660–1700*, 31.2 (2007), 43–64.

Brant, C. and S. E. Whyman (eds.). *Walking the Streets of Eighteenth-Century London: John Gay's* Trivia [1716], Oxford, Oxford University Press, 2007.

Clark, P. *British Clubs and Societies 1580–1800*, Oxford, Clarendon Press, 2000.

Corfield, P. 'Walking the City Streets: The Urban Odyssey in Eighteenth-Century England', *Journal of Urban History* 16 (1990), 132–74.

Hammond, B. S. 'The City in Eighteenth-Century Poetry', in *The Cambridge Companion to Eighteenth-Century Poetry*, ed. J. Sitter, Cambridge, Cambridge University Press, 2001.

Hitchcock, T. *Down and Out in Eighteenth-Century London*, London, Hambledon, 2004.

Hudson, N. 'Samuel Johnson, Urban Culture, and the Geography of Postfire London', *Studies in English Literature* 42 (2002), 577–600.

McKeon, M. *The Secret History of Domesticity*, Baltimore, Johns Hopkins University Press, 2005.

McRae, A. '"On the Famous Voyage": Ben Jonson and Civic Space', in *Literature, Mapping and the Politics of Space in Early Modern Britain*, ed. A. Gordon and B. Klein, Cambridge, Cambridge University Press, 2001, pp. 181–203.

Ogborn, M. *Spaces of Modernity: London Geographies 1680–1780*, London, Guilford Press, 1998.

Rogers, P. *Pope and the Destiny of the Stuarts: History, Politics, and Mythology in the Age of Queen Anne*, Oxford, Oxford University Press, 2005.

  The Symbolic Design of 'Windsor-Forest': Iconography, Pageant, and Prophecy in Pope's Early Work, Newark, University of Delaware Press, 2004.

Wall, C. *The Literary and Cultural Spaces of Restoration London*, Cambridge, Cambridge University Press, 1998.

5 Staging London in the Restoration and eighteenth century

Brewer, J. *The Pleasures of the Imagination: English Culture in the Eighteenth Century*, New York, Farrar, Straus, and Giroux, 1997.

Cowan, B. *The Social Life of Coffee: The Emergence of the British Coffee House*, New Haven, Yale University Press, 2005.

Daunton, M. J. *Progress and Poverty: An Economic and Social History of Britain, 1700–1850*, Oxford, Oxford University Press, 1995.

Gerzina, G. *Black London: Life before Emancipation*, New Brunswick, Rutgers University Press, 1995.

Linebaugh, P. *The London Hanged: Crime and Civil Society in the Eighteenth Century*, 2nd edn, New York, Verso, 2003.

McDowell, P. *The Women of Grub Street: Press, Politics, and Gender in the London Literary Marketplace 1678–1730*, Oxford, Clarendon Press, 1998.

Mackie, E. *The Commerce of Everyday Life: Selections from the Tatler and the Spectator*, New York, Bedford/St Martin's Press, 1998.

Newman, G. *The Rise of English Nationalism: A Cultural History 1740–1830*, New York, St Martin's Press, 1997.

Perry, R. *Novel Relations: The Transformation of Kinship in English Literature and Culture, 1748–1818*, Cambridge, Cambridge University Press, 2004.

Roach, J. *Cities of the Dead: Circum-Atlantic Performance*, New York, Columbia University Press, 1996.

Rosenthal, L. J. *Infamous Commerce: Prostitution in Eighteenth-Century British Literature and Culture*, Ithaca, NY, Cornell University Press, 2006.

Rosenthal, L. J. (ed.). *Nightwalkers: Prostitute Narratives from the Eighteenth Century*, Peterborough, ON, Broadview Press, 2008.

Shoemaker, R. B. *The London Mob: Violence and Disorder in Eighteenth-Century England*, London, Hambledon and London, 2004.

Turner, J. G. *Libertines and Radicals in Early Modern London: Sexuality, Politics and Literary Culture, 1630–1685*, Cambridge, Cambridge University Press, 2002.

6   London and narration in the long eighteenth century

Besant, W. *London in the Eighteenth Century*, London, A. and C. Black, 1902.

Byrd, M. *London Transformed: Images of the City in the Eighteenth Century*, New Haven, Yale University Press, 1978.

Copeland, E. 'Remapping London: *Clarissa* and the Woman in the Window', in *Samuel Richardson: Tercentenary Essays*, ed. M. A. Doody and P. Sabor, Cambridge, Cambridge University Press, 1989.

George, M. D. *London Life in the Eighteenth Century*, New York, Harper and Row, 1964.

Hunter, J. P. *Before Novels: The Cultural Contexts of Eighteenth-Century English Fiction*, New York, W. W. Norton, 1990.

Picard, L. *Dr Johnson's London: Life in London 1740–1770*, London, Phoenix Press, 2000.

Restoration London, London, Phoenix Press, 1997.

Rogers, P. *Hacks and Dunces: Pope, Swift, and Grub Street*, London, Methuen, 1980.

Rudé, G. *Hanoverian London 1714–1808*, Berkeley, University of California Press, 1971.

Sherman, S. *Telling Time: Clocks, Diaries, and English Diurnal Form 1660–1785*, Chicago, University of Chicago Press, 1996.

Stallybrass, P. and A. White. *The Politics and Poetics of Transgression*, Ithaca, NY, Cornell University Press, 1986.

7   London and nineteenth-century poetry

Freeman, N. *Conceiving the City: London, Literature, and Art 1870–1914*, Oxford, Oxford University Press, 2007.

Heffernan, J. 'Wordsworth's London: The Imperial Monster', *Studies in Romanticism* 37 (1998), 421–43.

Janowitz, A. 'The Artifactual Sublime: Making London Poetry', in *Romantic Metropolis: The Urban Scene of British Culture, 1780–1840*, ed. J. Chandler and K. Gilmartin, Cambridge University Press, 2005, pp. 246–60.

Karlin, D. 'Victorian Poetry of the City: Elizabeth Barrett Browning's *Aurora Leigh*', in *Babylon or New Jerusalem? Perceptions of the City in Literature*, ed. V. Tinkler-Villani, Amsterdam, Rodopi, 2005, pp. 113–24.

Parsons, D. *Streetwalking the Metropolis: Women, the City, and Modernity*, Oxford, Oxford University Press, 2000.

Richards, B. 'The City', in *English Poetry of the Victorian Period 1830–1890*, 2nd edn, London, Longman, 2001, pp. 193–206.

Sharpe W. C. *New York Nocturne: The City after Dark in Literature, Painting, and Photography*, Princeton, Princeton University Press, 2008.

Unreal Cities: Urban Figuration in Wordsworth, Baudelaire, Whitman, Eliot, and Williams, Baltimore, Johns Hopkins University Press, 1990.

Stange, G. R. 'The Frightened Poets', in *The Victorian City: Images and Realities*, ed. H. J. Dyos and M. Wolff, 2 vols. London, Routledge and Kegan Paul, 1973, Vol. II, pp. 475–94.

Thesing, W. *The London Muse: Victorian Poetic Responses to the City*, Athens, GA, University of Georgia Press, 1982.

Vadillo, A. P. *Women Poets and Urban Aestheticism: Passengers of Modernity*, London, Palgrave Macmillan, 2005.

Webb, T. 'Dangerous Plurals: Wordsworth's Bartholomew Fair and the Challenge of an Urban Poetics', in *London in Literature: Visionary Mappings of the Metropolis*, ed. S. Onego and J. Stotesbury, Heidelberg, Universitätsverlag C. Winter, 2002, pp. 53–82.

8 London in the Victorian novel

Alter, R. *Imagined Cities: Urban Experience and the Language of the Novel*, New Haven and London, Yale University Press, 2005.

Goode, J. *George Gissing: Ideology and Fiction*, London, Vision Press, 1978.

Maxwell, R. *The Mysteries of Paris and London*, Charlottesville, University of Virginia Press, 1992.

Nead, L. *Victorian Babylon: People, Street and Images in Nineteenth-Century London*, New Haven and London: Yale University Press, 2000.

Nord, D. *Walking the Victorian Streets: Women, Representation, and the City*, Ithaca, NY, Cornell University Press, 1995.

Schwarzbach, F. S. *Dickens and the City*, London, Athlone Press, 1979.

Spiers, J. (ed.). *Gissing and the City: Cultural Crisis and the Making of Books in Late Victorian England*, London, Palgrave Macmillan, 2006.

Van Ghent, D. 'The Dickens World: A View from Todgers's', *The Sewanee Review* 58 (1950), 419–38.

Walkowitz, J. *City of Dreadful Delight: Narratives of Sexual Danger in Late-Victorian London*, Chicago, University of Chicago Press, 1992.

Welsh, A. *The City of Dickens*, Oxford, Clarendon Press, 1987.

White, J. *London in the Nineteenth Century: A Human Awful Wonder of God*, London, Vintage, 2007.

9 London in Victorian visual culture

Armstrong, N. *Fiction in the Age of Photography: The Legacy of British Realism*, Cambridge, Harvard University Press, 1999.

Arnold, D. *Rural Urbanism: London Landscapes in the Early Nineteenth Century*, Manchester, Manchester University Press, 2005.

Barthes, R. *Camera Lucida: Reflections on Photography*, trans. R. Howard, London, Cape, 1982.

Corbett, D. P. *The World in Paint: Modern Art and Visuality in England 1848–1914*, Manchester, Manchester University Press, 2004.

Crinson, M. 'Georgianism and the Tenements, Dublin 1908–1928', *Art History* 29.4 (2006), 624–59.

D'Souza, A. and T. McDonough (eds.). *The Invisible Flâneuse? Gender, Public Space and Visual Culture in Nineteenth-Century Paris*, Manchester, Manchester University Press, 2006.

Donald, J. *Imagining the Modern City*, London, Athlone Press, 1999.

Dyos, H. J. and M. Wolff (eds.). *The Victorian City: Images and Realities*, 2 vols. London, Routledge and Kegan Paul, 1973.

Fox, C. *Londoners*, London, Thames and Hudson, 1987.

Freeman, N. *Conceiving the City: London, Literature, and Art 1870–1914*, Oxford, Oxford University Press, 2007.

Gruetzner Robins, A. *A Fragile Modernism: Whistler and His Impressionist Followers*, New Haven, Yale University Press, 2007.

Gruetzner Robins, A. and R. Thomson *Degas, Sickert and Toulouse-Lautrec: London and Paris 1870–1910*, London, Tate, 2005.

Hallett, M. 'The View across the City: William Hogarth and the Visual Culture of Eighteenth-Century London', in *Hogarth: Representing Nature's Machines*, ed. D. Bindman, F. Ogée, and P. Wagner, Manchester, Manchester University Press, 2001.

House, J., P. ten-D. Chu, and J. Hardin. *Monet's London: Artists' Reflections on the Thames 1859–1914*, St Petersburg, Museum of Fine Arts, 2005.

Lochnan, K. (ed.). *Turner Whistler Monet*, London, Tate, 2004.

Meisel, M. *Realizations: Narrative, Pictorial, and Theatrical Arts in Nineteenth-Century England*, Princeton, Princeton University Press, 1983.

Olsen, D. *The City as a Work of Art: London, Paris, Vienna*, New Haven, Yale University Press, 1986.

Porter, R. 'Capital Art: Hogarth's London', in *The Dumb Show: Image and Society in the Works of William Hogarth*, ed. F. Ogée, Oxford, Voltaire Foundation, 1997.

Ribner, J. 'The Poetics of Pollution', in *Turner Whistler Monet*, ed. K. Lochnan, London, Tate, 2004, pp. 59–63.

Sennett, R. *Flesh and Stone: The Body and the City in Western Civilization*, London, Faber, 1994.

Sharpe, W. and L. Wallock. 'From "Great Town" to "Nonplace Urban Realm": Reading the Modern City', in *Visions of the Modern City: Essays in History, Art and Literature*, ed. W. Sharpe and L. Wallock, Baltimore, Johns Hopkins University Press, 1987, pp. 1–21.

Shesgreen, S. *Images of the Outcast: The Urban Poor in the Cries of London*, New Brunswick, Rutgers University Press, 2002.

Treuherz, J. *Hard Times: Social Realism in Victorian Art*, London, Lund Humphries, 1987.

White, J. *London in the Nineteenth Century*, London, Jonathan Cape, 2007.

10   London in poetry since 1900

Adams, A. *London in Poetry and Prose*, London, Enitharmon, 2002.

(ed.). *Thames: An Anthology of River Poems*, London, Enitharmon, 1999.

Barry, P. *Contemporary British Poetry and the City*, Manchester, Manchester University Press, 2000.

Barton, N. *The Lost Rivers of London*, rev. edn, London, Historical Publications, 1992.

Bavidge, J. *Theorists of the City: Walter Benjamin, Henri Lefebvre and Michel de Certeau*, London, Routledge, 2011.

Brooker, P. *Bohemia in London: The Social Scene of Early Modernism*, Basingstoke, Palgrave, 2004.

A Student's Guide to the Selected Poems of Ezra Pound, London, Faber, 1979.

Hague, R. *A Commentary on the Anathemata of David Jones*, Wellingborough, Christopher Skelton, 1977.

Hamner, R. D. *Epic of the Dispossessed: Derek Walcott's Omeros*, Columbia, University of Missouri Press, 1997.

Hutchins, P. *Ezra Pound's Kensington: An Exploration, 1885–1913*, London, Faber, 1965.

Jones, P. (ed.). *Imagist Poetry*, London, Penguin, 1972.

Kerr, J. and A. Gibson (eds.). *London from Punk to Blair*, London, Reaktion Books, 2004.

Phillips, L. (ed.). *The Swarming Streets: Twentieth-Century Literary Representations of London*, Amsterdam, Rodopi, 2004.

Rennison, N. (ed.). *Waterstone's Guide to London Writing*, London, Waterstone's, 1999.

Rogerson, B. (ed.). *London: A Collection of Poetry of Place*, London, Elan Press, 2004.

Sinclair, I. (ed.). *Conductors of Chaos: A Poetry Anthology*, London, Picador, 1996.
(ed.). *London: City of Disappearances*, London, Penguin, 2006.
Lud Heat and Suicide Bridge, London, Granta Books, 2002.

Skelton, R, (ed.). *Poetry of the Forties*, London, Penguin, 1968.

Soja, E. *Postmetropolis: Critical Studies of Cities and Regions*, Oxford, Basil Blackwell, 2000.

Terrell, C. F. *A Companion to the Cantos of Ezra Pound*, Berkeley, University of California Press, 1980.

11   London and modern prose, 1900–1950

Biddle, T. D. *Rhetoric and Reality in Air Warfare: The Evolution of British and American Ideas about Strategic Bombing, 1914–1945*, Princeton, Princeton University Press, 2002.

Harrisson, T. *Living through the Blitz*, London, Collins, 1976.

Hillman. *London under London: A Subterranean Guide*, 2nd edn, London, John Murray, 1993.

Parsons, D. L. *Streetwalking the Metropolis: Women, the City, and Modernity*, Oxford, Oxford University Press, 2000.

Trotter, D. 'Phoning It In', in *The Uses of Phobia: Essays on Literature and Film*, London, Wiley/Blackwell, 2010, pp. 140–55.

Walkowitz, R. L. *Cosmopolitan Style: Modernism Beyond the Nation*, New York, Columbia University Press, 2007.

Welsh, D. *Underground Writing: The London Tube from George Gissing to Virginia Woolf*, Liverpool, Liverpool University Press, 2010.

Wilson, A. N. (ed.). *The Faber Book of London*, London, Faber, 1993.

12   Immigration and postwar London literature

Ball, J. C. *Imagining London: Postcolonial Fiction and the Transnational Metropolis*, Toronto, University of Toronto Press, 2004.

Baucom, I. *Out of Place: Englishness, Empire, and the Locations of Identity*, Princeton, Princeton University Press, 1999.

Fryer, P. *Staying Power: The History of Black People in Britain*, London, Pluto, 1984.

Gikandi, S. *Maps of Englishness: Writing Identity in the Culture of Colonialism*, New York, Columbia University Press, 1996.

Gilroy, P. *'There Ain't No Black in the Union Jack': The Cultural Politics of Race and Nation*, Chicago, University of Chicago Press, 1987.

McLaughlin, J. *Writing the Urban Jungle: Reading Empire in London from Doyle to Eliot*, Charlottesville, Virginia University Press, 2000.

McLeod, J. *Postcolonial London: Rewriting the Metropolis*, London, Routledge, 2004.

Nasta, S. *Home Truths: Fictions of the South Asian Diaspora in Britain*, Basingstoke, Palgrave, 2002.

Procter, J. *Dwelling Places: Postwar Black British Writing*, Manchester, Manchester University Press, 2003.

Sandhu, S. *London Calling: How Black and Asian Writers Imagined a City*, London, HarperCollins, 2003.

13 Writing London in the twenty-first century

Ackroyd, P. *Thames: Sacred River*, London, Chatto and Windus, 2007.

Ahmed, I. *Sorrows of the Moon: In Search of London*, London, Constable, 2007.

Bhabha, H. K. *The Location of Culture*, London/New York, Routledge, 1994.

Cleave, C. 'The Story behind *Incendiary*', www.chriscleave.com/main/?p=28, 2008.

Diken, B. and Laustsen, C. B. 'Zones of Indistinction: Security, Terror and Bare Life', *Space and Culture* 5.3 (2002), 290–307.

Gilroy, P. *After Empire: Melancholia or Convivial Culture?*, London, Routledge, 2004.

Gunning, D. 'Cosmopolitanism and Marginalisation in Bernardine Evaristo's *The Emperor's Babe*', in *Write Black, Write British: From Post Colonial to Black British Literature*, ed. K. Sesay, Hertford, Hansib, 2005, pp. 165–78.

Hall, T. *Salaam Brick Lane: A Year in the New East End*, London, John Murray, 2005.

Head, D. *Ian McEwan*, Manchester, Manchester University Press, 2007.

Hussain, E. *The Islamist: Why I Joined Radical Islam in Britain, What I Saw Inside and Why I Left*, London, Penguin, 2007.

Moss, L. 'The Politics of Everyday Hybridity: Zadie Smith's *White Teeth*', *Wasafiri* 39 (2003), 11–17.

Phillips, C. *A New World Order: Selected Essays*, London, Secker and Warburg, 2001.

Rushdie, S. *Imaginary Homelands: Essays and Criticism, 1981–1991*, London, Granta, 1991.

Sinclair, I. *London Orbital: A Walk around the M25*, London, Granta, 2002.

Ware, V. *Who Cares about Britishness? A Global View of the National Identity Debate*, London, Arcadia, 2007.

14 Inner London

Barber, S. *Projected Cities*, London, Reaktion, 2002.

Benjamin, W. *Charles Baudelaire: A Lyric Poet in the Era of High Capitalism*, trans. H. Zohn, London, New Left Books, 1973.

Brooker, P. *Modernity and Metropolis: Writing, Film and Urban Formations*, Basingstoke, Palgrave, 2002.

Brunsdon, C. *London in Cinema: The Cinematic City since 1945*, London, BFI, 2007.

Burgin, V. *In/Different Spaces: Place and Memory in Visual Culture*, Berkeley, University of California Press, 1996.

Calhoun, C. (ed.). *Habermas and the Public Sphere*, Cambridge, MA, MIT Press, 1993.

Dimendberg, E. *Film Noir and the Spaces of Modernity*, Cambridge, MA, Harvard University Press, 2004.

Timms, E. (ed.). *Unreal City: Urban Experience in Modern European Literature and Art*, Manchester, Manchester University Press, 1984.

Vidler, A. *The Architectural Uncanny*, Cambridge, MA, MIT Press, 1992.

INDEX

Cambridge Companions to ...

AUTHORS

TOPICS

Twentieth-Century Russian Literature edited by Marina Balina and Evgeny Dobrenko

Utopian Literature edited by Gregory Claeys

Victorian and Edwardian Theatre edited by Kerry Powell

The Victorian Novel edited by Deirdre David

Victorian Poetry edited by Joseph Bristow

War Writing edited by Kate McLoughlin

Writing of the English Revolution edited by N. H. Keeble